COLLEGE

D0635640

1022

762

The resolute and intelligent expression on the face of this Eskimo hunter reflects the crucible of survival in northern latitudes. The rain parka he's wearing, which was sewn from the lining of sea mammal intestines, is rarely seen now, except in museums. (Photo by Alim Kiryushin, Magadan)

Native Libraries

Cross-Cultural Conditions in the Circumpolar Countries

Gordon H. Hills

The Scarecrow Press, Inc.
Lanham, Md., & London
1997

NORTHWEST COMMUNITY
COLLEGE

SCARECROW PRESS, INC.

Published in the United States of America
by Scarecrow Press, Inc.
4720 Boston Way
Lanham, Maryland 20706

4 Pleydell Gardens, Folkestone
Kent CT20 2DN, England

Copyright © 1997 by Gordon H. Hills

All rights reserved. No part of this publication may be reproduced,
stored in a retrieval system, or transmitted in any form or by any
means, electronic, mechanical, photocopying, recording, or otherwise,
without the prior permission of the publisher.

British Library Cataloguing in Publication Information Available

Library of Congress Cataloging-in-Publication Data

Hills, Gordon H.
    Native libraries : cross-cultural conditions in the circunpolar North /
Gordon H. Hills.
        p. cm.
    Includes bibliographical references and index.
    ISBN 0-8108-3138-4 (cloth : alk. paper)
    1. Libraries and Eskimos. 2. Libraries and Indians. I. Title.
Z711.8.H55 1997   96-48793
027.6'3—dc21   CIP

ISBN 0-8108-3138-4 (cloth : alk. paper)

⊖™ The paper used in this publication meets the minimum requirements of
American National Standard for Information Sciences—Permanence of
Paper for Printed Library Materials, ANSI Z39.48–1984.
Manufactured in the United States of America.

To my parents
Willis Holden Hills and Barbara Hoyt Hills

Contents

To Honor
Irene Charley Shale .
(Shoalwater Elder)
December 8, 1909–February 21, 1985
Tokeland, Oakville, Taholah, and Hoquiam, Washington State
Auntie 'Rene took care of the children,
believed in education, wanted tribal unity,
and worked to preserve and pass on the Heritage.

In Memory
of
Martha Simon Kanuk
aka Martha Middlemist
(Tsaninermiut)
March 10, 1942–July 23, 1991
of
Kwigillingok, Kipnuk, Bethel, and Anchorage, Alaska
Wife, Mother, Free Spirit, Healer, Health Care Provider
"I live in two worlds."

Acknowledgments

I feel such a debt to so many people in being able to finish this book that it is difficult to know where to begin. I think of more than 100 library workers all over the circumpolar north and across North America who have helped out when I asked for special favors. These encounters were always gratifying and encouraging.

I look back to the paper by Julia M. Cruikshank, "Legend and Landscape—Convergence of Oral and Scientific Traditions, etc.," whose approach struck a strong chord of agreement with my own thinking, as I formulated the idea for a monograph.

For locations in the Lower 48 of the United States receiving special attention, I'm especially indebted to Conrad Lafromboise and Rosemary Austin on the experience of the Plains Tribe, and Hazel McKenney and Irene Charley Shale (deceased) of the Coastal Tribe for their inspiration. In Alaska, I'm most grateful to Audrey Kolb, Mary Jennings, Barbara R. King, Margaret Liebowitz, Mary H. (Moe) McGee, Judith F. Monroe, Juliet M. West, and Teddy Wintersteen. On Alaskan Native languages, I'm appreciative of help given by Gerald R. Domnick in going over some of my interpretations at an early stage.

Henry N. Michael's generous exchange of translations encouraged me to include the Soviet/Russian half of the Arctic, and help from O. Diakonova, L. P. Shvab and Yu. A. Grikhanov of the (then) Lenin State Library added impetus, as did an interesting tour of the Anadyr Central Library with Lyubov' Ivanova Vergeichik and another staff librarian whose name, I regret, escapes me. Russian and Chukchi friends found while in the Anadyr region brought the Russian north to life, especially those reindeer herders on the high tundra in August and their band of children with accompanying little dogs of equal number. Translation assistance, many key referrals, and indispensable advice from their lifetime of experience in Soviet and Russian studies were gratefully received from Stephen P. Dunn and Ethel Dunn of Berkeley. Finally, I am most indebted for help, information, and materials received from E. B. Artem'eva and her husband, Alexei Kvashnin of Novosibirsk, M. G. Bokan of St. Petersburg, and Z. P. Sokolova of Moscow.

For Canada, I'm grateful to Carolyn Robertson, Stella Etherington, A. Brian Deer, Vivian Cummins, Leith Peterson, Asen Balikci, and Yves Bernie, among others, and especially Marion Pape. Also thanks to John Murray, who acceded to my request to look over the Canadian portions of the text and offer comment. Information on Greenland would have been scanty and less current had it not been for the ready responses of Henriette Aabo Hansen, Ase Reymann, Marianne Olsen, and Danish translators

vii

Gracia Swenson and Rohn Gustafson. News of late developments and detailed comment on my text were provided by Klaus Georg Hansen of the Groenlandica Collection at Nunatta Atuagaateqarfia, Nuuk, whose gracious and refreshing commentary brought my ideas about Greenland nearer to reality, along with two multilingual books from Greenland publishers, including the catalog of the Groenlandica Collection (see Hoyer). For the Saami area of Fennoscandia I'm most appreciative of the more recent materials sent to me in 1995 by Paivi Alanen of the Lapin Maakuntakirjasto (Lapland Regional Library) in Rovaniemi, Finland.

Although they were not within the geographical scope of this book, Patricia M. Donnelly of New Zealand and Anne Bannerman of Australia provided a variety of most interesting relevant materials and comment. And thanks to the young computer specialists of Timeframe computer services in Anchorage for repeatedly rescuing an older customer from the quicksand of constant and confusing change in computer applications, to which he was a recent initiate.

Most of all I owe a great deal to the many Native people who encountered me as I visited and worked in their communities, trying to understand what relevance a librarian's work has among them, and confronted me with the right kinds of questions that needed to be answered. Finally, I assume full responsibility for all statements, opinions and interpretations herein. As for criticisms I may make of past policies and decisions, I've tried to balance that by recognizing and accepting responsibility for mistakes I believe I've made as well. Hindsight is the clearest and easiest kind, however, and I can only hope that my approach may find some helpful resonance or regard in the reader's view.

Gordon H. Hills

Preface

In the winter of 1980-81 I traveled to a Yupik Eskimo village at the mouth of the Yukon, close by the Bering Sea. As the newly hired Coordinator of a village library project for the area community college, I was beginning to make the rounds of nine village libraries that had been started by my predecessor, a younger, married man who had abruptly left his job the year before, the remoteness, harsh climate and much flying time away from his family perhaps persuading him to give it up in mid-stride.

The one taxi in the village—which was a surprising discovery in itself—was out of commission at the time, so I walked in a gently falling snow through this remote community of a few hundred, strung out along a winding slough for a mile or more, heading for the "village library," which was at one end of town. It was mid-morning, and all the children were in school. Our long flight out to the coast, which had required a change of small planes at one point, had encountered some snow squalls and gusty winds as we made our descent. Now the new and old snow combined to muffle all activity, and hardly a soul was to be seen.

For me the situation was almost bizarre, simultaneously a product of the working life—my job—and a mysterious and challenging odyssey. Just the fact of my being in this part of the world was a feat in itself. Jet travel from Washington state a few weeks before, then by smaller planes at lower altitudes out here, now on foot over permafrost—and all this with one goal in mind: to see how the new village library was doing in this subsistence village, a little arrow on the topographical map taped to the wall over my desk back in the regional library.

New to this remote part of Alaska and making one of my first "on-site" visits, I hadn't made any friends yet in the village. At that time there wasn't even a library committee to contact, only the village administrator. I'd been told simply where the library was. No one had had time, that morning, to give me a lift out. I recall there was a good deal of accumulated snow. It was slow walking.

Reaching the cluster of buildings owned by the federally constituted Traditional Council (as opposed to the village corporation established by Alaska state law), I trudged on through to the one where I thought the library was located, though I now was confused, because all the buildings looked the same—long trailers colored a faded yellow, juxtaposed in long pairs or at right angles. The drifts became deeper, and I passed one building where an end door was missing. I stepped over to look inside, half expecting to find an abandoned library. There were the ruins of a former weight-training room, with all the expensive equipment lying around, trash

ix

and debris scattered everywhere, obviously a vandalized place. The windows and door were gone, allowing wind and snow to scurry about.

Trudging on, scanning the unmarked trailers and fingering the key I'd been given inside my mitten, I was apprehensive now, wondering what the state of the library would be. The location at one end of the long narrow village was terrible, and the surroundings were unpromising, to say the least. Finding the one trailer of a pair that appeared to be the library, as there was a pile of empty book boxes in the arctic porch that joined them, I keyed a padlock and pushed the warped outer porch door open. Darkness. Feeling for a switch that turned on a light, I stepped inside with a rather tenuous aplomb, trying one locked door which had a colorful homemade sign on it saying "Adult Education Center," then went to the only other door, which was unmarked and unlocked. I went in, and turned on the nearest light switch.

I had heard the library "wasn't open yet," but the scene before me was startling in its "freeze-frame" aspect. Here was a village library that had received its materials, shelving, supplies and trained library aide over a year before, yet almost everything was unopened, still lying about the floor in carefully wrapped boxes. It reminded me of those diaramas in the better museums, where an activity from daily life has been stopped by a zealous museologist so that the public can better savor the antique heritage. It looked as though someone had earnestly begun unpacking boxes of books and started to set up one of the three large bookcases (which had been damaged in the process), and then stepped to a phone, or gone to lunch, or . . . called it quits. And they had, about a year ago. Everything was preserved from that precise moment, as I later learned.

In retrospect, this was the first big lesson of a very long series of lessons that were to come, and continue to arrive now, in my mind, regarding libraries in Native communities. Standing in that stillborn village library, abandoned just like the weight-training room, I was in cultural shock. The first impulse, of course, was to start putting things right physically, which I did for the remainder of the visit, along with training a new library aide. But the later impulses were mixed and vexing, anxious and groping. The next three years were to be a powerful learning experience, and I still go over my lessons, long afterward, trying to "put things right," at least in my mind. . . .

Bethal, Alaska, Winter 1990
and Anchorage, Fall 1995

Introduction

". . . That gulf of misunderstanding that exists between people."[1]

A series of events and revelations has gradually impelled me to the writing of this book. The catalyst was work in library development among Yupik Eskimo villages of western Alaska for a regional community college in the early 1980s, the lack of any cross-cultural orientation for non-Native field workers, and frustrations surrounding the premature termination of that project. Secondly, over the years of work as a librarian, I've come to realize how bureaucracy predominates among librarians, and how this library-centeredness affects community relations, community services, and the dim prospect for initiatives in these and other community-oriented aspects of library provision.[2]

Another reason was the frustrating experience I had in a graduate library school, which resulted in my acquiring an abiding interest in library education, to make it more field-responsive and therefore more active in research into future trends in library and information science management and provision. Not that individual librarians, or individual libraries, haven't been enterprising at times, and future oriented. In fact most of the progressive gestures in the library and information science field have come from individual librarians or the private information management sector—rarely from library systems, library organizations or library education. Yet there has been no lack of studies, task forces and recommendations from these quarters. There is a heavy irony in the fact that one of the traditional guardians of cultural preservation and transmission for the dominant western civilization—the library—becomes, in the global electronic information community of the late 20th century, a kind of reliquary, increasingly preoccupied with preserving itself. Yet another impetus for this book has been the observation that traditional and mainstream librarianship has had a great deal of difficulty accepting and implementing policies and programs of multicultural librarianship.

There has been a positive side to this impetus. It is the genuine interest in locally controlled library provision, heritage preservation and Native information management expressed by Native library users and managers. It is the intellectual stimulation and encouragement of sharing these ideas and actions with both non-Native and Native colleagues and public. This book is a further attempt to share. At times we slip into a more informal and humanistic style, rooted in daily life. Because the text has relatively amateur ethnographic descriptions, as well as cross-cultural observations and judgments, we have followed the practice common in such literature, by including some personal background in chapter 7.

Library development in Native communities has gradually taken on a special importance over the past decade, and yet the little information available is scattered through the periodical and grey literature. This book is an attempt, however flawed, to consolidate or at least go over most factors affecting this development.

Though the requirements and procedures for establishing and operating a tribal community library are covered from a variety of perspectives, this is not intended as a manual or handbook for managing a Native library. There are already excellent sources of information on this subject, for example the series of thirteen booklets made available by the National Indian Education Association,[3] and the comprehensive yet concise *Tribal Library Administrative Procedures Manual* produced by the TRAILS Project (1985-87), directed by Lotsee Smith Paterson.[4] These are listed in the Bibliography/Reference List I.

This is an interdisciplinary examination of conditions in Native areas vis-à-vis library development and services. Our concept of a "library" and the services associated with it may become transformed as it reflects the wants and needs of an individual Native community. The geographical scope is circumpolar, though the United States and especially my own experience in Alaska and with two tribes in the Lower 48 are featured. Certain aspects such as library education, cross-cultural experiences and multicultural librarianship have a wider scope, both geographically and contextually. The countries examined are Canada, Greenland, the former Communist Soviet Union and present-day Russian Federation, the United States (selectively) and, very briefly, Northern Scandinavia.

Though I have tried to be thorough, if I have left out notable developments or persons, I regret the oversight and can only plead that I've used a selective approach and have been hemmed in by time and circumstances, as well as a desire to complete the project. It is a subject in constant flux and flow, and the landscape out there is changing along with it.

The original text of *Native Libraries* was completed in 1990. In 1995 I went over it carefully, editing and updating wherever possible, as time permitted, utilizing information from additional research and consultations. The Bibliography/Reference List and Source Notes were expanded accordingly, into a Part II, not only to bring them up to date, but because it was the publisher's wish to have as current and complete a list of sources as possible, a gratifying invitation for any nonfiction author. It has a high percentage of annotations, and nearly all the sources cited were examined by the author. The reader is encouraged to browse through bibliograpies. Due to the preponderance of the transliterated and translated titles in Russian, the Russian Source Notes and Bibliography/Reference List are found at the end of that chapter.

My special interest is the cross-cultural character of library development among Native peoples, whose heritage has traditionally been orally transmitted, whereas the western, science-based European heritage has been written and otherwise encoded in a variety of relatively static, standardized media, such as print, graphics, and audio and visual recordings. It is a meeting between living persons and a record of living persons, between life and recorded history. It is often a meeting between those for whom libraries are, at least initially, foreign, ethnocentric, irrelevant and subversive, and those for whom libraries are comfortable repositories of knowledge and cultural brilliance. In the worst sense libraries in a cross-cultural setting are a decided invasion by the dominant, or European-based culture. In the optimum, Native-controlled mode, they will possibly be more inviting places (for Natives) to visit, documenting the tribal memory both traditional and modern, for young people today and those to come.

In the earliest colonies of the modern era, the idea of installing libraries in Native communities was not part of the "civilizing," Christianizing and exploitative processes introduced by Europeans. Once their military, trade, governmental or demographic predominance was assured, libraries or what passed for them were informal or private collections for the use of intellectual settlers, community leaders and the clergy. The few Natives with the "privilege" and literacy to use them learned to swallow their monocultural, ethnocentric and racist offerings. It has been only in recent years that libraries in Native communities have begun to be tailored to fit real Native information and educational needs.

Funding for high quality as well as appropriate Native libraries has received only token support thus far. The Native peoples have traditionally been the wards or dependants of the dominant society that conquered or eclipsed them. Their low social status in this new setting, endemic economic poverty due to loss of subsistence rights and lands, and scattered population have relegated them to the most remote backwaters of national life. Funding for the infrastructure of essential services has come almost entirely from the central government, with the Native communities contributing little revenue, their labor, and all the resources of their homelands in return. Thus obtaining funding for cultural "extras" like libraries and higher education has had enormous difficulty. The trend for the 21st century, however, may be for the Native traditional governments to receive grants directly, instead of through the costly, "foreign" and inefficient bureaucracies of the central government, which enforce narrow and inflexible "standards" that further alienate and frustrate.

The arrangement I've chosen is to select various aspects of Native community life and use these as a baseline for a discussion of library development. If it sometimes seems that undue attention is being paid to cross-cultural subjects and little to conventional library considerations, it is precisely because we choose to emphasize the former, for the benefit of the latter. This sometimes necessitates extended descriptions and analyses in order to define library development in terms of a particular real-life situation. In some cases I've used the experience of one geographical area, which seems to best illustrate the factors or conditions being featured. Further, it is indispensable to treat Native groups as entities, rather than to dissect them for purposes of study and analysis, in the western manner. To compare the hindquarters of the Arctic fox, the seal, the caribou, the beaver and the grizzly bear is fine from the point of view of western anatomy or zoology, but will tell you very little about how they live and relate to one another in the larger ecosystem of earth and the spirit world. We are treating here of durable, relatively continuous traditional communities, hundreds of generations in the making, which for our purposes only resemble each other in an ill-defined, general sense.

In considering the various aspects of this complex subject, one should note some major overall conditions that describe Native communities and the dominant factors in their struggle to enter the 21st century. These are: 1) the loss of lands, reduction of subsistence economies and a marginality of self-determination; 2) the overwhelming invasion by Europe-generated population, with its tenacious and ineluctable cultural impetus, its modern technology and science and bureaucracies; and 3) the profound dislocation and confusion caused by modern, urbanizing society, whereby the Native man and woman are equally propelled into a future-oriented world of multiple life-options and unprecedented fantasy provocation and anti-social temptations. . . .

There is a mind-set with varied cultural baggage that the Caucasian should objectively recognize, from his or her own long heritage, from far across the Atlantic Ocean, and against which it is indispensable to juxtapose, on equal terms, the Native community:

> Our Western-based [tradition of] reason and judgement [applied to northern societies is] a confusion about the differences among information, knowledge and wisdom. [We] establish an 'objective' meaning for ourselves. But it is often a Western-biased meaning, and not necessarily universal. Our science is therefore value-laden in what it chooses to acknowledge as important and to study, and what it chooses to ignore. There is a scientific blindness in our perception of the vibrancy of northern societies. . . . No amount of scientific information can offer the experience of even the quickest glance. If only there were a means of really seeing, of really knowing. . . . But the question 'why?' permeates all that we are. It is the internal compass that guides what each of us does, yet it can never be objectively defined or explained. It can only be experienced. . . . Aboriginal societies have more awareness of the 'why?' . . . There is a treasure there that must be acknowledged even if it cannot be understood. [From] a new humility, a broader awareness, and a refined sense of responsibility . . . will emerge a new kind of knowing and a fresh wisdom on our mental as well as our geographic frontiers.[5]

For library workers, the links among libraries, library education, multicultural librarianship and Native librarianship are becoming closer, and this is the trend of the future. At the same time, Native library services will evolve in their own way, Native-controlled. Museum-related, archival, educational, and documentation activities will be part of this effort, undoubtedly along with more appropriate sociability and new priorities and protocols.

The population of Earth (or Oceania, as it ought to be called) continues to increase, and by far most of this increase is and will continue to be in peoples of color. Even in North America, in another two generations the so-called "minorities" will be the majority. Couple this with the dramatically increasing amount and importance of information, whether raw data, predigested or selected, plus the enormously increasing power and sophistication of information and communication technologies . . . and prospects for a very different Native "library world" of the future become manifest.

The ultimate goal of these pages, therefore, is hopefully to stimulate a corresponding expansion of professional orientation among those librarians who may read them, and increased attention to cross-cultural and multi-cultural librarianship, including services by and for Native peoples, thereby giving librarians, library and information managers and library and information science educators everywhere a stronger and more coherent professional role to play in the future.

Notes

1. Quote from Hilary De Vries' pre-opening review of the Broadway musical "Miss Saigon," entitled "From the Paris Sewers to Vietnam's Streets," which appeared on pages 5 and 43 of the Arts and Leisure section, *New York Times,* Sunday, September 17, 1989, p. 43.

2. "Every bureaucracy is host to both progressive and conservative forces. . . . There is a perpetual struggle to determine the pattern of slow advance. . . . Their dynamic processes are astonishingly similar to those of 'natural communities'. . . . The most successful guided technological development occurs when program planners and technical specialists recognize the two sociocultural systems within which they work—their bureaucracy and the target groups—and have some understanding of the processes of change that characterize both of them." From *Traditional Societies and Technological Change,* by George M. Foster, p. 77.

3. National Indian Education Association. Project ILSTAC. Series of 13 booklets on starting and operating a tribal library or library services for urban Indians.

4. TRAILS, Training and Assistance for Indian Library Services. *Administrative Procedures Manual* (for tribal libraries). Program Director, Lotsee Smith Paterson, School of Library and Information Studies, Univ. of Oklahoma (funded by U.S. Department of Education).

5. Gamble, Donald J. "Crushing of Cultures: Western Applied Science in Northern Societies," *Arctic,* Vol. 39, No. 1 (March 1986), p. 23.

    For, " . . . just as technicians are sensitized to cultural differences and their meanings, for cross-cultural professional practice, so must they be sensitized to the bureaucratic world that provides their home base, and which in myriad ways, at conscious and unconscious levels, affects their perception of problem and mode of operation." From *Traditional Societies and Technological Change,* by George M. Foster, pp. 177–8.

1.

Preservation and Continuity of Heritage: A Sampler

The values of all peoples are a function of their way of life and they cannot be understood out of context.[1]

The Plains Indian Tribe[2]

Plains Indian community college is located in a small, economically depressed and isolated Indian community, near the mountains. The town is the largest on the reservation and is located at its center. The neighboring snowy mountains line the horizon, seemingly from pole to pole, like an endless row of ancient silver teeth. In fact they are called the Shining Mountains, and have a significant spiritual place in local Indian lore, legend and ritual. There are two other types of libraries in the town, outside of the college library: school libraries in the junior and senior high schools, and a local town public library, but of course neither type offers much direct support for the college community's needs.[3] The nearest city with a large library is almost 150 miles away. The college library is therefore isolated, but one would look for it to become the major postsecondary level library in this part of the state, and a center for research on the local tribe's heritage.

In terms of postsecondary and continuing education, as well as community information services, the academic and other library needs of the students and faculty, not to mention the community at large, are clearly evident after spending some time on the reservation. Students' experience is usually confined to the schooling and sociocultural environment of Indian communities, where the economy is invariably depressed and undeveloped.

There is only limited direct involvement with the different standards, priorities and social experience found in off-reservation communities, where much of the local consumer buying has to be done. In other words, young adults are rather conditioned to being satisfied with less opportunity for personal success, and therefore have lower expectations. And there is always the reservation environment to return to, with its protective skein of family life and government and tribal programs aimed at keeping one alive and a part of the Plains Indian tribal family.

However, one should not underemphasize the importance of the strength and reliability of traditional ties and support in the tribal community. It is a very ample, generous and ready "safety net," not only socio-economically and culturally, but psychologically. With all the family and relatives around, it is usually impossible to be abandoned and left to do harm to oneself or others, or to cultivate dereliction and ruinous ways for very long. . . . [4] In fact, it appears to be impossible, even if one leaves the reservation. And everyone will eventually know about it! As with most other Native communities, the tradition of sharing and caring is still very much alive, and is probably the single strongest aspect of the heritage to continue to this day. But in terms of the surrounding western economic society, the larger world of which everyone is ultimately a part, there is much to be done, and the tribal community college has slowly but surely been addressing its developmental needs.

Achieving accreditation several years ago, the college and its local supporters in the tribal community have been planning and working toward a wider array of curriculum offerings, including science courses with laboratory facilities, more vocational-technical programs, workshops with practical and timely value for the community, better coordinated college transfer credits, stronger adult education and remedial courses and facilities. It has also been organizing its support in the tribal community more effectively, to involve businesses, the various government agencies, the school district and alumni.

Housing and furnishings of the college library in 1986 were comfortable and adequate. Though a little crowded, it used the space efficiently. At one or two points during the day almost every one of the almost 30 seats were occupied. On average, it was almost always being used by several students and perhaps one or two faculty members, and also served as an unofficial student lounge, though at various times there had been a snack shop or student lounge set up in other buildings of the college's modest campus. It shared the same building as Student Services, some classrooms, and a room set aside for the student government. The library had received preferential treatment in terms of its housing and furnishings, and was a pleasant, well-outfitted library for a small community college. There were several tables and carrels, four microform reading stations, smoking and eating were permitted, and music played softly in the background. From time to time coffee was vended at one end of the circulation desk. Because it doubled as a study hall, there were plans to expand the library in a year or two into an adjoining room, once new classroom space became available. Despite its multiple use, the library was usually quiet, and students appeared to respect the need to maintain an atmosphere conducive to study. Later the library did in fact take over the large room next door, which doubled its size. In the fall of 1990, however, even this amount of space was limiting, and a nearby smaller room was assigned as a library workroom and storeroom. (Then the college applied for and received a Federal library construction grant, and in late 1993 a 5,490 sq.ft. library was dedicated. This added more space and seating capacity, new furnishings, and better lighting. A 1995 update is added at the end of this section.)

Staffing of the library has varied considerably, from the wife of a faculty member or an untrained former student to MLS librarians (all these last non-Indian). Budgetary constraints were the main reason for the variation in staffing standards. Sometimes there has been quite enough staff, with an MLS librarian, a full-time library assistant (who may or may not have library training or experience), and several work-study staff. At other times it can be like a one-man band: one librarian with a few work-study staff, who mostly worked evenings and whose conscientiousness was often in question. Use of the library in the evening, by the way, was minimal. For whatever reasons, students seemed to want to get all their library work and study time done during daylight hours.

After 1986 the library director job was held successively by two (non-MLS) masters degree holders and a Ph.D., who was too research-oriented. Since 1989-90 the librarian has again been an MLS librarian. Under the highly developmental conditions of the college, the librarian position should be either an MLS librarian or someone with at least a bachelor's degree who has background in libraries and knows what needs to be done in terms of daily operation and basic services. Either person should have had experience working in Native communities. The ideal would seem to be a tribal member who is an MLS librarian, but this is an almost impossible ideal at this time, there being so few such Native librarians available. During most of one academic year the library was operated by those with no library training whatsoever, although they had worked as library assistants (before there were any training opportunities, however).

If budgetary constraints become so severe that truly drastic cuts are necessary, it would perhaps be better to have no funds budgeted for library materials, if the alternative were to lose a diligent, knowledgeable and user-oriented library director. Granted, any college library should have a materials budget, but the conditions the tribally-controlled community colleges operate under make them a special case, though it would sometimes seem that college administrative costs might be reduced to ensure a stronger academic program. Future staff development plans might include training incentives or grants for a tribal college graduate, probably in education if not library science, to be the college librarian. The benefits in stability, commitment, role-modeling and community understanding with a home-grown college librarian would be manifest. On the other hand, there is the realistic argument that perhaps it is better to have an "outside," non-Indian librarian, who will not be involved either in local or tribal politics or be hampered with the identity of a "foreign" tribe!

Training for staff and library orientation for students have varied. Until the spring of 1985, no funds had been spent to send the library assistant or any other library staff for library-specific training, or even for tours and orientation at outside libraries, though they might be funded to attend out-of-state annual or other general Indian education conferences for four or five days at a time. This should change, as a policy required by the college, and not remain at the discretion or whim of a changing college librarian. There should be regularly budgeted travel funding for library staff other than an MLS library director to attend library-specific training within the state, and to attend annual meetings of the State Library Association. Work-study staff in the future need to have had at least introductory computer courses, and be trained to operate the library's Mac Plus computer in most library management areas. Any library assistant hired in the future would need the same computer training or background. For the past few years library staff have continued to receive training in library procedures.

Some kind of library instruction was offered to students from time to time during the 1980s, both informally and in credit courses. During 1985-86 a comprehensive, three-credit course in Library Research Strategy and Techniques was offered. This included sessions on study skills, oral and written communication, even music appreciation and other aspects of intellectual growth. It was found that for most students' library skills were only superficially developed, and even some faculty had to be helped to recognize and use the available library services and resources. A few students who had been to Native junior colleges or progressive high schools, or who had spent time at a university, were at home using the library. Others hadn't the slightest idea of the role a library can play in a student's work and personal growth, let alone how to use one effectively. Much coaching and encouragement and positive outcomes are needed to bring such students into active and confident library use. A library instruction course continues to be offered by the current library director.

There is always a need to further stimulate the growth among community college and undergraduate students of some basic intellectual habits, such as intellectual curiosity, the desire to learn, initiative, objectivity, a critical and interpretive approach, study skills, a broadening world view, and self-discipline toward academic achievement. This is particularly true for those Indian and other Native students whose world experience is often confined to that of the highly supportive and undemanding rural reservation or isolated and tradition-bound village life, though we must also rec-

ognize the many disruptive and debilitating effects of incoming urbanization and modernization, which bring world experience to the reservation in
seductive and exploitative ways.

At Native colleges such as Plains Indian Community College, the oblig-
atory array of remedial and developmental courses may sometimes have a
negative side. Too many such courses can be discouraging to students want-
ing to pursue degrees and higher education generally, as time and the funds
available to them dwindle.[5]

On the Plains Indian reservation, where slower, easier days and more casual attitudes prevailed than are found in the dominant culture's open-
economy communities outside, a tendency or perhaps even a tradition
seemed in place, that students and even occasionally faculty could miss
classes or be late with relative impunity, that this was the way one went to
college—although the administration did from time to time admonish and
exhort everyone to attend classes regularly, and to complete assignments on
time. In 1985-86 the point was being made in faculty and general staff
meetings that the college should be a model in the community, not only of
modern standards of postsecondary education, but in addressing community and economic development needs of the tribal community in a responsible, professional manner. Salient features of a model regimen should,
as a matter of course, include good attendance and punctuality, among
other supportive and productive habits.

There is even good-humored consensus that the much revered and af-
fectionately invoked "Indian time" should perhaps be phased out, at least
in terms of meeting one's academic or professional commitments at the college. To be accurate, there were only a few who abused this otherwise
healthy custom at the expense of others. After all, it is mostly the urbanized
and partially automated modern man and woman who actually choose to
live according to a timepiece on their wrist, showing the instant time in
hours, minutes and seconds, along with today's date!

The strengths and benefits of a bicultural and bilingual background—
the unique value of being Native American—need to be recognized by all
educators. Almost all the faculty for courses other than Native American
studies were non-Indian, and this tended to place a different value or subtle character difference on the non-NAS curriculum. One sensed that a student was asking himself or herself, if unconsciously, "If the non-NAS
courses are taught only by whites, will I have difficulties that are cross-
cultural in origin, and will I make it? Do I really want to apply myself, and
learn these things on their terms, as they say I should learn them? Are these
courses really relevant for me, and the tribe? Does it matter if I drop out or
fail this time?" For knowledgeable students other factors might enter into
their thinking: "Why are these white people here teaching, when the salaries
are below standard and there are no benefits [in 1986], and our reservation
town and nearest communities have so little to offer them, compared to

what they surely must be used to. They must in some way be sub-standard faculty, and we are getting a second-class education, so why should I try very hard, or be worried? Perhaps I'll transfer to another college anyway."

One shouldn't conclude that this is altogether the situation, but given the very uncompetitive terms on which faculty have been hired, at least until the 1990s, there was the possibility of such psychological losses among the students. Real and equitable improvement in faculty status was badly needed. The quandary here was not only for non-Indian faculty, who did not have access to the local Indian Health Service Hospital at that time, nor local housing advantages or other benefits available for homegrown Indian faculty and staff. There were even tribal faculty who had taught for several years and who were authorities nationally on the tribal heritage, yet they had never received a raise or tenured status. One white faculty member with a doctoral degree, who also had several years' service at the college, was earning 40% more than the remaining ten full-time faculty members. On at least two separate occasions faculty went through the motions of drawing up a salary schedule and insurance/retirement plan, at the administration's request, but with no result either time. (In 1990 we learned that a medical plan was finally available for all faculty.) In the past the turnover of non-Indian faculty has been high and there was little monetary incentive to remain, except that the work of teaching at the college is personally as well as professionally rewarding, and in other respects every effort was made by the college administration to make one's stay there as comfortable, fulfilling and stimulating as possible. The ongoing exceptions of salary raises, comprehensive benefits, tenure, and better housing alternatives really reflected on the Tribal Business Council itself, which seemed not to be receptive to the College Council's recommendations. In fact, Tribal Council members on the College Council (the governing body) were rarely at meetings. As a faculty member, which the librarian is, one is well involved in almost all aspects of the college's operation.

The tribally controlled community colleges in the United States were established in 1978 by passage of Public Law 95-471, "The Tribally Controlled Community College Act," which was amended and extended by Public Law 98-192 in 1983. It has brought Federal funding to set up and maintain a number of community and junior colleges on reservations or in areas with a heavy Native population. These are new ventures, just over 15 years old, with many and constant start-up problems. In 1986 there were 22 community and junior colleges in the American Indian Higher Education Consortium (AIHEC). Some, like Haskell Indian Junior College, have been in existence for much longer. In 1994 the tribally controlled colleges received land grant status from Congress, but the long-term benefits or consequences of this remain to be seen.

The materials budget for the library has improved significantly since the mid-1980s. Earlier, like faculty salaries and benefits, the materials budget persisted at a consistently inadequate and substandard level. The college then depended heavily on donated books and occasional small grants for what amounted to normal maintenance and growth. Collection development, in terms of supporting the curriculum, could only be said to have achieved a degree of success in the popular area of Native Americana generally. But materials on the tribal heritage itself were only at a beginning stage of development. One reason for this situation is that the tribal heritage materials tend to be retained by users for a long time, or be passed around and hence be regarded as "missing."[6] And tribal cultural programs like Native American Studies sometimes have their own, grant-funded collection of materials, which are only accessible by permission of an instructor until the grant-funded program comes to end, sometimes years later. In the mid-1980s there was no coordination of collection development in this area, so that the library might at least know what other tribal heritage programs had in the way of specific holdings on the tribal culture, if not administer some access to the materials. However, if a working relationship could be established with the Tribal Heritage coordinator, this situation should improve.

In the mid-1980s most periodical files were print, and the Western Library Network (WLN) database was on microfiche. The library acquired or received a variety of donated periodical files, which, though intellectually stimulating, had little to do with "curriculum support." However, it was a collection that rewarded serendipity and was impressive enough to be noted by the State Librarian. This happy condition was achieved through the retention of almost all periodicals received. The purpose here was to expose students in this isolated academic environment to as much academic stimulation as possible through an extensive and diverse display of periodical literature, with depth in some subjects of curriculum usefulness.

Ten years later, standards had markedly improved. Three areas of increased strength included bibliographic access tools, computer applications, and the acquisition of periodical files and tribal archival records on microfilm. By 1990 it had a Macintosh SE30 with a laser printer, and later added an IBM PSC2 for ILL purposes. The Western Library Network was accessed through a subscription to periodically updated CD-ROM disks, and about half of the collection had been put into the WLN database. Resources at Montana State University libraries could be accessed by modem, including databases like ERIC and the Wilson indexes. There was one older computer for student use, but they had to provide their own software.

The library also served increasingly as a de facto public library, and in 1990 the Tribal Business Council designated it as the tribal library. The periodical collection had grown through a combination of subscriptions and donations with this eventuality in mind. Thus in 1986 one found forty years of *Scientific American* (with the bound index), about twenty years of *Progressive,* a total of about thirty years of *Science* in a broken run to date, with current issues received. There were many key titles in aviation and space, and files of several standard titles in library science. There was a print file of over ten years of *The Chronicle of Higher Education,* with the half-yearly indexes accumulated in slightly reduced size into one folder. The same grant mentioned above also brought almost a thousand dollars worth of microfilmed tribal archival records (55 rolls) from the National Anthropological Archives.

The second area receiving a boost during 1985-86 was the social sciences, through a collection of several hundred titles passed on to the college by a former State University social sciences department head. These were not out-of-date materials, by the way, but current or recent titles. Another source that was utilized was the Library of Congress Exchange and Gifts Division's Surplus Books Program, located in Washington, D.C. This consists of books discarded by government libraries everywhere, and sometimes includes very useful material for developing libraries with small budgets. For example, many reference titles are replaced almost every year, such as the *World of Learning.* Certainly an edition one or two years old still has a great deal of reference value.

But the area needing most support in the collection remained the curriculum specifically. Although earlier there was a small library materials budget from the college's general fund each year, there was too much dependence on donated materials or "handouts" from other areas of the academic affairs or general college budget. This created a condition of haphazard or random collection development. However, there was an effort to begin to address this situation. The college president issued a directive that required all program grants to have, if legally possible, a line item for curriculum materials, which would be housed in the library. This policy continues today. That step alone helped a great deal toward providing an adequate curriculum materials component for the library collection. In addition the Department of Academic Affairs, which oversees the library, has provided steady support, and by 1990 the library was receiving from 7 to 12% of the college's annual budget, including a regular library materials component.

The audiovisual equipment of the college was controlled by the library, and improved annually. Funds for purchase, maintenance and repair came out of the overall academic affairs budget. In 1985-86, within the library were a dependable photocopier, two microfiche readers, and two other readers usable for either microfiche or microfilm (one with the image rotation feature). One of the latter was a reader-printer, but unfortunately without image rotation (it was acquired before my arrival and was found unopened in a storage area). In microforms the library had, in addition to the microfilm mentioned earlier, a large collection of microfilmed periodicals by and about Native Americans, and a large collection of pamphlets about Native Americans on microfiche. The microfilm collection was split between 35mm and 16mm, and the microfilm readers did not have automatic feeding, so there was a little more hand-work involved in reading microfilm. One microfiche reader, stationed at the reference desk, was dedicated for use of the Western Library Network (WLN) Resource Directory, a database of over 1.7 million titles (1986) held by many Northwest libraries. The range of audiovisual equipment available included television in both Umatic and VHS formats, video production equipment in Umatic, 16mm movie projectors, filmstrip/slide projectors, opaque projectors of two different types, phonographs, and an audiocassette recorder/player.

In 1986, bibliographic access tools included a conventional card catalog, the WLN Resource Directory on microfiches, the *Readers' Guide to Periodical Literature, Facts on File,* and various in-house files for accessing information on specific subjects in collections of materials lacking indexes. When the WLN microfiches and ILL service were first offered to college faculty in that year, the response was immediate and heavy.

In mid-1995 we received the following update: The new library facility, which now includes a separate archival area, had been in use 18 months, and among the new users were workers at the local Indian Health Service hospital. A working relationship with the Tribal Heritage coordinator had yet to be established. Public employees' medical insurance was available to all employees, the majority of it paid for by the college. The state's Job Service (statewide job-placement listings and help finding a job) had a kiosk and touch-screen database terminal. There was computerized genealogical searching available in the Archives area, and course textbooks continued to be placed on reserve in the library.

Twenty-seven colleges are now in the American Indian Higher Education Consortium (AIHEC), and there remained the problem of making the same amount of funding available cover an increasing student population. AIHEC libraries did not have a formal organization at that time, but a Montana Indian Tribal Libraries Group had formed. And finally, the Tribal Business Council no longer oversaw the college directly, and their relationship was likened to that of a university system and state legislature.

One goal of this and other tribally controlled community colleges is accreditation by their regional Association of Schools and Colleges. From the beginning, pressure is on a college's administration to raise faculty and academic standards, which also includes the (sometimes distant) goal of an MLS librarian for their institution. The budget for each college's fiscal year is determined by the enrollment of full-time Indian student equivalents in academic quarters preceding the current year, and the approved Tribally Controlled Community College (TCCC) Act budget, both of which fluctuate from year to year. There has been an increase in both the number of TCCCs and the number of Indian students, yet until recently the Congressional appropriation remained unrealistically inadequate. Thus, the college was constrained in offering relatively low, non-competitive salaries to prospective faculty, and in the early years the library had to survive on very unreliable funding, usually quite "soft." We learned of library situations at other TCCCs that were much worse off, some without even the beginnings of an appropriate collection. In the early developmental mode that these colleges are in, it seems essential to have the very best trained librarian possible, ideally an MLS holder or its equivalent, or the library may be relegated to low status and service energy. Just as important is to have strong advocates for quality library resources and services in the college, which in the optimum case would be both the librarian and his or her supervisor. It also helps to have support on the college council, and even the parent tribal council.

The librarian at another, nearby tribal college, though neither an Indian nor an MLS librarian, was a graduate of a prestigious northeastern university and was raised in the area. He was an enterprising library administrator and helped bring a superlative library building to his college through a Federal Library Services and Construction Act grant.

With its limited Federal funding, the college tried to increase its funds by various means. There was fund-raising in the relatively poor local tribal community and among the few merchants and corporations serving the area. There were restricted grants, which were constantly being applied for from the Federal government, and modest grants from the Tribal Business Council. The tribe, however, needed to give the college more fiscal support. The bond issue for a new and modern physical plant had been on hold for years. In the 1980s there was no assigned housing within the town for college faculty, the majority of whom commuted from "bedroom" and market communities just off the reservation, twelve to thirty-five miles away, which can be a distinct hardship during the winter months. Housing in the town for anyone was extremely difficult to find, and often of marginal standards—however, it's the kind of housing many permanent residents have. And while Indian faculty and staff had access to medical services at the new Indian Health Service Hospital, until the mid-1990s this was not available to non-Indian personnel except in life-threatening cases, which made for rather harrowing health care at times. As for tribal government, recent tribal elections give some indication that perhaps more progressive politics will be advanced, and from these the college and its faculty and staff can only gain.

Is a tribally controlled community college good or bad for the Indian community? And if it is wanted, accepted and developed according to the standards that accreditation brings, what more will be lost of the traditional culture? These are questions the leaders and elders of the tribe will be wrestling with over the coming years. Such questions are also closely linked to issues like economic and community development, all of which will bring the white man's thinking, ways and values still more strongly onto the isolated and insular tribal reservation, poor economically but still rich in tradition and with the dependable network of family and mutual support so characteristic of most Native communities. Improvement of socioeconomic welfare and the accompanying benefits of capitalist community development will also tend, however, to overwhelm and eclipse the conservative traditions, perhaps bringing the "needless harm" foreseen by tribal elders. And the college library will inevitably be an integral and significant element in this transformation. The desirable tangential direction of these two forces is to keep a healthy balance between western and traditional education, in order to maintain the strength, character and control to "enhance" their future life, garnering the best of both cultures for coming generations.

Therefore, this tribal community college, along with others (funded almost exclusively by Federal monies, namely Title 3 of the Indian Education Act), has to deal with this permanent dilemma, in terms of education goals. It wants to balance its curriculum and extension efforts between preserving the tribal heritage and preparing its students and the tribal community to survive and be successful in terms of the dominant society's economy and pervasive cultural influence. Yet in 1985-86 one got the impression and sense that perhaps the tribal leaders really only wanted to survive, to keep going along with their marginal ranching economy, heavy with unemployment and welfare, and didn't look forward to entering into the white man's full-scale capitalist economy (through oil and gas development on the reservation)—although there was an active chamber of commerce group and reformist elements that wanted very much to break away from conservative retrenchment policies.

A further compounding factor was that the vehicle for resolving this dilemma was the community college concept, as officially introduced and monitored by the outside society's regional Association of Schools and Colleges. Western educational structure and its bureaucratic relationships do not always allow for Indian ways of leadership, governance and communication, so that a certain tension is inherent in the process. (It has been suggested that a separate association of Indian/Native schools and colleges in the U.S. be organized to carry out accreditation for the TCCCs.) Then there is the relationship of the college with the Tribal Business Council that created it, which is still evolving toward improved trust and independence. But on a personal level, especially for those tribal faculty and staff who may have limited experience of living and working in non-Indian educational settings, the difficulty of reconciling reservation working concepts and relationships with mandated institutional goals can be a source of ongoing stress and confusion. In fact, at almost any college meeting discussing goals, new programs, relations with the tribe, the community and outside institutions, and development generally, these vexing cross-cultural considerations underlie one's thinking. It is seen as an impossible task—achieving a balance between the tribal heritage and the surrounding and infiltrating dominant culture—but all efforts are directed toward the most achievable compromise. (For an inside analysis of the dilemma Indian educators face, see Hampton.)

An interesting point is the relationship of relatively urbane, higher-degreed faculty to this remote, undersized library. It can be ambivalent at times, to say the least, especially for new non-Native faculty. Their previous experience has often been with university research or similar academic libraries, and the young tribal college library can be a huge letdown. From their perspective, which is often a specialized one, the collection is invariably seen as appallingly limited. A few faculty who come to this tribal college are working on higher degrees. Most want to be kept informed of developments in their field, or scan the ads in professional journals for better paying jobs elsewhere! There was a need for the library to bend over backwards to improve services for faculty, and to thereby indirectly increase library use by students as well. The goal was to work on eliminating the attitude that reflects low expectations of the library, by consistently improving it in every area of perceived or manifest weakness. Some of the faculty and administration who were taking extension courses in education from one of the state university's visiting faculty depended very heavily on the library's interlibrary loan service.

Working as a town-resident, non-Indian librarian for the Plains Indian Community College brought professional challenges and intellectual stimulation, though a significant degree of personal isolation among the somewhat closed and conservative domestic society of this Plains Indian Tribe. The vehicle I had at the time was in such poor mechanical condition that I couldn't leave town with it. During the summer months we ran a soccer program for youth (boys were the only participants), and this had the support of both the tribal recreation department and the town AAU club. Later, we attempted to contact the well-developed soccer program of a related tribe close by, but shortly after that I decided to return to Seattle to be near my son, then five years old. We took a load of boys to play a distant team and celebrated our defeats by going to a local "water slide." I wrote a few letters to the editor of the reservation paper, attended local pow wows, Indian dances and stick gambling, went often to the community swimming pool, which had a sauna and jacuzzi for relaxation, and shared my house with an Indian companion for the winter. As a transplanted rural Alaskan, I felt right at home.

The Bay Indian Tribe

From a remote plains Indian location, we go west to the coast. This is a story about looking for the heritage of a Native people where only fragmentary, peripheral or obscure sources exist, either living or recorded. The people are what we shall call the Bay Indians on the Northwest coast, with a reservation located on a few hundred acres at the entrance to the bay. I was employed as a CETA-funded heritage researcher for exactly one year, from Labor Day 1980 through Labor Day 1981, until the advent of President Reagan resulted in the elimination of almost all CETA jobs. However, in subsequent years, during my first Alaskan work stint, I returned each summer to volunteer time to produce a series of heritage publications for the tribal Heritage Committee, the main title being an exhaustive, computerized tribal bibliography on the heritage and history of the Bay Indians.

The Bay Indian tribe is comprised of two primary tribal stocks that came together on their present domain about two hundred years ago when diseases decimated both. Its tribal enrollment totals just over 100. It was finally recognized as a non-treaty tribe early in 1971, and the heritage program started in 1977. As a non-Native librarian with a curiosity about the Native heritage of place, wherever I am, I was familiar with some of the usual sources one consults in retracing and recreating the Native heritage and the ancestral domain. But on the bay I soon realized that there was a lot more than books, microfilms and artifacts to look into. There were the coastal people themselves—specifically the Bay Indians. The first Bay Indian elder I became friends with was one of the last surviving children of the last hereditary chief of the Bay Indians.

I had arrived on the reservation for the job interview after a 100-mile Trailways bus ride, and on stepping off the local bus from the coastal market town an hour's drive away that hot August afternoon I couldn't spot a soul moving about. There were houses clustered at either end of the reservation on the coastal highway, about a half mile apart, with tidal marshes on the seaward side and low, wooded hills to landward. I was walking around tentatively in the small housing area when suddenly I heard a stentorian voice. An old woman was calling from a back porch about 50 yards away. It was clear she was calling to me and I went over to have lunch and a chat with this venerable and wise elder, who I learned later was so favored by the reservation children. I tried my best to be the polite guest, but soon learned that she wanted to get acquainted, and to talk. Her wry, infectious humor soon came out, and I felt a part of things right away. At that time she was the primary elder working on "salvaging the heritage," and though I talked with the business manager later on, it turned out that my visit with this gentle yet strong-charactered lady was my main job interview. On looking back, this was also one of my first encounters with the oral tradition, the web of talk, familiarity and curiosity. This, combined with kinship bonds, however remote in time, blood or place, binds the Native community and carries the otherwise little-documented heritage forward.

The heritage program had begun three years earlier, and a quantity of material had been accumulated. This included copies of newspaper and magazine articles, books, maps, government documents, and a collection of oral history tapes that had been made of elders throughout the area. There were transcripts of most of these tapes, but I was dismayed to find, on listening to them, that these weren't the usual one-on-one interviews, but involved three or four participants, sometimes all talking at once! I would often hear the coordinator, a young white woman, gently trying to draw out the interviewee, a grandmother, on some point, as the "elderlies" visited back and forth animatedly. Then on one tape the earnest coordinator finally blurted out the revelation, "It's wonderful you're all visiting like this!" There it was: the wonderful grant funds from the National Endowment for the Arts had brought together tribal elders who hadn't seen each other for many years. It was an opportunity to renew acquaintance, to share news of families and memories of childhood and youth. There was heritage information as well. A few tapes had been made during car rides around the area, when sites of oldtime activities were identified, with Indian names.

One elder knew the language better than anyone and had taught it now and then as part of the heritage program. She developed a working relationship with a university scholar in Indian languages of the Northwest. However, this knowledge was mostly comprised of vocabulary lists and fragments of grammar. Although there are aluminum disk recordings in the National Anthropological Archives of her language and others of the region that were being spoken fluently, by the time funds are acquired to transfer these recordings to audiotapes, the elders who are conversant with their languages will have passed away.

Early on I learned that a grant had been received years before from the National Endowment for the Humanities for a heritage project to promote tribal and public education, but due to administrative mishaps it had had to be abandoned. I was puzzled and surprised, because no one had mentioned it until I found the papers while digging through the files. Anyway, we managed to resurrect it, but when we were ready to start, President Reagan took office and I lost my CETA (federally funded) job; no one was available to take it over. So when I left, it was dropped. We were disappointed, but I sensed a certain resignation, as if such things were expected. As for my own survival, by sheer luck I had been offered a high-paying community college job in Alaska (see chapter 2) and immediately went north.

In the following years I returned during my summers off and stayed on the "res." With permission I decided to start work on a series of heritage publications, drawing on the two files crammed full of resource materials. I was determined to make up for the failure of the old project. Several titles were confected on aspects of the ancestral culture and environment, some stories supplied by elders, and there was an exhaustive bibliography of sources. I spent considerable time discussing the various subjects with elders and other resource people outside and running down sources that could further verify any statements made. Final drafts were again shared with both elders on the reservation and outside experts.

When it came to publishing them, there was no money. There seemed to be a reluctance to venture the tribe's or the heritage committee's meager funds, as if this modest venture might also "fail." We finally found a donated paper supply and donated printing by an area Indian service agency. Seven years of steady work by the heritage committee and two coordinators had borne fruit. The publications were copyrighted and are still selling.

The absence of accomplishment in heritage projects was due to several factors. Anthropologists and other independent researchers were profoundly distrusted. There was a suspicion that heritage knowledge and artifacts would be claimed and taken over by these workers, who from time to time offered their contractual services. Negotiations over terms of their work had repeatedly broken down. There was possibly an underlying resentment that these outsiders might know more about at least some facets of the Bay Indian heritage than even the Bay Indian elders themselves. There was disagreement among the families as to whether or not to allow these academics and other white professionals to do such work for the tribe, when what they really wanted was to acquire this training and do the work themselves. It seemed that those who were receiving pay to work on the heritage were always whites—including their own hired heritage researcher!

A question came up about the need for the oral history master tapes to have backup copies in another location, and a nearby university offered to make copies free, on one condition: that the university be able to make its own set, and that these tapes be made available for researchers. This offer was declined. Even though the conditions for access could have been made as stringent as the tribe wanted, it was still not secure and private enough. I sensed that there was a strong reluctance even to let these tapes leave the tribal community center, for fear that somehow unfriendly hands would get hold of them. I once heard another librarian, one prominent in the history of areas just inland and an author of a number of short tracts on local history, in referring to Indians and their alleged disinterest in studying their heritage in libraries and archives, ask, "Aren't they interested in their own ethnology?" It's curious how quickly those from the dominant society forget or quickly gloss over the experience of Native peoples in Indian-white relations in North America, and how blind and insensitive they can be to the profound disruption, dislocation, decimation, deprivation and other losses endured by the yet surviving descendants of the original inhabitants. As for their non-use of libraries, more on that later.

The Bay Indians were "canoe Indians" in the old days, yet not a sign of this was evident to the reservation visitor, though in private everyone believed they should be able to fish and collect (or grow the today necessary imported stocks of) shellfish in the bay as their ancestors had done. But state and federal laws prohibited this, and besides, such resources had long ago been depleted to the point where close regulation was essential for the survival of most species. What few fish and shellfish there now were, were heavily harvested on the bay, on the rivers leading into it, and on the ocean for anadromous species.

How are we to know today that the Bay Indians had a flourishing marine culture? They were always in the water harvesting shellfish and pursuing seals and waterfowl or collecting grasses and other plants, traveling over it in their ubiquitous and versatile carved wooden canoes of various shapes and sizes, or beside it, in their settlements and fish camps, and at gathering and trading places. Their water trails went across marshes and up strings of small lakes on the coast, up sloughs and rivers, along the seashore (just beyond the surf), across shallow estuarine bays and coves (keeping to channels as the tide ebbed), on the tidal crest of rivers inland and back out, portaging to the nearby great river mouth for the spring and summer salmon runs.

Can we tell that the canoes were made from great cedars growing at the water's edge or near it—though the original growth has long since been cut down? That beached whales were regularly a part of the economy, and produced important trade items—though the whale population along the coast is only a fraction of what it was in pre-contact times? That the salmon fisheries were unlimited and far more than the local populations of early settlers with their unbridled acquisitiveness could consume? (Though today the multiple dams, drained wetlands, pollution, and many more fishermen have decreased salmon stocks to an alarming level.)

Although I wasn't working for the Bay Indian Tribe as a bona fide librarian, my job included various library-related and archival tasks and problems. As well as the oral history tapes and transcripts to look over, and the heritage publications to work on later, there were two file cabinets crammed full of collected materials that were arranged in a homemade filing system that took a while to figure out. (After about six months of contending with it, I finally went through every drawer and folder, almost literally with a magnifying glass, ignoring file folder headings with arcane codes—there was no time to organize everything more conventionally.) There was also no tribal library collection as such, but some books and documents had been collected over the years, and they have become the nucleus of one. For a long time these were locked in a file drawer for safekeeping. Later on, the business office staff in the new tribal community center established some of their shelves for the display of these and other library-type materials, which could be consulted by anyone allowed admittance to the office. They could also be signed out for home use by tribal members.

Gradually the collection has been growing, through occasional purchases and gifts. It now includes, of course, the tribal heritage publications. One of these is of main interest to librarians, and was the most time-consuming publication worked on. It is an exhaustive and computerized bibliography on the heritage and history of the Bay Indians, with many entries annotated. Now although this is not exactly a best-seller—the illustrated stories are the most popular—it was felt that it would be an indispensable tool for accessing information and sources of all kinds (including resource people) on the tribe. Brought together in one database is every source found in seven years of heritage work, in all media. It will be utilized more in the future. The software used was the Personal Bibliographic System, using an Apple II+ computer, and selective bibliographies could be produced on many specific aspects of the heritage. By 1985 there were more than 400 entries. Now, of course, computerization of heritage resources could be greatly enhanced, but the extent of progress since then is unknown.

In pursuing research for Native people, being an experienced librarian can be a help or a handicap (depending on one's flexibility), and having a background in the antiquarian book trade plus archival training opened the mind to other approaches. A familiarity with the very special subject of research on the Native peoples—not to mention that dealing with specific tribes or bands, etc.—is something that has to be appreciated in practice. Research for the Bay Indians was especially vexing because of the lack of enough elders with memory going back before the days of advanced acculturation. Seemingly there was one generation's knowledge missing, and one wished more documentation could have been done 50 years previously. There are still many sources in repositories yet unbreached, and one hopes that more will be learned. In recreating some of the heritage through the publications, it was sometimes possible for elders to make clarifications and additions, but more often than not there was little comment. Reliance was heavy on outside, non-Indian-generated sources. However, the many oral history tapes hold a great deal of information about the historical period, at least, and await a future researcher. My main interest was in the ancestral environment and aboriginal conditions, and for this I had to rely on bits and pieces from a variety of sources (primarily early Euroamerican descriptions, anthropological and archeological studies and other scientific work, as well as government surveys and other documents), along with extrapolations from sources on adjacent peoples or that generic to the southern Northwest coast.

Diseases and dominance brought by the Euroamericans barely 200 years ago eventually eclipsed the Bay Indian world almost totally. Today, one could say there is only a slight shadow of the material heritage to be seen. The changing U.S. administration and policies in Indian affairs nationally also helped to discourage and dissipate the old ways of thinking and living. Not that the Bay Indians would choose to return to them. Not at all. But they do want their fair share of access to the fraction of subsistence resources still remaining to be harvested in season, and efforts at litigating such aboriginal rights into a commercial reality are being pursued from time to time.

I've followed with interest the various disputes that come and go in Bay Tribal politics. Frustrating as these developments sometimes are to the tribal worker (whether Native *or* non-Native), they baffled me for a long time until I found that the opposing factions are the various extended families involved, and that this is about as ancient a condition as one can find in the heritage. For it is the extended family that is the strongest constellation of prideful individuals in Native life, a ready-made force that guarantees the stiffest natural competition for survival and dominance. However, with modern demands for cohesive and coordinated management of tribal resources, traditional ways have had to adapt again so that the whole tribal community benefits, us and them, young and old, now and future generations.

As an amateur researcher and sometime librarian for the Bay Indians, I've had the privilege of being able to learn as much as I can about their heritage. I hope the future will bring more opportunities to learn, and perhaps to discover more of the ancestral life and conditions. Time spent with the Bay Indians eventually lets one feel the thin yet durable fabric of heritage that is still intact in modern times.

The Connection Between Libraries, Archival and Museum Projects

From an oral tradition, and having had most untrustworthy and uncertain relations with Euro-North Americans, the Native peoples have not been disposed to entrust their efforts at archival organization to outsiders. In the United States, funds are available for tribal archival projects from the National Historical Publications and Records Commission, the National Endowment for the Arts and the National Endowment for the Humanities. Although an increasing number of tribes and Native organizations are embarked on archival projects, this progress can only be judged as meager, relative to the quantity of material needing management. One should also distinguish between tribal government and private records, and Federal government records about the tribe. The former types remain within the tribe, whereas the latter ends up in the regional Federal archives. There is a growing debate among archival authorities due to the movement among the tribes, especially those with active archival projects, to have all records on the tribe returned to it.[7]

Until recently the Plains Tribe discussed earlier had no archival program of its own. Its records were stored in scattered locations like former agency sites, various buildings, and even private houses. The first need is to identify these locations, to officially take possession of them (or make copies) as part of the tribal archival program, and to take steps to inventory and securely store the records for future processing. There were also maps and photographs stored in various locations, some in private hands, and these originals or copies should be brought within the tribal library and archival programs.

In some remote Native communities a proto-museum in the form of a secure display case or two, plus some modest documentation efforts toward an archival program, would perhaps be even more attractive and fitting for a Native community than a small library alone, unless the library is tailored by local control to provide the most appropriate information available in the most attractive formats—which implies more graphic materials. Interest in the past heritage, in families, places and local activities has a natural relevance and appeal. A museum *per se* or a professional archival program is an expensive and highly sophisticated operation needing a suitable building and some professional management at all times. A small library operation, on the other hand, can at least start with a very modest outlay in funds, housing and staff. And it can also house some beginning museum and archival projects.

Technical assistance is now available for starting and maintaining a tribal archives, and workshops are scheduled from time to time across the U.S. and Canada. The best initial contact would be the Society of American Archivists. The book *Native American Archives, An Introduction,* by John A. Fleckner, lists a variety of helpful materials as well as "sources of assistance" for any Native entity considering the establishment of an archives.

Another controversial aspect of heritage preservation is the recall of tribal artifacts from museums and other collections around the world. But before such a relatively large-scale enterprise can even begin, a professional museum facility is needed, and a small but growing number of tribes are establishing such facilities. The next scale up, then, would be to have a tribal library with archival storage and a small museum area attached.

The issue of "recalling" tribal artifacts from museums, universities and even private collections around the world, and especially in Europe and North America, for the express purpose of installing them in new tribal museum facilities, is coming to the forefront in both Native communities (with or without museums) and among collectors, both private and public. Douglas Cole, in his book on "the scramble for Northwest Coast artifacts," reminds us how these materials were acquired, primarily in the 1880s and 90s:

> Anthropological collecting had special impetus behind it: the realization that time was essential, that civilization was everywhere pushing the primitive to the wall, destroying the material culture and even extinguishing the native stock itself . . . the amount of collectible materials was enormous . . . the Northwest Coast was one of the few North American areas of rich and striking material cultures which remained relatively unshattered at the advent of the Museum Age. Only in the far western and northern portions of the continent could fairly complete collections still be made. Secondly, on the coast the impact of western culture was simultaneous with the collector's work, and in great measure assisted it. The calamitous decline of the native population from contact until the latter decades of the 19th century [due to diseases brought by Europeans—GHH], for example, must have created a surplus of many objects at precisely the period of the most intense organized collecting.

. . . Thirdly, the introduction of European tools and the changes in native society from post-contact wealth led to a fluoresence of artistic production in the 19th century. . . . In the great population movements [one of which created the Bay Indian Tribe out of two previously existing and adjacent linguistic groups—GHH], spurred by disease and the introduction of canneries and missions to the north coast, many villages were abandoned, occasionally almost intact. . . .8

Much trading and negotiating was involved in these transactions, as well as deceit and occasionally outright theft. Skulls and skeletons could only be acquired this latter way, for example, "A poor fishing season meant a good collecting winter." Household items that had European replacements, like pots and pans, blankets, weapons and the whole range of tools used in hunting, fishing and gathering, were easy to get, whereas "cultural items still used were much harder to come by." Often these belonged not to one person, but to a family or a secret society. Then there were those artifacts that were simply given as a gift, usually priceless pieces that were heirlooms from the far distant past.

When a local professional museum program has been established, the tribe is in an excellent position to negotiate the return of these relics of the heritage. However, progress on this issue is at a stage similar to that of the return of tribal records of all types to a tribal archives. These future trends, along with Native library development that is Native controlled, are part of the Native cultural renaissance of the future.

St. Mary's on the Lower Yukon
The Library as Curator, The School as Village

The former village administrator (a non-Native) of St. Mary's on the Lower Yukon explains:

> I think libraries [in remote Native villages] have the best chance to survive if they become repositories for local history. . . . Perhaps a library in combination with a small museum is a better concept. If the library can be a place to which people can come to be reminded of the past, reminded in the form of books, photographs, artifacts and other items, it will then become a place people will want to keep.9

Another point he brings up is the foreign, "imported" character of the library started in a Native community. In such an atmosphere, which is common enough, it requires one committed supporter or a few dedicated and interested people to keep the library going, at least for some time. The village administrator did not see village libraries as being very viable, at least as presently operated (in the Yukon-Kuskokwim delta of Alaska), because of the many other pressing public necessities. Further, . . .

> . . . It is not likely that the library in a village would continue beyond the provision of state grants specifically for libraries. For the most part, I think people are generally indifferent to the library, if for no other reason than that a library is not a familiar or expected institution in a village. . . . On the other hand, the same can be said for almost every service now available in the community, including such basic services as police, fire, water and sewer. . . . At some point library services may become something people in the villages would prefer not to do without. I do not despair for the fact that libraries did not come as a result of community action, because over time the people in the villages will make of the library *what they want it to be.* If libraries are important, they will remain [my emphasis].[10]

In the same village, by the way, there has been a Catholic boarding high school for many years, but it closed in 1987: the St. Mary's School. Establishment of K-12 schools in almost all Yupik Eskimo villages resulted in a steady decline in St. Mary's student enrollment, which was almost entirely Yupik. A poor school economically, many of its staff were Catholic volunteers from the "lower 48." It had a library, but its collection was old and consisted mostly of donated books, including a lot of discarded Alaska school system textbooks. However, it was popular and was used for studying and counseling, as well as reference, probably because of the high value placed on learning, study and intellectual growth in the school, the main attraction and catalyst being the special relationship between students and staff:

> Highly personalized relationships were the scaffolding through which students acquired the behavioral structure of the majority culture. . . . White teachers and Eskimo students negotiated new forms of social interaction at critical points of cultural conflict. . . . St. Mary's taught new behavior—such as class participation and leadership—by presenting them as expressions not of individual assertion but of the group supportive cultural ideal.[11]

The above quoted author comments on the school library and its function in the school:

> . . . the library was much in use. Students studied there frequently. It was also the site for a lot of informal teacher/student exchange. Many of the conversations about books and ideas on a person to person basis took place in the library. . . . The library at St. Mary's was important as a social center. . . .[12]

In essence the St. Mary's School's success, including that of the library, despite a poverty budget, was due to its having been a kind of Yupik village in itself.

Notes

1. Definition of cultural relativism by Geo. M. Foster in *Traditional Societies and Technological Change,* p. 87.
2. "Plains Indians Tribe" is a pseudonym for the actual name of the tribe. A few features identifying the tribe's location have been slightly altered toward a generic description. "Bay Indian Tribe" is also a pseudonym, and the same treatment has been used regarding identity.
3. The public library in town was the branch of a regional library system, but it was totally inappropriate for the local Indian community. Most of the collection was unimaginably dull and belonged elsewhere, the reference collection was tiny and out of date, and only a few (count them on one hand) current periodicals were received. Patronage was very low, and the elderly white woman in attendance appeared to have had no library training. The library had recently been offered as a gift a quantity of up-to-date reference books (duplicate copies acquired by the college through the Library of Congress), but had not shown any interest in them. The offer went unanswered, despite repeated queries.
4. The widespread and intergenerational prevalence of alcohol abuse is, however, a singularly depressing fact of life for many tribal community residents. If one doesn't have an alcohol problem now, one has probably had one in the past. Alcohol abuse and consequent harmful domestic activity seem to be accepted as a normal condition, and drinking and driving is a usual leisure-time pursuit for too many.
5. Paraphrased from pp. 91–92 of the University of Alaska, Fairbanks Self-Study, 1989–90 (First Draft), March 15, 1990. This was submitted to the Northwest Association of Schools and Colleges for Reaccreditation Review.
6. On looking over the shelf list during a summer of cataloging many donated books, the author discovered that an alarming number of titles on the Plains Indian Tribe and related tribes were long, long overdue. Through quasi-detective work, discreet yet persistent inquiry, and finally, notices of Small Claims action in the Tribal Court, almost all of these were gratifyingly returned. One cache of expensive Native American art books was returned from an abandoned house on the northern fringe of the reservation! It was not at all a matter of theft, but of coveting good books and sharing their contents.
7. Personal communication from Mark Thiel, Assistant Archivist, Memorial Library, Marquette University, Nov. 2, 1987. He has been very active in training tribal archivists, and has written a manual, available from Educational Services Institute (ESI), Falls Church, VA.
8. Cole, Douglas. *Captured Heritage, The Scramble for Northwest Coast artifacts.* UW Press.
9. Personal communication, June 11, 1987, from Tim Troll, village ad-

ministrator at St. Mary's for several years, later with the law firm of Beaty, Robbins and Morgan, Anchorage, AK.

10. *Ibid.*
11. Kleinfeld, Judith S. *Eskimo School on the Andreavsky, A Study of Effective Bicultural Education.* Praeger Studies in Ethnographic Perspective on American Education. New York: Praeger, 1979, pp. 131–132.
12. Personal communication, Judith S. Kleinfeld, September 18, 1987.

2.

The Subsistence vs. the Capitalist Culture: Subarctic Eskimos[1]

"Library service of any quality in rural areas is a very new, indeed a revolutionary concept: as revolutionary in its own way as computers or satellite communication. . . ."[2] Couple this with the fact that both computers and satellite communication (including television) are joining libraries in Yupik Eskimo villages across the Yukon-Kuskokwim delta of Alaska, and we assuredly have, in terms of access to new information, a revolutionary situation.

The Village Library Project of Kuskokwim Community College took place in the Yukon-Kuskokwim delta of southwestern Alaska, fronting on the Bering Sea. About the size of the State of Oregon,[3] the delta is almost entirely tundra, with the Yukon River forming the northern edge against hills and the Kuskokwim River flowing southwesterly into the bay of the same name. Mountains to the south and eastward complete the encirclement of this vast region, creating, in effect, a unique geographical homeland of wet tundra. A maze of tributaries and sloughs characterize both river courses. Viewed from the air in the summer months, the innumerable ponds, lakes and serpentine sloughs over the vast tundra area in between give the impression of a waterscape, rather than a landscape. Spruce and deciduous forests are found on drier tundra upriver and in the hills and mountains bordering the delta on all sides.

The region is located just south of the Arctic Circle and has a climate of long, rather harsh winters and relatively short but lush summers. Winters are characterized by short days and zero or below-zero temperatures, with periods of wind and icy thaw, but the summers more than compensate with endless daylight and bountiful subsistence resources across the land and waters.

The Yukon-Kuskokwim delta is the largest and most heavily populated contiguous area of Native settlement, subsistence culture and Native speak-

24

ers in North America, after the Navajo area of the southwestern U.S. All but a small fraction of the population is Yup'ik-speaking Eskimo, living in 57 villages ranging from 150 to about 400 in population, with a few having between 700 and 800. Bethel, the regional center on the lower Kuskokwim, has 4,800 of a total 20,000 for the region.[4]

Euroamerican or western values and development policies and priorities have been supplanting or at least strongly influencing the traditional economies and other cultural ways at an increasing rate. This is especially true since the Alaska Claims Settlement Act was passed in 1972. It brought Native local and regional corporations into gradual control of large areas of Alaska, culminating in total land and resource control in 1991. However, Alaska Native Claims Settlement Act (ANCSA) ended aboriginal fishing and hunting rights of Alaska Natives; control over tidewater development or any projects impacting subsistence lands and resources remains controversial and litigious.

The extent and convertibility of this control continue to be adjusted in follow-up Federal legislation, legal actions, and administrative decisions by the U.S. Department of Interior's Board of Land Appeals, as one task of the Act is to balance retention of Native corporate ownership with the desire of some Native shareholders to sell their stock. A sign of the growing ambivalence many Alaska Natives may be feeling, regarding the balance between protection of subsistence resources and resource development on subsistence lands, was seen at the 1995 Alaska Federation of Natives convention in Anchorage, which voted in support of oil drilling in the Arctic National Wildlife Refuge (ANWR) on the northeast Arctic coast, location of the calving grounds of the huge, international Porcupine caribou herd. Threatened drastic cuts in Federal funding for Native American programs by a Republican Congress plus a constrained Alaskan economy were apparently the motivating factors behind the vote.

During the first half of the 19th century Russian explorers were followed into the Y-K delta by missionaries of the Russian Orthodox, Moravian and Roman Catholic faiths. After sale of Alaska by Imperial Russia to the United States in 1867, the U.S. government slowly and paternalistically began to assume responsibility for the welfare of the Native population in the Territory of Alaska. In this century, the U.S. Bureau of Indian Affairs, through Federal law, and more recently the Alaska State government (statehood came in 1959) and utilizing huge oil revenues from the Prudhoe Bay field, have introduced local government options and funded countless capital projects. After the Molly Hootch decision[5], K-12 schools in every village, gradually replaced the BIA secondary schools. Telecommunication networks and modern transportation services developed by government, the military and the private sector are the equal of any in the world, for a region so sparsely populated and remote. One main lack is interconnecting highways, prohibited by, among other factors, the exorbitant cost of building and maintaining roadbeds over permafrost. In Alaska, however, air travel has become a system of "interconnecting highways." Any local roads are confined within a village or connect with a nearby airstrip.

In a word, in terms of access to information and resources for modern development, the Yukon-Kuskokwim delta is being catapulted straight into the 21st century, and many of the Yupik people are most anxious to have their hands on the controls. The traditional subsistence economy is already under pressure from a growing population, and easier transportation (snow-mobiles, called snogos or snow machines, in winter; outboard-powered, of-ten homemade, flat-bottom river boats during the warm months; and a va-riety of winged aircraft by scheduled and charter carriers all year round). There is regular barge freight service from the mainland U.S., and both jet and turbo-prop airliner service between Bethel and Anchorage, 400 air miles due east. (There are also two other regional sub-centers whose run-ways can handle jets, one on the Lower Yukon, and the other 150 miles up-river from Bethel on the Kuskokwim.) Presently oil and gas exploration and dam proposals are posing dramatic changes for the subsistence economies, which flourished relatively undisturbed for thousands of years.[6]

Public desire for library development in the Y-K delta was expressed dur-ing a series of meetings sponsored by the White House during the winter of 1978-79 ("Speak-Out" for libraries, etc.). Possibly some of this interest had been stimulated by previous school library development, which was strong in at least one of the three school districts in the region, the Lower Kuskokwim School District. Financial and technical assistance was needed to start a program of library development in the remote villages desiring li-braries.

The Librarian of Bethel's Kuskokwim Consortium Library since the early 1970s (serving both the residents of Bethel and Kuskokwim Com-munity College, the latter providing about 80% of its funding) started a search for funds that eventually resulted in a large state appropriation go-ing directly to the college for a village library development project. Prepa-rations were begun and a Project Coordinator was hired for the 1980-81 fiscal year. Nine villages participated the first year, which was perhaps too many.

The criteria for accepting a village to participate in the project were al-tered over time. At first the existence of community college programs in the village was a prime factor (Adult Basic Education Center, extension courses taught by contracting with qualified school teachers in the village). Later, of necessity, other factors became more important: the surety of a heated, lighted place for the library; the interest and commitment of local officials; the availability of a qualified resident to be a library aide; population; re-moteness; community-wide interest and support. (Ultimately other, less obvious factors became of prime consideration: these will be brought up as we proceed.)

Interestingly, we found that it was often easier to establish a library in a small, poor village than in a large, affluent one, due to the fact that there is usually a dominant family or clan in a small village, whereas the large village of several hundred may be wracked or disorganized by opposing power factions, or having difficulty managing all kinds of grants for a variety of projects. The city manager (village administrator) may be supportive—or uninterested. The traditional mayor may or may not be strong on the library. And with each election, each change in village administrator, the local climate for the library may well shift, for better or worse.

And there were traps in dealing with a village administrator (often non-Native), who knew very well what a library was and with whom we dealt monoculturally. In the enthusiasm and impetus of project work, it was sometimes all too easy to gloss over the fact that behind him stood 300 or more Yupik Eskimos out in that remote village—and we really had no idea what they thought of a library in their village. We had the logistical support of the village administrator—there was the library open and ready . . . and only later would we realize that a great deal had been missed in not approaching the Native community itself, and inviting their direct involvement in the project from the very beginning, assuming they even wanted to consider it.

Another problem was inherent in the position of village library aide, and the fact that initially there were no village library committees. So this lone key person was selected by the village council, which sounds fine on the face of it, except that our standards and recommendations were too ambiguous in those early days. Too often it was someone from a dominant family who had no special qualifications, someone with a problematical background, or a teenager looking for some spending money and with the right connections who was simply given the job—something to do (in a subsistence village very short on jobs in the cash economy). Of course, this method also had its brilliant choices: the occasional superlative and enterprising library aides who could be a potential Native library training cadre, role models in delta library development and provision.

In return for the village's contribution of a heated, lighted place for the library, the project provided transportation and per diem for the resident library aide to attend two 3-1/2-day training workshops in Bethel, a "core collection" of library materials, library furnishings in the form of sufficient shelving, subscriptions to about 20 periodicals, a cassette recorder/player, cooperative extension materials, a Yup'ik language course on audiocassette with supporting literature in print form, plus two visits during the first year by the project coordinator to help set up the library and get it operating. During the first year of a village library's operation, the project paid the village library aide for ten hours work each week for about six months, until approximately the middle of May. In the following years the project funded one annual on-site visit per village by the project coordinator, and an annual workshop/meeting of all library aides, plus ongoing consulting support to "resolve any problems." These sometimes necessitated additional village visits.

Training of the founding village library aide has emphasized the most basic procedures for: 1) establishing the library, and 2) operating the library. The aide was pivotal in every respect, since he/she acted as the agent and liaison for the project once the project coordinator left the village. Over four years' experience, however, we found that one must be in as close touch with village officials as with the library aide or library committee, in order to make realistic progress. Belatedly, as the funding and support services for the project were being phased out by Kuskokwim Community College during the final year, 1984, we recognized that both the mayor and village council should have been included in the initial briefings, as well as continuing liaison, perhaps through annual presentations by the coordinator each fall. Also, village library committees badly needed some training themselves, but there wasn't provision for this. All these measures would have provided the expertise for effective village governance, and would probably have generated more interest and support in the community. In some villages such engagement occurred naturally, as opportunities arose, whether spurred by the coordinator, the aide, or others in the village. But in others, where the village administrator seemed "in charge" to a Kussaq (Caucasian) coordinator who was only just learning the socio-cultural ways of the Yupik villages, there was no contact at all with the traditional leaders—and in some villages it can be seen in retrospect that this omission significantly handicapped the viability of these libraries.

A background in cross-cultural relations for non-Native college field staff, those who work in the remote villages, is important. And opportunities for learning the Yup'ik language, although not required, have been available for these workers, whose clients are almost exclusively Yupik Eskimos. Admittedly the trend is for more and more young Yupik people to be, if not bilingual, then exclusively English-speaking, but many from the parental and grand-parental generations—certainly in some of the more traditional villages—can be totally illiterate when it comes to written English, though they may have a fragmentary acquaintance with spoken English. As a college field worker I received no cross-cultural orientation, and no encouragement to learn the language. This in a region where, except for Bethel, the villages are almost entirely Yupik Eskimo, with a high percentage of Native speakers.

On one memorable occasion the indispensable usefulness of learning the Native language was reinforced for me with unexpected humor and surprise. At my final briefing with the Chefornak village council, I opened by giving in Yup'ik a statement I'd carefully and conscientiously practiced. I said, "I'm sorry, but I don't speak the Yup'ik language . . ." Whereupon everyone at the table burst into laughter! For I had done just that, and communication in at least one sense was total. For the rest of the session I needed the help of an interpreter, the village library aide, but the lesson was not lost.

In the 1960s and most of the 1970s, cross-cultural accommodation was left almost entirely to the Yupik Native, and the Kussaq staff at the college was turned loose to learn about delta life by hit-or-miss, seat-of-the-pants encounters. Later, in 1987, I learned that the college still did not give such orientations to its staff and faculty, yet the college's own Yup'ik Language Center regularly gave cross-cultural orientations to outside agency personnel and delta visitors when requested! With the arrival of a new college head at the beginning of 1988, along with a reorganization of the University of Alaska that eliminated the separate community college system and made this field campus a subordinate unit of UAF, there were signs that some of these oversights might be addressed, though implementation would be more difficult, requiring approval from Fairbanks, which included the Y-K delta in its service area.

In 1990, delivery of college courses was by mail, supported by audio-conferencing, and there were no longer full-time college staff in the field. An Adult Basic Education program, administered in the villages for many years, utilized local residents with associate (two-year) degrees as "facilitators" in helping ABE students, but not those taking college courses through Distance Education, which were also provided by the college, although some facilitators were taking these courses, as well as coming to Bethel for training twice a year. The coordinator of these programs visited each village (ten in 1990) two or three times a year. The facilitator positions were part-time, occupying three evenings per week. By 1990, community libraries established by the college in the early 1980s and others begun since were still not actively integrated into the college field programs, but there was some interest and movement in doing so.

The original project coordinator, who did a creditable job in helping set up nine libraries the first year (although two or three almost failed from insufficient appropriate follow-up support), appears to have had enough difficulty with the remoteness of the delta and, as he had a small family, with the innumerable flights alone to remote villages (20-25 trips per year was the average the first three years, with each village visit lasting 2-3 days), that he resigned early. His successor, who was myself, worked from the second year to the end of the project. My own cross-cultural knowledge was picked up informally, and by close observation and study. I had worked just previously for the Bay Indian Tribe on the Washington coast, living outdoors most of the time, and thus was perhaps better prepared for bush conditions and cross-cultural encounters generally. It also helped that I was unmarried, though I had a dog team in Bethel, which some would say is almost like being married!

The core collection of each village library consisted of forty-five linear feet of fiction and non-fiction, meeting standards of a basic collection for a beginning very small public library. This was placed in three shelving units having a total of about 17 shelves, along with whatever additional shelving and furnishings the village was able to provide. In the first nine villages, enough extra money was available from the project to purchase attractive folding tables and chairs as well. The non-fiction portion of this collection was strongly reference in character, and the fiction shelves predominantly juvenile, science fiction, westerns and romances. Added initiatives brought more adult fiction in donated paperbacks and back files of magazines like *Alaska Magazine* and *National Geographic*.

Eventually the villagers were informally solicited for recommendations, and this resulted in the addition of practical repair manuals, local Alaskana, high interest sports books and audiotapes on specific sports, local maps, sectarian religious books, business and trade skill texts, and materials on life-coping skills. Anything pictorial on Alaska was of high interest. Illustrated adult fiction would be popular, but there is very little commercially available. One yearned for the old Classic Comics of the '40s and '50s. (In the 1990s, there are various such series available again.) Cassette tapes of music, Bible readings, and on other subjects (e.g. coaching basketball and wrestling—the two most popular team sports) are also available. (See concluding pages of this chapter and the article in Appendix A for ideas promoting innovative village library activities and materials.)

Regarding the original "core collection" we used, which was selected by my predecessor from the Wilson *Public Library Catalog* to "represent all man's (*sic*) knowledge," it should have been my initiative to immediately form a project advisory committee from the Yupik community, not only to review the contents of this collection for its appropriateness, but to ask for its guidance and recommendations overall. I can only plead that I was learning many lessons too fast, and besides there was no time to reassess the core collection and order a whole new constellation of more appropriate materials, let alone reevaluate the entire project in mid-stride, as it were. In time the excesses and omissions in these collections will hopefully be modulated and supplanted to fit each community.

One "default" trap to be avoided in selecting materials for Native libraries is to rely only on the major library suppliers and selection aids for acquisitions. One should be more open not only to alternative media, but to alternative sources for materials. The excuse that expenditure deadlines and staff time limitations necessitate resorting to the convenience of mainstream sources reflects rather the dominant society's priorities, instead of those of the Native community.

By 1984 at least one village had purchased a microcomputer for use in its combined library/Adult Basic Education[7] Center building. Another possibility is to have a television monitor and video recorder/player, especially if the village has cable television, which is slowly spreading among the larger villages. Pat Smith, former Chief of Library Services of Canada's Northwest Territories, gave a paper on "Northerners' Needs for Northern Information" for the 8th Northern Libraries Colloquy (Edmonton and Whitehorse, June 1–6, 1980), which speaks to the need for non-print materials in Native libraries:

> . . . paradoxically, or logically, the needs for northern information expressed by northerners (read: Native population) lead us to consider the unexpressed needs. The needs, perhaps, that people are unaware of: information about developments and events which are going to affect their lives and homes. If oil and pipeline companies and those conducting surveys and inquiries are really serious about informing and consulting with the people of the north, not just the leaders of the people of the north, understand what is happening. Information must be conveyed graphically, by videotape, by slide and cassette programs, and, above all, by using the experimental satellite channels on television to reach into people's homes. (p. 149)

During the period of my first residence in the delta, an advertisement appeared regularly in the regional newspaper. An oil company, ARCO, one of those that wanted to work on the Bering Sea continental shelf, offered to loan to anyone interested a series of video cassettes, in either Yup'ik or English versions, on oil exploration and drilling, etc. They also produced a single cassette, celebrating the Yupik Eskimo heritage. Utilizing local elders and subsistence village life, it was of such high quality that we regularly showed it to tourists and visitors in the Bethel Visitors Center. Native delta residents liked to watch the Yup'ik version, because they knew the people in the film!

KYUK-AM-TV (Bethel, Alaska) has produced over 40 video programs on the Yupik area of western Alaska, all of which are available for purchase. Most are in English versions, but several are available in Yup'ik as well. KYUK-AM also broadcasts Central Yupik religious music, the best known being Peter Twitchell's "Local Gospel Hour" on Sunday mornings. He also produces three other series of programs with high oral history content: "Yupik Profiles," "The Old Ways," and "Yupik Stories." For purposes of archival preservation, in 1989 duplicates were made of the master tapes of these series, which are stored in the local library. Most of these are in the Yup'ik language. Other public service programming encourages continued communality among Yupik residents throughout the delta. Three times a day there were emergency message programs called "Tundra Drums," a daily community Bulletin Board, a "Swap and Shop" radio classified ad show, and most popular of all a "Birthday Call-in Show," on which one can wish someone a Happy Birthday! And there are others, including two nightly news programs following each other, in English and in Yup'ik versions. Other than KYUK-AM-TV, there is KYKD-FM in Bethel, the latter being a Christian station that combines prerecorded material out of Chicago and some local programming. It "targets" primarily teens and young adults. Villages on the Lower Yukon can usually receive Nome radio station KNOM and KICY more easily.

When I first arrived in Bethel (1981), I attended the last movie held in the only local movie theatre, which then closed, as Bethel Cablevision was becoming well established. (KYUK-TV, the local combined public/commercial television station and the Alaska State Television Project channel had already been on the air for a few years.) Following this, and with the ready availability of videocassette recorder/players, videotape stores have opened, and a number of remote villages have acquired their own municipally operated cable systems with satellite dishes. This arrangement gives the village council control over what television channels and programs villagers watch. The Kuskokwim Consortium Library's video collection was expanding rapidly by 1989, and a television monitor and videoplayer were available for in-library public use.

Telephone service, by the way, has steadily evolved from the one village phone of 15 years ago to individual phone service (for those who can afford it) in almost all villages. In the future undoubtedly lies the prospect of computer networks, and audio-conferencing is already common. All villages with television sets can receive at least the two channels mentioned above (local and state): the former, under RATNET (Rural Alaska Television Network) providing local, general, public TV and Yup'ik programming; the other, operated by the State of Alaska and formerly called Learnalaska because of its predominantly academic programming but now named the State of Alaska Satellite Television Project. This latter is a melange of national network and urban Alaska programming, plus some state informational productions such as Aviation Weather. In 1995 RATNET, which served 120,000 mostly rural and Native residents, was threatened with severe budget cuts, and a proposed merger with KYUK was accepted. It is now called the Alaska Rural Communications Service (ARCS) and is administered by a combination of the four public TV stations in Alaska and private cable companies.

Five villages were accepted during the second year (1981-82) of the Village Library Project, then two more in 1982-83. Progress for all libraries has ranged from adequate to very uncertain. In the fall of 1987, fourteen were open and two were closed, "temporarily." Actually these two libraries had their collections and furnishings in storage, and one village wasn't sure where its was. These same two have had difficulties from the beginning (1980), 15 years ago, mainly due to lack of adequate housing for the library, but also due to a lack of real interest and commitment to get one started and operating—as well as flaws in the methodology of the Village Library Project. Over the years there has been almost constant change in the status of each village library, due to the fact that each one has been evolving in its own village circumstances and environment along lines of either improved or deteriorating quality, some with an increased role and use, along with changing housing, budget and grant management and library aide performance.

After difficulties encountered during the first year, it was evident that local political support should be emphasized and continually monitored. Formation of a village library committee was strongly recommended, rather than having the village council act as the library committee. Most local liaison work had to be done by the library aide, who was coached in workshops and reinforced by other, more experienced aides in ways to bolster the standing of the library, as well as the standard of library services offered. However, such orientation should have been done at the outset, in gaining the support and understanding of local officials on behalf of the library. As it turned out we were working at long distance solely through the local library aide and the (usually white) village administrator, with occasional encouragement from travelling college staffers (but not the college administration!).

The role of the coordinator, as agent for the creation of new libraries and an advisor for those already established and operating, was all too significant, not to say fatefully crucial. The main goal of the final, phasing-out year of delta-resident technical assistance was to make the village libraries as independent as possible. A handbook was prepared for the use of village administrators and village library aides. (This was never distributed officially, but was made available informally by the former coordinator, who had sole responsibility for its writing.) The coordinator facilitated and expedited improvements for the individual village libraries and monitored their progress by phone calls and on-site visits to help directly (especially in training new aides, which for a while was done almost entirely in the home village), and passed on timely information and advice about changes needed in order to meet requirements for the State of Alaska's Library Assistance Grants.

Almost all the villages needed these grants to keep their libraries going. They were consumed mainly by the aide's salary and heating fuel costs. But then these subsistence villages are dependent—for non-subsistence services—on a variety of large state grants and a variety of governmental agencies, for everything from building and maintaining airstrips to operating K-12 schools. The old U.S. Bureau of Indian Affairs schools were turned over to local, state-funded or other newly formed independent school districts, and the remaining few distant boarding high schools for Natives and Indians were phased out,[8] as almost all the villages now have their own K-12 systems. (Earlier we mentioned the closing of the St. Mary's School on the Lower Yukon for the same reason.) The salaries of village government and state school district employees were provided through state sources. Although jobs in the private sector exist in a remote subsistence village, they are few in number, and the cash economy is developing very slowly and as yet without any major basis or resources. So far it's confined to limited commercial fishing, a Native crafts industry, one or two village stores, and some trapping.

The cross-cultural nature of the project presented other interesting problems. Training of villagers to be library aides evolved from schooling sessions in Bethel—which took villagers far from their home village to the regional center, with its diversions, temptations and relative anonymity for the visitor—to on-site village visits by the coordinator for one-on-one instruction, coaching, and just plain visiting and getting acquainted in the aide's home village.

As a visiting professional, it is crucial to establish good relations in the village, to know the community better and to be known oneself. As well as making friends, this effort also gives the aide confidence and recognition, and the library a start toward acceptance and community status, by eliciting the interest, support and some pride by local officials in a new community service. In going to a home village, the coordinator chose to "go with" community pride and cultural strengths in order to reinforce the training, rather than pulling a villager into the mostly "Kussaq"-dominated regional center of Bethel, far from family and friends.[9] (Kussaq equals white man or woman. The Yup'ik term is derived from the first Russians who entered the delta, the military element of whom were Cossacks.) Speaking of Kussaqs, there was one point of view among them which said that establishing libraries in these villages was *not* replacing anyone's cultural values, and that the villagers have been used to libraries for some time. Then there was the opposite stance, which said that libraries-in-the-villages are premature, and that they will fail if not constantly nurtured. I must disagree with both these positions, because the truth lies somewhere between the two extremes. It is rather a matter of the kind of library development, the way it is introduced, and, most important, by whom.

Another cross-cultural question involves the position of males and females vis-à-vis the public library in a Yupik Eskimo village. Does it make any difference if the aide is a young woman or a young man? It appears that it does in some villages. Some men may not go to the library, simply because it is operated by a woman and is thereby made a "woman's place." In one village the library was placed on the second floor of a city building, where the village administrator's office was located. Both the village administrator and the library aide were young women (Native), and there was also a space on the 2nd floor where the women's sewing circle met! As if to literally underscore this relationship, the first floor of the building was reserved for men's activities.[10]

Recognizing such culturally specific conditions, we have also thought to suggest designating certain shelves in the village library as "Men's Books" and others as "Women's Books," just as some have always been labeled "Children's Books."[10] This is not overly accommodating, nor is it sexist; it is an attempt to make the libraries more acceptable to all the villagers on their terms—especially for men, who carry the traditional authority in Yupik culture. Women and children and some of the educated adults use the library, but men generally may well not if the library aide is a woman. But I can sense the protest of some readers at these suggestions. Keep in mind that we are not foisting one of the dominant society's urbanized small libraries onto the Native village—along with its baggage of cultural biases and social issues. Quite simply, we are trying to make possible the organization of a small community library in another cultural milieu. That statement in itself must wipe the slate clean of cultural predilections, beyond that of the objective concept of a community library. The reluctance of some men to use certain facilities "open to all" in a village because of this gender identification is also seen in the use of the Adult Basic Education centers in some villages,[12] where some young men are said to be unwilling to show a lack of prowess in academic and related skill areas by being seen entering the place, although they might go in to get acquainted with a young woman personally! Hunting, fishing and trapping are the men's traditional, subsistence domain; the women are at home with children, or gathering plant resources, making or washing clothes, preparing and cooking food, or processing game and hides brought in by the men. Of course, some activities were shared by men and women alike, and these vary from village to village.

Taking all the above into consideration, I personally believe that non-Native, female library consultants travelling to these traditional villages *may* have further compromised efforts at library development in *some* of them. In fact, probably my *own* participation, as a male, in a kind of community activity (indoors, and working with children) often perceived as women's work, was equally compromising and confusing! We simply weren't considering how these switches in traditional gender roles might impact our image and the status of a "library" in the eyes of Native villagers, especially the male leaders. Were the books and information contained in the library (and the schooling experience with which they were identified) primarily for women and children? And if a young man was associated with them, would he compromise his self-image and role as a man in the village?

In order to qualify for Library Assistance grants and matching money available from the Alaska State Library after the village library was established, each participating village council had to pass a library ordinance or resolution and have the library open at least ten hours per week for 48 weeks of the year, although for a few years the State of Alaska allowed for "alternative library services" to be offered during the summer months, when subsistence fishing takes precedence over all other community activities. This usually involves placing an exchange paperback and periodical collection in the village administration offices, which are open throughout the year. (However, as of the mid-1990s the State Library was less convinced of the need for this policy, as some Native subsistence villages had no difficulty keeping their library operating in the summer months.) Passing a library ordinance or council resolution with that proviso makes the village public library an official arm of village government. Another type of supporting grant available to these villages is issued under Title 4 of the Federal Library Services and Construction Act, but thus far such grants haven't been used very much.

The State Library Assistance Grants, funded through LSCA Title III, are for operation and improvements for an existing public library,[13] but not for starting a library or construction of a library building. There were other state funding sources available for the purpose of new construction in those years, but as of this writing the only one available for construction is under the Federal Library Services and Construction Act. Orientation and advice were given at all workshops for the library aides, regarding the requirements and preparations needed to qualify for such state grants and any other funding available for libraries.

The type of housing utilized for a village public library takes many forms: rooms in community or recreation halls, or in other village government buildings, former clinics or vacant houses, government trailers or school classroom buildings, and lastly, combined school/public libraries that are set up in the local high school's library area. The latter arrangement has to be negotiated between the village's school advisory board and the village council. Wherever desirable and feasible, for its apparent economy and efficiency, the project supported such combined or multiple use of the village library area, as did the college administration. For example, some villages hold their Adult Basic Education classes in the library, or the village library aide doubles as the ABE monitor (ABE aide in the village).[14]

On the face of it, one would think that it would of course work out best in these small, isolated villages—many of them quite poor—to have the high school library and public library combined in one facility. However, under the prevailing cross-cultural conditions this is not easily done, and is often not wanted, although attitudes are slowly changing. Of the 16 villages that joined the project as of 1990, not one had retained combined school/public library housing, although several started out that way. The villagers apparently prefer to have total control over their own library. On the other hand it seems clear that the village library joins most logically with the local ABE program, for these combinations are relatively easy to effect, and the ABE program is also administered by the regional community college. In villages where school districts are administered by local Native government, on the other hand, combined school/public libraries are more natural and desirable.

As well as offering public library services, the village libraries are also there to provide some preparation and support to high school graduates in the villages who may be considering higher education, and to do the same for students in distance education courses of the community college. Library assistance for ABE students has already been mentioned. Interlibrary loan is encouraged, as well as any other mutual assistance and sharing. In

1982 one library was totally lost when the community hall in which it was housed burned to the ground.[15] In a few weeks a quantity of new and duplicative materials was being donated by other village libraries as well as by the regional library in Bethel, and shortly the village had more than enough good library materials to open in a new location. The strongly supportive response from the other libraries also boosted the spirits of the "burned out" library aide, who, instead of quitting his library job, took on a new enthusiasm which eventually resulted in the library re-opening, furnished with all-new shelving and furniture purchased with remaining grant money and some village funds.

The library aide position in most villages being only a part-time job, the aide usually has other part-time jobs as well as subsistence activities to pursue. As a resource person the library aide is sometimes able to obtain employment in the local school as a teacher's aide, to help take care of the school library as well. We have also found that the aide really needs to be a high school graduate. Then, with library training and regular coaching, he or she is more likely to operate the library in an effective, enterprising way, responsive to villagers' needs. Experience with high schoolers has shown that they are too peer-influenced and self-oriented, regardless of training, and use their library hours mostly as a trysting time with their friends![16] However, they are usually better educated and are more "acculturated" to the conventional library concept (which may or may not be relevant to the larger Yupik community).

Funding for the project itself, after the first year's direct appropriation from the state legislature to the college for this purpose, developed a checkered character, but at all times originated, directly or indirectly, with the Alaska State Department of Education and the University of Alaska. Funding for the second and third years came partly out of the continuing appropriation to Kuskokwim Community College, plus two grants: one from the Alaska Commission on Postsecondary Education, the other from the Alaska State Library. The fourth and final year's funding came from the college, plus a supplemental grant from the State Library for a project evaluation. The project fortunately began at a time of ample state funds and the availability of a local state legislator with much seniority. It ended at a time of reordering of the college's priorities, which did not include any further village library development (only some annual technical assistance from the State Library), and a precipitous downturn in state revenues, brought on by a slump in the world oil market. In 1987 the economy had just about bottomed out, but the village libraries were still able to receive the $5000 annual grants plus matching funds. (As we have noted above, however, these grants may not be so readily available in the future.)

The annual (biennial as of 1995) meeting of library aides, which continues today (though they must now pay for their own transportation and expenses out of their individual budgets), takes place in a different major village each time, to take advantage of not only the economy of meeting within the delta, but the strong cultural reinforcement and sense of community so prevalent throughout the region. The village setting also offers an opportunity for outside guest instructors to experience the cultural and environmental conditions that predominate. From the author's perspective, to say that working with village people and the aides has been as much a learning experience as it has been one of instructing others would be an understatement. One recommendation made toward the end of the project was that any future project should have a Native advisory group, to ensure that villagers control policy formulation for library development in their communities.

During mid-winter of 1983-84, an evaluation of the Village Library Project was done by two consultants, one from the Alaska State Library and one an independent consultant with years of educational experience in the delta, as well as Third World library experience. Much that follows will draw on their 93-page report, entitled "The Yukon-Kuskokwim Village Library Project, An Evaluative Study, Prepared for Kuskokwim Community College and the Alaska State Library," and dated January 8, 1984. Other material covered thereafter includes the final recommendations and three-year statistics submitted by the project coordinator before his departure in March, 1984. The author, aka the former coordinator, assumes sole responsibility for opinions and interpretations expressed regarding the Evaluative Study.

The final mandated acts of the project, along with the outside evaluation, were a successful annual meeting held in February, 1984, at St. Mary's on the Lower Yukon, which was attended by 11 out of an available 14 delta library aides; and production of a *Village Library Handbook* of about 90 pages in length with many appendices of information, intended for distribution to village officials and library aides. This annual meeting was an unusual joint one, bringing together librarians and library aides from Nome, the Seward Peninsula and St. Lawrence Island, as well as the Y-K delta.

One of the lingering vexations of work in these Yupik Eskimo villages was the silence or uncritical reaction on the part of villagers and village officials, caused in large part by the absence of Native involvement in the conception and implementation of the project—and undoubtedly a lack of understanding by many villagers as to what exactly the library was for, in the village. There were failures in cross-cultural orientation and liaison as well, because at the time such basic communication and local control issues didn't seem important to me, preoccupied as I was with the logistics and schedule of the project.

To some degree the villagers participated in the final evaluation. In the end the project was voted out of existence by the governing body of Kuskokwim Community College, the Community College Council, under the leadership of the college's president, who was neither Native nor a supporter of the project (it was funded just before he was hired). Nevertheless, the makeup of the council at the time of the vote was representative in every way of the delta communities, including ones with village libraries. A major regret and frustration of mine, however, was that the project coordinator—the primary resource person—was never contacted or called in at a time when the project was being voted "up or down." In fact, during the three years of my work I was never asked to report on progress, and the only meetings I had with the college administration were annual ones, at my request each and every year. (During the second year, at my insistence, I was finally able to work together with coordinators of the college's other village programs.) One of the ironies that couldn't be escaped—and there were many—was the fact that, from the coordinator's point of view, the project was being phased out at a time when he had finally become effective in working with village councils, and had seen the need for training library committees, having Native oversight, expanding and diversifying the Native library concept, etc.

The Yupik people by custom do not usually criticize or reject the offerings of visitors, which might explain why no negative comment was ever directly received by the coordinator. (Another, more relevant explanation would be, because they had never felt sufficiently involved, or informed, to make any comment.) Some questions, comments and even criticisms were passed on by second or third hand, to be sure, but it is difficult, not speaking the Native language or living in any of the particular villages whence such information came, to accept them as 100% negative. It goes without saying that there are many start-up problems when community development schemes and money are brought in from the western culture, predominantly by Alaska State government. And one consultant commented that too often it has been the case that such development projects are ended too early, before the new services or benefits can be understood, accepted and institutionalized in Native village life and society.

The evaluative study concluded that these small public libraries in the remote villages should not be developed as mini-urban public libraries, because they have a "broader, more culturally adapted educational role as . . . village literacy and learning center[s]." An awareness should be cultivated "on all levels that the three primary institutions in the village—school, library, college—have a broad common purpose of encouraging literacy and learning." A "strong working relationship should continue to be developed between the college and the village library [as well as the school], since such a relationship is mutually supportive." Lastly, these libraries are "creative opportunities for developing new modes of learning which are available to all community members on an ad hoc rather than highly formal basis."

Many recommendations made by the study were already operative, or were being addressed. One that was underlined was to find ways to increase the scope and status of the library aide's job in the village. "Sources of funding should be found to provide broader library-related services; village governments should be encouraged to provide increased training opportunities for the aides, and recognition of the village librarian's role in the village should be provided through a variety of means." Another need pointed out was to develop networking among the village libraries themselves, and with the rest of Alaska. The annual (or biennial) meeting is one way, then encouraging telephone and mail contact, and perhaps a newsletter edited by the aides themselves. Each aide should join the Alaska Library Association, in order to receive news of interest to Alaska libraries and library workers. With the purchase of a microfiche reader, each library could utilize the Alaska State Film (now Video only) Library Catalog and the Alaska Library Network (ALN) Catalog, both of which were available on microfiches, for ordering audiovisual software and print materials through Interlibrary Loan, drawing on all major Alaska libraries. Such in-house bibliographic resources increase the service capability of a village library many times.

General recommendations of the coordinator included some that were listed in the Evaluative Study. In addition, for a village library to best support college field instruction in the remote village, the library aide should be included in beginning-of-semester meetings and audio-conferences of part-time instructors, Adult Basic Education staff and distance-learning instructors. Library hours should be convenient for students. Combining of the ABE center and library in one facility should be encouraged, if conditions are right. Any interlibrary loan to a village having a library should be routed through that library. This would help acquaint the aide with interlibrary loan procedures and bring villagers and educators into the library.

A main feature and benefit of the periodic training meetings is the role of peer training and example. They have proved to be very popular, and when held in a remote village there are various advantages. The status of the host village librarian is enhanced at home, the host village library is improved for the occasion and is usually the recipient of gift materials, other village librarians can identify with and share with the host librarian most effectively, the network among the village librarians who attend is nicely cemented under the most conducive circumstances, the villagers feel most at home because they are "on their own turf," and this factor undoubtedly increases the acceptance of those Kussaqs who attend the meeting. In a remote village there is usually no alcohol readily available, and few other distractions during the day to draw participants away, except possibly some shopping, sightseeing and visiting with relatives who happen to be living in the village. This last phenomenon provides some the opportunity to visit with family not seen in several years.

Various training options were found that could help make up for the lack of a village libraries coordinator from the college who would help train the village librarians and library committee members, and consult on village library management problems. A new aide could be taught by a former aide. Since the aides are all village residents, the former aide is almost always available. The newly hired aide could visit another nearby village library, especially if it's a model library with an experienced aide. Various manuals for rural Alaskan, Native American, and small libraries and the project's own Village Library Handbook could be studied, and correspondence, audio-conference or televised library courses were occasionally offered through the efforts of Alaska State Library. However, since the Library Assistant program at Tanana Valley Community College has been terminated for many years, such distance learning courses are being offered somewhat less often than before. Besides, these are not cross-cultural in character, and none are designed with Native villages specifically in mind. (See Epilogue for new developments and future potential.)

Another recommendation that would help new library aides in remote villages is to have training videotapes and computer-assisted instruction produced with particular Native village groups as the target audience (Yupik, Athabascan, Inuit). Video programs, to be effective, would have to use Native actors and Native settings. Such tapes, if available on loan, could supplement the manuals and handbooks nicely for self-training at home. The logical agencies for producing such videotapes, as well as any software that might utilize computers, now commonly found in the village schools, for example, might include the Office of Instructional Technology at the University of Alaska, Fairbanks, possibly with the help of the Consortium for Alaska Municipal Training. On the other hand, perhaps the State Library could arrange the same through cooperation with regional Native organizations such as the Association of Village Council Presidents in the Yupik area. Some villages have their own municipal cable system, MCTV channel and video production equipment. Video production might therefore be arranged more cheaply and beneficially by using these local facilities, further involving Yupik people at the village level. The computer software, if Native-oriented, might have to be especially written, perhaps with Yup'ik versions, even using the new written orthography. It goes without saying that both the videotapes and software should be produced in close cooperation with advisors from the Yupik community. (See *Church Conference*)

A training and orientation visit or in-service training stint might be arranged at the Kuskokwim Consortium Library in Bethel, and the Alaska State Library regional coordinator could be contacted to see if a training visit might be possible, to help a new library aide. (See the last pages of this chapter on the idea of training a resident Native library training cadre, who would to a large degree replace the non-Native Alaska State Library Coordinator, because the ASL Coordinator would be training them instead of trying to reach all village library aides once a year, which is demonstrably impossible. The present training policy has been operative in the Y-K delta for 15 years, almost unchanged.)

The Kuskokwim Campus, UAF (formerly Kuskokwim Community College), as the main source and vehicle of funds for the Kuskokwim Consortium Library budget, should not close the door on any future proposals to fund the establishment of new libraries out in the villages, or to increase the networking capability and cooperation generally among the village libraries. KCL is the "area center (or regional) library for the Yukon-Kuskokwim delta, and as such is the sole vehicle for any future library development in the villages." This recommendation by the coordinator is important because of the possibility of changing policies of succeeding college administrations, as well as the College Council, and the fact that the State Library can only recognize KCL as the regional library for purposes of library development and interlibrary cooperation throughout the entire delta.

In the project it was naturally hoped that trained library aides would stay on the job as long as possible. Correspondingly, the villagers would like to see the same library trainer year after year. However, due to staff turnover, program changes, reorganization efforts and funding shifts or reductions, the college's image in any one village has changed, with few exceptions, almost every year. In the author's judgment this continuing unreliability on a personal level "seriously erodes any solid liaison built up over the years with every village affected."

Incentives, recognition and rewards should be developed for non-Native college personnel to learn something of the Central Yup'ik language. Though I am not aware of any official policy of this kind, the Yup'ik Language Center at the college now has a sequence of excellent courses aimed at a practical knowledge of the language for non-speakers. For one not to make any effort along these lines could be seen as a show of disrespect and harboring of ignorance regarding the indigenous, host culture. Indeed, such avoidance tends to strengthen an "us-and-them" mind set when one is surrounded by Native speakers in the remote village and not able to listen, understand and share. The fact that Yupik children are learning English in school holds promise for increasing acculturation into western civilization, but the increasing self-determination movement among the Yupik villages shows how their parents feel about the lopsided bicultural balance prevalent in the delta thus far.

To the dismay of Yupik elders, one encounters a significant and steadily growing percentage of Yupik young people who cannot speak their own language. But today and for many years to come the Euroamericans will continue to work with their parents and grandparents, many of whom are clearly uncomfortable, embarrassed or generally at a disadvantage when they have to communicate exclusively in English with college representatives. There are now Yup'ik language programs at all grade levels in the schools, which will perhaps ensure the survival of Yup'ik language proficiency among the young.

In the early 1980s the author attended meetings in remote villages where the visiting college representatives (all non-Native) knew no Yup'ik whatsoever, and could not understand their Yup'ik-speaking audience. Instead, they brought along interpreters. One or two non-Native college field workers had apparently acquired some fluency in Yup'ik, but nothing was made of it. For those unable to attend courses on the Bethel campus, there are textbooks and audiocassettes to supplement some private tutoring out in the Yupik population. A graduated testing program could offer merit pay or other rewards, or at least a certificate of recognition to those who achieve a "getting along" capability in Yup'ik communication, with speaking, reading and writing categories at levels of increasing fluency.

Until 1990, there were no tests by which Yupik students of the college could receive academic credit for oral and/or written proficiency in their native language. Now plans are underway to make this possible.

Some will look for more quantitative measurements or the lack of them in the Village Library Project, and there are some limited figures and comparisons we can offer. However, it is relevant to cite the remarks of another evaluator, who was looking at statewide training of village public safety officers:

> I have eschewed the use of statistical analysis in looking at any aspect of the program for three reasons: first, the program was continually growing during the period of observation; second, the number of [library aides] was too small for secure statistical manipulation; and third, different [library aides] were and are at different stages of training completion and job longevity, thus making statistical comparisons meaningless.[17]

All but two of the 16 village libraries that were started between 1980 and 1984 became operational on a regular basis. The remaining two did not do so for the following cumulative reasons: a housing situation that became poor or unstable or that has never resulted in adequate housing; the State Library assistance grant was repeatedly not applied for; the coordinator did not visit the village on successive years; the trained library aide abruptly "resigned," not being interested in working in a library that never opened!; and village officials and staff changed completely after an election, which pulled the bottom out of whatever impetus there had been for a community library. Obviously the problem in these two villages—both of which had expressed interest in having a library, and even passed a library ordinance or resolution—was that neither village was sufficiently involved, informed, or united to enable "the library" to get under way, let alone take root.

In retrospect, after many years of being able to think on these matters, I can say that some of the reasons for their failure included the lack of enough orientation and mutual consultation in the community as a whole to introduce the idea of a library properly, so that the village officials could have provided direct implementation and governance for it from the outset, knowing what it needed and what its potential was, and because the library was an unknown quantity and the villagers either didn't know or weren't interested in the library the Kussaqs brought to them. (But they might have been more interested to know how to build a truly community library.)

In one village, the smaller one, it required much more preparation to acquaint everyone with a library's possibilities and to directly stimulate interest. (This is the library that never actually opened.) The original villagers who acted as our liaison were a white couple, though the Native village officials received us. The core collection was initially installed (and neglected) in what "we" thought was a poor location. The space designated was a shelved corner in a little used, old community hall. There were no windows and access was too limited. In the meantime the makeup of village government changed.

Before the library opened we could have enlisted the help of the newly hired and trained library aide in giving demonstrations as to what a library is about, by showing films of strong historical interest to the village, either out in the community or in the school to the village children, or videos about its own life, using high schoolers to document activities in the community by videocamera. Or a collection of professional quality, 8" × 10" photographs about village life could have been taken by these same young people with loaned cameras, then put on display. Or a series of interviews with elders and esteemed adults could have been videotaped in the village, and shown at a community meeting.

But all of these ideas should have been proposed in meetings with and presentations before the village council, not unilaterally arranged by the coordinator. The introductory effort should engage directly with the village leadership. And the ideal presenter in a Native village is not an outside, non-Native person, but a Native who is known and respected, and preferably one who can speak the language and answer the questions of elders. For example, at the college there were a couple of well-known Yupik faculty members. If these could have been enlisted to help give presentations in these particular villages, it might have made a difference.

In the second village, which is one of the largest in the delta, and where for 15 years now the library still has not found a stable, permanent home, I believe the same effort might help convince local leaders, of all factions and families, to make a permanent home for the library, comfortable and of adequate size. Because when it has been open—and it has been open in at least three locations that I have direct experience with—it has been popular and successful. In fact, one of the frustrating as well as ironic reasons it has moved so much is that it has been used too much and been too crowded with people (mostly children)! The problem here seems to be, again, a lack of enough resolve or interest to make the library a permanent and dependable part of village life, which probably means the library should "prove itself" on the terms that adults in the village value most. And that would require getting the village adults directly involved in the planning and governance of the library, again using esteemed Native individuals to ease the way.

The potential is certainly there, but it will be almost like starting all over again, and close monitoring and follow-up will be essential. But this will have to await either initiative from within the village or a healthier state budget after the recession of the late 1980s and state budget reductions and retrenchments of the 1990s, before more funds become available for village library development.

All sixteen villages passed a library ordinance or resolution. Ten out of the sixteen had a library committee, and these operated with varying effectiveness (no library committees have received orientation or training of any kind, to my knowledge). All villages that applied for their state library assistance grant and followed the requirements received them, each year. In turnover of library housing sites, at the time the project ended about half were in the original housing location; the other half had moved, usually to better quarters, and often to a better (more central) location as well. About one-third tried at one time to be a combined school/public library, but none stayed that way. By 1984 almost half had combined ABE center/library operations, however, and this trend will probably continue in the future. All the libraries except one had, at one time or another, college instructional programs in the village. Of course, where there is a library, it is a "beachhead" (if you'll excuse the use of this term to describe the initial step in an invasion of some kind) for the college to bring instructional programs to that village, or to improve them.

On the turnover of library aides, in 1984 (one to three years after the project started, depending on the village) 50% of the libraries had the original aide; in 1987, 20%—which after several years is really not much at variance, if at all, with the average longevity of librarians in one job. In 19% of the villages in 1984, they had their second aide; 1987 information showed there had been additional turnover of an unknown number. I only recognized three names on the list of aides for 1987, because all three were aides in the same villages in 1984. Which means there are a large number of Native residents in most villages, approximately two to six, who have had direct experience working with library materials, and most of whom have received some training or orientation with a non-Native trainer, attended training meetings, etc.

Of the fifteen (1984) operational libraries, the annual circulation statistics ranged from 17 items circulated in a new library (open only a few months), to between 800 and 2,300 for the top five. Because the village library (as opposed to whatever library collection the high school and elementary school may have) is a new feature in the village, the aides were asked to also keep a record of visitors to their libraries, along with circulation.

Here is a chart of the total funding received by the project over the four years of its duration:

Funding received by Village Library Project From Alaska Commission on Postsecondary Education Grants (Only Available for Two Successive Years)

FY 1982	Grant No. 335490	$19,974.00
FY 1983	Grant No. 335610	$15,494.00

KUCC Matching Funds:

FY 1982	$30,956.00
FY 1983	$31,202.00

FY 1981 FUNDING CAME FROM A $110,000.00 direct appropriation from the legislature to the college for the Project.

Total Funding Received by the Project

FY	college	ACPE Grants	State Lib. Grants	Total
81	110,000.		16,000.	$126,000.
82	30,956.	19,974.	22,000.	$ 72,930.
83	31,202.	15,494.	37,801.	$ 74,497.
84	23,009.		17,522.	$ 40,530.
				$313,957.
			Village contribution (see below)	$173,250.
			Grand Total:	$487,207.

Village Monetary Contribution to Village Libraries (total of 16)

NOTE: Estimate of $1500. per year per library for fuel and utilities
$150. per month for housing × 11 months per year

9 village libraries for four years (FYs 81–84)

5 village libraries for three years (FYs 81–82)

2 village libraries for two years (FYs 83, 84)

Fuel, etc.
9 × 4 × 1500 = 54,000.
5 × 3 × 1500 = 22,500.
2 × 2 × 1500 =   6,000.
$82,500.

Housing value estimated average
$9 \times 4 \times 11 \times 150 = 59,400.$
$5 \times 3 \times 11 \times 150 = 24,750.$
$2 \times 2 \times 11 \times 150 = \underline{6,600.}$
                                                90,750.
                                      $\underline{+ 82,500.}$
Total village $\underline{\$173,250.}$
    contribution

In 1983 the Alaska State Library granted the Village Library Project enough funds so that any and all village library aides from the Y-K delta could attend the Alaska Library Association Conference, held in Fairbanks at a large motel with conference facilities. As soon as this idea was brought up, I wondered about its usefulness at such an early stage of library development in the villages. It meant jetting the aides to Anchorage, where they would change planes to get to Fairbanks, a trip of close to 1000 miles, taking most of a day. Not only was this a great expense, but it was all being spent in going outside the home region to attend a highly sophisticated meeting of degreed, experienced mainstream librarians. I had to agree that it was good to rub shoulders with fellow library workers, to make some contacts and to see the profession of librarians come together. It would emphasize the network concept, and show that the village library aide had a lot of help out there, in the form of interlibrary cooperation and available expertise.

However, I thought I knew the villagers and the village library situation well enough to have justifiable qualms about the whole enterprise. The agenda had almost nothing that was really relevant for the villages; it had to do with more advanced library problems and issues than the village libraries faced. There was one 60-minute session very early in the morning on the last day called the "Bush Librarians Coven," as if those in rural areas were a species apart (which in a sense was true, but not to the degree of being witches!). As we got underway, it became apparent that a trip of this kind was a major personal experience for most of the aides, and for a few, traumatic as well. The fact that they were going to a "library conference" was, at least until we arrived and attended the first sessions, almost an afterthought. For a few, I seemed like a chaperon, a guide to the big city, a counselor on personal or family problems (created by our distance from home). Under these pressing circumstances, I found myself having to squelch some paternalistic inclinations.

This kind of situation occurred when, due to the readily available alcohol, some of the aides imbibed enough to miss sessions, even most of a day. I was criticized by State Library staff for allowing this to happen, as if the village library aides from the Y-K delta were my wards. In fact I was their library trainer and advisor, once their first year of library operation was completed. But such alcohol availability was a big mistake, and impacted the Native people adversely—the ones from the delta being the only Natives in attendance at this statewide meeting, as far as could be discerned from appearances. This in itself was a revelation. From our rooms we had to go right through the cocktail lounge to reach the conference hall and meeting rooms, each evening there was a no-host bar in the foyer, and for the nightly suppers there were carafes of wine liberally distributed on all the tables. I felt a resentment at having to contend with the alcohol factor, the "false spirit" so thoroughly identified with the Kussaq, or white man (though most of the conferees were white women).

The Bush librarianship session in one of the smaller rooms turned out to be crowded and rushed, with little time for deliberation. A few village library aides made it to this one relevant meeting, of which only a small part could be devoted to problems of the beginning Native village libraries of the Y-K delta. My afterthought was that all that money might have been better spent in improving the village libraries themselves, or investing in more training of the aides at home. What we had experienced was in the tradition of "total immersion," with no consideration at all for the Native sensibility or the real needs of the Yupik village libraries. In retrospect, I can see now that the most important networking needed at that stage was among the Yupik library workers themselves, not with non-Native librarians from distant towns and cities, despite our links with them.

Distance learning has of necessity been developed throughout the north, from correspondance courses to the most sophisticated interactive electronic media. The Alaska State Library has offered courses to rural village library workers by audio-conference from time to time. Individual units of the University of Alaska system have also experimented with state-of-the-art distance learning hardware. Chukchi College in Kotzebue, located on the Bering Sea, uses an interactive "Telelearning" system that enables a math teacher to work problems and correct students' work directly on a television monitor screen seen by several students in scattered remote villages. The students can work problems on this "electronic blackboard," with the teacher able to make corrections and show examples on the same display. This is a vast improvement over audio-conferencing alone, with its disembodied voices and lack of visual stimulation and intimacy. Most villages have a full audio-conference setup with a convenor (open speaker). These kinds of learning situations, along with others involving culturally appropriate television productions and computer programs could be developed for teaching and sharing at least some aspects of Native library management in the future.

Community librarians in the Northwest Territories of Canada take correspondence courses through the Rural Library Training Project, Southern Alberta Institute of Technology, Calgary, Alberta. Northwest Territories Public Library Services believes that these should be reinforced by some audio-conferencing, however.

We haven't said much about any extra training needs for the college field worker or coordinator who already has a college degree or two, except that he or she should have an orientation to village conditions and cross-cultural communication, and be given some real incentives to begin learning the Native language. I believe that, as field workers, they should be able to assist villages in other ways than just teaching or advising on library management. Why not give them special intensive training courses in bookkeeping and accounting software, auditing, tax-preparation, and similar skills essential to village government? That way they would be more valuable and practical resource people, and make the transportation and per diem expense of their village visits more efficiently spent.

Audrey Kolb, former Northern Coordinator of Alaska State Library and based in Fairbanks, has many years' experience working with rural and Native libraries and library workers across mainland Alaska, as well as consulting background. In personal communications she commented on some of the above training ideas.[18]

On the possibility of peer trainers recruited from among the village library aides, she points out that,

> due to the part-time nature of their job in the village (1/4 time), there has been a turnover which tends to keep the competency level from rising. To ask selected aides to train others would be a dubious undertaking, unless more pay, time working, and overall incentives for increasing individual expertise and job satisfaction were in place. However, in principle this seems to be a good idea. As more library systems are established throughout Alaska, development and training programs will be available. This would be a natural benefit of increased governmental infrastructure and its inherent stability. . . .

"Another possibility is for Native corporations to establish a position for a trained librarian or library technician to coordinate training or offer centralized services." However, Kolb adds, "thus far there hasn't been any interest in this idea from those Native organizations which have been approached."

"The X-CED program[19] seemed a viable possibility for training," she said. But there was no interest, "on the basis that the mission of the program precludes programs resulting in degrees below the bachelor level, and it requires enrollment as a full-time student."

The State Library also looked into the University of Alaska's Correspondence Study program as a method of training rural library workers. Unfortunately it has requirements for one-to-one tutoring with no audio-conferences. Also, it is aimed more at students with a "strong academic background and a goodly amount of self-discipline. The 'typical' successful student is a teacher, not the audience we are trying to attract." Perhaps these conditions will change as more young Native people complete high school and standards for education and communication skills in English increase.

"The (library education) courses being developed and taught through Rural Education are an attempt to provide some training," adds Kolb. "My goal is an instructional program consisting [of] a series of courses, the completion of which will result in an AA or AAA degree. I think most of the courses could be taught by audio-conferencing and educational television, plus a variety of materials and media. In addition, an internship is absolutely necessary. Village libraries are too inadequate in materials, organization and programming to serve as the only training site. The problems are *so basic.*" (emphasis in the text.)

Looking at the new electronic technology available, she says that "videotapes and computer programs are certainly a possibility. Commercially developed ones are not likely to meet the basic needs of Alaska's small libraries. Media programs are expensive to produce. Viewers are pretty sophisticated because they watch a great deal of commercial television; consequently, any television training materials need to be well done."

Finally, adds Kolb, in-service training has been utilized, and apparently has been very successful, as it has been elsewhere in training Native workers. This involves the Native village library aide spending a short period of time working in a larger library, either an area center library like Bethel or Nome, or a larger metropolitan library in Fairbanks or Anchorage. During this time the aides are trained in a range of typical library tasks and put to work. In this situation they receive a volume of sophisticated experience probably worth several months of developmental coping in a struggling village library.

Margaret Leibowitz, former Deputy Alaska State Librarian, now retired, made the general comment that most of the above ideas with any merit will require extra funds, and in view of the severe downturn of the Alaska economy in the latter 1980s due to the depressed world oil market, it will be years before anything significant could be attempted. Her pessimisim was well founded, as all Alaska state agencies had their funding reduced by 15% or more for FY '87. Alaska state government revenues are in large part derived from oil fields on the Arctic coast. And oil income is even more uncertain in the 1990s, as oil fields become depleted, though drilling in some new areas may begin before 2000.

Kolb commented further on library development in Native areas of Alaska, citing a development project on the Seward Peninsula in the northwest that was carried out by the non-profit Kawerak Corporation. The Association of Village Council Presidents (AVCP) is the corresponding non-profit arm of the Calista (Native) Corporation for the Yukon-Kuskokwim delta:

A logical first step would probably be to work with AVCP and the [Alaska] Department of Community and Regional Affairs to get across the concept of libraries combined with adult learning centers. It was Kawerak which applied for the grant to build six adult learning centers in their region. I got involved so libraries could be a part of that program because I believe learning materials are important in education and training.[20]

In the latter months of 1990, I attempted a mail survey of all villages in the Y-K delta, to get a sense of the status of library development. Returns came back from over half the villages, and the results presented a fragmented picture. Less than half of the original 16 project villages responded, and only a few of these said they were open and receiving their state library assistance grants. The rest reflected a lack of knowledge about the availability of the grants, or said the village council had not seen fit to keep the village public library open. Of the total number (about 30 out of a possible 50-odd), several expressed interest in having a village public library, and some project villages wanted to reopen theirs. (Three mailings were used, sending a brief, one-page questionnaire with a stamped, self-addressed envelope.)

We should mention that library development in other Native areas of Alaska has been successful. We have tried to explore the reasons for its failure thus far in the Central Yupik area, and I believe that a fundamentally different approach is needed under the unique conditions that prevail, due to the high concentration of many subsistence villages and a large indigenous population in one geographical region, where the Native language is still spoken by a significant percentage.

To close this evaluative dialogue, I will offer some conclusions that reflect my belief in eventual Native control over Native resources, including information and libraries. This will undoubtedly bring a new approach, innovative concepts, and a distinctively Native-oriented character to new libraries.

The key points in Native village library development, then, are local control, reliable and adequate funding, access to appropriate training, interlibrary or network support, appropriate materials, programs and services, and qualified library workers.

Local control starts (ideally) with a (bilingual) Native library advocate properly introducing a diversified and flexible library concept to local officials, elders and the village administrator, once the village has expressed interest in starting a community library. Local control also means a village library committee or board, selected by village government from residents most interested in and knowledgeable about the library concept. Orientation and training of library board members is essential for effective and long-term viability of the library. The resident hired to staff the library should have at least a high school education, and arrangements should be made for training him or her as soon as possible, emphasizing the village library setting. (There is some debate as to whether mainstream library training is better than training in the village setting.) It is critical that library services adapt to the nature of the Native community, and not vice versa.

Reliable and adequate funding can be problematical or marginal in difficult economic times, even with well-coached and knowledgeable library boards, supportive village governments sending in grant applications in timely fashion, and a well-trained village library aide who dutifully files annual reports. This underlines the importance of community control and technology transfer, which translates into more community interest and pride, enabling a village library with reduced funding to continue, even in the hardest of times, and able to turn successfully to volunteerism for staffing if need be—an option which is not yet very practicable. Eventually, of course, it would be natural and necessary for some combination of funding from village and regional corporations and state and federal sources to maintain a system of community libraries in the 50-odd Central Yupik villages throughout the Y-K delta.

Library education and training in Alaska is presently available through an area center library or educational institution, or the State Library. The paraprofessional library education program at Tanana Valley Community College has been closed for years. Bringing an outside trainer/consultant to a remote area is an expensive process, difficult to maintain, especially in times of a depressed economy and a severely reduced state budget. Annual meetings or workshops and "on-site" village visits address ongoing problems only momentarily, and the expertise is gone for another year when the non-Native, non-resident trainer/consultant leaves the area. Under present conditions of a statewide shortage of library training opportunities, some Native village libraries could conceivably go two years before having a training session, especially if village visits are delayed or the present village library aide either quits or for any one of a multitude of reasons can't get to periodic training meetings or workshops in regional centers. And in such an early developmental situation as we find in the remote villages, problems are the norm, not the exception. A library can close for months due to what might elsewhere be considered a momentary mishap.

Reminding ourselves of the self-determination movement that is gaining prominence among Native peoples of the circumpolar north, the clear trend for the future involves equitable settlement of claims and Native control over a portion of lands and resources, especially when they involve subsistence economies. Corollary to this is the increasing role being played by Native peoples in the administrative and technical management of their communities and resources, as trained personnel become available. For the long term, then, the dominant society's library infrastructure supporting Native library development should more decisively enact technology transfer, and not persist in policies that are still, however inadvertently, rather neo-colonialist, guarding or delaying the acquisition of indispensable library management expertise by Native library workers in de facto Native "library systems."

At this time the availability of appropriate library training is almost directly proportional to the funding available for someone to come in from a distant metropolis, usually a highly qualified (if not overqualified) professional trainer/consultant. This is aside from any staff development funds that may be available in larger organizations locally. Such measures can be supplemented by various distance learning options, again originating from non-Native institutions holding village library management expertise.

In the author's view, avenues should be pursued that give selected resident library workers (or prospective workers, like X-CED graduates) intensive, village-specific, small library management training, with the proviso that they spend a certain period in the home area as a library tutor/trainer. One Native trainer per constellation of 6-8 villages, with an alternate, would be a start. In other words, an outside professional trainer/consultant would now be giving intensive, short-term, paraprofessional library training to this Native library training cadre, rather than trying to get out to personally train all village library aides, always with uncertain, uneven and usually transient results. In-service experience at a larger urban library would be an effective training reinforcement for these trainers. Some kind of credentialing mechanism would be needed, to give the Native training cadre definite status and authority as paraprofessionals. Higher pay for the Native trainer and the prospect of regular increases would also benefit the Native libraries. Regional annual meetings or workshops should be planned and run by these Native trainers in equal collaboration with professional library coordinators, and with direct input from village library boards of the region. The regional area center librarian from Bethel should continue to be one of the coordinators.

Pursuing this training scheme further, and looking at it in practical terms of the here and now—and the best current candidates might be certain promising village library aides within the Native regions, or former model aides—this would in fact accomplish several things. With a partial reallocation of funds into the Native sector, overall costs would be reduced in the long run because with local peer "paraprofessional" help close at hand, villages would probably be more involved and their libraries would become stronger, do a better job and be less likely to falter; having a local Native library tutor/trainer would boost the status of both the village libraries and the village library aides, increasing morale and probably reducing turnover; the village library aides would have a peer role model within the cultural community to emulate and aspire to; assistance would be more quickly available more often; and knowledge of the local Native language for briefing library boards, village councils and elders, etc. would hold immeasurable benefits for the libraries' acceptance and support within the Native community. There would also be a stimulus here for Native library workers to consider libraries, small museums, Native archives, documentation, and related fields as viable career alternatives. At least there would be a visible rung on the ladder leading to more prestige and higher income, something not much in evidence in any professions exercised among the Native peoples.

Appropriate materials, programs and services, focussing first on village life and villagers, need to employ the full range of audio-visual, video, graphics and computer resources, along with print. Innovation should be the byword, and the whole oral tradition in all its aspects should be creatively mined.[20] The extended interlibrary network could be utilized to search for and obtain resources from wherever they are found, on northern peoples, resource management and control, land claims and sovereignty issues, Native politics and organizations, and business opportunities, marketing, etc.

Interlibrary support or networking within a region would also benefit from having a resident Native library training cadre available to travel to designated neighboring villages. The State Library trainer/consultant, either directly or acting through the area center librarian, could provide them with information about the availability of needed materials, a task often requiring special knowledge of distant sources, as well as unusual effort. Here the State Library's extensive bibliographic resources would be very helpful. The state grant for the village where the Native tutor/trainer resides could have limited inter-village travel and other essential costs added in. More important, however, is the fact that the whole regional Native "library system" would be given more status, stability, training and support—from within the Native community.

A qualified and conscientious Native village library aide implies a satisfied, confident and respected worker and village resident. With an active and informed library board, reliable and adequate funding, the ready availability of coaching and training by peer Native resident tutor/trainers, attractive and appropriate materials, programs and services, the beginnings of a Native library network, plus an already strong community and cultural pride enhanced by all these things, libraries and Native communities will have a much better chance to survive the hard times and hard decisions.[22]

Increasing resource development and land and resource management responsibilities for the Native and village corporations, a growing cash economy and the need for better trained personnel for the infrastructure administering all of the above, not to mention the basic services provided by Federal, state, local and regional entities, imply a constantly growing need for information of all types in the delta, as elsewhere across the north. The need for continuing development of library services throughout the region seems clear, and they will have to be of increasingly higher standards and levels of technology to meet the needs and demands of the 50-odd Yupik Eskimo villages around the Yukon-Kuskokwim delta.

It is certainly a difficult and delicate task to insert a foreign cultural institution into any community, and then to ask the residents to operate it alone. In the long run, however, it is the only way it may be accepted and integrated into community life and activities. In the past, the traditional

Yupik "library" has been the oral tradition maintained by elders. In the Village Library Project, we looked for ways to benefit and grow because of this oral tradition, to eventually bring the village library effort into concert with it. Through the children, who are more acculturated to libraries, or at least library-type collections and activities (as whites know them), this can be achieved more quickly and readily as times goes on.

There is much to know and respect of the Yupik Eskimo life and culture in this world of accelerating socio-cultural, infrastructural and economic changes. All the funding in the world cannot buy rational and humane progress in cross-cultural development if the ancient traditions and the integrity of local authority and customs are ignored. Perhaps, long after the "Village Library Project" is gone, the Native-administered village libraries throughout the Yukon-Kuskokwim delta will not only support orderly and responsible regional development, but will help maintain a healthy balance between modernizing pressures and traditional values.[23]

Epilogue

In 1994-95 I found that all the librarians I talked to in Alaska expressed increased awareness and concern regarding the inadequacy of library services for Natives and other minorities, and the need to realistically and effectively address this situation. Ironically, it was felt that it is now up to Native communities and their resource entities (like the Native corporations) to share in or initiate any new library ventures. Almost everyone recognized that only through Native control can long-term progress be achieved. Native corporations, the University of Alaska, the State Department of Education, and State Library could combine their resources toward strengthening higher education and other training for Natives, institutionalizing appropriate museum, archival, documentation, and library services, and helping in the sociocultural, economic, and psychological recovery of Native/Indian communities overall (See under Napoleon in Bibliography/Reference List II for a brief description of the Native holocaust theory.)

In the Y-K delta, though only a few of the original 15 Village Library Project libraries still operate and receive their state Library Assistance Grants, other village libraries are being established, operating year-round, and finding additional sources of funding, such as the more flexible Federal LSCA Title IV grants, and Special Grants for library construction. The three Yupiit Nation libraries are combined school-public types, under the control of the Yupiit School District. Though there are no library boards or advisory committees, these villages are small and closely linked, and the Library Coordinator has feedback from the library aides and the community, such as longtime library advocate Mike Williams, a prominent local resident and member of the school Board.

Although the 50-odd villages throughout the delta are insular domains and very independent, no two being alike, the Yupiit Nation would seem to be a viable model for the future. (In the Fall 1995 elections, several more villages in the Lower Kuskokwim area rejected state municipal government and reverted to the federal traditional council.) Each library has a computer and CD-ROM reader. There is no public card catalog, and patrons utilize the computer program *Follett Cat Plus* to access (or find out the) holdings of their own collection. Print-outs of the holdings of the other two district libraries are also at hand. Another program, *Brodart* on CD-ROM, is used to download full MARC records for in-print titles ordered, and a shelf list card is printed. This is the only print "card catalog" maintained. For interlibrary loan and availability of out-of-print titles, etc., there is now an 800 (no cost) telephone number to call, available statewide for all small rural libraries. The number of library workers in the district is six, including the non-Native Coordinator, or about two per village.

The Coordinator (a degreed librarian) trains Library Aides, who also attend workshops within and out of the region, and occasionally Alaska Library Association (AkLA) conferences, funding permitting (for which they sign an agreement to be alcohol-free).

Programs of the Yupiit Nation libraries have included museum-type displays of local Yupik crafts, personal collections, and photos of elders. Documentation is through videotaping of sports events, school graduations, Eskimo dancing, and interviews with elders. An archival role is fulfilled with collections of school yearbooks and local imprints. All videotapes recorded locally are kept in the village library. There are occasional social events, children's programs, and occupational training programs, the last of these coming through satellite TV channels. Two sources for these are the Distance Delivery Consortium (DDC) out of Bethel, which provides such programs as Health Aide training, and STAR Schools of Spokane, Washington, which provides a wide variety of educational programming, some of it Indian/Native oriented.

For the rest of the delta, the annual training workshops in Bethel have currently become biennial, and although experienced Native library paraprofessionals of the region like Sharon Reichman and Maxine Beaver of Bethel assist with presentations and are bilingual (Reichman in Siberian Yup'ik and Beaver in Central Yup'ik), the main presenters continue to be non-Native, some local and others from the State Library and elsewhere. Participation by Yupiit Nation library aides and those from other state school district libraries is highest. They are paid more than workers from independent village public libraries, often work more hours, and receive more training. In looking over evaluative comments by many workshop participants, Native and non-Native, one has to note the mixture of diversity and ambivalence. Attitudes, and the degree of acculturation in either direction by library workers, cover a wide range.

The Alaska Library Network (ALN) bibliographic database was last issued on microfiche in 1992 and is still in use in many Alaska village libraries. (They can use the above-mentioned 800 telephone number to learn about newer titles and to request materials.) Out of a total of more than 70, the only western Alaskan communities that can afford to have the CD-ROM version of ALN in the computer program *LaserCat* are the regional centers of Bethel, Kotzebue and Nome.

To my knowledge, there are no Native librarian associations in Alaska yet, that I know of. *Tracings,* a newsletter edited and issued by the State Library, is aimed at all small rural libraries, with no special attention to Natives. AkLA conferences still have alcohol beverages available, though not quite as prevalent as in the past. Native attendance and participation has increased somewhat, especially when the venue is in a location more easily accessible to surrounding Native communities. At these sessions, sometimes special Pre-conferences for Native library workers and others interested are held. It is exasperating that in 1995 these still need to be designated "Pre-conferences," falling into the old syndrome of treating nonmainstream librarianship as somehow odd and extra, as if bush Alaska library development, let alone that serving Native communities, both rural and urban, didn't merit full status in the eyes of normal librarians. (One could also ask, Why there are so few, if any, sessions on serving Alaska's other minority populations?) Anchorage conferences of the Alaska Library Association have emphasized seminars and speakers on the latest in library technology. The 1995 conference was in Juneau, in southeast Alaska, and except for half-hour programs on Native American literature for children and WLN (Western Library Network) and SLED (online "Statewide Electronic Gateway" to library databases and other services) users, the rest was primarily urban-oriented, taking up many sophisticated and "trendy" subjects. No programs or presenters were evident on Native community (rural or urban) or other minority library services.

Finally, in late 1994 the Alaska Governor's Advisory Council on Libraries, which oversees the State Library, had no Natives among its 12 members, although apparently there had been a Native representative earlier. No mention was made of other minorities. A Democratic governor took office early in 1995 and may make the council more ethnically representative of the state population.

A "Village Library Project" in New Mexico?

In the fall of 1994 I learned of a very similar project being started among Apache, Navajo, and Pueblo communities in the hot deserts and dry mountains of the Southwestern United States. As I read over the materials sent to me by New Mexico State Library, I experienced feelings of déjà vu, and impulsively sent off a long letter full of gratuitous advice, for it seemed so much like a replication of the project I'd helped manage in subarctic Alaska.

It was the "New Mexico Native American Community Libraries Project," and though similar in purpose and many details to the one in the Y-K delta, there were significant differences. There was a large Native American Libraries Advisory Group, and there was consultation and input from Navajo advisers from the outset. The communities are connected to each other and city centers by roads, and each one has full computer applications, including automation and telecommunications capabilities. A generous legislative appropriation also provides a much larger collection expenditure ($7,500) for each of six community libraries, along with furniture and modern equipment. Each community had to provide a *paid* library aide and utilities, phone, etc., as well as housing, a council resolution establishing the library, and an advisory board. Training is a key component, and this is the Project Coordinator's responsibility.

The headquarters library at Crown Point will be incorporated into the Navajo Community College, now under construction. The Native American Advisory Group will provide ongoing oversight for the project. The initial number of six communities will be expanded over a five-year period to about 50, including the Native American Studies Center at the University of New Mexico in Albuquerque. This seems overly ambitious for such a short time period, but perhaps the addition of close and direct Native American monitoring, the commitment of the state legislature (and available federal grants, etc.), and the other improvements will allow it to go well. An association of Native American library workers, the T'a a Dine Library Association, has already been formed in New Mexico, and will include Arizona and Utah. The current president of the New Mexico Library Association is a Navajo.

Notes

1. The first part of this chapter is taken in large part from an article by the author entitled "The Village Library Project, Yukon-Kuskokwim Delta, Alaska," that appeared in *Rural Libraries,* Vol.III, No.2 (1983), Clarion State University, Clarion, PA. Used with permission.
2. Sharr, F.A. "Functions and Organization of a Rural Library System," *Unesco Bulletin for Libraries* 26:1, p. 24.
3. Identical with the Calista Native Corporation area.
4. This estimate provided by the Association of Village Council Presidents (1990).
5. *Hootch, Molly v. Alaska State Operated School System. Pacific Reporter,*

2nd ed., Law Library, pp. 793–816. This beame the 1976 decision "which mandated the establishment of local high schools in the smaller communities of the study area which had until that time sent their children to boarding schools in Bethel, St. Mary's or outside the region," sometimes as far away as southeast Alaska and the Pacific Northwest states. (Feinup-Riordan, p.267)

6. The best single source-book on contemporary Yupik life in the Lower Kuskokwim and coastal villages is, in the author's view, Fienup-Riordan (1982). She is an anthropologist who has specialized in the Central Yupik area, publishing many titles on the Yupik people, their heritage and history.

7. Hereinafter also referred to as ABE.

8. In view of growing delinquency problems in remote Yupik villages in 1990, reconsideration is being given to keeping the distant government boarding schools open, as an alternative for troubled youth. In Bethel, the regional center, there is also growing recognition of the need for an alternative high school, for the same reasons.

9. "Anthropologists have noticed an innate dignity in personal bearing and a pride in their way of life characterize the peoples among whom they work." Foster, George M. *Traditional Societies and Technological Change,* p. 88.

10. The same problem has been found in other cross-cultural service situations. See Kaufert and Koolage (1984), who cite difficulties female Native medical interpreters have had in serving male Native patients, "who were reluctant to accept their role in advocacy." p. 285.

11. Extending this thinking further, we can reconsider which are "adult" materials and which are "children's" in this cross-cultural, bilingual setting, where literacy differences may exist between the generations and even between villages. Villages differ in the degree of Yup'ik spoken according to how traditional one is, whether the village is on the coast or upriver, and whether the village is Catholic, Russian Orthodox, or Moravian, certain missions having been less tolerant of Yup'ik language, customs, and ceremonies than others, sometimes deciding to totally eradicate them. (See pp. 57–70 of Fienup-Riordan [1982] for a detailed historical discussion of the differing policies of these churches and their clerics in the field.)

It therefore sometimes seems logical and natural to include titles with easier English and illustrations among the adult books, in order to stimulate and encourage the hesitant adult to take one home. Also, to be guided by one's dominant society concepts of what is adult and what is children's literature, in terms of "reading level," "interest level," etc. is to risk falling into another trap of cross-cultural ignorance and insensitivity. My predecessor in the Village Library Project was a history major in college. When he put together the founding "core collections," he apparently included library-bound copies of every scholarly title his favorite history professor/author had written! This was an extreme case of cross-cultural blindness.

12. ". . . Literacy generally becomes important only when villagers begin to see that those persons who are literate have extra advantages, or when they come to feel they are less likely to be cheated by city people if they can read. As standards of living are raised and there is increased travel and contact with the remainder of the nation, conditions become increasingly favorable for presenting adult education programs to rural peoples. But until such time arrives, slight sucess is the usual rule." Foster, George M. *Traditional Societies and Technological change*, p. 169.

13. In 1990 the Alaska State Library was reviewing these grants to possibly make them more restrictive, adding sufficient service levels and more local commitment as further requirements for their issuance, an arbitrary and unilateral shift in policy that will only adversely impact the remote Yupik village libraries, as presently supported.

14. The number of hours a village librarian works turns out to be a multi-faceted factor in longevity on the job. Rather than looking for ways to find additional work hours for the village librarian elsewhere in the village, the optimum approach might be to increase the library hours themselves, but his would depend on the librarian's capacity for enterprise and initiative, and the kind of residual support found in the village. For libraries that include learning center facilities, services and programs, such as the six specially built Library/Learning Centers in remote villages on the Seward Peninsula in northwestern Alaska, it is easier to raise the hours to 20 or 30, which makes the village librarian position much more attractive. In those villages with a library alone, or perhaps joined informally with an ABE center, where the hours go below 20 per week, it has been found more productive to be open fewer days and longer hours. This not only increases use but gives the village librarian, or aide, a better schedule of free time. (From information supplied in part by Audrey Kolb, formerly of Alaska State Library.)

The location as well as the nature of a Native community library is open to innovation and departure. I was reminded by a long-time faculty member of the Kuskokwim Campus, UAF, in Bethel that, instead of making that town's separately housed, joint city-college library more inviting by adding a Yupik hospitality room just inside the entrance, such an addition should rather be situated in a large, centrally located shopping center in town, "where the people are" . . . (A similar trend is occurring in cities, where occasionally we find a new branch being installed in a large, suburban mall.)

15. Again, early in 1988, another library was burned out when the village offices where it was located were swept by fire due to an electrical short circuit during gale force winds.

16. For a detailed look at the complex cross-cultural ambivalence experi-

enced by Natives training and working in Kussaq paraprofessional situations, see the article "Training of Indigenous Non-Professionals: An Analysis of Eskimo Welfare Workers' Perceptions of their Role," by Graham P. Andrewartha.

Worth considering, too, is the advice of Lotsee Smith in her paper, "Indian Community Libraries in the New Mexico Pueblos," one of four such papers in "Profiles of Four Indian Library/Information Programs," by Nellie Buffalomeat et al., for the 1978 White House Preconference:

> . . . it is imperative that someone from the local community serve as 'librarian.' Knowledge of the people, the culture, the language and community information needs is a more important prerequisite than knowing the Dewey Decimal System or other library skills. . . . Experience has shown that a mature person who is interested in the library and is stable in the community makes the best librarian. Young, unmarried people, while quite good at the job, tend to leave it for a better or different one at the first opportunity. (p. 33)

There are arguments for either a younger or older person in this position, but one has to admit the wisdom of having an older "librarian" in a conservative, traditional community undergoing a complex array of acculturating changes—the younger generation being affected the most.

17. Hippler, Arthur E., on p. 1 of "Final Report to the Commissioner of the Department of Public Safety on the Village Public Safety Officers Program" ("VPSO"). Institute of Social and Economic Research, University of Alaska. October, 1982.

18. Personal communications, Audrey Kolb, August 21, 1986 and January 19, 1988. She is the author of *A Manual for Small Libraries in Alaska,* cited herein. Though the manual mentions at several points the Native culture and its community ways, and the need for all Alaskan libraries to be informed on the Native heritage, cross-cultural conditions per se in Native library development are not addressed.

19. "The X-CED (Cross-Cultural Educational Development) Program is the off-campus delivered teacher education program to prepare students to serve the unique educational needs of Alaska's multicultural population. . . . [It] offers full-time undergraduate course work for students seeking a B. Ed. degree." p. 61, University of Alaska-Fairbanks 1986-87 Catalog. A useful document for understanding the nature and limitations of the X-CED program is: *Program Review, Alaska Rural Teacher Training Corps (ARTTC) and Cross-Cultural Education Development Program (X-CED), 1970-84,* by John M. Booker. College of Human and Rural Development, Center for Cross-Cultural Studies, University of Alaska, Fairbanks. June, 1987, 61pp, 17 1.

20. Personal communication, Audrey Kolb. Late 1986.

21. For anyone working as a librarian among Native people where the oral tradition is still strong, I recommend a reading of *African Libraries, Western Tradition and Colonial Brainwashing,* by Adolphe O. Amadi. Libraries originally evolved out of the oral tradition, yet they have become highly bureaucratized and ethnocentric transmitters of western cultural concepts. Amadi's unblinking examination of the implication of both "before" and "after" has revelatory as well as poignant implications for library development in Native areas today.

22. Alaska State Library administration expressed interest and qualified support for some of the ideas expressed above, at least theoretically, but they point out that more funding would be needed to start any new programs. The state library has a wide range of missions to fulfill, and improving services to Native communities is only one aspect of one of them. The flush fiscal days of the 1970s oil boom are gone, and a tight state budget severely limits any prospects for innovation.

23. The final pages of this chapter are largely taken from a short article published in the Alaska Library Association journal, *Sourdough,* Vol.25, No.1 (Winter, 1988). Used with permission.

     As for increasing the percentage of Native professionals in the region, one school district has apparently been above average in this respect. The Lower Kuskokwim School District has about one-seventh of its teaching staff that are Natives, with another seventh that are white who have married Natives and will therefore probably stay in the region for some years. (From remarks of the district superintendent, Sue Hare, before the Bethel Chamber of Commerce, September 29, 1988.)

3.

Oral and Written Traditions, Literacy, and the Native Orthographies

The white man writes everything down in a book so that it will not be forgotten; but our ancestors married the animals, learned all their ways, and passed on the knowledge from one generation to another.[1]

As literature pours into society, people measure themselves against the widespread norm and begin to doubt their self-worth. The standardization of print with its emphasis on literary style accentuates the differences among people in their oral and written discourse. . . . Being functional in contemporary society requires not only the ability to read and write but also the ability to be articulate in conversation and dialogue.[2]

In past ages, contact and exchange with foreign cultures was, with the exception of migrations and invasions, rare and incidental; even the invasion of conquest might take decades, and a migration generations. Things moved at the pace of the foot soldier or beast of burden, and of primitive sails over the uncharted seas. Societies were much more fixed in place and tradition, and their world ended at the limits of their domain—or not far beyond. The rest was fabled. In any case, there was no need or call to go beyond, to "the ends of the earth," and all such mad contemplation was full of terror, foreboding and peril. But in good time contact and exchange and trade slowly increased and spread, and form the 16th century these experiences came faster and with more intensity, on a scale that seemed to acquire dimensions previously nonexistent. Humanity was changing and evolving over time, both in its relations with natural forces and resources, and in relation to itself. To use Edmund Wilson's trenchant phrase in another, somewhat analagous context—at the beginning of the historical era urbanizing humans underwent a "shock of recognition," as individual self-consciousnessness was ushered through the tool of writing, which objectified and fixed social transactions.

In the late 20th century, when the human world is imploding culturally, compressing back into almost a tribal community again, with the help of a steadily increasing percentage of literacy, relatively quick means and ready availability of circumglobal travel for at least the better educated and affluent minority, and communication by electric and electronic media, both audio and video forms, for many of the rest who cannot leave home at all or so easily, one can still find the original oral tradition here and there, especially among the Native peoples and in Third World nations. In North America, we often talk about Native peoples as though they were the only ones with their original homeland, or at least still having close daily ties with their original cultural heritage. Relatively speaking, that is our definition of Native people and their communities. But for the rest of us, if we cannot point very exactly to one homeland and one uninterrupted line of heritage back to antiquity, we often yearn to do so.

Walter J. Ong, in his book *Orality and Literacy, The Technology of the Word,* described the oral and written modes of human expression and their respective world views and intellectual life. Thus, the oral world:

> Human beings in primary oral cultures, those untouched by writing in any form, learn . . . by apprenticeship, by discipleship . . . by listening, by repeating what they hear, by mastering proverbs and ways of combining and recombining them, by assimilating other formulary materials, by participating in a kind of corporate introspection. . . Orally-based thought and expression is additive, aggregative, redundant (copious), conservative or traditionalist, close to the human life-word, life-as-struggle (as in a contest), empathetic and participatory, homeostatic, situational . . . Language is so overwhelmingly oral that of all the many thousands of languages—possibly tens of thousands—spoken in the course of human history only around 106 have even been committed to writing to a degree sufficient to have produced literature, and most have never been written at all. (pp. 7, 9)

The old-time oral tradition was, to quote Eric Havelock's[3] phrase, the tribal encyclopedia, the living reference collection that ensured the preservation and transmission of known information about past experience, subsistence skills, origins, and right conduct. We can hardly imagine today what this experience was like, to live by and partake of the oral tradition on a daily basis, when it was the lifeblood and survival story of the people— "our people, and how we came to be in this place." Tales and chronicles, incantations and prayers were recited and repeated, intoned and sung, celebrated and danced, dramatized and ritualized, murmured and whispered and echoed, since the most ancient times, times almost geological in their remoteness and obscurity. During those seasons of the year, usually the winter or indoor months when increased idle time and darkness forced even closer company in communal dwellings expansive for just this purpose, the ear and mouth—and the entire body in ritual, display, response and performance—combined to ensure the longevity of the heritage, to the accompaniment of a crackling fire or flickering oil lamps. The young fell silent and listened to their elders, to those who knew by heart the old stories and memorized heritage, who knew how to be a good hunter or a productive wife, who respected the sacred, mysterious, and often fearsome ways of shamans.[4]

The closest many of us can come to knowing what this experience was like might be those bedtime stories we were told or read in early childhood, in semi-darkness and semi-wakefulness, as we listened to the magical, droning, older voices, carrying us far away and yet pulling us closer and closer as we drifted off to sleep and security. For the oral ways had a magical hold, and not just for the "storytelling" experience, for that was only one small part of cultural transmission in aboriginal times. Just as in antiquity there was no such thing as "wildlife," so there was no time or place for pure poetry or "entertainment," in and of itself. Everything was tied to subsistence survival ensuring the perpetuation of our kindred, though of course one could also be enchanted and entertained while being caught up in one of many ritualized activities.

To survive and endure in aboriginal times, one could not be alone (in spirit and personality), and in fact one did not even think of oneself alone as we do, for psychologically there was no self-consciousness and ego as we know it today (though there is more than one theory on the evolution of human consciousness). The world was made and maintained by the common thought of one's own people, and in harmony with everything within reach, within sight, and all else imaginable. To question or even doubt this status quo usually brought either death or banishment. The rare individual who might have signs of such aberrant behavior would certainly be considered "possessed," or literally "out of his mind"—or he might become a shaman. . . .[5]

The round of daily life and the progress of the seasons were filled with precisely scheduled tasks that responded to the dynamic of the cycle of subsistence resources. Each task was accomplished in a certain way at accustomed places by certain kinship or tribally related individuals—or by slaves among some peoples. Things made for the communal household were always of particular materials, always of a proven design, always put to a specific, time-honored and revered, sacred use. Else how could life go on, if things were not done in the prescribed way, to honor and praise our sacred origins and spirits who supplied all that we know, our ancient home since time itself began, that we might live and prevail forever in these ways?

What some would now call superstitious practices and observances adhered to every feature of daily life, and the world around was peopled with spirit life every bit as powerful and sensitive as the human kind, and which in fact preceded it, and from which we evolved. Therefore, we must study and watch these things all around us, to learn about ourselves, for we are mirrored and contained within the watery circle of earth and sky, the realms of wood and leaf, fur, fin and feather, noon and night, blood and stone, birth and death, smoke and spirit.

In the sophisticated world most of us know—urbane, literate, global, rather cynical and very self-conscious, egotistical and self-indulgent—we still have many vestigial ties to our most archaic oral traditions, maintained by folk culture. And we have an inherent sense that much of this folk culture is really true, despite over two thousand years of Plato's scientific tradition carried forth by European civilization and its accompanying technology. For if our innermost feelings were expressed, we have a certain yearning for the security and surety of ancient traditional beliefs that were unquestioned and so well preserved, enabling our cultural river to flow to this day. And certainly for us now there is a sharpened edge to this yearning, due to the holocaustal nature of modern war, the anxieties attending poorly understood threats such as hazardous waste, uncontrolled afflictions of the body, and even seemingly innocuous "technological advances" that one day turn out to be inherently lethal to humankind.

The very new phenomenon of modern worldwide culture as a tribal, communal experience is an unwieldly and almost volatile thing to contain. Yet at the same time it feels very familiar, almost déjà-vu. Every day on television we see and hear of the activities of our kind around the world, almost instantaneously, thanks to satellite communications technology. Over the past few centuries the pace of life in every way has been increasing not just steadily, but at an increasing rate, in an upward bending curve.

But in contemporary Native and Indian communities there are activities of an oral tradition, at least in the modern, self-conscious and limited mode, that are more active and cultivated than is generally known.[7] In fact the "oral tradition" isn't really mentioned as such, because it is very much alive in practice, and with a dynamic all its own. In my own experience, it is the time I went to ask someone for a ride to town, and stayed over two hours listening to an elder tell about conditions in his childhood instead. It is caring for family first, the tight web of extended family still well-preserved beyond subsistence times. It is the profound and sacred role of funerals, not only to say goodbye, but to say hello—how everyone leaves his daily work to attend, not just for an hour, but for the day, to keep company and attend the "crossing over." Another elder has gone to the spirit world, where nothing has changed for one's grandfathers, and from whence they may return when one least expects it, in myriad ways, to let us know they are still with us, still watching, and remembering. In more traditional communities, it is the regular singing and dancing shared with the young—the voice of the people that speaks from the past and to the present. At pow wows or dance festivals, the spiritual power and "good medicine" of songs is displayed and exchanged among the tribes. The spirits of all things are abroad as always, and need to be allowed for, listened to, respected. Vision quests are followed only in the most traditional communities, but these needs are still discussed, and sometimes an individual will be gone away for this purpose.

Until the end of the Middle Ages and the invention of the printing press, communication was primarily face-to-face, and, when information was first recorded and propagated, it was by hand, and for a very long time even beginning literacy was quite controversial, "highly developmental" (as we would say now), and utilizable only by the tiny number of "specialist" recorders and scribes and a privileged few from among the elite and powerful.

It has been said that the developing, planetwide consciousness of our "modern" world of the twenty-first century needs new and more inclusive, ecumenical archetypes, and until that need is fulfilled, there will be strife among the many ancient ethos surviving today. Unfortunately, those Native peoples in the Fourth World of the north are at risk of being swept aside unless empowered to define and defend themselves in modern terms, which necessitates education and communication far beyond mere written and oral literacy in one's Native tongue, and encompassing far more than one's original homeland.[6]

Transportation by human feet and astride animals or propelled by sails over the seas remained limited to that pace until the steam engine powered the first railroads and ships early in the nineteenth century. So we could really say that modern transportation has only arrived within our own era. All these momentous developments have helped to bring about the present widespread multiplication and intensification of strife between peoples of differing cultural ways and different gods.

The faculty of storytelling needs exercise and cultivation, enrichment through retelling and exchange of stories, with various versions. The old stories involve human-like animals and birds encountering people straddling both worlds, half-human and half-spirit. All of nature participates; imagination and sentience serve to teach lessons, provide amusement and humor, offer warnings, relate the past, explain what is, bring in food, and prevent disaster. If we will only listen to all the voices around us—and from within—we will learn what we need to know. Traditional healing and medicines are also shared and passed on from generation to generation.

Traditional visiting often reinforces and clarifies very complex and subtle relationships. It involves catching up on kin, exchanging news and judgments, sharing traditional lore, tales and gossip, harking back to the past and looking at what we have become. It includes the expected food and nourishment, perhaps the exchange of small gifts, or performing a needed or helpful task. Through these gestures, trust and bonds are affirmed, and commitment to the renewal of heritage and guarding of kinship is understood.

Pow-wows are held weekly all over the United States and Canada. These involve traditional dancing, including dancing competition in costume and usually several "drums" with singers, a potluck "feed," and sometimes gift-giving. Old-time stick or bone gambling draws big crowds, as much for visiting as to watch or play.

Among the modern Central Yupik there are Eskimo dance festivals, family reunions, lavish birthday parties, and "anniversaries," when the passing of someone is commemorated after one year. These latter are convivial if respective occasions, and the host family offers food and gifts to the guests. A child's birthday party is much more than that: a house will be filled to overflowing with adults and children alike, with gifts and plenty of food. The Russian Orthodox Church celebrates its Christmas during "Slavic," in early January, and orthodox villages have house-to-house processions where singing and feasting take place. These have become much more than rituals for the devout, however, and many in the community share in these festivities. I remember those oral history tapes of the Coastal Tribe and how important visiting on a regular basis was to the roomful of elders chatting and how the one-on-one "oral history interview" often seemed awkward and contrived in their eyes. "Why can't we all sit in?" I'd asked, and I had no good and reasonable answer for them, being their friend.

So, in pursuing any comparisons between oral and written forms of language, we had better remind ourselves that we do so in the literate tradition, which is to say that we are imposing literate concepts onto a very different tradition, the oral expression of language. An excellent and provocative discussion of this predicament is found in Jack Goody's book, *The Domestication of the Savage Mind,* and other published writings by him. He points out various ways in which literate analysis of oral forms of language can project inappropriate, culturally conditioned and limited concepts onto what is a much more complex cultural matrix than we have been led to believe. In other words, there is ambivalence and equivocation in the oral tradition as in the literate tradition, and Goody also claims that early literate forms of ordering or expressing relationships established a bias that continues to this day: for example, the use of dichotomies, of sorting phenomena into either/or arrangements with a European interpretation, or into lists of objects or categories and tables reflecting values that only partially or even erroneously reflect relationships in another oral language. Not that oral systems of language didn't have such intellectual tools already, but inscribing data as a record onto a surface gave it an abstract and detached character that was to alter the very thought processes of those who pondered them. When it comes to comparing the oral and literate forms of language (and some assert that this is a three-sided affair: orality, literacy and language), non-Native observers have sometimes been too willingly subservient to the constraints and order imposed by a European intellectual tradition thoroughly steeped in the mechanization of thought that we revere as "literacy."

The underlying patterns of communication in Indian/Native life and work are reflected in a more visually oriented basis for social relationships, especially in connection with work and athletic recreation and ceremony. It is a more personally supportive, face-to-face, non-competitive society, less linear and more group-oriented in the most profound and comprehensive sense. The eyes and what they see and reflect are perhaps more important than the mouth and its utterances. The young traditionally learned by observation and experimentation, rather than listening to the lectures and explanations of a "teacher." Public meetings are traditionally arranged with people sitting in a circle, with more faces to respond to. Discussions are more open and wide-ranging, not following the parliamentary logic and "agenda" order of the white community, but allowing more people (primarily the older adults) to share in keeping things going and giving all the adults the opportunity to speak up, even if the public dialogue goes from one "unrelated" subject to another—because in fact all the concerns of tribal or village members are of equal worthiness, and comprise the whole of tribal community life. The consensus is that all matters of concern are interrelated, just as everyone's lives and work are. There is therefore a natural logic in human affairs at play here, a culturally different approach to human interdependency and community "problem-solving," as modern technocrats would call it.

One highly unsettling effect on Native society of acculturation to western ways is a change in the status of Elders. From our experience with the dominant society's relegation of its "Senior Citizens" to inactive and rather irrelevant modern status, we can perhaps learn something from the Native Elders' traditional role, which was to serve as stabilizing community leaders and spiritual counselors for younger tribal members. Nowadays they can also perform as trainers and role models in making cross-cultural development and training more effective, as well as better balanced and appropriate for the tribal community. Two provocative papers published by Joseph E. Couture[8] (Cree) in 1979 describe the "best" format for training Natives, and the role Elders can play in it. However, trainers need a "clear awareness" of several factors beforehand: the drive for self-determination, and that collective concerns override others; Indian administration will be transferred to local control; economic development should be a humanizing experience, with individual fulfillment; the land is sacred; and the Native decision-making style is also collective, group-oriented and noncompetitive.

Natives training Natives introduces a new acculturation dynamic, and Elders can be a part of it. Couture relates:

> Elder opinion is that Indian cultural/spiritual heritage is the ground out of which Indian identity arises . . . Elders completely understand the nature and purpose of current person and community development technique . . . The inclusion of Elders in a training workshop is the clearest and also easiest

operational effort that trainers can make to assure appreciable cultural impact
. . . One learns about Elders through relating over a period of time. The Elders apply a learning-by-doing model, counselling and teaching focus on the
doing, on one's experience. Respectful observation eventually yields evidence
of remarkable, incisive intellect, of tested wisdom, of sharp and comprehensive observational ability allied with excellent memory recall, and of well-developed discursive ability—abilities and skills which constitute the main cognitive qualities of Elders' mind.[9]

Part of the source of these abilities, out of an oral tradition and a tribal subsistence community, can be ascribed to Native child-rearing practices and
traditional decision-making. The Native was educated in a holistic way, developing all the faculties, both cognitive and intuitive sides of the brain, in
a way more balanced than modern education (formal and informal), where
the cognitive side is emphasized and the intuitive side is neglected or even
denigrated.

The old oral tradition pervaded all aspects of life, from listening, learning and memorizing to watching and miming, from participating and following (in the sense of following a story) to replicating and duplicating. It
integrated life's needs, fears and reverence in forms of physical shape and
decoration. It was the sound and movement of human ritual and play, the
grimace and gesture of persona acting out the mysteries of social and spiritual relationships. Yet it also linked people to the past, which it emphasized.
Temporal relations among kin were uppermost. Concerns were of the here
and now, which was everything. "Future planning," in the sense we understand it today, of projecting objectified lives into the distant future, was
nonexistent. Knowledge was based on social cohesion and moral order.
Consensus was built on the sharing of a mutually affirmed and celebrated
"world-view" (our world being here, in this place), engendering a feeling of
always "belonging," literally a bonded member of the landscape and elements and spirit realm. (And to a minor degree these traditional values are
still held, still lived. They often affect the Native approach to modern life.)

Then it happened, obscurely and incidentally, in various times and places
long ago, that incised symbols and signs represented the objects we sought,
and acquired a separate existence in and of themselves. Tags of ownership
on objects became tags of identification and these were eventually noted
down in lists and tables. Thus a written record became civilization's memory, and one that could be referred to again and again, as its authority was
cumulative. Literacy and the written record transformed both human nature and the human condition, adding a new dimension and new order to
intellectual development and evolution, for good or ill.

> The invention of writing was highly significant for the development not only
> of language, but of society, and favored the progress of commerce . . . It con-
> firmed the power of priests through the trained scribes . . . It fixed historical

tradition, and thus strengthened social cohesion . . . that led to the expansion of city states into empires . . . With the rise of an urban mode of life, there appeared technical vocabularies characteristic of higher civilization . . . The existence of a literary tradition exerts a conservative influence on linguistic development. . . . Even in the ancient world, the part played by language in society had manifested itself in such a way that very few really new features have come to light since. . . [10]

To write is to read,[11] and for about 2000 years humans have been increasingly recording and reading, to the point where we now talk of the "information explosion" and crises in literacy. Linked to these activities have been the increasing capabilities in travel and communication, to the point where someone on the moon can be seen and heard talking directly with someone—or everyone—on earth. We are in the midst of what has been called the Age of Information, when access to and accurate interpretation and effective use of "data," or more intellectual messages, is the road to success, progress, and further evolution in the scientific view. In fact, we equate this capability with state-of-the-art human experience. Redigesting and refining our cultural ways more and more has become life itself for the more sophisticated human societies among us, and our origins in the subsistence life and its traditional economies recede further and further into the distance and the subconscious.

The printing press, according to Ong, was a "psychological breakthrough of the first order." Text itself involves both sight and sound. Sound was left over from the days of manuscripts or lists of accounts being read aloud, when early "readers" declaimed to themselves and most texts were written to be read aloud anyway. Sight was rendered much more efficient by the alphabetical letterpress, through the greatly increased uniformity, clarity, spacing between letters and more standardized format. The press "imbedded the word itself deeply in the manufacturing process and made it into a kind of commodity . . . One consequence of the new exactly repeatable visual statement was modern science." Printed text took on a finality and authority, an "unanswerability" all its own.

The Socratic method of latter day oral cultural times—which were also the earliest times of writing—featured the agonistic or contesting mode, whereby public dialogues consisted of just that: two speakers giving and taking, or a speaker and audience playing off each other verbally, in an unrepeatable exchange, although the attentive and devoted memory of those times meant that such oral displays were remembered and repeated and passed on, eventually to be recorded for all time—for the "future," in the new "writing."

In Native societies of North America today, the arrival of literacy and western culture brought by the Europeans is only a few generations old in many areas, especially the north. Its new concepts are only recently being understood and utilized by many Native people. Native languages have acquired alphabets, a written form and style. Dictionaries have evolved from the pioneer efforts of early missionary proselytizers and later modern linguists. In fact, the teachings of the Bible and church ministrations as translated by missionaries provided the impetus for the first serious attempts at Native alphabets, and printing for colonized Native populations. Dictionaries today are academic products attempting to pinion in two dimensions the orally learned medium of aboriginal speech, which contained and conveyed a Culture in every sense that one can imagine. Agents of western culture were anxious to set down and translate Native utterances in written form, usually for the purpose of bringing western cultural ways (like literacy in Christian texts) more effectively to partially assimilated Native peoples, through texts in their own, newly created alphabet. Admittedly, a critical sampling of the Native cultural continuum was also preserved in this way, propelling it into the modern era.

The development of writing and its marriage partner, reading was part of the evolution from orality into literacy. In the latter, we think about ourselves and our ways. And we think about ourselves thinking about ourselves. The relatively recent arrival of this self-consciousness, which begins with historical time and literate ways, is what sets modern humans utterly apart from those in the aboriginal, solely oral epoch, which is a few million years old. Therefore, it was a few seconds ago, figuratively speaking, when humans became aware of themselves objectively. In fact, we have a distinct feeling of omnipotence, along with a little nostalgia and even discomfort, do we not, when seeing an anthropological documentary on television, where a few shamans from the modern world—scientists—are observing and studying one of those last pockets of aborgines. It is a feeling that comes from the undisputed knowledge that they are totally under our dominance, and we can examine them just as objectively as we might some organisms on a slide under a microscope. Ever since Plato, we have been dissecting and manipulating our own nature, as well as everything else in the environment around us, for the sole purpose of extending and bettering our lives, as we like to think. Why nostalgia or discomfort? Because aborigines are so close to us—it was not so long ago, and our psyches still remember. . . . The discomfort is from the just-forgotten—what we have let go yet apprehend from that earlier time, before the historical era with its accelerating modernization.

But what is the written form, compared to the oral tradition? It has been described as a pile of standard grade lumber next to the living tree. The oral tradition was a dynamic of everyday life that occupied everyone without exception and with only a communal conscience. It was shared and practiced communally. The written tradition, called the "gunpowder of the mind," suddenly isolates the individual, alone and usually silent, to decipher and interpret symbols imprinted apart from everything else, with no meaning except that given to it by the "reader." The mind is given a power that is from within, not without, a totally new and peculiar uniqueness really devastating to the tribal consciousness, which was subjective only in a social sense. The power to objectify one's surroundings, and oneself, was the death knell to the oral tradition in its strictly verbal form.

Ong asserts that "more than any other single invention, writing has transformed human consciousness. . . . It takes only a moderate degree of literacy to make a tremendous difference in thought processes. . . ." Whereas the oral or spoken word is an experience of sound which unifies and interiorizes the thoughts expressed in the moment uttered, before it vanishes forever, writing and print isolate. It is a visual experience of the reader alone. "Writing and reading . . . engage the psyche in strenuous, (textually) interiorized, individualized thought of a sort inaccessible to oral folk." They are of a fixed, linear pattern, now exactly and infinitely reproducible through modern printing processes. Science and writing, and especially print, developed hand in hand. In modern times, "the feeling for human existence has been processed through writing and print." The development of dictionaries, or lists of words—in English over a million in modern unabridged dictionaries—was only possible through writing and print. The oral tradition might only need several thousand words.

Yet we are still talking about and alluding to the old oral tradition, even within the modern era of worldwide instantaneous mass communication. Still in evidence among the Native and illiterate peoples and subterranean elsewhere, it is commonly much diluted, and regarded for the most part in an objective, self-conscious way, but we insist on the necessity to at least garner an interest and even deferential regard for it. Its most powerful purveyor is the Native language, with its syntax and concepts from that ancestral time, the tribal world. And where the language is about gone, and no more full-bloods survive, we still find remnants of heritage celebration—the custom, display and ancient spiritual predilections that bring comfort and reassurance, identity with The People of antiquity.

The written tradition used to be called the "key to civilization" or "key to salvation" for Native people. Now it is called the "key to the future," or "key to survival," literacy, education and "development," the catch-all modern term meaning institutionalized acculturation and assimilation into western socioeconomic and cultural ways. Expertise, knowledge and skills in the western written and scientific tradition are increasingly seen as the only way left for Native people to prevent total dominance by non-Natives. In Alaska, for example, this means preventing a total takeover by non-Natives of the Native lands and resources after 1991, when provisions of the Alaska Native Claims Settlement Act were to open up Native corporation stock to anyone. However, the Native organizations through their U.S. Congressional delegation were recently successful in amending the act to severely limit access to control of Native corporations by outsiders.

An obvious irony lies in the probability that in pursuing the white-man's pervasive literate and educational tradition, the Native is acculturating himself or herself right out of the oral tradition, if not the Native heritage altogether. But what other choice does one have? For the Native people of the contiguous 48 states of the U.S. in the 19th century, it was a matter of submission to the invading Euroamericans, or death in warfare. In Alaska and other northern regions, it is a different kind of conflict, but the end result will be the same: gradual and inexorable assimilation into the dominant western scientific tradition, with its attendant technology, exploitative of the environment (lands and waters), and without any serious regard to the subtleties or even the survival of any past heritage and traditional subsistence economies. The difference is that the Native peoples will still be able intellectually and emotionally to partake of the eroding and diluting traditional culture, but the profound psychological experience of a tribal consciousness will be gone, except in vestigial, momentary and symbolic ways. This experience is not unique to Native Alaskans, of course, but is a trend seen all over the world, affecting all nations and all peoples. . . . The current resurgence of autonomy and self-government among northern Native peoples, as well as other colonized peoples of the world, though indispensable and long overdue for their survival and well being, cannot override, it would appear, the basic, long-term evolution of humanity toward an increasingly interdependent and conciliatory social system, in my view. It may even be essential to it.

For hundreds of years the most remote Native villages of North America have been veritable islands—self-sustaining, self-governing, and confident in their traditional subsistence ways. Now the surrounding sea of the ascendant culture is gradually rising to flood, with its incredibly more efficient means of travel and communication, that bring outside methods and values into every Native household in the village on a daily basis. Within the remote subsistence community, though as much as 75% of survival needs (fuel, clothing and food) may still come from hunting, fishing, trapping, gathering and the accompanying crafts, massive amounts of state and federal funds are accelerating its transformation into a Euroamerican- or Eurocanadian-style community, with all the required infrastructure and institutions. Yet to come in many areas of Native and Indian rural habitation—"Indian country" in the U.S. lower 48 states, the Native corporate lands of Alaska, and Native areas of northern Canada—is the intensive development of renewable as well as non-renewable resources. Such development is understandably feared in highly subsistence areas, because of the expected critical impact on subsistence resources and traditional concepts. For the rest, Natives and Indians in most areas are preparing to take over management and control of their lands and resources, if they haven't done so already, with the help of constitutional law, congressional or legislative acts, executive orders—and their own organizational initiatives.

Where K-12 education becomes available to every Native child, there is the probability of loss of some of these young people to the dominant society. They may leave the village for good, to return only for visits. Now there is an increasing number of Native young adults who, after finishing some kind of postsecondary education, are returning to stay and help govern and protect traditional interests and resources, or to provide the desperately needed expertise to upgrade the tribal economy and quality of life, albeit in modified, non-traditional terms.

"The Plains Indian Community College will provide post-secondary education which enhances the Plains Indians without needless harm to their sovereign way of life." (See opening section of chapter 1.) After beginning work as librarian for the college, reading this sentence in the mission statement of the college's self-study gave me some pause, especially: ". . . without needless harm to their sovereign way of life." It still comes back to me from time to time, underlining the librarian's seemingly impossible task in a Native American community. In other words, they will remain the same but stronger as Plains Indians. And "without *needless* harm to their sovereign way of life." So there will be "harm," but it should be kept to the minimum possible.

This dichotomy often made itself known in both general staff and faculty meetings. It seemed that every issue that arose had a bicultural price tag, socioculturally speaking. The administrative model and its accompanying self-studies and long-range plans, policies, procedures and bureaucratization brought onto the reservation by the Regional Association of Schools and Colleges, the accrediting body, put the Plains Indian Community College administration, staff and faculty constantly on the spot. The "standards" of the Regional ASC must be met, for accreditation to be granted. Accreditation means that the college is accepted into the nationwide community of "postsecondary educational institutions," and credits earned by students are transferable. Yet at the same time, the college is perceived by the Plains Indian tribal community as doing some harm to it. The goal, however, was to achieve a balance between cultural preservation and education—"education" meaning the white man's kind.

I remember visiting a Yupik village in the winter of 1982–83 on the Lower Yukon, and being invited by the person I was staying with to go talk with a council member about the village library which was just being set up. We entered the small prefabricated house—one of several in a row, part of a tract of new housing for the village on the hillside above the great river. Typical of such dwellings, it was essentially one room, eventually to have cloth or plywood partitions separating sleeping areas from the living area. A man was sitting on a bare mattress in the main room, watching TV. There was little in the place, as this was a newly constructed house, and the man had just moved in. He had the house all to himself. After leaving our boots in the arctic porch, we sat on the floor to talk and drink coffee. The only light was from the black and white TV on the floor, flickering and glaring into our faces like a campfire. There was a small stack of books beside the man, who was propped up on one elbow. We got talking, and it was apparent that he was well educated and articulate. He was in a thoughtful mood that night, and we talked about the library. There was no question in his mind that it was needed. The question was, where to put it. This had been a chronic problem in the village, though it is one of the largest and most monied on the Lower Yukon. It was a question of priorities, and what the dominant families in the village wanted. There were so many projects going on each year, and a great deal of state money was being adminis- tered—money from revenues generated in recent decades by that hidden non-renewable resource, oil.[12] We talked only briefly about the library, as he was more interested in getting acquainted and visiting.

The TV sound was turned down, and now only the video's light flared and sparked in our eyes. Gazing silently at television is just as mesmerizing as staring at the oldtime campfire, with or without the voices telling stories. Both TV and firelight provide us with uncontrolled images and dreams, but eventually we must break the trance and face prosaic reality. Though the relatively new and bizarre experience of "television viewing" appears to strengthen the oral tradition, in fact it fiercely acculturates into the ascen- dent, worldwide Western culture and the print tradition. Hence the in- creasing relevancy of libraries in the foreseeable future, for Native commu- nities, as well as related services like archives, museums and documentation, and all the cultural activities supporting them.

The traditional ways were still strong, and the harsh climate and isola- tion of the village kept them so. Parts and supplies flown in or shipped in by ocean-going barge cost cash money that only a limited number of village adults earned, mostly through commercial fishing permits, though a few had jobs in village government or stores. The rest depended almost entirely on government transfer payments and subsistence, which might include selling garments from hides obtained in hunting or trapping to acquire ex- tra cash. But the main source of cash was a limited number of commercial fishing permits, whereby salmon and other fish caught in the river were sold to fish processors. Travel out of the village for those without cash could be accomplished by having medical reasons, when a federal agency would foot the bill. And the young people traveled thanks to the state-funded school district, going to nearby villages for athletic and cultural events, and as far away as Anchorage, Seattle and even Washington, D.C. for conferences and tours, and to see the Federal government in the national capitol on special "Close-Up" programs.

Literacy, however, whether linguistic or cultural, isn't enough. Nor is a high school education in one of these tiny villages, or the elementary so- phistication that comes with outside travel. Training in the regional com- munity college is a start, but university and corporate training applicable di- rectly to developmental needs in Native home areas is a necessity. I say "home areas," because Native villages are communities close-knit by blood relations, and it often isn't comfortable, in the long run, for Native workers to live and work in another village. They are strangers and have no kin support. But this depends on the village and how traditional it still is. For some educated Natives this is the attraction of cities; one can live there without the problem of acceptance by the population (aside from racism). And for one who is now socially experienced and literate, the written tradition will offer comfort and confidence, both in the big city and the foreign village. Non-Natives are usually accepted as guests and neighbors in the village because they are, in the long run, real "visitors," who eventually leave.

Undoubtedly, as the literate, urbane, bureaucratic and individualistic ways of the non-Native society become imbued within the fabric of village life, the old ties of kinship and family rivalries will recede somewhat, allowing for the more aggressive and less principled competition of modern society, in which the young may challenge or divert the established order, and a new capitalism (or socialism) with its doctrinaire excesses will gain ascendance over the socioeconomic landscape, as it has already begun to do. Perhaps by combining Native values with modern western methods of development and management, the Native community will find that balance so desired between the past and the present, the oral and written traditions.

Ron and Suzanne Scollon[13] of the University of Alaska, Fairbanks, associated over the years with the Alaska Native Language Center and the Center for Cross-Cultural Studies, have produced many articles, papers and books on the practical as well as theoretical considerations in Native/non-Native communication. They point out that literacy is found in many gradients, and isn't simply a matter of being able to read and write, either the dominant language or a Native orthography. Their work has been primarily among Athabascan-speaking Indians of Alaska.

First of all, there is a fundamental difference between the respective heritages of Native and non-Native communication. The non-Native or western conditioning is toward a highly focused, assertive, unilateral kind of sense-making. It tends to be egocentric and ethnocentric, and adopts a stance of non-negotiability in person-to-person encounters. The Caucasian tends to be always "speaking-for"—i.e. for his or her cultural group, an institution, or the recognition or dominance of the non-Native laws or ethics in question or deemed applicable. Modern technological and bureaucratic institutions require focused interaction, the Scollons point out, because of time constraints, crowding, social complexity and widespread communication through distancing media. There is also the "gate-keeping" situation, whereby the non-Native acts as the giver and withholder of access to goods and services, expertise and advantage generally—as held by non-Native institutions.

Throughout these encounters, the conduit model of communication is used—a linear, point A to point B medium for transferring information. "There are other ways of viewing language," say the Scollons. Non-literate communication, by contrast, involves a high degree of mutual respect and negotiation. The Athabascan Native believes that "mutual sense-making must be mutually accomplished. It's the first thing to be negotiated. . . . To the extent one works through literate modes of expression, one is forced into non-negotiated forms of making sense. . . . This distancing of the medium . . . is in direct conflict with a central human value, the value placed on mutual sense-making. To the extent that this value is a significant Athabascan value, literacy is a threat to Athabascan identity."[14]

The stereotypical Native is seen as "withdrawn, shy, uncooperative and unaccepting of unilateral sense-making." More appropriate models for communication might be traditional activities like picking berries, "chewing the fat" (a phrase derived from a Native activity and accepted by non-Natives as meaning person-to-person gossip and visiting), and preparing buckskin. Let us look at the latter model as an example.

> The work is slow and takes much care [so as not] to tear or mutilate the skin. As the tanning progresses and the skin gets more pliable it can be treated more easily with less concern about its tearing. Once it is well tanned it takes on a toughness that is a result of its softness. Then it can be used. This metaphor is used to talk about relationships. New relationships are fragile, susceptible to tearing and subsequent uselessness. Relationships must be worked slowly, mutually, by all parties until there is a tanned buckskin between them. Only then can that buckskin be safely treated instrumentally to accomplish other ends.[15]

This situation assumes, of course, that both parties are speaking the same language, almost always a non-Native "official language." Another writer comments on how children are affected: "If we accept the role which communication plays in social interaction as an important aid to language acquisition and cognitive development, then the indigenous language as the medium of communication must take precedence to enable the children to come to terms with their cultural environment."[16] One of the problematical situation in many Native communities has been that children speak, read and write English in school and speak their Native language at home.[17] It is not our intent to examine here this particular cross-cultural oscillation any further. Instead, we will take up something closer to libraries and information transfer: literacy in the Native orthographies across the north, and the availability of texts in them.

As mentioned earlier, missionaries have always been the primary agents for inventing orthographies of the spoken Native language. This occurred in Greenland in the 18th century, and in Alaska and many parts of Canada in the 19th century. Unfortunately, from the present Native point of view, these are not of a single uniform system, so we have a variety of types of orthographies in use. Most use the Latin alphabet, however, with variations in the use of special punctuation, accents, and other signs and marks. Only the Inuktitut syllabics of the Canadian eastern and high Arctic depart radically from this norm. Actual present-day use of these Native orthographies

or alphabets varies considerably, and is mostly related to the date of introduction, in some cases the earliest being the most widely accepted and used.
Other factors affecting acceptance of a missionary-created Native orthography were how closely it approximated the spoken language, how much literacy in the orthographic system itself was introduced to the population,
and the amount and nature of printed materials produced.

Thus in Greenland the Greenlandic orthography is almost universally
used for printing and writing. It is now the official language. In Canada the
situation varies, again depending on the province or territory, and which
Native orthography is indicated. Syllabics is widely used among the Inuit
of the eastern and high Arctic and northern Quebec, for example. A Roman
alternative orthography for the syllabics is now available, which corresponds
fairly closely to the Greenland orthography, and refinements are continually being made from both sides in an effort to reach a common Inuit orthography. Literature in syllabic is abundant in periodical form, but much
less so in books. This is probably a natural development and is reflected similarly in the United States, where the "Indian press" (in English) has been
very extensive and articulate for decades, and only in recent years has produced monographs and fiction in any calculable quantities (almost all in
English). Word processing programs have been developed, by the way, that
convert syllabics into the Roman orthography, and in a short time the reverse
will be available. Inuit of the western Arctic use a Roman orthography. The
Inupiat (or Inupiaq) people of Alaska's arctic slope use a similar orthography.

In the Russian north, orthographies in the languages of the numerically
small peoples began to be created during the first half of the 19th-century,
as part of Christianizing efforts. (We will draw heavily here on articles by
Kazarinova, and Khudaverdyan and Khamakulova, cited in the Russian
Bibliography/Reference List.)

As in all Fourth World communities, there is always the overwhelming
and relentless influence of the dominant or ascendant culture of the surrounding and invasive population. In Russia, since the 16th-century, Russification of northern peoples across the north has been increasing with time,
but accelerated and intensified during the Soviet period, especially during
the 1920s and 1930s, after Lenin's death. The idea was to put out an insis-
tently helping hand to enable the Native societies and cultures to make the
great leap forward into the advanced and enlightened Soviet peoples' Communist utopia. Literacy and reading was required, and initially alphabets
were constructed for practically all the small peoples, as if this would auto-
matically provide the key to the civilizing experience. Publishing was begun
in these new orthographies, as directed from central authorities in Moscow,
which emphasized socio-political tracts, literary works from the Russian tradition, and children's stories, all purposed to bring the Native children into
the Great Russian family, despite Lenin's earlier policy to keep native cultural 'forms' intact, the better to receive 'socialist content.'

Kazarinova cites some of the factors militating against the acceptance and use of materials published in Native orthographies. First there is the great difference between the oral language and the printed or written orthographies, and the Native's attitude toward words on paper, and how much to trust and use them, points covered elsewhere in this chapter. Teachers weren't trained to work with Native languages, and few knew them in the printed forms anyway. And Native-generated texts, what few were available, were poorly promoted by librarians.

Publishing after the Great Patriotic War (WWII) increased, but there was still a dearth of materials of practical use (relating to subsistence-based economies), all but a minority being published in Russian. Titles on the cultures of Native peoples were only available on a very limited basis, the print runs were very small, and few if any were available for circulation outside of town libraries. So those who might have benefited from them the most went unserved, because due to losses in the field from passing around of popular titles, libraries weren't prepared to lend them to brigades and remote villages, whence the irony of restricting access to books because they are too much in demand!

In 1963 the publishing scene as it affected the northern peoples changed. Centralization was increased, and small local publishers ceased working independently. Press runs of titles of special interest to Native workers were further restricted, and Russian became even more generally the publishing orthography. In addition, despite the influx of millions of new workers and settlers into northern areas of resource development all across Siberia and the Russian Far East during this same period, creating the need for more rather than less publications for everyone, there was no corresponding increase in publishing for the population of this vast region, except of one type. This was the generation of scientific and technical publications for specialists. But even these were under difficult constraints, as they depended on regional publishing agencies for their relatively small printings. Often years would go by as technical titles were shunted from one publishing schedule to the next and so on, making them obsolete or irrelevant by the time they reached readers' hands. And few of these were in any Native orthography.

In 1990, major publishers in the Magadan region didn't even know about *past* public demand and use of published materials, let alone current needs and wants. They were publishing 'blindly,' only noting the numbers of orders to fill. Market assessments weren't part of the process, though at all levels of government there were agencies that should have done so, but apparently did not. Their position was that titles in Native orthographies were of the 'lowest sort' (based on what?) and there was no demand for them. In 1989 and 1990 book wholesalers actually returned over a third of copies of books in Native languages, claiming that demand was nonexistent. Yet, for example, few if any libraries at the village level had even a dictionary in the local Native language!

Hence, the current legacy of low publishing in Native orthographies across the Russian north. But, as in any specialized publishing plans, there will always be low press runs and a limited readership. This is nothing new. For the time being, however, under the current difficult economic conditions, ways should be found to increase publishing in needed subject areas and to meet public demand for more publications in Native orthographies. This will also support the revival of interest in Native cultures and economies, as promoted by several new organizations militating for self-determination in many homelands of Native peoples across the Russian half of the circumpolar north.

Khudaverdyan and Khamrakulova (also listed in the Russian Bibliography/Reference List at the end of the Chapter 6) make this point in a telling argument that links the survival of northern ethnic identity with publishing in Native orthographies. A book is not an abstract thing, having, on the contrary, a highly personal character and close import for the individual reader. It is generally recognized that, for any people, its ethnic integrity and wholeness is nurtured and passed on through its Native language. Therefore, if highly pragmatic and desirable books are published in an attractive format, books in Native orthographies by Native authors, written by and for a Native home readership, they will increase literacy and usage of such literature. But before this is possible and effective, such publishing ventures must be based on a thorough knowledge of the potential market and its wants, something lacking at this time. Combining this effort with the slowly rising rate of publishing in Native orthographies currently, and the increasing teaching of Native languages in school systems, there will be a place for libraries and everything they represent in Native communities. (The article doesn't discuss the effects or potential of electronic media in oral or written literacy, now or in the future, nor the possibilities in computer applications.)

Ways to fund publishing of titles wanted by northern readers, and especially Native ones, might include temporary subsidies from the central government, at least until regional governments and other entities (not to mention a stronger national economy overall) are sufficiently strong to help sustain these Native area and local publishers. The consensus seems to be that, as the Russian Federation hopefully survives the difficult and prolonged transformation into its own version of a 'market economy,' Native publishing across the north, as well as other aspects of economic development benefiting the Native peoples and their struggle toward self-determination, will strengthen.

The subarctic Central Yupik Eskimo area of southwestern Alaska is the largest single concentration of Native speakers anywhere within the United States, second only to the Navajo of the southwest U.S. If we use the rule-of-thumb of the Language Bureau of the Department of Information of the Northwest Territories, which says that if there are 5,000 Native speakers of a language, it has an "excellent chance of survival," the future of the Central Yup'ik language is bright. The new Yup'ik orthography developed by the Alaska Native Language Center of the University of Alaska, Fairbanks, which is supposed to be an improvement over a Moravian orthography that has been used for many years, is only beginning to be learned, primarily by the young in schools. (The earliest orthographies in the area were produced by the Russian Orthodox and Roman Catholic missionaries, but were not as widely accepted.) There are now grammars, language tapes, and a series of college courses being taught in the Yupik area community college, including use of the TPR or "Total Physical Response" method of James Ashwer. General and specialized dictionaries have been produced, and training for interpreters is being developed more fully. Serious consideration is being given to making available simultaneous translation facilities for all public meetings. School districts in the region are presently embarking on an extensive Yup'ik language reinforcement plan, treating it as both a second language and a primary language, depending on a student's given proficiency.[18] A major lack is enough printed materials in the new Yup'ik orthography, but in time perhaps this will improve, as it has in other parts of North America. New advances in computer instruction are making possible some innovative and exiting Yup'ik language materials in multimedia format, also being produced at the college and its Yup'ik Language Center.

Concern over the survival and preservation of Native languages has risen in the Yukon Territory in recent years. There are six major and three minor Athapaskan Indian languages, with Tlingit at the extreme south central end of the territory. Daniel L. Tlen's survey of the status of the languages (the latest of a series of such surveys), entitled *Speaking Out*,[19] found that "there is a very positive and broad-based perception of the importance of maintaining and promoting Yukon Native languages." Yet he reported that there were no formal provisions for teaching the young, no promotion of language use in all situations where Native speakers are found, and no recognition of the need for official recognition of the Native languages in the public process.

However, there has been some Native language teaching, and some teachers being trained to teach the Native languages, but these programs must be expanded, and many other recommendations acted upon before the Native languages can be expected to be passed on to future generations. These include full Native community participation in the planning and implementation of language maintenance, and extension of Native language programming into the radio and television media. The role of library and teaching materials in the Native orthographies will play a part in this linguistic renaissance, and the use of audiovisual forms of literacy propagation, like "talking books."

Tlen's recommendations are comprehensive and aggressive, reaching firmly into every facet of life, both public and private, Native and non-Native.

He feels that only in this way can the Native languages endure. And his survey, which included sampling of views from all segments of Yukon society, seems to reflect a consensus among Yukoners that preservation of the Native languages is worth supporting. But, "many people stated that 'a person must *want* to learn a language!' To learn a language one must hear and use it—in story-telling, singing, playing games, dancing, or in a conversation." So the burden is equally on the Native community and non-Native authority to provide a province-wide environment that is conducive and supportive for Native language learning and use, in the most common, everyday situations.

The Yukon Native Language Centre of the Council for Yukon Indians is funded by the Yukon government. Programs of instruction during 1986/87 in schools throughout the Yukon totaled thirteen, mostly in rural communities and including five Native languages. The centre has aims that will sound familiar and compatible to every librarian:

1. "to provide technical and practical support to native languages programs . . ."
2. "to train native Yukoners to read, write and teach their languages"
3. "to conduct basic scientific work on all Yukon native languages in order to document them for the benefit of future generations"
4. "to develop dictionaries and educationally sound teaching materials for the languages"
5. "to respond and transcribe stories, legends, and local history which may be edited for use in the classroom."[20]

Education generally in the Yukon is being examined to ensure that Native peoples begin to control the acculturating process as it affects their children—and the children of non-Natives as well. The "Final Report of the Joint Commission on Indian Education and Training"[21] lists four major recommendations, which point to the need for equal access to education, for recognition of Native cultures as integral to Yukon public life, for a separate Indian Education Commission, and for the reform of laws, policies and infrastructure of Yukon to serve Native peoples equitably and appropriately.

Certainly a symbolic gesture of Canada's building resolve toward making the Native peoples full citizens and realizing the united equality of all her nationalities can be seen in the singing of the national anthem at the opening ceremonies of the 1988 Winter Olympics at Calgary, when the above-mentioned linguist and singer, Daniel Tlen, dressed in full buckskin outfit, sang it in Southern Tutchone.[22]

In the Northwest Territories alone there are six separate orthographies in use (Inuktitut, and 5 Dene, or Athabascan), and in 1986 the Task Force on Aboriginal Languages issued a report[23] that made many recommendations, which can be summarized in one: make the aboriginal languages just as official and commonly available as English/French. (The usual manner of treating Native languages has been to regard them as Native dialects and patois, and not real languages for government, commerce and education.) The Government of the NWT gave its response,[24] which was in surprisingly high agreement. The result is at least a definite effort to greatly widen and strengthen the place of aboriginal languages, in both oral and printed forms, in all areas of life in the Northwest Territories.[25] Included in the Task Force Report were statements supporting government funding to enable libraries to provide materials in all formats in the aboriginal languages, for a Northern publishing house that can produce materials in these orthographies,[26] encouragement and development of aboriginal writers, and lists of materials in these languages made widely available, both in and out of government.

The reference to libraries in the slightly more than one page Executive Summary of the Report is tacked on, however, in this way: "The Task Force supports other efforts to enhance the use of the aboriginal languages including renaming place names and developing aboriginal language resources in libraries and museums." The Government's response doesn't comment on or make any reference to the role of libraries or cultural centers in this sense, but its general agreement, support and array of initiatives seems to imply that increased aboriginal language resources would certainly be needed,[27] not to mention Native library staff, to provide appropriate services and liaison to Native speakers and those learning aboriginal languages.

Use of Native languages is in the majority in the eastern two-thirds of the Canadian arctic. In the west and southwest (Yukon Territory and SW NWT), non-Native languages predominate. The history of Dene language orthographies (in five dialects) of these regions, and the infrastructure to support refinement and standardization has always been behind the Inuktitut areas, but a recent survey shows that these languages are alive and well in almost all communities surveyed.[28] A very high 82% of respondents said they could use their Native language, and barely a majority could also use English. *Analysis of the Dene Language and Information Review*[29] from which we are drawing our information, was "undertaken by the Department of Information in the spring of 1983 in order to help define (the role and tasks of the Dene Section of the Language Bureau of the Department)". The Dene Section, like the Inuktitut Section of the Bureau, "involves extensive translation of printed materials into" the respective Dene dialects, but it was established much later.

In terms of literacy, orality and the Native orthographies, the quandary facing librarians working in Native communities is of a complex and subtle kind—the more so because the situation facing them is a dynamic one, and intensely cross-cultural. Yet there are parallel experiences in cultural conditions; e.g., the shaman of old and the artist and writer of today. And there are signs all around us, claims Robin Tolmach Lakoff, that "Deep in our hearts, we are no longer a society that values literacy."[30]

Lakoff points to the Nielsen ratings on how many Americans watch television, the declining sales of books and attendance at movies, and the growing trend for at least certain kinds of books to be written from movies, television mini-series, documentaries and the like, not the other way around, as used to be the case. We should also add cable television and especially the ready availability of videocassette player/recorders (VCRs) and videocassette movie rentals, all of which have further isolated people in their homes and apartments, to watch the world through a TV window. As television technology, production and artistic concepts become more closely turned to the public's desires for entertainment and stimulus in the oral tradition, we tend to turn away from silent, lonely, print forms of leisurely preoccupation. The most popular television programs are increasingly interactive with the viewer (game shows), or involve highly vicarious formats, such as the daytime dramas ("soap operas") and sports, and shows where a celebrity guest or panel addresses a personal or controversial topic. Even radio has spawned a proliferation of talk shows, a format in which listeners can call in by telephone and offer their comment on a wide range of controversial issues, as pontificated upon by the host or moderator (usually male), who becomes a kind of parental figure, scolding or encouraging by turns, all before a vast nighttime radio audience. Here we have the oldtime oral tradition again, voices in the dark reassuringly discussing life's perplexities, acknowledged authority figures boasting and scolding, whose claim to fame is, unfortunately, mostly bombast, hearsay and demagoguery on a national scale, though directed one-on-one with a listener at home, in an outrageous parody or caricature of the confessional booth. Looking back to my own childhood, movies in home communities and neighborhoods used to be community gatherings, and listening to the radio was usually a family affair. Most movie houses of 50 years ago have disappeared, replaced by the rental of video movies for home use, watching television movies on a variety of cable TV channels, or patronizing multiple-movie complexes where often only a handful of moviegoers are found in each small theatre.

The literate tradition of reading and study has two sides, between which one can look for a balance. It can prepare you for an active public life or make you a cloistered loner. I had a long-time friend who spent her entire life, after a divorce, reading novels and biographies in bed and on a couch in her quiet living room. Always complaining about her low income, she was never able to bring herself to try teaching in a local community college, choosing instead to keep her wide knowledge and understanding of English and American literature quite at home. And excessive television viewing can do the same thing—it also is two-edged, but on the side of the oral tradition. One can become stimulated and inspired to "become active in the community," "get out and do something," using TV to broaden one's intellectual horizons and community involvement, even become a voracious reader, or one can become a "couch potato," staring vegetatively at endless cable television fare for hours and hours and whole days, utterly a spectator, even resentful of household chores drawing one away from it.

There are other, less obvious signs of our preference for the oral mode. In the bureaucracies and corporations we prefer information meetings (especially over lunch) and make appointments to see and talk with people face to face, rather than poring over reports, studies and memos. We try always to have money in our budget to travel to field locations or attend conferences. And travel itself to all parts of our nation, and increasingly throughout the world, is becoming the modern lifestyle, at least for inhabitants of First World Nations. We would rather, given the funds and leisure time, see and meet people and cultures and new environments face to face, than read about them or see them on television. A generation ago train travel was an opportunity to meet many new acquaintances face to face over a trip of several hours or days as one wandered up and down the fully-equipped train. Nowadays a long jet flight can be made sitting literally elbow to elbow with someone who remains a total stranger from beginning to end. In jet travel, we are actually being thrown from one place to another, with the possibility of only perfunctory social amenities, due to the crowded conditions and speed of such travel. And the word "thrown" is quite apt, in terms of the culture shock often experienced, and the "jet lag" we always complain about.

Computers and their applications have added a new and exotic dimension to the lives of those they touch. Sitting at a computer console combines the typing experience, television viewing, and a sort of "pocket theatre," the latter because we are interacting with the monitor, determining what we shall see on the screen. Computer use has been described as "non-threatening" and "user friendly," which is another way of saying that previously employed methods and means of learning have been, for some, intimidating and unfriendly—difficult and uncompromising to use. Now that games are a part of computer applications, they can also be playmates.

For librarians, who tend to be tradition-bound (mostly print-oriented), to be surrounded by all the above changes can be overwhelming and depressing, even threatening. But any second thoughts should cause one to know one's clientele better—both actual and potential. Looking further ahead, as future-oriented we must, there is also the obligation, as publicly-funded, university-educated, professional specialists, to not only respond to the perceived or asserted needs of a client group more effectively, but to advocate and promote progressive changes, to anticipate the future rather than be confronted by it. (That is the non-Native heritage.)

But how can the oral tradition properly strengthen Native libraries? A stimulating guide in this direction is Adolphe O. Amadi's book[31] on African libraries, which points out that ignoring traditional ways of communication and cultural transmission runs the risk of not only inflicting psychological and social deprivation, but the "freezing up of creativity and the intensification of misdevelopment."

. . .print mentality and bureaucratic rationality go hand in hand. p. 186

. . . literacy is the separation of thought from emotion and behavior. p. 187

[For students], their habitual, holistic world outside the school is in complete dissonance with the new literate and closed universe of classified and alphabetized information. p. 188

[The Native attitude] toward work, the concept of time, and the codification of reality . . . tends to be holistic, rather than lineal and fragmented. p. 188

The basic technique of oral librarianship . . . is the collection, processing and dissemination of eye witness or who-knows-what accounts. . . . p. 213

. . . the primary responsibility of the custodian or gatekeeper of knowledge is to burrow into, decipher and disseminate knowledge of clientele. p. 214

. . . if librarians are to become relevant institutions for the bulk of the population, the following must constitute part of the blueprint for action: debooking, deprogramming, deprofessionalization, de-alphabetization, debunking, reorientation, as well as the deschooling of society itself. p. 215

. . . most of the devices utilized by libraries become a means for burying and mystifying information rather than making it accessible. p. 219

[Native communities should have two "levels of service":] academic, research and documentation centers, or libraries, and popular information or community centers. . . . p. 220

[The latter] . . . should combine the services and expertise of journalists, social workers, educators, public health nurses, and librarians, among others. p. 221

Amadi argues, with documentation from many sources on the role of western institutions among Native populations, that the Native library's mission should lie in interpreting and distributing "needed and relevant" information drawn from the oral or written "transcript" of the culture and what Natives believe it to be, "which in turn largely determines and directs . . . individual and group behavior." (p. 221). As we shall see in Canada, and in a lesser and distorted way in the former Soviet Union, the most appropriate (or effective) Native peoples' library and information services are holistic culturally, tending to combine a variety of desired community activities with them.

Writing and speaking and listening, the audiovisual media, computers and their increasing capabilities, books and periodicals, AM and FM radio, telephones and telecommunications, television and its refinements, video and audio production, storage and playback devices, communication satellites, Native and colonial languages (oral and written), the performing arts (both live and in any medium), photoduplication and transmission services, microforms, remote and outreach services—what an incredible array of tools we have in the "library and information" field alone! But many of these are useless if the minds of library workers and technicians, line librarians, supervisory and administrative librarians and related service providers in a system or community are still myopic and two-dimensional, too bureaucratized to stretch, too "survival" oriented to take initiatives, too culture-bound to see or comprehend—let alone embrace—the modern multicultural world.

Notes

1. From D. Jenness, "The Carrier Indians of the Bulkley River," *Bulletin* no. 133, Bureau of American Ethnology, Washington, D.C., 1943. Quoted on p. 37 of *The Savage Mind,* by Claude Levi-Strauss, Univ. of Chicago Press, 1966. (English translation from the original 1962 Librairie Plon, Paris edition: La Pensée sauvage).
2. Battiste, Marie Ann. *An Historical Investigation of the Social and Cultural Consequences of Micmac Literacy,* pp. 20–22.
3. Havelock, Eric. *Preface to Plato.* Cambridge, MA: Belknap Press of Harvard University Press, 1963.
4. For a view on the relevance of the oral tradition in modern education, as well as a comprehensive discussion in one article of the whole orality/literacy balance in our lives, see Egan (1987).

    To go back to the pre-verbalization, pre-consciousness days of human communication, when movement, gesture and non-verbal utterances predominated, see Jousse (1990).
5. "In the old days, there were no strangers!" This exclamation by a friend knowledgeable of Yupik Eskimo life summarizes the insular and inbred village life of aboriginal times. Strangers might, in fact, be killed on the spot.
6. ". . . Unless the people desire modern values and have enough control over other aspects of their lives to enable them to carry out their goals, modernization and economic development through literacy will not occur. Rather language and literacy, as history has illustrated, have been powerful tools used to submerge masses into subordination, and to change consciousness, values, and traditions . . . and the phenomenon continues unchecked through formal governmental education that is indifferent to the language, culture, values, and needs of the peo-

ple and through political subordination of native peoples to the interests of a colonizing government." Battiste, *ibid., p.* 187.

7. For a detailed yet useful description and analysis of personal and public Native communication patterns, with comparisons to non-Native ways, see Chapter 4 of *The Invisible Culture, Communication in Classroom and Community on the Warm Springs Indian Reservation* by Susan Urmston Phillips. New York: Longman, 1983.

   Another illuminating source for understanding at least Indian (Lower 48 U.S. Native peoples) ways of socializing is Steven Bryan Pratt's *Being an Indian Among Indians.* Univ. of Oklahoma Ph.D. dissertation, 1985. (Ann Arbor, MI: University Microfilms International.)

   Protocol in Native settings varies considerably, and polite inquiries should be made before speaking to Native groups. Perhaps an elder or respected male should be the spokesperson or presenter. In mixed Native/Western meetings, it might be useful to poll everyone present on questions, otherwise non-Natives, for cultural reasons, will tend to dominate the talk every time. General or "intertribal" meetings tend to be more democratic in that sense, but in Native/Indian society—especially at the tribal or village level—it has been and still is the custom for elder males to be the public voice. To ignore this tradition, for whatever reasons, is to court nonacceptance or silent rejection.

8. Couture, Joseph E. "Native Training and Political Change: Future Directions," 1979.

9. ————-"Next Time, Try an Elder!" 1979.

10. Singer, Charles, E. J. Holmyard and A. R. Hall. *A History of Technology.* Oxford University Press, 1954, Vol. 1, pp. 102–106.

11. ". . . In pre-industrial societies, writing was not a means of communication in the modern sense but a magical and religious activity." Benge, Ronald Charles. *Cultural Crisis in Libraries of the Third World.* London: Clive Bingley; Hamden, CT: Linnet Books, 1979, p. 95

12. The winter of 1987–88 brought very different economic conditions (that, in more than one measure, have continued into the 1990s):

    > Bush villages, including many in the Yukon-Kuskokwin delta, are in serious financial trouble this fiscal year. . . . A readily identifiable cause of the fiscal squeeze—especially for remote, bush villages whose economies are in reality more linked to subsistence than cash—is the state's 32% reduction over the past two years in its revenue sharing and municipal assistance programs. One of the villages close to declaring bankruptcy at this time was the one we were visiting.

    "Bush Villages Cutting Essentials, Says Survey on Rural Fiscal Health," by Michael Fagan. *The Tundra Drums.* (Bethel, AK.) December 12, 1987, p. 1.

13. What the Scollons and other Alaskan cross-cultural scholars have

learned and shared in numerous publications and appearances has not been sufficiently recognized and integrated into cross-cultural relations by either the private or public sector of Alaska, especially the educational bureaucracies. The reasons for this include the fact that many Natives live in remote areas of the state and encounter relatively few whites, and those who come to the cities often endure discrimination of various kinds and end up on welfare, in trouble or in menial jobs, thus in marginal and prejudicial social status. The turnover of non-Natives in rural areas is fairly high and constant, precluding the chance that they will learn sound cross-cultural attitudes. Non-Native professionals also tend to keep their own company (as do Natives). Finally, the dominant non-Native educational institutions are in principle (and idealistically) organized to achieve largely theoretical academic goals, which may or may not be transferable or even translatable to the workaday world of rural and Native Alaskans.

14. Scollon, Ron and Suzanne. "Literacy as Focused Interaction," *Quarterly Newsletter of the Laboratory of Comparative Human Cognition,* Vol. 2, No. 2:26–29.

15. *Ibid.,* p. 13 in a draft copy.

16. John, Magnus. "Formal Education and the Role of Libraries," *Int. Lib. Rev.* (1984) 16, p. 396.
    In the same article: "The nature of oral-traditional societies itself inhibits formal education. The kind of communities in which people live and the issues which affect their lives relate more than anything else to the question of survival. Face to face contact is such a powerful communicative force . . . that questions of how to survive seldom rise above local level. Immediacy . . . is a characteristic phenomenon which pervades the modes of thought and feelings . . . Any requirement, therefore, of the individual to come to terms with his environment through formal education requires such a mental leap that it makes the prospect of new ideas for development a scarce commodity." p. 404.

17. A study of effective teachers of Native students in boarding and regional high schools disclosed that the "Supportive Gadfly" type, characterized by "personal warmth, active, demandingness" was the best, whereas "Traditionalists," "Sophisticates" and "Sentimentalists" fared much less successfully. Rather than beginning "business at once" in the classroom, the supportive gadfly "might spend the first days getting to know the students and helping them with non-academic problems . . . and "made sure that the students knew each other." Demandingness with this kind of preparation became "one more facet of his personal concern for them." Kleinfeld, Judith. *Effective Teachers of Indian and Eskimo High School Students,* 1972. See also: Kleinfeld, Judith Smilg. *Eskimo School on the Andreavsky,* 1979. The same approach would benefit librarian-Native clientele relations.

18. The same friend quoted earlier, who has spent a number of years in the Yukon-Kuskokwim delta and has much understanding and patience in cross-cultural relations, believes that in a generation the region *will* be monolingual. The only way to retard this development, he claims, would be to no longer use "stateside" or non-Native teachers, "who look down on Natives" and are monolingual and monocultural. (And condescension has often colored church/Native relations as well.)

Michael E. Krauss makes a similar argument in *Alaska Native Languages: Past, Present, and Future* (1980), including television among factors that work to terminate Native languages and otherwise bring about cultural genocide among the Native peoples. He also places little value or hope in bilingual language programs in schools. As the saying goes, "When they start teaching the Native language in the schools, that's a sure sign of trouble."

In fixing the "blame" for erosion of Native language use, however, one has to remember that cultural imperialism includes many more factors, also discussed throughout this volume. It is a universal dilemma, involving social, economic, political and even military influences. To try to defend and strengthen a Native language under conditions of such comprehensive modernization is very difficult.

The Alaska Native Language Center at the University of Alaska, Fairbanks, which published Krauss's paper, issues a series of booklets that attempt to "provide a basic introduction to the characteristics of each language group": *Athabascan Languages and the Schools; Inupiaq and the Schools;* and *Central Yupik and the Schools.* Each is from 50 to 80 pages in length. They orientate the non-Native teacher to the communication problems apt to be encountered in these Native communities.

The first Circumpolar Conference on Literacy was held in Yellowknife, N.W.T. in the spring of 1990. Debate featured definitions of literacy (in dominant or Native orthographies), "the problems of loss of Native languages among the young people, lack of written materials in the traditional languages, and the influx of 'colonial' languages." *Bright Lights* (N.W.T. Public Library Services), April, 1990.

19. Tlen, Daniel L. *Speaking Out, Consultations and Survey of Yukon Native Languages Planning, Visibility and Growth.* "Prepared for the Government of Yukon and the Council for Yukon Indians." Whitehorse, Yukon, August, 1986, 76 p.

20. Yukon Education. Public Schools Branch. *Annual Report, 1986–1987,* p. 6.

21. Joint Commission on Indian Education and Training. Kwiya. *Executive Summary.* (August 28, 1987.)

22. "Olympic singing makes native language point," *Whitehorse Star,* Thursday, February 18, 1988.

23. *Report of the Task Force on Aboriginal Languages* (to the Government of the Northwest Territories), 1986, 55p.

24. Government of the Northwest Territories. *Response to the Recommendations of the Task Force on Aboriginal Languages,* October 21, 1986, 13p.

25. Cserepy, Frank A. E. *Native Languages in the Northwest Territories.* Chief, Language Bureau, Department of Information, Government of the NWT, (1984), p. 2.

26. Burnaby, Barbara. *Promoting Native Writing Systems in Canada.* Toronto: Ontario Institute for Studies in Education, 1985, 222p. Occasional Paper 24. See especially these articles: "Six Years Later: The ICI Dual Orthography for Inuktitut, 1976–1982," by S. T. Mallon; and "A Syllabary or an Alphabet: A Choice between Phonemic Differentiation or Economy," by John Murdoch. The Inuit Cultural Institute's attempts to standardize both Latin and syllabic orthographies has met with clear success since its inception in 1976, and the alternatives of either Latin or syllabics meets the needs of separate areas of the Canadian arctic to sustain what progress has already been achieved. Standardization into Latin orthographies is unlikely in the near future, as Murdoch explains: ". . . 'scientific' arguments used to justify Euro-Canadian efforts to displace the syllabic system with a roman, phonemic system are more indicative of what Euro-Canadians know of their own industrial, or high food society, rather than what they know of hunter-gatherer, subsistence (low food production) societies." p. 127.

    Though conventional printing in syllabics is more difficult and expensive, the growing availability of computer programming options utilizing syllabics should increase use.

27. An excellent example of a bilingual text on the heritage of the Inupiaq is: *Puiguitkaat, The 1978 Elders Conference.* Transcription and Translation by Kisautaq-Leona Okakok. Edited and Photographed by Gary Kean. North Slope Borough. Commission on History and Culture. (Barrow, Alaska, 1981), 653p. The Northern Quebec Elders Conferences are also available in trilingual (French, English, Syllabics), print form: *The Wisdom that Comes with Age,* for 1981, 1982 and 1983. Available from Nortext Information Design Ltd., Suite 200, 16 Concourse Gate, Nepean, Ont. K2E 7S8.

28. Northwest Territories Education. *Language and Society,* (1983).

29. Northwest Territories, Government Department of Information. *Analysis of the Dene Language Information Review.* Prepared by M. Devine. December, 1983, 50p.

30. Lakoff, Robin Tolmach. "Some of My Favorite Writers are Literate: The Mingling of Oral and Literate Strategies," in *Spoken and Written Language: Exploring Orality and Literacy,* ed. Deborah Tannen. Norwood, NJ: Ablex Corp., n.d., p. 257. Related source materials include: "The

Myth of Orality and Literacy," by Deborah Tannen. in *Linguistics and Literacy,* ed. by William Frawley. New York: Plenum, 1982.

Jack Goody's *The Domestication of the Savage Mind* (NY: Cambridge U.P., 1977) attempts to reconcile the oral and literate traditions by examining "the means as well as the modes of communication that enabled man [*sic*] to make . . . advances in human knowledge."

31. Amadi, Adolphe O. *African Libraries, Western Tradition and Colonial Brainwashing.* Metuchen, NJ: Scarecrow Press, 1981.

4.

Urbanization, Modernization, and the Migration to Cities

To many Natives that have never experienced a city life, city is a place where they can escape the norms of the village life. City is a place where no villager watches him any longer; that is, he is able to do things that he normally does not do in the village. So he gets in the city, as it is a kind of pioneering all the way.[1]

The indispensable lesson taught by failures to transfer institutions is that modernization must be systemic if it is to be durable. It must involve indigenous people in behavioral transformations so manifold and profound that a new and coherent way of life comes into operation. Institutions cannot be transferred; they must be transformed. Lifeways cannot be adopted; they must be adapted.[2]

We usually think of Native peoples as being in rural areas, on reservations, reserves, pueblos or rancherias. We've already looked at remote Eskimo villages, far out on a tundra that is frozen in winter, a marshland in summer, with no roads joining them to the outside world. The Plains Indian Tribe described earlier is very isolated, a condition that has reinforced its traditional conservatism. The nearest city of more than a few thousand population is more than 100 miles away, over a range of mountains. The Bay Indian Tribe is located on a sparsely settled coastal estuary that has never known extensive modern development. We who live in heavily populated areas, or in larger towns, rarely see Indians or Natives.

Yet, paradoxically, more than half of all Native peoples live in urban centers, usually the larger cities. This is a trend that is worldwide—Native populations migrating into towns and cities. While the tendency of many of the more affluent non-minority city dwellers is to emigrate into outlying rural or suburban areas, Native and other minority populations are doing the opposite, part of the effect of modernization, as well as urbanization, and worsening economic conditions for the poorly educated. City life always attracts the acculturated modern Native, for good or ill.

The first impact of European or western culture was through visitors, and the goods they brought with them and used in trade. The new metals, more efficient tools and strange foods, the different clothing, and their strange speech introduced an authoritative new invading culture. Often, in some regions, mostly the temperate latitudes, there were new and terrible weapons to confront, when the conquering Europeans demanded land and its treasures.

Then it was through the technology these bearded strangers brought with them that a whole new world opened up, a magical and unprecedented world, powerful and inescapable. The great ships, first sail-borne, then steam-driven, that came from unheard-of lands so far away that one could not believe they really existed; the airplane, that could come out of the sky and land on water; the train, a monster nothing could stop, that could carry a whole town or army. Aviation suddenly swept away weeks of travel and changed it into hours of effortless, wondrous transport to distant places.

In recent decades the reliable and relatively trouble-free but labor-intensive sled dog teams, for example, have been replaced by the snowmobile,[3] snogo or skidoo. With skis for front wheels and a broad belt for power at the rear, it can go very fast and far—as long as there are no breakdowns or accidents. And if this happens, it can mean death in below zero weather far from habitations. The social impacts of the snogo can also be something less than unmitigated progress: the cash cost of having one can be prohibitive, leaving a family at a disadvantage in subsistence gathering; snogo travel and operation generally favor younger men over mature men, who used to be the main hunters; snogos push Natives into the cash economy, where they must now meet payments and operating costs that did not exist with the traditional dog team, which are primarily fed from junk subsistence fish; a stratifying effect comes into place, when some snogo owners do better than others in trying to balance their budget with whatever subsistence goods they gather and sources of cash. The advantages of snogos (when they're running) are their convenience, speed, low maintenance, and the greater social interaction possible when men can return home at night after hunting at a far distance, instead of camping out for days.

But the inventions that most stirred the imaginations and expectations of Natives across the north were the "invisible" short-wave radio, broadcast radio, the telegraph and telephone, citizens' band radio (the "CB"), and finally television. The phenomena themselves were amazing, voices and images arriving out of the air or traveling through wires, but the information they brought gradually described an incredible culture, the home of the restless, invasive, acquisitive white man. Images of his highly urbanized, sophisticated, and technologically developed society soon were universally impressed on the Native psyche.

It took centuries to create "developed nations" through modernization, which came about through essentially unplanned development in an extended, circuitous evolution involving many civilizations that rose and subsided, or were absorbed or transformed. The pace of change was much slower for most of that time, gradually increasing at an accelerating rate since what we call "historical time" began. In the last 100 years—and especially within the lifetime of the oldest of us—the changes have seemingly reached an intensity and ubiquity almost impossible to inventory, let alone comprehend. They are changes in every facet, every realm of our existence.

Long before the historical era, urbanization (featuring the formation of large settlements and market towns) began to transform aboriginal society. Its onset coincided with the beginnings of primitive bookkeeping, and astronomical calculations along with more earthbound measurements probably preceded all of these things. Incipient modern technology began about 3000 years ago, and intensified further as the currents of invention and early science came together in Europe, with some contribution from the Far East and Near East.

Within the past fifty years the pace of progress in literacy worldwide has markedly increased, and the nature of literacy itself has become more complex and resplendent, much as a beam of daylight becomes a spectrum on being directed through a prism. The prism is modernization.

Urbanization compounds social change and relations when large numbers of people come together to live in one place. Modernization occurs when urban goods, services and information—as well as sophisticated urban-dwellers—are encountered by those from rural areas. Modernization is the process of change from a relatively isolated, "undeveloped" nation or society into an increasingly urbanized and integrated, "developed" society.

From our standpoint, the effects of urbanization are important for many reasons. They have a profound impact on the subsistence culture, drawing people into towns from their traditional hunting, trapping and fishing camps. In the town they are surrounded by the values and activities of the white man's cash economy, though there may only be a small number of jobs available for Natives, who usually have far less education and technical skills than non-Natives. If they remain in town, they often are no longer within the network of village kinship and community support. They encounter the anonymity of town life.

In the Yukon-Kuskokwim delta, for example, the regional center of Bethel (pop. 4500) is the "metropolis" for 57 remote villages. Villagers can come here and do things they would never dream of doing in the home village. Therefore, the cases of drunkeness and assault are endemic, if not an epidemic. It is an area crisis. People don't know or greet one another the same way. There are many people in Bethel who don't know each other, whereas the opposite is the case in a remote village. There are many more cash-paying jobs, the subsistence life is in the background now, there is more freedom for excess in personal life—and privacy.

In the remote village or other isolated rural Native community, "privacy" as the white man knows it is almost nonexistent, or at least harder to find, and justify. For many Natives this is a new experience, and either an un-settling one or an intoxicating one (usually both, figuratively and literally!). For those who don't speak "Village English" well, the first language is prob-ably the Native one. Or the same in Quebec, with Pidgin French. And so on. For the Native woman, modernization and "big city" life are usually a liberating experience, because she has many more opportunities opened to her, in jobs and career options, and more freedom in social mobility. Hence, the emancipation of women has played an important role in the acculturation experience at the Native community. There are many more services of all kinds, some not available at all in the home village. There are more consumer choices, more advanced communication and trans-portation, better educational facilities and health care. One feels at the cen-ter of a power base, where authority is administered.[4]

On the other hand, there are the negative aspects of town life. If alcohol is sold in bars, supermarkets or state liqour stores, it is always available. Or, if not, there is always the bootlegger, helping to foster alcohol abuse and crime. Then there is the relative isolation and anonymity of town life. There are many young men unemployed, fewer subsistence opportunities, and everything costs money, which is hard to come by. The family is mostly back in the home vil-lage, so one may feel lonely or bored a lot. Air fare to visit the home village costs dearly, so one can only go there once in a great while. The authority of the elders doesn't matter much in the larger towns. And usually the whites are in control of everything. The Native women usually seem better able to get the good jobs, but the Native men sometimes have a hard time getting hired, no matter what their skills or education. It depends on the local situation.

The effects of modernization are not confined to those living in cities and towns, but are exported to the remote villages and settlements through ra-dio and television. Many Native communities now have access to satellite cable systems, and the deep city life of the south is delivered right into the sitting rooms of Eskimos living in arctic remoteness. The effects on Native people of these electronic media and their messages from foreign cultures are profound, and have a central role in accelerating modernization as well. Because they are so commonly experienced, and so strongly a source of modern information, recreation and education, we shall begin by discussing radio and television in the north and their effects on Native people, then the effects of modernization on the Native worldview, and lastly library and information services to Native people in the cities. They are all tied together in the fabric of Fourth World life in the late twentieth century. (Fourth World: areas of indigenous population under the total dominance of an-other, usually invasive population and culture.)

The first telegraph land lines that were operational in the north joined military posts, and were also used for public and commercial traffic. This was around the turn of the century. Native peoples had no direct use of them; they were to provide communication between outposts across the north and headquarters forts and population centers where the small numbers of whites had established settlements, for the beginning trade and territorial administration. Such telegraph lines had been established in the south since the U.S. civil war, and were a factor in the subjugation of continental U.S. and southern Canadian Native peoples.

"The first successful wireless system took to Alaska airwaves in August, 1903. It was the world's first application of radio-telegraph technology."[5] Think of these fragile lines of communication into the remote regions of the north as feelers and antennae for the southern culture of Euroamericans and Eurocanadians, extending their authority and control over the entire North American continent, from the Rio Grande to the arctic tundra. High frequency or short wave transmitter/receivers were then developed to more easily communicate over vast distances using voice. These again connected government outposts and trading posts, and occasional were used for medical purposes. Though there were occasional regional experiments to try to improve reception, requiring costly technology to connect remote communities, it took the emergency situation of World War II to establish dependable northern communication networks. The White Alice communications system of powerful transmitter/receivers, developed in the 1950s across Alaska, connected major population centers and military posts. But remote villages and smaller towns still didn't have direct communication to the outside world.

In the late 1960s the Alaska Communication System operated by the Radio Corporation of American (RCA) was established, after earlier inadequate attempts to start an Alaska-wide telephone service. RCA utilized COMSAT, the first communications satellites launched by NASA (U.S. National Aeronautical and Space Administration) in the early 1970s, and by the mid-1970s one telephone per remote Alaskan village was installed. When I arrived in the Yukon-Kuskokwim delta in 1981, of the 20-odd villages I had to contact, almost all still had the single village telephone in a city building somewhere, sometimes in an unheated area. But by the time I left in 1984, over half the villages I worked with (15) on a regular basis had individual telephone service available (if it could be afforded), and the rest were in the process of having them installed. In 1987 almost all villages had individual phone service to some degree, and in these villages an average of about half the households had their own telephone. The rate of this kind of development is indicative of the speed with which modern communication technology has come to remote northern communities.

Before individual telephone service was offered, most village homes had citizen band (CB) radios, which acted as a public address system and intercom within the village. School districts used high frequency radio tele-phones to maintain daily communication between the district office and in-dividual village schools. The informal CB radio system is still popular in many villages, as it acts as a common communication channel joining the entire village on one open "party" line.

A similar course of development took place across northern Canada, as the difficulties of radio communication in the higher latitudes were over-come. In the late 1960s Canada's TELSAT Corporation launched the sec-ond communications satellite in the world (the Soviet Union having the first, the U.S. the third), its main purpose being to extend television cover-age to the Canadian north.

Radio, whether point-to-point or broadcast, has served a number of pur-poses in remote northern communities. As well as exposing northerners to southern culture, attitudes and priorities, it brings people closer together and brings services of larger towns into remote communities. Add to this a growing air service in all parts of the north, scheduled as well as charter, with all types and sizes of aircraft available, and the web of western tech-nology can be seen to have gained a firm grip on the north, from every di-rection.

One special use of regional or local broadcast radio in the north is for send-ing personal messages to persons in remote locations. It is still used today, to reach those who still only have radios, or whose whereabouts are unknown. On KYUK-AM radio in Bethel, Alaska, there is a 15-minute "Tundra Drums" messages program in the morning, mid-afternoon, and evening. This service is free, and anyone can put a message on. The messages one hears can give a definite flavor of the north, such as: "Charles Patka of Napaskiak, come to AC, your snogo parts are in," or "A runaway dog team with ten dogs was found near Steamboat Slough on Sunday evening. Call —— for information," or "Tom Andrew of Stoney come home. We're almost out of fuel!", or "A pair of men's bifocals with dark frames was found at the Riverfront Restau-rant, call ——." KYUK-AM reaches all over the Yukon-Kuskokwim delta, a re-gion larger than most states in the continental U.S. This program opens with community announcements about meetings, hearings, courses being taught, and outside visitors or representatives of the note who are in town—events the community should know about. It's called the "Community Bulletin Board."

Thomas Clark Wilson, in his master's thesis, "The Role of Television in the Eastern Arctic," reminds us that in the early days, communication was a function of transportation. One traveled over land or water to the person one wanted to talk with, or sent a message by someone else, who went to that person. One characteristic of aboriginal communities is that they be-lieve they are the only people in existence, and that they are at the center of the world. The Polar Eskimos of northwest Greenland thought they were alone at the center of a world covered by perpetual ice and snow. The

Blackfeet Indians, until they acquired horses via Spanish sources in the 17th century, migrated on foot with dogs dragging diminutive travois. On the northwest coast, a variety of canoes carved from the halves of (mostly hollow cedar) trees made travel in that watery environment much easier and faster. In the north, skin boats, kayaks and sledge dogs increased the mobility of hunters and gatherers.

Television—the electronic transmission of visual images and sound from one place to another—makes it possible to see and hear someone far away—live. In the early days of radio and television, tapes were used to supply northern communities with programming from the urban centers of the south. Now live transmissions are commonplace. Imagine the thoughts of an Inuit family in the high arctic, on first talking to someone in a village 100 miles away by telephone, or while watching a first-run movie, commercial advertisement or live broadcast from Ottawa for the first time on television. To many Native people, technological marvels such as tape decks, cable television and computers are much easier to understand and use than the conventional library, and much more interesting and compatible. But the cultural dislocation and disorientation that accompany them is called modernization. Not only is the Native culture transformed, but the Native finds himself or herself in an unending personal metamorphosis.

Wilson describes the educational system and television as "southern artifacts which have been parachuted into the Canadian north." What is one to think of these enigmas, these marvels? Tony Lentz comments: "If writing is twice-removed from knowledge, television is even more seductive because it is a pseudo-oral tradition." Walter J. Ong in *Orality and Literacy* compares television, which he calls "a secondary orality," to the primary tradition:

> This new orality has striking resemblances to the old in its participating mystique, its fostering of a communal sense, its concentration on the present moment, and even its use of formulas. But it is essentially a more deliberate and self-conscious orality, based permanently on the use of writing and print, which are essential for the manufacture and for its use as well.

In fact, the average person, whether a functionally (English/French-) illiterate Native living in a remote settlement or one who has become an assimilated city-dweller, can only be intrigued by this new status symbol of modernity, at least passingly prideful of this icon of the "new religion."[6] That is how we receive these products of an accelerating scientific and technological progress. We accept them with anticipation, because once acculturated to modern technology we *expect* these new gadgets, aids and extensions of ourselves. What a contrast to the slow and laborious development, by trial and error over millenia and at what human cost, of the tools and creature comforts of our aboriginal forebearers. In considering the impact and significance of communications technology and information services generally on remote and isolated Native communities, it is indispensable to know what the past has been like, to stand back at a palpable distance and see our experience as history, to be aware of how recently our contemporary technology arrived on the world scene. Not to be able to make these projections is to be like the Polar Eskimos of the last century, thinking we are at the center of the universe, surrounded by an eternally righteous and omniscient "science and technology."

The interactive modes of electronic communication are most readily accepted by Native peoples: the telephone, CB radio and two-way television,[7] where the participants can see, hear and talk to each other simultaneously. Earlier we mentioned a successful experiment in teaching math, using a technology that enables the participants not to see each other, but to see each other's work on an electronic blackboard. Experiments with two-way television in the north have been very successful, as well as very expensive. But the technology is becoming more common, and cheaper. The interactive modes strengthen the oral tradition of face-to-face communication, which reinforces community bonds.

Over the years Indian and Native groups in northern Canada have lobbied for better communications in their areas. A 1975 paper by Thomas J. McPhail[8] listed their needs. The Native people wanted their communities to be connected to *each other* by two-way communication, not just to population centers in the south. Secondly, they wanted Eskimo- and Indian-language programming, including educational and career-oriented programs. Third, interactive television was needed in the fields of education, medicine and some commercial groups, like those exploring for energy sources. Lastly, the non-Native population needs to have English-language programming for its own cultural needs in the remote north.

Broadcast radio and television from southern metropolitan centers, on the other hand, produce controversy and problems. This is the direct, one-way insertion of non-Native, highly urbane and popular culture straight into Native homes. In villages which have their own satellite dish operated by the village officials, some control may be possible over the viewing fare of local residents. I know one instance in western Alaska when a local program was being televised from the village community hall one winter's evening; all outside channels were turned off and only the municipal cable television channel could be seen! The point was to focus on the village, on the culture, and to encourage people to come to the community hall.

Wilson, in his study of Canada's eastern arctic, found that the new values as shown on TV were understood mostly by young people. Elders would ignore it, or were very critical. A helplessness, or feeling of decreased control, was felt. Loss of "internal locus of control" lowered self-esteem, induced dependency and self-doubt, lessened pride and motivation. With more local control, Native-produced TV and exchange of programming among Native peoples, television and radio can become an integral and healthy part of Native community life. In the fall of 1987, producers of the Sesame Street children's program out of New York City filmed children of a Bering Strait community in Alaska. Seeing themselves on national TV the following year would give them a place among the other TV persona, a kind of special identity and recognition in the modern world of electronic images.[9] As the deceased pop artist Andy Warhol is reputed to have said, "In the future everyone will be famous for 15 minutes."[10]

A study[11] of the effect of television on Native Alaskan children newly exposed to TV showed that the practice of visiting fell off sharply, and the movie theatre (if there was one) lost most of its customers. Adults continued their book reading habits, but children's reading dropped and continued at a lower rate. Magazine reading increased, but dwelled more on teen pop culture material. As for the use of English, slang increased, but vocabulary growth was not stimulated. Now that videotape players/recorders are commonly found along with TV monitors in many homes, all kinds of movies can be rented, including those that are "R" or "X"-rated for whatever reason.

It was also found that "the longer rural Alaska children are exposed to TV, the more likely they are to believe that what they see represents expected and usual behavior, even when they know programs involve actors and acting." Sex-role stereotyping increased among the children, regarding the suitability of careers. As we all know, TV also stimulates a desire for material possessions, and for travel, but at the same time these Alaskan children rated themselves and their group the highest in importance. In conclusion, Forbes said that when parents watch TV with children it lessens the exotic and bizarre effects of TV viewing on their young and impressionable minds. "The potential (for good) has a greater chance of being realized in Alaska than it does in the rest of the U.S. because the control of, and responsibility for, the form and content of TV ultimately rests in the elected hands of the viewers rather than in the hands of commercial interests." These remarks may apply in those communities carrying only the State of Alaska Satellite Television Project channel, or programs from a local radio/TV station, or where a local cable system is also locally controlled or deigns to accept the guidance of a local advisory body.

Whether the foreign, non-Native television will be sufficiently balanced for Native viewers who have not only Native television programming but Native-owned broadcasting and production facilities, such as those held by the Inuit Broadcasting Corporation in Canada, itself supported by relatively "soft" federal funding sources, remains to be seen. The IBC has program status, rather than being an integrated broadcasting service or a separate network. There are many other issues clouding the future of Native broadcasting in Canada, and these are cited and discussed in the IBC's "Position Paper on Northern Broadcasting" (revised October, 1985).[12]

However, the 1987 report of the IBC President, Rosemarie Kuptana, projects an optimistic picture of Native broadcasting in northern Canada for the future. The federal Northern Native Broadcast Access Program, the "main source of production funding," was renewed, and northern broadcasters proposed a TV Northern Canada (TVNC), a "dedicated northern system that would relieve many of the scheduling bottlenecks" the IBC has contended with. A journalism training program was developed at the NWT's Arctic College, and a special children's series was inaugurated, called Taguginai, complete with popular hosts and puppet friends. More convenient time-slots and flexibility for IBC programming have been arranged by "renting airtime on a satellite transponder," and "an historic agreement with Alaskan Inuit and Greenlanders to exchange programming on a regular basis" has been signed.

Some say that the effects of prolonged television viewing on Native peoples have yet to be clearly seen, but other studies, some cited here, see harmful effects. Elders and other Natives in the north feel the power of southern television, along with the IBC itself:

> Without control over the local distribution of southern television, and without Inuktitut programming, Inuit fear for the survival of their language and culture. . . . Extensive southern television viewing decreases communication between the generations, causing stress in some communities and reducing time children spend engaged in traditional activities with their parents. [It] also leads to a decline in the use of Aboriginal languages. . . .
>
> In surrendering its language, a society surrenders its capacity to plan for and control its development. To be masters in their own homeland, Inuit must not surrender their right to communicate in Inuktitut.

The impact on newly exposed Native children is known, but what about the long-term effects? Tony Lentz of the Pennsylvania State University, Department of Speech Communication, says: ". . . It is particularly unnerving at a time when the young people we teach appear to be losing their writing skills as well. How is it possible that modern children could lose both their ability to speak *and* their ability to write? Can it be that we are witnessing a decline in *both* oral and written traditions at the same time?"[13]

A study of Oxford House Cree in northern Manitoba over several years produced some disturbing as well as illuminating observations.[14] The reduction of subsistence resources forced men to go away for summer jobs and thus the families were split for the warm months, sometimes into fall. Family allowances and welfare became available in the 1950 and 1960s and became an "acceptable means of earning a living." Still, the unemployment rate remained high. The usual Native school experience had a further alienating effect: children had to be in school in order for families to receive government benefits, and the older ones went away in those years to residential schools. When they came back with their Kabloona (White man's) education, they were unfit for village life, and dissatisfied. Elders and these young people were alienated, their upbringing were so different.

> A main concern of the Cree relates to modern communications and transport; while both ease the physical hardships of the north, they also tie the people firmly to a money-based economy that cannot be supported by indigenous resources. 'Progress' is therefore often perceived as restrictive. [The same applies to schooling and television. Such 'gifts' of modernization turn out to have a price tag:] "the price is the Cree's loss of ability to direct and shape their own destiny, and that of their children. . . .

Narrative—the oral tradition—is now replaced by films and television. People don't care to listen to the elders much any more for lore and entertainment. Even long-time favorites like bingo and Eskimo dancing programs are drawing smaller audiences. The bingo has to have big enough prizes and the dancing program has to be maybe better than average and with some other benefits for young people to be attracted. Modern, urbanized behavior as shown on non-Native television tends to support aggressive and disrespectful behavior among the young, even overt aggression (vandalism, theft, assaults, rapes), especially when combined with substance abuse. Earlier, fear of shamanistic reprisal helped keep hostility down, along with the respected position of elders and the traditional roles of men and women. In the Yup'ik Eskimo language, there are various degrees of "shyness," which characterized the Eskimo personality of old, and of which vestiges still remain. "If television is replacing narrative, the method by which people were taught to channel aggression will be lost, and social norms for young people will change irrevocably." In the future, one way to counteract this trend is to have Native television offerings, and locally originating television production. This is already happening through new programming by the Northern Service of the Canadian Broadcasting Corporation (CBC), and the IBC.

We can go back and recall visiting a council member in his new house one winter evening in a Lower Yukon village, talking with us as his black and white TV flickered "like a campfire" on the floor of his nearly bare front room. . . . Continuous TV viewing resembles the campfire-staring experience, hypnotic and compelling, at once state-of-the-art electronics yet homely, primitive. But the images in this case might as well be from a distant planet, a remote culture. They are not of the mind's close and comfortable imaginings, as a campfire, but of mind-manipulators—whether benevolent or cynically mercantile—a synthetic world of the mind, assuredly, but a mind apart from our natural and conventional acquaintance.

Modernization is a process or, in human terms, an experience, whose definition has changed as much as the modern world. What used to be called anglicization (or turning into the likeness of a particular colonial power) or Europeanization or westernization (the scope broadening) is now generally referred to as modernization: the "process of social change whereby less developed countries acquire characteristics common to more developed societies. The process is activated by international, or intersocial communication."

This involves not the simple transfer of information, goods and services, but transformation of the Native society—socially, politically and psychologically. Such broad and profound cultural changes can only take place if individuals themselves experience change. The "mechanism of transformation" is empathy—putting oneself in another person's situation. If one is not disposed by nature to emulate an intruding culture, there is mass communication (print, radio, film, television) to facilitate the expansion of horizons. Another definition of empathy is "psychic mobility." Physical mobility is relatively accessible, but social mobility (change in "lifeways") is more difficult, and fraught with dangers. Psychic mobility amounts to profound changes in the psyche of the Native: changes in values, attitudes, priorities, relationships, wants, desires and fantasy. These changes in turn affect one's regard for and relation to both the traditional and the incoming culture. This creates a psychosocial oscillation, the Native alternating between subsistence traditions and modernizing surrogates that are not replacements, the whole being in reality a new metamorphosis, of which the Native people are the medium.

Modernization brings "secularization, commercialization, industrialization, accelerated social mobility, restratification, increased material standards of living; the diffusion of literacy, education and mass media (almost all of the incoming culture's terms); and the expansion of popular involvement and participation." But what appear to be the benefits of Progress are, as we have seen, full of duplicity and ambiguity:

> . . . [T]he new organization of knowledge brought about by modernization come[s] into traditional societies as invading armies. Reality is redefined and reclassified in almost every sector of social life . . . there is also a new social distribution of knowledge. . . . In a society in which wisdom used to be associated with old age there may be a sudden reversal as the young and the very young can plausibly present themselves as privileged interpreters of the mysteries of modernity. In such situations the dethroned elders naturally have rather mixed feelings about the change. Modernization legitimates new experts and simultaneously delegitimates old ones. Some of this legitimation may be informal . . .but there are also highly formal and institutionalized processes by which the new experts are legitimated. The most important of these . . . is the school. . . . Its very presence serves to bestow status upon those who have begun in whatever measure to acquire the new lore . . . [and] it is not at all necessary that [it] be coherent. . . . Indeed, it may be argued that something is gained by incomprehensibility. . . . The religion proclaimed by this new universal church is the mystique of modernity.[15]

In Toronto, Ontario

In 1974, Richard Ficek, a student at the Faculty of Library Science of the University of Toronto completed a remarkable Community Services Practicum entitled "Information Needs of Native Peoples in the City of Toronto." He looked at the total situation of Native people in the city, from demographics to social problems and community activities of every kind, gradually working into the information needs of Native people. It is a no-holds-barred critical approach, with all sources listed at the end of the each chapter. The study is based on many personal interviews, all of which are documented. Finally there is a series of recommendations, each of which is accompanied by a frequently eye-opening "justification." Some of these are singular insights, not found in the usual study on urban library services to Native people—and here we paraphrase.

Popular programs should be repeated, and not be one-shot affairs. They should be accurate (not glosses or generalities) and respectful of Native beliefs and sensibilities. Programs should be open-ended, without a cut-off time, to allow for natural socializing. They also shouldn't be about Native culture only, but relate to the urban setting everyone is living in, and how Native people can make positive contributions in the city. Collections in city libraries can be improved by adding to the materials mentioned in the National Indian Education Association series of booklets, Native and Indian newspapers, Native recordings, and by housing everything about Native peoples in one place in the library. Many Native people find the intricacies of the Dewey and other conventional library ways of organizing materials, which scatter Native materials all through the collection, a big barrier to feeling welcome in libraries. In some places a bookmobile could stop at Native social centers, or agencies serving Natives, Native alcoholism treatment center and the like, with shelves assigned for this purpose arranged beforehand. Remedial reading and other literacy help can be programmed, along with the sessions on coping and survival skills and information, and alcoholism counseling. If someone on the library staff, preferably a Native person, were experienced in alcohol counseling, this would alleviate any problems from intoxicated persons frequenting the library, which could have a good connection with local detoxification and treatment services. The important point in all these recommendations is to accept the conditions Natives contend with in a straightforward fashion, and to help to improve them.

In Tacoma, Washington

The Northwest Room of the Tacoma Public Library, serving a middle-sized city with a significant Indian population, is a special collection on the heritage, history and contemporary life of the Northwest, with an emphasis on

Tacoma and surrounding Pierce County. But a serious effort was made to make the collection fairly representative of all parts of the Northwest—Washington, Oregon, Idaho, Montana, British Columbia and Alaska. Personal contacts and liaison were established and maintained with historical societies or area libraries throughout the region. Being among the first Federal depository libraries in the state of Washington, Tacoma has many rare, scarce and out-of-print titles on the Northwest. The Northwest Room opened as a public service area just before the National Bicentennial Year, 1976. The idea was to make available to the general public all possible materials on a circulating basis. In the beginning, very few materials were for "library use only," and even these might be loaned out if the patron were known and trustworthy.

Most such collections are for reference only, so this was an attempt to jump that sacrosanct gap, conveying rarities on regional history into the hands of the history-oriented public, including students of all ages, reporters, authors, researchers from out of town, and city officials. Items with roughly less than 100 pages, if out of print and in the public domain, were photocopied, and the photocopies bound and loaned out. The same was done with selected articles from standard periodicals on Northwest history, of which the library had complete runs, or others of special interest or of a seminal nature.

A major sub-collection in the Northwest Room was in Native Americana. An effort was made to reach out to Indian tribes around the Northwest, to discover any tribally produced materials. A large, representative collection of the Indian press (in print form) was begun through subscriptions. A microfilmed collection of backfiles of Indian periodicals (by and about Native peoples) was purchased. The Indian press provides important documentation of current events and issues in the Native community, despite the fact that some library-oriented librarians may sniff at its often homely and amateurish format. These qualities simply reflect the fact that Native journalists and publishers are often very poor and cannot afford or do not have access to sophisticated editorial and printing services. The content is there, and it is current and most relevant. (For further documentation of this, see Chavers, and Whiteside, in Bibliography/Reference List II.)

In later years while working for the Bay Indians on the coast I spent some time working on a series of heritage publications. When these were ready to be published, we went searching for a local printer. The prices quoted for minimum printings were far higher than the tribe's poor heritage committee could afford. Finally we learned through Indian sources of a local printer who had done some work for other tribes at very reasonable cost. But even this was too high, so we ended up producing the first 100 copies through the print shop of a regional Indian organization serving small tribes in western Washington, using a supply of excess paper they wanted to get rid of! The Bay Indian elders were justifiably apprehensive about committing too much money to this first-time publishing project, and went about it very conservatively. The printings were then put together by heritage committee staff and helpers on the reservation, using the most economical bindings.

For the Northwest Room, liaison was established, or begun, by contacting the Tacoma Indian Center. After talking with Indian instructors for the center's educational programs, they were invited to visit the Northwest Room and bring students. Almost no Indians had been library patrons until then, for many reasons. Local Indians and the authorities have not gotten along well over the years, due partly to disputed land claims, controversial business activities in the Indian community, and occasionally open conflict over Indian treaty fishing rights. There is a widely held prejudice against Indians in the region, primarily due to a controversial Federal court case, the "Boldt Decision," which gives half the harvestable salmon caught in the jurisdictional area to Indian fisherman.

For many Indians and Natives, entering the white bureaucratic world for any reason is a distinctly alienating experience. One of our goals was to help overcome this feeling of being "spooked" in a library, and to help Indians utilize what we had to offer, which included a respectable percentage of Indian-generated materials. It is certainly possible for Native students to also find value in the most racist and ethnocentric materials produced by observers and scholars of non-Native background. One should critically and perspicaciously extract the information accessible in them, cultivating and adapting that objective approach which disciplines oneself to override any cultural antipathy one may understandably feel.

Too often urban public libraries still ignore or slight the ethnic groups in their service area, not taking the trouble to find out if they exist, or establishing and maintaining regular liaison, including them on advisory committees, and utilizing outreach services and innovative programs to serve them in appropriate, community-oriented ways. It is especially easy to pretend or believe that Native people are not resident in the neighborhood, because they keep a low profile and stay away from places and company where they believe they're not exactly welcome. Yet there is certainly a tradition in public libraries, and now community college libraries, to target and serve those most needing library services for advancement in American society. Immigrant groups and minorities trying to make headway have, from time to time and in various places, found help in libraries. But this is not a universal experience in all libraries.

Library collections and the variety of materials they offer, well-staffed services and the occasional ethnic program all combine to attempt to interest these groups through conventional library provision. However, such offerings need to be less library-generated and more community-generated. Hence the need for boards of trustees to include representatives from immigrant and minority groups, rather than the usual pillars of society or their spouses, or friends of city council members, who are usually white. In a city like Tacoma, the public library trustees ought to include an Asian, a Black, and an American Indian, because all these groups have significant populations in the area; possibly an Hispanic board member as well. Friends of the Library should be more inclusive and empowering by inviting local Indians and other minorities to make presentations, put on programs, and to join the Friends of the Library community. Library staff should include members from minorities, which would tend to bring more relevant programming and service approaches into library planning. Of course the ultimate preference, for bringing Native people into library use, is to have them on the public service professional staff. The most progressive library systems will do everything possible to help the library schools and their funding agencies to provide opportunities and grants for Native bachelor degree holders to obtain advanced library education. But library schools themselves can also do more, along with libraries, and we will discuss this at length in chapter 8.

Regarding the Northwest Room in Tacoma Public Library, a special advisory committee could be set up to represent the Tacoma population, and to some degree the Northwest as a whole. To those who say that certain minorities aren't interested in being involved in the library, I would say that the library hasn't done its homework and needs not only to get out and know the community better, but to bring a realistic representation of the community into library involvement, especially non-user groups.

Are Indians and Natives "interested in their own ethnology"? Certainly they are, and to some degree they are still living it. For them, it's not ethnology, it's life. Then why are so few Native people seen in dominant community libraries? The reality of the situation is complicated, but perhaps John Marshall's comments strike a realistic-sounding chord:

> . . . few Native people ever make use of libraries. Why? . . . Aside from those who do not read, i.e. are functionally illiterate, would-be Native users are put off by the architecture of buildings, the bureaucratic procedures encountered in the library, the formal arrangement and confusing classification of the collection, the brusqueness and lack of cultural understanding or empathy on the part of library staff, the paucity of materials relevant to Native life or to their immediate personal concerns, etc. It all seems part of a larger, dominating, majority culture which is alienating to all but the most persistent and the most acculturated Natives. . . .[16]

Other reasons cited earlier are: the absence of Native library staff, lack of appropriate library materials and services, lack of liaison with the Indian community, the monocultural threat implied in the institution called a library, with its heavy acculturating and authoritative image, and prejudicial expectations of non-Native library staff. In a word, if there is to be library provision for Native people, they would prefer to have their own libraries, and that is what started happening in the 1980s, in the U.S., Canada, and elsewhere. The are interested in their own heritage, but not as condescendingly or superficially offered to them in conventional libraries, in bits and pieces scattered throughout the building. In the meantime a library branch in the city can take special, tailor-made steps to serve an Indian or other ethnic community—if it has good liaison with that community.

Los Angeles Public Library

In the United States there are a few urban library/cultural centers for Native city dwellers. The American Indian Resource Center of the Los Angeles County Public Library is a good example of one.[17] Started in 1980 by a federal Library Services and Construction Act grant, it is now a permanent part of LAPL services. Information about the center, the LA Indian community and the center's experience in serving it is revealing. There were estimated to be between 48,000 (by 1980 census count) and 70,000 Native people in the greater Los Angeles area. There are no identifiable Indian neighborhoods, however, which makes delivery of library services a challenge, due to the vast area of Los Angeles County and the economically deprived character of the Indian community, which has a very high unemployment rate. Indians cannot afford to come to the center, at least not on any regular basis. So the center goes to them. The liaison and outreach programs and services of the center are multiple and extensive.

Being a part of the LAPL system, it "can send materials for pickup at 91 Los Angeles County libraries scattered all over the county's 4000 square miles." Photocopying of materials is governed by a "liberal policy" when they are sent to someone's home. But there are barriers to library provision, even for the center, which is adequately funded:

- no geographical focus, or single cultural and social services center.
- poor transportation; both public and private forms are discouraging.
- communication by the usual means is inadequate and delayed.
- the oral tradition is a factor; "live and direct" actual presentations are preferred.
- past experiences with non-Native institutions, missionaries and government policies have created resentment and distrust; so libraries have inherited some of this negative image. Their experience in both public and government boarding schools amounted to cultural genocide.
- literacy problems are a factor; consider functional illiteracy and school dropouts.

The center has utilized outreach very effectively and imaginatively:

In fiscal year 1985/86 we made 86 outreach ventures of which 26 were away from the library and in the community. Of these 26 ventures, 18 involved book displays. The results astounded us: a circulation increase of 134% and a reference increase of 156%.

Basically we went to pow-wows with a table, a two-wheeled shopping cart full of books, flyers and smiles, There are three scheduled pow-wows in Los Angeles each month for dancing and socializing. We attended any gathering where we could meet Indians: from church potlucks to a senior citizen luncheon.

We also work closely with Indian services agencies and organizations, which is what we've been stressing this fiscal year. Last summer, for example, we co-hosted with a tutorial project a picnic for Indian children and their families: films, flyers and library tours were structured around games and lunch in our park.

We have two displays in our repertory: THE INDIAN HERITAGE (mostly art books and tribal histories) and NATIVE AMERICANS NOW (contemporary artists and poets, contemporary issues and concerns in the Indian community; books that place Indians firmly in 1987 rather than 1887).[18]

The new librarian continues to be a non-Indian, with a Native American assistant or aide. Tom Lippert, my original informant, died a few years ago. His assistant was a Navajo. Navajos appear to be the largest group in the service area, although most major U.S. Native American cultures are well represented, except those from the far Northwest. An important feature to note about the center's operations is its open-minded and freely responsive approach to its particular community's library and information needs. The center is serving the Los Angeles Indian community on its own terms, not on the library's terms. There seems to be little indication of bureaucratic hassles or inhibiting administrative protocol to overcome. In a phone conversation, the library director at the time, Joanne Bliss, reminded me of the constantly changing availability of materials and services for Native Americans, due to a variety of factors. Funding or support from municipal, state, and federal sources, for example, is always at the mercy of shifting political winds.

The collection has some special features that need highlighting. The Indian press is well represented by subscriptions or back files to many Indian newspapers from all over the country. (Indians in the city aren't necessarily from the surrounding region. The LA Indian community has a large segment from the northeastern Iroquois nations, for example.) Special interest newsletters are also received. There are over 300 recordings of traditional music. (One other popular library activity could be viewing of past pow wows on videotape, to look at dancing styles and to see friends and relatives dancing.) There is a Vertical File with articles and all types of ephemera on subjects of interest to Indians, not using the usual vertical file subject headings. They have a large collection of films and a steadily growing videotape collection. "One is a series of storytelling sessions in Indian languages with English subtitles." Then there is a well-used Information and Referral File. When Indian patrons call in asking how or where to get information about community services, events and the like, this file provides the answers. It's very important to keep such a community referral file up-to-date. In building the collection, the emphasis is on materials showing the Indian perspective. Types of material shunned are "captivity accounts and mission/church history"—unless the Indian point of view is shown.

Though the center uses the Dewey Decimal Classification and LC Subject Headings of the LAPL system, it is not at all happy with them. The collection has therefore accommodated to user-community convenience by arranging materials according to tribe. To further facilitate user-access to Native materials, some slight adjustments have been made in a few DDC numbers to bring materials on the same subject together, instead of leaving them arbitrarily and irrationally scattered (in the Native's ideological scheme of things). For example, Native biography that used to be split between 920 and 970.2 have been combined in 920. And a number of alternative subject headings and needed cross-references are used, following the terms used by Indian patrons. This is a fundamental and comprehensive problem—the "logical" organization of materials—and needs to be addressed realistically, using Native concepts of reality, so Indian users can feel comfortable looking for things in the library. An inquiry in 1995 disclosed that the center continues its work, with an expanded collection and more services.

Friendship Centers in Canadian Cities

Across Canada there is a unique network of over 85 "Friendship Centres" in cities and towns, whose function is to make urban life for Native people less threatening and more promising, as well as to help them maintain ties with their heritage and home areas. The first one was started in Winnipeg in 1958. Six are in Quebec, with more planned. Most are in Ontario, with the highest provincial population and largest cities in Canada. British Columbia has slightly less, and Saskatchewan, Manitoba and Alberta have about a dozen each. The Yukon and Northwest Territories together have nine, and the towns they are located in are the few larger towns in the north. Nevertheless, they serve as intermediate stops on the way to deep city life, much as Bethel, Alaska is the intermediate town between the remote villages and Alaska's large cities. Finally, the Atlantic provinces each have one Friendship Centre, in the capital in each case.

Self-started by Native people and their city friends, the centers soon qualify for Federal funds through the Canadian Secretary of State, and for provincial funding in some provinces. Local fund-raising is used, and some are included in charity campaigns. Each center is autonomous, with its own governing board, employing 3-6 persons. Federal support has been increased, and will emphasize training opportunities through these popular and efficiently run service centers. Although they usually do not have library collections as such, it turns out that they perform many of the cultural and documentation programs and information and referral services associated with libraries. In Quebec the variety of such Friendship Centre offerings is an indication of their vitality: hostel facilities, crafts workshops, theatre troupes, drug and alcohol abuse programs, Native cultural projects, newsletters, recreation for youth, liaison of all types with the non-Native community, meeting rooms, social services liaison, escort and interpretation services, and even savings and loan credit services in one center. But underlying all these activities is—to quote from the "Quebec Association of Native Friendship Centres" booklet by the same name—"moral, emotional, social and cultural support for all Native persons in difficulty."

For example, the Calgary Indian Friendship Centre, established in 1964, has been funded by a variety of local and provincial sources, through fundraising campaigns. Incidentally, if anyone ever wondered if Native people understood what libraries, documentation, archives and museums and information services have to offer, we can quote "Pat Weasel Head, a Blood Elder, [who] was once asked what he thought about recording sacred gatherings. This was his answer: 'You asked what I think of pictures and writings. I think it is very good to make a record of what goes on. Life is changing very fast. Soon these scenes will only be memories. The young people will never know how we operated our holy ways if they cannot see and read and hear records that can be made today. We all have treasured photographs of our long-gone chiefs and relatives and camps. In the same way, our grandchildren will someday treasure a record of things that are today.'"19

The Calgary Centre started out as a social club. But the needs of Natives coming to the city soon became of equal concern. The Local Council of Women joined with the original Native Friendship Club and the Calgary Indian Friendship Society was formed. Its goals included some of the services and programs mentioned above, and in 1967 it found larger quarters, buying and moving into a house. Increased costs and service burdens led to a financial crisis, and in 1974 it changed its name to the Calgary Native Friendship Society, continuing to receive funds from the City of Calgary as well as the province. The Centre was also a part of the local United Way Campaign. Finally, in 1980, after a successful building campaign, the Centre moved into a million-dollar new facility on the site of the same house. Its modern architecture includes a sloping west wall extending from ground to roof, "creating an aura of light and height inside the building."

Its services and programs have been expanding to meet the needs of urban Native people in the Calgary region, and for Native visitors from other areas, including reservations just across the US border in Montana and the Dakotas. These now include: Court work, family counselling, Ladies Programs, Elder's Social Club, Urban Native Women Parenting Program, Hospital Workers Report, Rummage Sale, Life Skills Courses, Urban Orientation Program, Legal Clinic, Urban Referral Program, Public Speaking Class, Students Involvement Program, Tutoring, and Cree and Blackfeet language courses. Sports and recreational activities of every imaginable kind are run for both youth and adults, and cultural programs include crafts, drumming and singing, dancing, hand games, pageants, music and art lessons, film showings, and activities in connection with the annual Calgary Stampede.

But not a library! Notice, however, that a number of the activities are library-related. Thus Native communities in an urban environment generate their own beginning library and information services. "The Calgary Public Library does not provide any special library services for native people," and "none of [its] branches are in what you would call predominantly native neighbourhoods." However, the library system does carry "substantial amounts of information of interest to the native population." Also, through a fundraising program it is "seeking sponsorship for a new, more intensive collection of information about native North Americans."[20]

Anchorage, Alaska

In Anchorage in 1995, where about 14,000 Alaska Natives and other Native Americans reside, the Anchorage Municipal Libraries (AML) and the City of Anchorage seem receptive and concerned to better serve this client group, as well as other minorities. Though its budget has been increasing lately, some branches were closed several years ago due to budget cuts after state oil revenues fell off. But a recent pilot project that introduced a new, combined school-public library into a predominantly minority and low income neighborhood is being continued, with more local community control in its governance.

It is recognized that minority representation in various aspects of the system has been low and needs to change so as to serve the entire population of the Municipality of Anchorage, not only those for whom libraries have always been of service. AML utilizes a Regional Services grant from the State Library to administer the 800-number telephone reference service and institutional library services in the area. (See citation under my name in Bibliography/Reference List II for more information on the latter.) The headquarters library, Loussac, used to administer Bush Library Services, a books-by-mail program, to south central and western Alaska, but as of FY 1994 this has been taken over by the North Slope Borough Library in Fairbanks for mainland Alaska and by Juneau for Southeastern Alaska, which also administers the 800-number reference and ILL (interlibrary loan) telephone number for that region. Another new program available to rural residents and funded by the Library Services and Construction Act (LSCA) Title III is called SLED (Statewide Library Electronic Gateway) and provides online information from libraries, government sources, and Internet, as Susan Elliott of Alaska State Library explains in the August 1994 issue of *Newspoke,* Alaska Library Network News. In isolated Native subsistence villages, users of SLED will most likely be village and school libraries. Urban Natives and Indians may or may not know about SLED, unless they are library users or have access to a computer, neither possibility having much promise at this time, from our point of view.

The origin of funding for Regional Services grants is both Federal and state in nature. The Federal source is Title I of the LCSA. States must doubly match the amount requested from the U.S. Department of Education and also include "maintenance of effort" costs, as if the state itself were providing the Federally funded portion. This is seen by some as unnecessarily burdensome on the states, and there are other provisions that "lock" the state into continuation of increasing levels of library service provision, if Federal funds are to continue.

The magnificent, not to say palatial Loussac Library in mid-town Anchorage, built during the oil revenue peak of the 1980s, may last for many years and be handicapped accessible, but is it Native accessible, Native hospitable? Or minority accessible? Areas needing to be addressed are already being recognized. The advisory board and professional as well as paraprofessional staff have little minority and Native representation. Close liaison with Native and minority communities, acquisition of Native art, and special collections and programs are being considered as of this writing. To be noted are the differences in the oral and written traditions and how these determine one's expectations and the kinds of media that should be acquired and promoted in order to satisfy both. All are signs that auger improvement for future Native library services in Alaska's "biggest Native village," as well as for other minorities.

Notes

1. Translation notes for the song "I'm Lost in the City", by John Angaiak, from his record album of the same title, issued in the 1970s by the Eskimo Language Workshop, Department of Linguistics and Foreign Languages, University of Alaska, Fairbanks. Angaiak is a well-known Yupik vocalist and composer from the Yukon-Kuskokwim delta.
2. Lerner, Daniel. "Modernization, I: Social Aspects." *International Encyclopedia of the Social Sciences.* David L. Sills, ed. New York: Macmillan, 1968. Vol. 9, p. 36.

3. Pelto, Pertti J. *The Snowmobile Revolution, Technology and Social Change in the Arctic.* Menlo Park, CA: Cummings Publishing Co., 1973.
4. For a complete review of the variations in urbanization of Native peoples from a Canadian perspective, and how their requirements may be met, see: Gurstein, 1983.

   What is "city" to one is "country" to another, relative to one's own origins and "compared-to-what?"! In Bethel, one could find what seemed like curiously out-of-place behavior among the settled white half of the population toward newcomer-whites, customs that were exasperatingly akin to those found in the deep city life of the Lower 48. Newcomers and their greetings were often ignored, and pedestrians never offered rides—unless the one greeted or driving recognized and knew the other. The unfortunate person without his or her own vehicle could call one of five or six taxi companies to get a lift.

   In contrast, small town remembrance was available to the author when he returned to Bethel after a three-year absence. It was like Old Home Week. People remembered him, were pleased to see him back, and inquired after his situation. However, Bethel was as clique-ridden as any other isolated northern community where a minority white population is found in the midst of an established and larger Native population.

   While living on the Plains Indian Reservation, by the way, it was necessary to commute to work by hitchhiking from a hamlet 12 miles away for a two-month period. I was only late to work once—by about 10 minutes. Here, I was one of very few whites living an Indian community.

5. Reid, Sean. "Alaska Calling, Telegraphs to Satellite Transponders . . . Technology tackles Alaska's age-old problem of long distance communication," *Alaska Magazine,* May, 1982. Information on the history of Alaska communications development is drawn mostly from this article.
6. "TV—Better Than Shaking Tents and Dreams," *Psychology Today,* March, 1978, p. 109. Notice cites an article by Granzberg, Steinbring and Hamer in the *Journal of Communication,* Vol. 27, no. 4. Cree ritual whereby a shaman calls in persons from a great distance is compared to television. Findings of their research show that sex and violence depicted on TV have deleterious effects, causing nightmares and obstreperous, untraditional behavior.
7. One such experiment took place during the Christmas season of 1980. Two-way television joined six remote communities in Project Inukshuk, operated by the Native organization, Inuit Tapirisat of Canada (ITC). It was all programming in Inuktitut. No game shows or M*A*S*H* here. Each community presented programs, and joint "town

hall" meetings were held on issues of importance to Natives. The project was funded by the Canadian government for $1.9 million.

8. McPhail, Thomas L., Associate Professor, School of Journalism, Carleton University, Ottawa, Canada. "The Impact of Broadcasting Technologies on Northern Native Communications in Canada." A paper prepared for the International Communication Association Annual Conference, Chicago, Illinois, April 24–27, 1975.

9. A useful publication giving all particulars about radio and television services addressed to Native populations of Alaska, Canada and Greenland is *The Northern Native Broadcast Directory,* edited by Deborah Lee Murin, 1988. It lists all services involved, with their position papers and programming in a second section.

10. In the late 1960s and early 1970s, the author was involved in a number of Indian treaty and minority rights demonstrations in Washington State. They were organized with one eye watching for the media television coverage. Minorities with little-known or unpopular political views to advocate can, with some verve and determination—and thinking like a TV producer—find access to prime-time TV news, espousing their cause in the very living rooms of the elite and influential.

11. Forbes, Norma. "Television Effects on Rural Alaska, Summary of Final Report" (of) the study "Social and Cognitive Effects of the Introduction of Television on Rural Alaska Native Children," by Norma Forbes, Clark Ashworth, Walter Lonner and Danuta Kasprzyk. Alaska Council on Science and Technology, Contract 33–82, Center for Cross-Cultural Studies, University of Alaska, Fairbanks, Alaska, March, 1984.

12. Inuit Broadcasting Corporation. "Position Paper on Northern Broadcasting." Revised October, 1985.

13. Lentz, Tony. "The Medium Is the Madness: Television and the Pseudo-Oral Tradition in America's Future," in *Communications and the Future,* edited by Harold F. Didsbury, Jr., Bethesda, Maryland: World Future Society, 1982.

14. Hanks, Christopher C. et al. "Social Changes and the Mass Media: The Oxford House Cree, 1909–1982." *Polar Record,* Vol. 21 (1983), No. 134, pp. 459–465.

15. Berger, Peter, and Brigitte Berger, and Hansfried Kellner. *The Homeless Mind, Modernization and Consciousness.* NY: Vintage Books, Random House, 1974 (c1973), pp. 145–147. For a current look at the American brand of homelessness, see the special section in the May/June, 1990 issue of *Utne Reader:* "Roots, A restless nation searches for a place to call home."

16. The following account of the center's activities is taken from a draft supplied by American Indian Resource Center librarian Tom Lippert, author of an article which appeared in *News from Native California,* Vol. 1, No. 2 (May/June, 1987).

17. *Ibid.*
18. Quoted by Dennis Francis, Executive Director, in his message in the October, 1984 publication, "Twenty Years Anniversary of Calgary Indian Friendship Centre, 1964–84."
19. Personal communication, Calgary Public Library. April 5, 1988.

5.

Multiculturalism and Biculturalism: Native Library Progress in Canada and Greenland

I: Canada

Library Service to Native people is not an isolated issue. When speaking of library services you neither circumvent the issues of education, information, and communications nor avoid the implications of social and economic conditions. Library service to and in Native communities must be assessed and organized in response to the needs and uniqueness of the region, the community and the people.[1]

There are over half a million[2] of the Native peoples in all of Canada. The Atlantic provinces of New Brunswick, Nova Scotia, Prince Edward Island and Newfoundland altogether have a Native population that is very small, with a minor role in provincial affairs. Quebec has a similarly small percentage, but for various reasons which we will touch on later, the Native peoples have a significant place in the movement for self-determination and local control of development, including library development. Five large provinces march westward, held between the U.S. border and the 60th parallel: Ontario, Manitoba, Saskatchewan, Alberta and British Columbia. Above the 60th parallel, commonly referred to as the Canadian North, are, first and most prominently, dominating the continental heart and extending almost to the north pole, into the High Arctic, the enormous Northwest Territories. To its west is the second largest, the Yukon Territory, situated up against Alaska and above British Columbia.

Though we will briefly and selectively mention developments in the other provinces, we will focus mostly on Native libraries in Canada in four provinces: the Northwest and Yukon Territories, which are the most

119

northerly and the most rural; the Province of Ontario, which has the most urban centers; and Quebec, which is of special interest because of its crossroads position, between the Canadian arctic and Greenland, the Atlantic gateway and the interior, and where both English and French domination of the past have left their legacies and rivalries. It is also a province with a close mixture of Native peoples, and where the James Bay and Northern Quebec Agreement of 1975 has brought a controversial resolution of Native claims, and perhaps an ironic return to Native unity and renaissance in the New World.

But land claims negotiations between most Native tribal groupings and the Federal Government of Canada are still going on, and will take many years to resolve. The situation varies from province to province, as we will note. In 1990 disputes even arose between Native entities over conflicting land claims, and armed confrontations occurred on two reserves in Quebec over the issues of gambling casinos and land.

Canadian provision of library services to the Native peoples has varied over time and among the provinces, and in relation to the Federal government. There has also been variation from east to west, and between urban and rural areas. As elsewhere, the Native peoples were a small minority nationwide and lacked political influence, were economically as well as legally impotent and provided no tax base within their own communities for any educational-cultural services. Generally speaking, library services to Native populations have developed first and most appropriately in areas where there has been the highest concentration of Native people—the southeastern population centers. As our main interest is in northern areas, however, this will be our starting point; we shall move then to the southern provinces, and a survey of development on the national scene.

We look first above the 60th parallel, at the Yukon and Northwest Territories (NWT). Here, in vast northern Canada, is the highest proportion of Native people to the rest of the population: 18% in the Yukon, 58% in the NWT. In contrast to the relative autonomy of the provinces to the south, the federal government retains control over nonrenewable resource development and health care in the territories, though the newly created Nunavut Territory in the eastern Arctic along with the general trend toward autonomy elsewhere will bring more regionalization and Native control. And, of course, if eventually successful, the recurrent Separatist movement in Quebec (defeated by an extremely narrow margin in Fall 1995, for the second time), would drastically alter the Canadian sociopolitical landscape, much more so than we have discussed here.

The Yukon Territory has the smallest population of any Canadian province or territory: just over 23,000, of which more than 4000 are Native, comprising eight major Indian tribes. Public Library Services of the Yukon Education Department "coordinates the operations and acts as a consultant for the ten branch libraries and nine community libraries in the

Yukon. The branch libraries, found in the largest settlements, are run by independent citizen boards, except in Whitehorse, the provincial capital, and they employ paid librarians. The smaller community libraries are operated by volunteers."[3] A newsletter is circulated by Public Library Services to branch and community libraries.

The Libraries and Archives Branch of Yukon Education conducts training workshops for both community librarians and library boards, and distributes a policies and procedures manual for library boards. Archival management training is made available as well.

Regarding Native libraries, until recently "there [were] no written government policies in place . . . regarding library services to native people."[4] However, in late 1987 the Libraries and Archives Branch funded the position of Native Programs Coordinator, whose rather all-encompassing responsibilities were "to assist the Yukon's Native community to make full use of library and archival services available to them including the development of band libraries, archival collections, as well as co-ordinating a variety of library and archival services aimed at the Native community."[5] Discretionary funding for FY 1988 was intended to make available some funds for Native library support.

Land claims negotiations in the Yukon have gone on since 1973, and in November, 1988 "an agreement in principle" was reached between the territorial government and the Yukon Indians. However, final notification was delayed and continues to be discussed.[6] The Federal government has already settled with the Native peoples of Northern Quebec and the Inuvialuit of the Western Arctic.

Where there is no progress in self-determination, as in education and social services, and administrative authority and professional expertise remain on the non-Native side, impatience wears thin, almost according to a foreseeable timetable. Where there is no Native participation in decisions that affect their lives, there will eventually be protests, perhaps militant ones, especially from youth. As elsewhere, there is a tendency for the non-Native, dominant population to be ignorant about Native affairs and the real heritage and contribution of Native Canadians. In the Yukon Territory as elsewhere, rising public consciousness of the justice and necessity of Native claims has given those claims increased priority by both Native and non-Native coordinating elements, supporting an expeditious settlement. The installation of a Native Programs Coordinator in the Yukon Library and Archives Branch by 1990 was one of many signs that Native people of the territory are finally beginning to receive equal treatment and equity from the government.

For the past fifty years the scattered population of the Northwest Territories[7] has gradually been drawn into sixty-odd communities situated along waterways of the eastern and western arctic, and in a few towns in the southwest quarter of the territory, including the capital of Yellowknife. With a total population of just under 50,000 dispersed in these mostly quite small settlements—many are only a few hundred—the logistics of service, supply and communication are unique and difficult. The formerly nomadic Inuit and Indian hunters, fishermen and gatherers, most of whom still pursued subsistence ways into the 1960s, migrating between seasonal camps, have steadily moved into a relatively small number of permanent settlements, thus accelerating the effects of urbanization and modernization. Access to education, health care and a less precarious lifestyle are among the attractions of these settlements. Unfortunately this also brings a rise in individual and social problems.

Employment beyond the reduced subsistence economies (the types of which vary considerably from region to region) fluctuates wildly, depending on the occasional government or corporate infusion of money into special projects, such as the Distant Early Warning (DEW) radar line (now the North Warning System), oil and gas exploration, various surveys, expeditions, military operations and the like. Sources of income other than the few cash-paying government and service jobs are government assistance and the products of Native commercial arts marketed through cooperatives.

Politically, in recent years more autonomy has gone to the NWT (Northwest Territories) government, with control over education, culture, and libraries (under Culture and Communications), local government, housing and public works, and most renewable resources. Although the Legislative Assembly is elected, an overall Commissioner is appointed by the federal government. In recent years the Native peoples have come together in various organizations, as land claims and other issues came to the fore. The Committee for Original Peoples Entitlement (COPE) was mostly concerned with land claims. The following year (1971) the Inuit Tapirisat of Canada (ITC) was organized, representing the other interests of Native peoples across the arctic, Quebec and Laborador. Under its umbrella are a number of special purpose corporations and committees such as the Inuit Broadcasting Corporation (IBC); the Inuit Cultural Institute (ICI), which has its own library; the Inuit Development Corporation (IDC); and the Inuit Committee on National Issues (ICNI). The original COPE is now a regional affiliate of ITC. In 1991 a proposed homeland for 17,500 Inuit named Nunavut was tentatively approved by both the residents and the Canadian House of Commons. Five times the size of California, covering Eastern Arctic and Hudson's Bay lands, the huge region will be an area where Natives can manage their own hunting and fishing rights without interference from either NWT or Federal authorities. Included in the agreement is payment of $522 million over a 14-year period. A final agreement between the Tungarvik Confederation and the Canadian government was signed in 1993, establishing this semi-autonomous region.

The Dene-Metis Negotiations Secretariat has handled land claims for the Dene Nation in the western Arctic (Metis are persons of mixed Amerindian and French ancestry.) In 1991, a settlement proposal between the 13,000 Dene-Metis and the government was refused, and negotiations continued. In the mid-1970s the Secretariat joined with the Metis Nation in organizing Native library and archival development. The Dene Nation Library, for example, which was apparently the only Native-run library in the Northwest Territories, has become an excellent research library, with archival and records sections for the Dene Nation. It has limited access, by written permission, and has its own special classification system. There is also the Dene Cultural Institute, which is separate.

These demands for autonomy and self-government are found among most Native peoples today, to one degree or another, seemingly as more younger Natives return to the home areas with a modernizing education, to see non-Native governmental and corporate enterprises increasingly probing for access to resources under or on Native lands and waters, the severe curtailment of traditional subsistence options, and the accompanying social problems and their steady rain of personal tragedies impacting the lives of family and friends.[8]

Self-determination efforts also have implications for library development and provision, which have customarily been administered by non-Native authority and its relatively unlimited resources. If library services truly have any relevancy for Native community development, they will have to be seen as useful and supportive for Native self-determination. NWT libraries are increasingly aware of this, and are redoubling efforts to ensure that appropriate library provision is developed throughout the Territories, including lobbying with the territorial Legislative Assembly and the federal government.

From an interview with Marion L. Pape, then NWT Public Library Services Director, we learned more about efforts such as: 1) initiatives being taken to collect aboriginal language materials; 2) how local library collections are being fiscally strengthened so as to be more autonomous; 3) measures to enhance present collections and attract non-users; and 4) why NWTPLS is automating. More local Native librarians will be trained, as well as community library board members, and NWTPLS will encourage and support local libraries participating in territory-wide library programs (book festivals, reading programs, etc.).

A conference held at the headquarters of NWT Public Library Services in late 1986, on "Libraries as Community Information Centers," produced a list of "most important problems."[9] These were: "not enough Native materials in NWT libraries; a need to form representative community library boards to take the leadership role in library development; more training for community library staff; lack of library profile in the communities, and more paid hours for library staff and for longer public opening hours."

The Selection Policy for NWTPLS (April, 1987) emphasizes local input and control over local collection development, and greatly increased acquisition of materials in aboriginal languages, emphasizing video and other audiovisual formats. Due to the lack of sufficiently large academic or research libraries in the NWT, emphasis is also being given to strengthening the reference and research capabilities of the Headquarters Library in Hay River, near Yellowknife.

Most interesting, not to say invigorating, is the "Library Services Operational Plan, 1985–90." Emphasis here is on an array of ambitious and community-oriented activities aimed at fulfilling objectives that, when met, will see strong regional libraries[10] coordinating local library provision that is locally controlled and promoted, with more appropriate collections and programs, and easier access to outside information through a stronger Headquarters library in Hay River. It will also bring more efficient interlibrary operations through computerization and automation of library procedures. Having noted all this, we can look at the personnel and service concepts and learn how staff are to go about implementing these changes.

In other words, what philosophy is to help guide their daily work? The administration of NWTPLS sees this as having underlying importance for the success of its innovative policies. (Quoting from the Operational Plan):

> Library services needs to do more than simply make available information materials for all citizens. . . . The library has a responsibility to reach out and bridge the gap between what the library can provide, and what individuals are aware of. . . . Community information services cannot be based on the passive provision of printed information to users. . . . Information workers cannot be passive channels for information [which means that workers] must understand the information that they are handling. . . . [T]hey should be able to create . . . with the help of the local community, appropriate information sources if they do not exist. They must be able and willing to interpret, repackage and apply information to the user situation (the printed word may have to be put into the local language, or into audio or visual format). Finally, the information workers must, where necessary, help [users] act on the information that has been supplied. This implies workers who are fully accepted as part of the community they serve. . . .

This is the description of an activist, dynamic library and information services infrastructure fully integrated into the community which will, as the Operational Plan summarizes, take initiatives to coordinate appropriate access modes to the "immense amounts of material being . . . produced in the north by government departments, broadcasting corporations, and Native and other community-based organizations. . . . Libraries are at a turning point in their development in the NWT."[11]

Village libraries across the NWT are combining their facilities with other related and compatible cultural services, such as local mini-museums, tourism centers and elders' centers. Among the appropriate and desired programs being offered are oral history and other local documentation activities, archival collection efforts, visits by northern authors and artists, "video nights," traveling exhibits, literacy programs, writing contests and reading competitions, Children's Book Week and National Book Week. To quote one NWTPLS staffer's note: "The most thriving community libraries are those which combine local history, photographs, oral tradition and illustration types of activities." Library automation continues to be developed at Headquarters in Hay River, bringing online access by remote communities to their bibliographic database. A "book block" rotation system also serves the remote communities, with materials sent being based on community profiles.

The future for the Northwest Territories (NWT) may lie not only in further regionalization, but in division into more manageable entities that include control by the predominantly Native resident population. The creation of Nunavut has spotlighted the top-heavy character of NWT government and the need for more efficient and relevant local administration. (See Dickerson and "Formal Signing . . ." in Bibliography/Reference List II.) Even in Alaska, where the Native has been empowered by the Alaska Native Claims Settlement Act and increased self-determination, it is not inconceivable that a contiguous, Native homeland like the Yukon-Kuskokwim delta, with a three-quarters Central Yupik resident population in more than 50 villages and a high percentage of Native speakers, will someday become a semi-autonomous territory.

Although Ontario has a small percentage of Native population, it actually has the largest number of Natives, over 110,000. These are almost all Indians and Metis. Due to the presence of several large cities, including the nation's capital, Ottawa, urban library services to Natives figure prominently, and Ontario has been active in this area of library provision. It began in the early 1960s, when individual initiatives were made from the Native side and from a few librarians, including the Director of Ontario Public Library Services, who started a traveling library service to some bands in 1959. At this time there was no federal assistance at all for library services to Native people, who could only try to avail themselves of those non-Native community libraries that might be within reach. Isolated band councils here and there took it upon themselves to find library housing and what books they could, like discards from nearby established libraries in the Eurocanadian community.

The year 1966 seems to have been a watershed, when a survey of many regional and municipal libraries revealed that a large number had been approached to serve members of Indian bands. The Education Division of the federal Indian Affairs Branch drew up a plan to assist interested bands to join in existing public library services, the official policy then being to "enable Indians of Canada to enter the mainstream of Canadian life."[12] The Province of Ontario Public Library Act of 1967 "specifically refers to Indian band councils as equivalent to municipal authorities for the purpose of receiving library grants and signing library contracts."[13] Early in 1967 the federal Department of Indian Affairs and Northern Development developed a scheme for library grants to bands with a per capita formula, with the band contributing a fraction of that sum per capita as well.

Very quickly a wide array of problems revealed themselves. Professional and technical advice was needed by the bands; there was only one professional Native librarian in Canada at that time (David Sparvier); library materials of the kinds most needed and wanted by Native peoples were in very short supply, or were heavily biased and stereotyped against them. In the following years various summer projects took place, training Native students to then go out and assist bands to develop libraries and library services. Most band libraries became a part of regional public library networks. Regarding materials and their format, Adamson added: "Non-book materials are most important among those with limited educational background. Films, filmstrips, pictures, sound recordings, art and museum objects have a direct appeal, and libraries which serve Indians need to have rich resources in these fields."[14]

In May, 1970 the Indian Information Center was established at the University of Western Ontario. Its basic, grant-funded purpose was "to collect unpublished materials and to develop a bibliography of information contained in professional journals and other unpublished works. The focus of this endeavor was materials pertinent to Native studies."[15] The bibliography thus produced was to be computerized, and microfilmed for those (public libraries) unable to have a computer retrieval system.

Most of the chronic lacks in Native library service were identified at this early stage: the need for materials in Native languages and by Native authors and artists; the need for Native-produced films; the role libraries could play in increasing literacy and authorship among Natives; how they can help reduce school dropouts and help slow learners; how they can support the movement toward self-determination; the needed representation of Natives on regional library boards; the need for public and regional library representatives to reach out and contact bands, help them secure grants, offer advice and technical support, give demonstrations, etc. Finally, "the enrichment of regional library resources by the addition of more materials on Indians will make these available to non-Indians as well, and increase mutual understanding and respect."[16]

It's interesting to note how, as more and better library provision materialized throughout Ontario into the 1970s, the higher everyone's expectations and standards became. And Native leaders didn't always understand what libraries are able to do, and that they don't have to be replicas of the white man's urbanized and Eurocanadian-oriented libraries transplanted into the Native community.

In late 1975, John Marshall gave a brief to the Ontario Task Force on the Education of Native Peoples, entitled "Library Services for Native Peoples," which covered the various library and information services then operative for Natives, offering trenchant recommendations for improving their effectiveness.

At this point, the differences between band libraries and public libraries was the almost total inability of bands to provide local financial support, compared to support capabilities of the Eurocanadian communities.[17] Otherwise band libraries had the same access to provincial per capita and federal discretionary funds as other public libraries. The local support gap was so wide, however, that radical changes seemed called for, if standards of library provision were ever to reach equity.

In the latter 1970s, complaints and demands became stronger, as well as continued efforts at improvement and support. As an example, in 1976 the Canadian Association in Support of the Native Peoples (CASNP) issued *Information Access through Library Services: A Handbook for Native Groups,* compiled by Jenna Hofbauer. This was a how-to-do-it guide that provided a basic definition of what a library is, how it can serve the Native community, and how to go about getting one started. The single critical factor that gets slighted is funding, and one is referred to a booklet available from CASNP. In view of the complications of funding band libraries, perhaps it was just as well to make this referral! Even though both provincial and federal per capita amounts in the band library grants had been increased over time, the actual sums available to bands for a year's library service were pathetically meager, and many bands were simply unable "to develop anything that could reasonably be called a library, and even where a library of sorts exists, it is usually operated at minimal levels."

In northern Ontario, four regional libraries and the Ojibway-Cree Cultural Centre (federally funded) were in place, "to develop cultural services for the Native population including library services," but "the efforts of both these groups are blocked by the lack of viable facilities on Native reserves." The final recommendations of the brief just quoted from included no less than a 20-fold increase in the per capita amount, which would simply have brought band standards up to the level of public libraries. However, the same minimum amount continued until 1983, when through a "reorganization and decentralization of Native funding," the federal per capita aid to band library services was ended. Now there were certain nondiscretionary funds for areas like health and welfare, with all other social services like libraries having to compete for whatever discretionary funding remained, thus producing a lot of confusion and ill-prepared situations at the local level. The small provincial per capita aid continued as before.

Meanwhile, the several Indian cultural centres throughout Ontario were promoting research, study and public/band education of their respective Native heritages. In northern Ontario, 1979 marked the first of annual, week-long workshops for Indian library workers. Also there began in this year the Anishnawbe Kaskantomawin Native Information Service (AKNIS) of the Northwestern Library System. This service was to coordinate certain activities of all four northern regional libraries and the Ojibway-Cree Cultural Center, namely: to make available the Ojibway-Cree Resource Centre

Bibliography to all participants, promote the available library information services, develop an interlibrary loan and reference service, and "work toward the development and extension of library services" to all constituencies involved. Federal funds per capita allocated directly to regional libraries were reallocated to fund AKNIS.

Then 1980–82 produced more watershed contributions. These studies included one by a graduate library school student; one by a consulting firm under the direction of the Task Force on Native Library Services; and lastly a "report of the Ontario Public Libraries Programme Review for the Minister of Citizenship and Culture," which also addressed the situation of Native libraries.

Judith Carlson's report[18] as a student in library education at Ryerson Polytechnic Institute in Toronto provides us with, among much other useful information, a list of areas needing attention. It is worth noting here that, among all the American Library Association-accredited graduate library schools in the US and Canada, it is the rare instance where their faculty have produced research into the area of Native library services—or multicultural library services, for that matter. (See chapter 8 for more discussion of this issue.) Ms. Carlson was not working on an MLS thesis at all, but on a paper which was part of the 2nd year in a paraprofessional or vocational training program. It turns out that her report is still recommended by no less an authority than the National Library of Canada, so scarce was pacesetting research in those days, John Marshall's and others' contributions notwithstanding.

She noted the inadequacy and bias in the Dewey Decimal Classification System, when applied to the Native peoples. Subject headings needed to be looked at for revision and replacement, to promote ones that are more accurate and more intelligible for Native users, and that are less likely to perpetuate ethnocentrism and racism among non-Native users. The selection of materials on or for Natives required special caveats, due to negative or distorted stereotyping, arising for the most part out of ignorance and racism. She points out that by this time, most Natives in fact lived in urban areas, and library services must take this into account as well, both for the Natives on the reserves (who might be considering a move to the city) and for those already in cities. Native studies collections needed much infusion of funds and development, for researchers, students and public education. There was a need for bookmobiles and other mobile units to bring library services to the smallest bands, most of whom were in isolated and remote situations, culturally if not geographically. Liaison with Native communities was almost non-existent, and initiatives should be expected from librarians, not Natives. Native librarians were so rare as to be national celebrities, certainly in the library world, and public libraries serving Natives needed the help of Native staff members. In cities, especially, there was a need for libraries to have survival and coping information readily available and promoted. Funding should be reliable and adequate, to bring library services for Natives up to the standard routinely provided to public libraries serving other Ontario residents.

The second report was the most comprehensive and penetrating, and we will look it over in some detail. Though more professionally organized and thorough in its analysis, for the most part it offers the same data and findings as Carlson. It is the *Report* to the "Ontario Public Library Review on Native Library Services in Ontario."[19] The recurring appeal for more progress and commitment toward equity is again heard: "The level of library services to Indian communities in Ontario is so far behind other communities that only through a major commitment at all levels can this appalling situation begin to improve." The first major problem was financial, and the second was the "inability of the existing library system in Ontario to develop a culturally relevant service to the Native community."

There was a "need for the provision of a more stable funding for the ongoing operation of a band library as well as increased training of Native library staff. . . . The existing libraries are barely surviving and in many cases are doing so only through the efforts of one committed individual. In addition, as the federal government has discontinued funding [the direct per capita grants], some libraries have ceased operations over the past year. Bands who do not have library services presently are not encouraged by this situation to even consider the setting up of a library on their reserve."

A special section was devoted to cultural factors in Native community library development. "Community needs should dictate the type of services required as well as the priorities defined in delivering these services." This refers to the persistent tendency to impose urban, non-Native models onto Native communities and reserves, where libraries "need opportunities to develop at their own pace and to define their own needs." Citing the trend across Canada to promote the national yet multicultural heritage, the Native culture—or the original Canadian culture—needed to be studied and publicized much more.

Several factors cited by Carlson were mentioned. Some additional ones included: "cost of translating materials into various Native languages, lack of sensitivity of the non-Native systems and institutions, lack of a proper long-range plan based on a distinctive and unique philosophy and set of objectives as determined by Native people, problems of jurisdictional responsibilities involving two levels of government, lack of commitment on the part of those in decision-making positions to ensure proper and adequate delivery of services, and lack of assistance and encouragement of Native writers."

Finally, the network of community information services includes, in addition to AKNIS, several cultural/education centers and, in the towns, the Friendship Centres described earlier, although they don't have library collections per se. Federal agencies with an inherent interest in the development of library services to Native communities include the Department of

Indian Affairs and Northern Development, the Ministry of Northern Affairs, the Ministry of Education, the Department of the Secretary of State and the Ministry of Culture and Recreation. The report concludes, like Carlson, by recommending that a coordinating agency be created with province-wide powers, to ensure provision of needed funding, consultancy, training and development, appropriate community support services, appropriate library provision, and materials in aboriginal languages and works by Native authors.

The third report is "Ontario Public Libraries: the Provincial Role in a Triad of Responsibilities."[20] Two sections deal expressly with "Indian band libraries" and "Native Peoples Library Services," which are sections taken from the Public Libraries Act. Essentially it describes the problematical situation as we've come to understand it—the funding of Ontario's Native libraries—and offers this comment: "It is necessary to bring representatives of the Federal and Provincial governments together with Native people and their library consultants to begin to approach a solution to this problem." Both sections of the report quote statements from the Task Force report previously discussed, including the recommendation of a province-wide coordinating authority, and offers these two recommendations of its own:

> Recommendation 7.65—The Provincial Government establish a position to be filled by a Native person whose task is to develop library service programmes for Native People of Ontario and to design an organization and structure including the funding requirements for the delivery of library service programmes to the Native People of Ontario, both on and off the Reserves.

> Recommendation 7.66—The Provincial Government increase the population grant to operating Indian band libraries to twenty dollars per head, so as to begin to build a library service from the local level and arrangements be made through the Ojibway-Cree Cultural Centre and the Woodland Indian Cultural Education Centre for trained guidance in developing the Band Libraries.

Since 1982, a variety of measures have been taken to continually strengthen Native library services throughout the province.

Early in 1984, a communique or news release[21] from the Ontario Ministry of Citizenship and Culture announced the creation of the Native Library Development Project, with funding of $100,000 "in FY 1984 to help northern Ontario Native bands develop and maintain library services." This took the form of wage subsidies to band libraries, "to ensure greater continuity in the delivery of Library service," and support for purchase of materials "of special interest to Native people, and to meet specific training and development needs of Native library staff." The NDLP also had a Project Coordinator, who was available to evaluate and promote library services. The project was "in response to recommendations contained in a recent library review task force report," and "reflects efforts of Northern regional library boards."

Late in 1984 an "Advisory Committee on Native Library Services" was appointed.[22] Thus, after many ad hoc Native and citizens' task force efforts over the years, an advisory group became part of the Ontario Ministry of Citizenship and Culture. All five committee members were either Native or working for Native library/cultural organizations. Over the following two years grants to the bands continued. In July, 1986, "revised criteria" for the Northern Native Library Development Program (NNLDP) were issued. These set forth provisions for NNLDP financial assistance for band library staff salaries up to $10,000 per library, and for both per capita and special grants, which could cover practically every aspect of library operations except construction of a new library.

The Ontario Public Library Strategic Plan (April, 1990) addresses the chronic lack of funding for First Nation libraries, ensure that library workers receive cross-cultural training for serving Native communities and clientele, brings the quality of Native library services up to that of non-Native areas, and establishes a First Nations Library Advisory Committee for the Government of Ontario.

Quebec has a special and unusually interesting place in the merging of Native and Eurocanadian cultures and regarding library development in that setting. The ten Native (Inuit and nine Indian) peoples[23] of what is now Canada's Quebec Province first saw Europeans in the early 17th century, as the British, Danish and French went past their shores looking for the fabled Northwest Passage to the Orient. The rivalry of the French and British, at least for Quebec proper, was essentially ended as a result of the Treaty of Utrecht in 1713, which also gave the Hudson Bay Company exclusive trading rights, eliminating official French interests. By 1750 the HBC was in Inuit territory, and through the following century missionary, commercial and military interests came in waves over Quebec. But the inheritance from Europe had, from the first contact, a double image: French and English, giving "la vie quebecoise" forever a dual personality. But we leave out the underlying base—the residual Native population which has endured so much change and alteration over the past 500 years. Across the 19th century change came in the form of trading posts, whaling stations and American whaling ships, missionary pioneers, and claims by the U.S. and Scandinavia to Arctic islands.

The annual cycle of subsistence activities changed as well, in order to trade at distant or shifting coastal trading posts. "The effects of contacts and the attractions of Eurocanadian products and ideas entailed profound changes in the lives and settlement patterns of the Inuit of Arctic Quebec."[24] By the 20th century, competition was the theme played out in various realms: trading company rivalry between the HBC and Révillon Frères; competing jurisdictional pressures of the provincial and federal governments;

the Anglican and Roman Catholic churches as rivals not only for souls, with the Moravians, but as competitors in the provision of hospital services. The result of these unstable arrangements was that, in many areas, or over a period of time, there might be no trading posts, or no missions, or no hospitals, or no police, no government agents—or they were there in abundance, vying for the Natives' patronage. It is no wonder that from about 1910 to near World War II there was starvation, and many syncretic movements or cults arose, "only truly understandable in terms of shamanism and traditional beliefs about identity, reincarnation, and possession."[25]

In the 1930s and '40s the Depression and World War II brought more alterations—economic, social or military, as well as technological. The caribou almost disappeared and marine game resources were reduced. But government services at this time were beginning to reach into the north. In 1948 the family allowance transfer payments also began to alleviate some of the instability of life in northern Native communities. The first federal schools and infirmaries opened, sedentarization (the shift from nomadic lifestyle to towns) increased, seasonal camp use decreased, and schooling (in English or French, depending on the community) became a regular and normal aspect of life for young Natives. In less than two generations, the Native population of Quebec doubled.

But there were still dichotomies: neither the federal nor the provincial government was in control, as they jockeyed for power over forests, mining and hydroelectric projects, and jurisdictional control over populations. All this time the Native community life and culture, the languages and traditions, were at the mercy of transient agents of southern, non-Native interests. Out of this chaos arose two Native movements: one, the cooperative movement, which emphasized Native community power and control and older, traditional social relationships; the other, attractive to the young Native bureaucratic educated elite, patterned itself on the white infrastructure and development enterprises. The population was still increasing, as well as becoming more youthful than ever before.

In 1975 the young bureaucrats who, with their supporters, were in the majority and comprised the Northern Quebec Inuit Association, joined with the Grand Council of the Cree and the federal and state governments to sign the James Bay and Northern Quebec Agreement. This resulted, for northern Quebec, in a withdrawal of almost all federal interests, gave the go-ahead to provincial development projects, set up an autonomous education commission (the Kativik School Board), gave monetary compensation to the Natives for lands, along with Native bureaucratic control over most aspects of life, and reserved about one percent of the land for the exclusive use of Natives. Subsistence activities could use this land category and one larger category—as long as no resource development took place. Those communities that did not take part in the James Bay Agreement did not receive these benefits.

However, since 1975 there have been disillusions and deficiencies experienced over this agreement, with its emphasis on economic development and power struggles, and the result has been that the Native community has been drawn together as never before. It seems that the 1980s were characterized by an increase in cultural activities of every kind—and libraries and library-related projects were at the forefront of these changes. There was a magazine in both English and syllabics; radio productions were being made in Inuktitut; the Avatuq Cultural Institute was built at Inukjuak, in the northwest; Inuit Elders got together to set priorities; and future communications options were explored.

The Kativik School Board, which covers sixteen communities in northernmost Quebec is, in itself, of great interest. With headquarters originally located in Dorval for logistical reasons, it subsequently moved north. Its quarterly magazine, *Anngutivik,* published trilingually (English, French and Syllabics) in large format, gives news of education in all its aspects, including children's entries and glossaries of educational terminology and Inuit curriculum development. The Kativik Health Service manual is also trilingual. One item in Vol. 3, no. 2 (Winter/Spring, 1987) of *Anngutivik* recounts a visit to the Soviet Union by board delegates.

The 1985/86 Annual Report[26] for the Avataq Cultural Institute pointed out the need for Native language development and training, which was behind the Yukon and the NWT at that time. The Institute produces a series of publications which include the proceedings of the Inuit Elders Conferences, the Proceedings of the Inuit Language Commission and Remedies of the Inuit. Some of the recommendations of the Elders Conferences of interest to librarians are: finding Inuktitut geographical names, building a new cultural and museum center, and supporting the Inuit History Project, which has various facets: transcription of archival material in the National Archives, research on historical visual material in public and private collections, and completion of a bibliography on Native northern Quebec. Other projects included a chronology of Inuit history or prehistory, and a photo history book, as well as regional histories. There was also a separate agenda of archeological activities, during which Inuit were to receive training in archeological techniques.

Though there was no provincial funding assistance directly to Native libraries, library services were available through central loan libraries or affiliated municipal libraries. In addition, all "Amerindian," Cree and Inuit communities had school libraries, and some of these serve adult needs. One village had a municipal library administered by the local social club. A sign of increased official attention was seen in a projected provincial "study of the whole question of libraries in Amerindian and Inuit communities"[27] in 1988.

A *Mémoire*[28] of the Institute éducatif et culturel Attikamek-Montagnais (IECAM), which is located in extreme southeastern Quebec, is dedicated to bibliothèques publiques (public libraries). Issued early in 1987, it is entitled *Les Bibliothèques publiques en milieu Attikamek-Montagnais: savoir repondre a un besoin manifeste* ("Public libraries in the Attikamek-Montagnais region: How to answer an obvious need"). It also contained the following appendices of interest: "Maison de la Transmission culturelle" (House of Cultural Continuity), "Rapport de Recherche au suject (sic) De la consultation enterprise Sur le programme des Bibliothèques communautaires" (Report of Research on the subject of Consulting Services in the Community Library Program), and a 1986 document sent from the Canadian Department of Indian and Northern Affairs to the Ministère des Affaires indiennes et du Nord, proposing "authority to increase contributions for the Community Library Program."

There are some interesting concepts in the main report of this *Mémoire,* which perhaps gain enhancement by being expressed in the French language, another advantage of cross-cultural communication. The need for improved public library services is cited, and the description is one we have heard before: Native library services are below those enjoyed by the rest of the province; libraries are seen as an indispensable tool to both development and cultural diffusion and preservation, and the founding of the IECAM brought a new contextual highlight to public library development.

The report points out that underdevelopment of Native public library services is an historic phenomenon. The notion of Native culture itself is new to Native peoples, many of whom still live it and are immersed in it their entire lives. (In the same way a Caucasian is not normally an objective student of the particular cultural conditioning he or she has come from.) In the past, cultural transmission was through Elders; now urbanization, modernization, and education distract and claim the young for a new cultural amalgam. The present means or vehicles for cultural preservation and transmission have various sponsors, and lack a unifying, coherent and effective focus. The IECAM has endeavored to be a coordinating institution and agent in this effort.

Though many communities had a collection of books of some kind, library provision as needed and as it should be—services and programs of a wide range—fell far short. Since development schemes of the past have been aimed at communities of 5000 or more, this left area Native communities essentially without support for library services. Though certain groups of Native communities had access to regional library services, others had none. Cutbacks or minimal allocations of funds for cultural projects at times have indirectly retarded the development of library operations. In sum, provincial funds available in the past for band library development should be reinstated at a higher level, with a proportion of materials in Native languages, including teaching materials. Band councils have contributed some funds, with good intentions and good effect. In the best of circumstances this may cover the wages of a librarian working part-time.

Problems cited in the *Mémoire* included insufficient funds, poor federal-provincial coordination, and inept municipal authority in the administration of library services. Local libraries had low status, which meant they were more likely to lose their housing to other services, and be moved around, which disrupts service. Hours of opening were often only during the day, which resulted in working adults having little access. Collections were poorly maintained, and selection aids weren't readily available. Low pay and part-time hours do not attract well-qualified librarians. Most library users are young, and elder Natives are not attracted to libraries that are school-oriented. However, school libraries create a demand for good libraries in the community. Bilingual school curricula, standardization of Native languages and teaching aids adapted to the needs of Native cultural transmission all add to the demand for materials in Native languages.

Solutions offered can be summed up as sufficient funding, development that reflects the reality of Native community life, qualified personnel and coordination of public library services with efforts at cultural transmission.

As for the means of cultural transmission in the Attikamek-Montaignais area in southeastern Quebec, enabling more effective future preservation and continuity, the IECAM *Mémoire* first proposes a "House of Cultural Continuity" for each community, including a description of its goals and activities. There should also be a regional Centre for Technical Support and Production, for Centres for Promotion, and two Reception Centres. The House of Cultural Continuity would have three aspects: to preserve, to teach, and to communicate. Its services and programs would accordingly include: archives and documentation, emphasizing the value of heritage, arts and crafts, and collecting and preserving; then, school/Native community transition, youth recreation, and language classes; and thirdly, interpretive displays, shows and fairs, local history and lore, an audiovisual library, library, tourist center, and community radio and television.

The Mémoire adds a 1985 report on research to do with community library development in the province by the Québec Ministère des Affaires indiennes (MAIN). Funding for these libraries came through a modest per capita grant from MAIN, with a few rare instances of additional funding from other provincial or Federal sources, or local sponsorship, as by a social club. Although about two-thirds of these communities had libraries, the remaining third had none. The most common problems of existing libraries were: inadequate housing; inappropriate hours (evening and weekend hours lacking); not enough books with Native content; lack of information on new or more appropriate available materials and lack of selection aids; lack of promotion, publicity and attractive library programs; too many books not returned, and a shortage of qualified personnel. Financial requirements could be summed up in the need for adequate funds to: pay the salary of the librarian at an suitable level; to acquire the needed materials for the collection; and to maintain the library as an attractive community service.

Some other improvements requested by the Native communities themselves were: a centralized acquisitions system, and an updated bibliography of the variety of materials available about Native peoples; establishment of a regional center for the collection of Native materials, and for their circulation; provision of a training program that will make available more qualified library personnel (utilizing existing training organizations), and hiring by MAIN of a coordinator who is a specialist in library resources, who would work for a period to implement these improvements.

The final document in the Attikamek-Montagnais *Mémoire* is from the Canadian Department of Indian and Northern Affairs, dated January, 1986. It concerns a proposed doubling of the per capita grants to all Native community libraries, special allocations for equipping libraries, and providing the salary for 34 full-time or part-time library technicians, depending on the need. "This program is geared to assist in the organization and maintenance of public libraries on reserves, in collaboration with provincial services for public libraries."

We will comment briefly on Native library services and provincial support elsewhere in Canada. This is not to suggest that these other provinces have been deficient in providing library services to Natives, but for reasons of economy, as stated earlier, we have selectively fixed on representative areas of the country.

In Manitoba, the Public Libraries Act states that bands "can enter in agreements with existing library systems to provide local library service." However, "funding for this type of contractual agreement has been considered to be the responsibility of the federal government."[29] In Winnipeg in 1994, there was a Native Studies Collection in the St. Johns Branch, and special bibliographies had been issued. In addition, various programs on aspects of the Aboriginal community and culture were being presented.

In British Columbia, "the Library Services Branch (of B.C. Tourism, Recreation and Culture) has no separate and distinct program of developing Indian band libraries, nor any special funding arrangements. Native populations within existing library jurisdictions are included in our per capita support of public libraries."[30] An example of Native initiative in B.C. library development is the "Library Training Proposal Outline for the Secwepemc Cultural Education Society and the Central Interior Tribal Council Libraries." As the proposal states, the SCES and CITC libraries "serve a key role in the collection and access to information on issues and concerns affecting the Native people in the central interior."

The Saskatchewan Public Libraries Act states that "Indian bands may contract with regional libraries, and if so, have the same rights and responsibilities as other participating municipalities." Provincial funding goes to these regional libraries and is unconditional, as there are "no grants tied specifically to library services for Native people. The Saskatchewan Native Library Service *Newsletter*, which ceased publication in January, 1986, had much useful information on Native library development in the province. The Prince Albert Chiefs in north central Saskatchewan, by way of illustration, have taken initiatives to ensure appropriate library services for Native people. Most of their libraries have been located in schools, and have been exclusively federally funded. "Unlike southern communities, the northern reserves could not take part in a regional library system, nor was there a library consultant available through [the federal Department of Northern and] Indian Affairs to foster school library development."[31]

The Saskatchewan Library Association has had First Nations workshops for many years, and there has been a position in the Provincial Library responsible for services to the First Nations for equally as long. On the Native side, the Saskatchewan Indian Cultural College at Saskatoon has been concerned with library services to the provinces' bands since early this century, and there are other library systems with special mandates to serve predominantly First Nations populations. The Gabriel Institute of Native Studies and Applied Research has provided postsecondary education, teacher training, and Metis community library support since 1980. Lately, there have been First Nations training workshops across Canada utilizing telecommunications and computer applications, including computer-mediated conferences employing Unibase Telcom, for example.[32]

In Alberta, "provincial legislation has no provision for . . . specific grants" to Native libraries. "Legislation allows for annual operating grants to library systems, municipal libraries and community libraries. Indian bands are not included in any population calculations for this purpose. In order for this to happen legislation would have to be amended, after mutual agreement by the Indian band(s) concerned, the federal government and the provincial government."[33] However, the Native Education Department in Alberta is closely advised and controlled by Native educators. Materials used in Native community schools are reviewed for appropriateness, and updated regularly in the publication entitled *Native Library Resources for Elementary, Junior and Senior Schools,* issued by the Native Education Project of Alberta Education.

Throughout Alberta there are about twelve Native "cultural groups," including the Dr. Anne Anderson Native Heritage and Cultural Centre in Edmonton, which performs functions similar to those of the Ojibway-Cree and Woodland centers in the east. Its activities include teaching the Cree language, Metis crafts and arts, the history and uses of herbs, and operating a Metis Hall of Fame and a Resource Library and Research Facilities.[34]

Certainly one of the more interesting developments in the Canadian Native library scene is the existence of various Native library classification schemes.[35] There are about four versions in use, and below we will describe a prominent one by way of example, that used by the Ojibway-Cree Cultural Centre in Timmins, Ontario. The system created for the library of the

National Indian Brotherhood (now the Assembly of First Nations) in 1974–76 by A. Brian Deer, one of the first Native MLS librarians in Canada, has been the basic scheme on which others have patterned their work. His approach was not to adapt existing systems, or even to standardize his own, as he worked for various Native organizations.

> Each was drawn up from scratch in accordance with the particular interests and needs of the organization involved, the particular collection of papers they had, keeping in mind that things had to be simple since most organizations did *not* have a person whose only job was to maintain a library. . . .
>
> When I was at the Kahnawake Cultural Center, I used two classification schemes. One was a homemade scheme to handle material about Iroquois history and culture. The scheme was not a variation of the NIB one, but it was similar in notation. For books and articles on non-Iroquois subjects, I used Dewey. I devised my own subject Library Catalogue with the help of an Apple personal computer. The Library abandoned the card catalogue almost from the beginning. . . . I plan to standardize the subject headings in accordance with [the] *Unesco Thesaurus.* . . .
>
> My job [in charge of the Library at the Mohawk Nation Office, Kahnawake Branch] at present entails the monitoring, collecting and organizing of Six Nations Confederacy (of which the Mohawk Nation is a part) papers and correspondence, almost entirely 20th century. We maintain a book-style accession catalogue with name and subject indexes, with the help of an IBM-compatible personal computer. We use the two-volume *Unesco Thesaurus* (published 1977) for the standardized terms in the subject index, plus terms that I've added (e.g. Border Crossing, Condolence Ceremony, Great Law, Wampum, etc.) to handle topics special to the Six Nations. . . . The papers are *not* filed in a classified order, although there *is* a classified thesaurus in the *Unesco Thesaurus* for that purpose. Instead the papers are housed in filing cabinets in the same order as they are catalogued and are assigned 4-digit accession numbers for retrieval purposes, corresponding to the numbers used in the subject index. . . . [He also indicates that at some point he may put these materials in a classified order, again using the *Unesco Thesaurus,* and that standardization along these lines might also be a possibility—ghh.)
>
> Had the *Unesco Thesarus* been available in 1974, it probably would have been used at the National Indian Brotherhood library. Native libraries are in need of general classifications and subject headings that are modern and sensitive to Native concerns in the 20th century. The *Unesco Thesaurus* in its coverage gives particular attention to the social sciences (including human rights and law), and culture.[36]

To first scan the Ojibway-Cree Classification's Basic List and Subject thesaurus, as well as the OJICREE classification rules, is to enter another world, one where the Euroamerican world-view of Melvil Dewey or the Library of Congress is absent.[37] Here the central orientation is the Native North American peoples of the 1980s and 1990s: their world, their problems, their heritage and history. Some of the many innovative and practical headings are:

POLITICAL ORGANIZATION (meaning Native associations); PROTEST; BORDER CROSSING; CONSTITUTIONAL STATUS; INMATES; LIFE SKILLS; METIS; TERMINATION; TREATIES (between Native people and other governments); and URBANIZATION. Others are: ABORIGINAL RIGHTS; BAND TRAINING (meaning training of Indian band members); HISTORY (sub-headings are the names of many tribes and bands. Here the sub-headings "INTERNATIONAL" and "PROVINCES" refer to the history of non-Native entities); LAND CLAIMS; LOCAL GOVERNMENT (meaning band government); BUSINESS; CONFERENCES.

In the classification schedule itself, the major category Social Development is illustrative:

```
P—SOCIAL DEVELOPMENT
00—GENERAL
10—(unassigned: formerly economic resources - see S)
20—ECONOMIC CONDITIONS
21—EMPLOYMENT AND UNEMPLOYMENT
30—SOCIAL CONDITIONS
31—SOCIAL CONDITIONS OF CHILDREN AND YOUTH
32—SOCIAL CONDITIONS OF WOMEN
33—SOCIAL CONDITIONS OF MEN
40—CULTURAL IDENTITY (including assimilation)
41—CULTURAL ATTITUDES (including prejudice)
42—INTEGRATION AND SEGREGATION
43—INTERRELATIONS WITH OTHER GROUPS
```

All subjects have, first and foremost, a natural ethnocentric orientation, i.e. a Native focus. Also, the subdivisions appear to be specifically on Native aspects of a subject. Thus, in the Library Basic List the subject ENVIRONMENT AND NATURAL RESOURCES has the parenthetical clarification "(Mackenzie, James Bay, Hunting and Fishing, Energy, Alaska Native Review Commission," and the sub-subjects under LITERATURE include twelve Native groups like Cree and Haida, along with Juvenile and United States. In sum, one has the impression the collection is organized to be optimally useful for Native Studies and Native students and researchers.

As for the subject headings used, the matter is made much simpler with a wholly new, Native-focused classification. But then we must look at subject headings in non-Native public and academic libraries, where many Native students and future leaders and educators pursue their education. Some non-Native libraries are concerned about the many inappropriate, misleading, prejudicial or just plain inaccurate subject headings still being used, for the sake of "standardization" alone. A human catalyst in this area of needed housecleaning has been Sanford Berman, Head Cataloger of the Hennepin County Library in Minnetonka, Minnesota, whose widely distributed *Cataloging Bulletin* and many published articles provide an ongoing dialogue regarding the improvement of subject headings generally in libraries, including those to do with Native peoples, or "Indians of North America."

Native library classification is "one of the high priorities of the (Canadian Library Association) Interest Group on Native Library Development," according to one of its members, who adds:

> I believe that a student familiar with Native classification schemes would not have any more difficulty than you or I did, in deciphering the complex and sometimes confusing, though also orderly, LCC and DDC systems so widely in use elsewhere. And who knows, perhaps something new and beneficial will be learned from the Native schemes which are so useable. Something of value for the library community in this day of complexity of information systems and information needs. . . .[38]

In fact, one hears from various sources of local adjustments to the predominant policy that would standardize and homogenize library classification. One example is found on p. 278 of *The American Indian Reader— Education,* produced by the Indian Historian Press (cited herein). The Indian Historical Society's library first considered using the Library of Congress E, F and G classifications as the basis for its library, but decided to discard them. Instead, it has designed its own system, which is both simpler and comprehensive. It resembles the LC system, in its use of both letters and numbers, as well as decimals and whole numbers, but is simpler, and oriented to the Native community's major subject areas of interest. The library receives cards from the Library of Congress, but without the LC call number in the corner. Here is featured the library's own classification number, with the LC number just beneath. There are six major subject classifications: 100-History and Anthropology, 200-The Arts, 300-Education, 400-Law, 500-Reports, and 600-Fiction. Within each of these areas, the materials are arranged by author, using an initial letter that indicates the first letter of the author's surname. The card catalog is arranged alphabetically, but by author, title and tribe. Another example is the library at Inuit Tapirisat of Canada in Ottawa, which also planned to use a special Native classification system following a reorganization of the library.

> The Task Force on Library Services to Native People was established through the lobbying efforts of people concerned by the lack of recognition on the part of the mainstream library profession toward the problems faced by Native people in conjunction with libraries.[39]

This group of Canadians, formed in 1985 of concerned librarians and Native representatives, issued its report in October, 1986. We should note again that here is yet another example of a badly needed and long overdue initiative in the library field which has come from working librarians and representatives of a neglected client group—not from the library establishment, which includes faculty/researchers comfortably ensconsed in library education.

The report consists of three series of recommendations, offered respectively to the Canadian Library Association Board and/or Council, to a new task force on library service to Native people, and to the Interest Group on Library and Information Services to Native People. There are eight main areas that the twenty recommendations address:

1. Creation of a new task force to work on implementing the recommendations.
2. Creation of a single, standardized Native library classification scheme.
3. "Training packages" (distance learning and on-the-job training), which also includes pressuring library education generally to increase the Native librarianship component, and increasing Native scholarships.
4. Access to information: promote and explain library services and their potential to Native communities; include Native press in CLA press releases; have extra career days in Native schools; prepare profiles of library careers for the Office of Native Employment; and include Natives in CLA group publicity pictures.
5. CLA lobbying campaign: conduct a survey to find out current status of library services in Native communities; work to get a person of Native ancestry appointed to the National Library Advisory Board; "advise library-oriented policy-makers through consultation with local Native organizations to include Native people on their committees and task forces when they develop library standards"; find out the numbers of enrolled Native library students and the number of graduates.
6. Collections: make a comprehensive survey to obtain a single inventory of Native collections nationwide.
7. Funding of Libraries: work with government at all levels toward the designation of specific amounts of money for Native libraries.
8. A National Native Library Conference. (As of 1995, this had not taken place.)

Progress in the development of Native library services in Canada has accelerated steadily since about 1980. Some of the underlying and contributing reasons for this—impelling Native communities and concerned librarians to take a continuing series of initiatives—are the growing attention to Canada's northern rural and remote areas, not only in terms of resource development and settlement but simply to establish clear authority and control over its arctic borders. In the process, Native communities have asserted their own claims to land and self-determination. These and other factors have directly affected the direction and degree of Native library development, as well as related subjects such as: literacy in Native orthographies; Native language equality in society and public affairs; documentation of Native heritage, history and community life; support for the production of Native literature and audiovisual media, and the all-important Native-controlled radio/television production and broadcast capability. It has also been said that, in a natural and wise paradox, Canada has lately become more united while in the process of recognizing and celebrating its multicultural heritage—and her Original Peoples are hopefully on the road to full partnership in the nation's future progress.

II: Greenland

Greenland is an enormous island in the North Atlantic, the largest island in the world. A vast ice cap occupies the whole body of it, leaving only a fringe of coastal islands, headlands, seaward valleys and fjords, estuaries of the sea that create a deeply scalloped effect on the map. Greenland stretches from north to south, from 83 to about 60 degrees north latitude. Most of this island continent is north of the Arctic Circle. The ice cap is 2500 kilometers long and up to 1000 kilometers wide. At points along the center it is three kilometers thick. Greenland is located just a little over 160 kilometers across Davis Strait from Baffin Island, and Canada's High Arctic islands parallel the Greenland land mass until they almost meet at Ellesmere island and Greenland's northwesternmost coast. Iceland is the closest eastern neighbor, a relatively small island nation about 160 kilometers off the southeast coast. To the north of Iceland there are only arctic waters, constantly carrying icebergs southward, which then drift around the southernmost point of Greenland, Cape Farewell, up the west coast and later becoming hazards in the main North Atlantic shipping lanes.

Greenland or, in Greenlandic, Kalaallit Nunaat, is generally divided into three zones: western Greenland, where 90% of the 53,000 population now lives; sparsely settled eastern Greenland along the east coast; and the Polar Northwest, next to Canada's Ellsemere Island, where a few Polar Eskimo hunters live and the Thule airbase is located. "Western Greenland" is more accurately the subarctic southwest coast, which has the mildest climate and the most lands bare of permanent ice. In this area, a maritime economy is supplemented by caribou hunting and sheep farming. Districts to the north and on the east are mainly for hunting economies.

In several respects Greenland's history and blend of cultural heritage comprise a special case. In order to understand the situation and resources that Greenland librarians work with, we will review these in some detail.

Greenland's Native or Inuit heritage goes back to antiquity, when waves of Eskimos of several different cultures migrated east from Canada, one after another over thousands of years. Peoples of the Dorset culture settled along the habitable shores of Greenland from about 550 BC to 995 AD. Then a new migration, Eskimos of the Thule culture (pronounced TOO-lee), made first contact with Greenland Eskimos in the northwest, and at about the same time Eric the Red and fourteen surviving ships out of twenty-five filled with Norsemen from Iceland arrived in southwest Greenland (985 AD).

Some pockets from the last migration of Eskimos of the Thule culture remained out of contact with foreigners until the early 19th century, on the northern east coast and extreme northwest coast, the latter being the northernmost human population in the world. What the Norse found on the southwest coast were ruins and relics left by ancient Eskimos. There are also accounts in early Icelandic histories and Eskimo legends of encounters between the Norsemen and either the Dorset or Thule Eskimos. Several sagas written much later also give accounts of Norse/Eskimo mixing and conflict, which are supported by archeological and anthropological evidence.

In the 13th century Norway claimed Greenland, and a century later Norway joined with Denmark. It was during this time that the sagas were recorded. Then, when this union was ended in 1814, Denmark retained Greenland along with other colonial territories, and this tie has remained to the present day, making for much stability and continuity in Greenland's development. So one can say that there is a joint Inuit/Norse heritage going back a thousand years in Greenland, which is a unique and extraordinary situation from our point of view. Yet Greenland is considered a Fourth World nation, due to the ultimate authority of the Danish government and its support, and the predominance of Danish language and culture, albeit alongside the Greenlandic language and culture. The Eskimo legends referred to, by the way, were in the oral tradition and were systematically recorded until the nineteenth century.

The Norse, who occupied Greenland until possibly 1400, according to carbon-dating of remains found recently, also extended their travels to North America. As to why they disappeared from Greenland, there are various theories, the most scientifically plausible being that a climatic change weakened Norse husbandries (perhaps also making them more vulnerable to inroads by northern Eskimos), and they either died off or returned to Iceland or Norway, or emigrated and went on to North America, where archeological remains of settlements have been found on Baffin Island and Labrador. But the lore among Greenlanders favors more dramatic ends for the Norse (being wiped out in warfare, etc.), and it is from these that some Greenlandic literature has been drawn.

From 1400 on, Denmark-Norway and later the Dutch had whaling operations off western Greenland, and the Dutch even established trading with the Inuit residents, bringing in tuberculosis, liquor and sexual promiscuity, along with more pedestrian wares. Finally, in 1721, Denmark-Norway permitted a limited mission and whaling/trading station to be established where Godthab/Nuuk (the Danish/Greenlandic name, respectively) is today—the capital, administrative center and largest town. However, within several years it failed and withdrew. But the seeds of missionary work, trading and settlement were sown. Over the following sixty years or so other similar enterprises were commissioned and subsidized. Anthropological and ethnographic evidence was gathered during this time by the execrable practice of abducting Eskimos and learning from them. A German Moravian mission was permitted entry in 1733. Both this and the Danish missions grew in the coming decades. In 1774 the Royal Greenland Trading Department was established, and from this point a benevolent Danish trading policy toward the Inuit prevailed, the goal being to maintain the Inuit hunting economies in order to sustain the production of skins, blubber and whalebone.

In 1782 two Inspectorates were established, a Northern and Southern, still confined to the west coast. Government regulations set down by the Royal Inspectors actually protected the Inuit in their traditional ways and stabilized community life, the goal being, again, to maintain the harvest of marine mammals. The severest punishments and penalties were reserved for those unscrupulous non-Inuit traders who might take advantage of or abuse the Native people. This policy of Danish authority "protecting" the traditional Native ways, obviously for their own self-interest, has continued up until very recently, and some would say that this bias continues, but in less obvious ways. Intermarriage, forbidden in 1782, did not become more common until the mid-nineteenth century, creating a class of mixed-race Greenlanders, the underlying population group that eventually dominated western Greenland.

From the late 18th century various expeditions by Danish and English explorers started mapping and exploring Greenland. In 1789 the total population was just over 5,000. By the mid-19th century the Lutheran creed was predominant and literacy was almost universal. An orthography was created early for Greenland Eskimos, and translations were being made for the Bible, catechisms, and hymns. The first Greenlandic grammar was produced in 1760 and the first dictionary, in 1750, both by Poul Egede. Missionaries came to dominate Greenland literary efforts until well into the 19th century. In 1830 a couple of crates of books were brought into Greenland by a Danish professor by way of starting some kind of library service. This "Collection of Loan Books for Southern Greenland" ultimately became the beginnings of the present National Library. In 1835 an investigatory commission had a liberalizing effect, bringing training in the trade monopoly to some Greenlanders, with profits to be invested in Greenland. The year 1845 saw two teacher training colleges established, but due to a lack of students only one continued.

The "Collection of Loan Books for Southern Greenland," mostly books in Danish, German and English, may well have been the source of articles and translations that appeared in early issues of the first newspaper, *Atuagagdliutit,* which began publication in 1861, in Greenlandic. It was set, edited and printed by Greenlanders from the beginning, and for its first 90 years (until 1952, when it became bilingual in both Greenlandic and Danish) it was written only in Greenlandic, with illustrations made by woodcuts and lithography. By the mid-19th century both the Moravian and Royal Danish missions had schools that taught reading and writing, as well as the catechisms then in use.

Late in the 19th century the U.S. took an interest in Greenland, and several expeditions took part in explorations. By 1905 the population had doubled to 10,000. Robert Peary utilized Polar Eskimos for his expeditions to the North Pole from 1891 to 1909, and in 1910 Knud Rasmussen founded his famous Thule trading station, where the author-to-be Peter Freuchen minded the store.

From 1900 the Danish government took a direct interest in Greenland affairs. This was also the year the Moravian mission withdrew from Greenland. In 1907 a large training college was built. Governing legislation originating from consultation with Natives as well as resident Danes was introduced for the first time in 1862, following the creation, by Hinrich J. Rink in 1862, of *forstanderskaberne* (Boards of Guardians; at first one for all Greenland, later two for North and South). The trading monopoly with Denmark was reinforced still more. In the 1920s Greenlanders participated for the first time in an administrative commission. At the same time the State Inspection of Public Libraries began, and libraries were started in several outlying communities. In 1925 an administrative law was instituted that established local governmental structure and compulsory schooling, as well as providing for other education, health care and law enforcement. Boys were given the chance to attend high school in preparation for university studies in Denmark. Cod fishing was organized more systematically. Motorized boats, coastal ships and the first planes were to be seen, but dog teams were still common for winter travel, as elsewhere across the north. (Snowmobiles didn't start coming into common use until the 1960s.)

In 1926 Radio Greenland, or Kalaallit-Nunaata, was established, in the first instance by an individual radio enthusiast the year before. (Later, in 1965, another individual started Greenland television in much the same way.) From the beginning it emphasized Greenlandic programming, which today is 80% of Radio Greenland's fare. Thus it helped to preserve the language and further the concept of a united Greenland. Radio Greenland is administered by an independent board and the staff is almost entirely Greenlanders.

World War II isolated Greenland from Denmark and the world, and thus it was given its first experience of de facto self-government. American air bases were built on the island, introducing still more disruptive foreign influence. Library development in the settlements was suspended during this period. Greenlandic book production in the years just before the war, by the way, had been meager indeed—five or six titles a year. In 1945 Greenland was a second-class colony, with low standards in almost every aspect of infrastructural capability. For those born in Greenland, the life expectancy of men was an appalling 32.2, for women not much better: 37.5. But demands for equal rights and equal treatment as a Danish territory did not convey hostility toward Denmark. After the war a new Prime Minister visited Greenland, and a Greenland Commission was set up to study the situation and make recommendations.

In 1953 the new Danish constitution granted much more independence to Greenland. The population rose sharply, more Danes came, and from 1950 to 1970 the Danish budget for Greenland rose 400%, including inflation. The defense treaty with the U.S. was renegotiated, turning over a few airbases to Greenland. The newly constructed Distant Early Warning (DEW) Line of radar stations across the North American arctic had made these bases less important to the "Cold War" (over 40 years of international tension with open hostilities) with the USSR. Yet the greatly increased fiscal and economic investment by Denmark resulted in a flood of Danes arriving to take up the many new jobs thus created—and to be paid more for the same work. Alcohol use markedly increased, as did suicides, and the incidence of venereal diseases was 100 times that of Denmark. Yet there were benefits: health and medical services greatly improved.

But in the post-war period "normalization," or equality with Denmark, was the goal, at least initially. So "Danification" became the byword, and the cultural changes accelerated. Family planning was introduced, and the extended family gave way more and more to the nuclear family household. Further economic development and job opportunities helped to increase illegitimate births because of the lessening of parental authority. Sedentarization, or the population shift to larger settlements, increased, causing further social stress. There were now drastically fewer Greenlandic teachers in the schools, going from 85% in 1950, right after the war, to 29% in 1970. Yet, as in the past, there were developments that reinforced movement toward a national political consciousness. Greenlandic remained the "appropriate principal language." Radio Greenland continued in operation as always, the autonomous voice of Kalaalit Nunaat. Political parties emerged for the first time.

In 1956 a scientific book collection (called Groenlandica) was established as a small branch of the Central Library of Greenland—in the administrative center and largest town of Godthab/Nuuk. This was also the year when the first professional librarian (Danish) was hired, and these policies were instituted: Danish-language stock top priority; Danish-language children's libraries backed up the schools; and Greenlandic readers were provided with whatever books were available. Through the late 1950s about 100 outlying settlements established libraries, but there was almost no training available. Usually settlement librarians were local school teachers, who worked part-time. In 1968 the Central Library had a total fire, but this resulted, after some delays, in a much larger library facility being commissioned on September 24, 1976. From 1956 to 1975 there were 15–20 titles in Greenlandic published per year. People read such books over and over again, for lack of sufficient new titles. Until the late 1970s, library education was only available in Denmark's four-year school and no Greenlanders had ever completed this training. Then in 1975 an instructor-librarian was hired at the Central Library in Godthab/Nuuk.

At this time the Central Library had 24,000 volumes, with multiple copies of many titles. The Danish cataloging rules, which are a modified version of the Anglo-American Cataloging Rules, were used. Classification followed that used by Danish public libraries. In building the collection, selection emphasized the humanistic aspects of the Arctic, materials on other Inuit peoples, geographical descriptions and ecological conditions. In 1976 there were 8-1/2 full-time equivalent librarians working at the Central Library, including one who served hospitals only. Over the first 150 years of the Central Library's history (1830–1980), a wide variety of materials was acquired: early accounts of settlement life, Danish songs and Greenlandic adaptations of them, novels, collections of short stories and myths, plays, several sagas based on legends, biographies, historical accounts describing life in Greenland long ago, and novels with a science fiction twist, describing various visions of a future Greenland. There is also a strong poetry tradition, allied with poems put to song. In addition, theatre has been popular at times, as in the 1920s and 1930s. Some plays for radio have been produced. Finally, much foreign literature has been translated into Greenlandic. But despite all these efforts toward building a Greenlandic literary tradition, the volume of titles in Danish, especially in the category of new titles, predominates. A collection of films and slides was started. There are still important Greenland materials being held by the Danish Royal Library and many other Danish repositories.

Finally, Home Rule was granted by the Danish Parliament on May 1, 1979. The transfer of self-government to Greenland took place from 1979 to 1984, the only functions remaining for Denmark being foreign relations, defense policy, the financial system, the monarchy, and the administration of justice. The act states that "Danish must be thoroughly taught. Either language may be used for official purposes." By 1994 the percentage of Greenlandic school teachers had risen to 70 percent, and by 1990 the longevity of Greenlanders had risen to 60.7 percent for men and 68.41 percent for women. On January 1, 1980, education, Greenland radio/television and the library service were placed under Home Rule. The new organization of Greenland libraries changed from one in which a central library directly and comprehensively served many settlement libraries, to one where each of seventeen Municipal Councils, whose constituencies ranged from 500 to 4000, administered its own library through a Culture and Education Committee, with daily operations managed by the area Chief Inspector of Schools. Again, part-time untrained librarians, usually teachers, staffed these libraries. At first there was concern that this might work to the detriment of library provision across Greenland, but experience hasn't borne this out.

By 1980 most of the books being produced by Greenlandic authors were being published in Greenlandic, rather than Danish, and many of these were children's books. Whereas a very high percentage of Greenlandic books in the past had been translations from Danish authors, the proportion originally written in Greenlandic began edging upwards. As for library use, it was the children who were comfortable in them, because of their exposure to school libraries. Older adults, in contrast, weren't used to them, sometimes regarding books and libraries with a certain awe or reverence. And they probably only read Greenlandic. But library use steadily increased, even though in the Godthab/Nuuk library, for example, Danish borrowers still predominated. In 1995 this is no longer the case, though Danish librarians can be found in the local town libraries of Sismiut, Qaqortoq and Aasiaat, and in four libraries in Nuuk (other than the Central Library). Overall, however, the atmosphere and image of libraries has changed, and now one can see many Greenlanders frequenting libraries on a regular basis.

In 1980 there were, in addition to the Central Library in Godthab/ Nuuk, 107 libraries: 19 city libraries, 31 children's and school libraries, and 57 settlement libraries. The number of Greenlandic titles was so few—40 to 50 per year at this time—that they all went to libraries, which could purchase books in Danish on their own. Approximately 12 books per capita were being borrowed. Research classes from the university used the Groenlandica Collection, and library research techniques were taught. Greenland and related arctic resources in Denmark are found in the Royal Library, the State Library at Arhus, the Arctic Institute, the Institute of Eskimology, the Navy Library, the Geological Survey of Greenland Library and the Ethnographic Collection of the National Museum, the latter having already transferred some rare Greenlandiana back to the National Museum in Nuuk.

Training has been a chronic problem due to the isolation and part-time nature of work in settlements and the high turnover of Danish-born library workers, all of which rings a familiar-sounding bell across the Fourth World of the north. Training is given to about ten individual settlement librarians each year, emphasizing book selection. Annual group training in book selection is held for the northern and southern settlements. There are local Book Selection Committees. Danish titles are publicized in weekly circulars sent out by the Central Library, while Greenlandic titles are publicized in monthly letters.

There continues to be a shortage of Greenlandic titles. A new orthography was introduced in 1973, but is not popular with older readers. Regional libraries receive block grants for libraries in their area, and the Central Library's budget for supplementing regional library materials as been increased substantially, half being available for materials in Greenlandic. To get an idea of the difference in availability, consider that there is a total of about 500 Greenlandic titles available, many of them for children, while about 10,000 titles in Danish are available. However, Greenlandic titles are distributed free by the Central Library, which buys the books, while Danish titles must be purchased by individual libraries. Greenlandic titles translated into Danish naturally have a wider readership than the reverse translations, being accessible to the Danish reading population.

The population of Greenland is now 55,000 (1994). There are about 42,000 Greenlandic speakers, with various dialects. A Greenlander is a person born in Greenland (usually to Native Inuit parents) and who speaks Greenlandic. Though Danish is the language of administration and justice, Greenlandic remains the main language of the population. Among other languages taught or spoken is English. At times the author had difficulty learning of developments in Greenland libraries, because most library literature is available only in Danish. This doesn't mean that library literature is not available in Greenlandic. The translation services I had available included the Nordic languages, but not Greenlandic! Other vexing considerations for Greenland librarians may be the priority given domestic versus foreign requests, academic versus public library needs, dealing with sources using various languages, expenses of multilingual publishing, and the fact that Greenland still doesn't have a national library per se: the Central Library in Nuuk serves as one. Very few Greenlandic materials have been translated into more languages, and if this happens, it is a major event (as it would be for any author). However, in the 1990s, books with trilingual texts are being published (Greenlandic, Danish, English). There is one full-time publisher, Atuakkiorfik, and a few smaller ones. Some families are split-lingual, in various combinations, and a few Greenlandic authors write in Danish, then translate their own work into Greenlandic.

Godthab/Nuuk today is a city of 12,000—a sprawling metropolis by northern standards. Eighty percent of the people are Inuit. There is a Scandinavian look to the city, and another contrast one notes is the large Native middle-class population. The biggest health problem, as elsewhere in the north, is alcohol abuse and its anti-social side effects. The suicide rate is also high, one of the concomitant effects of continuous and unrelenting social transformation. Coupled with the overpowering American influence on the culture is the predominantly Danish influence in libraries.

One interesting institution joins with other pan-Inuit educational and cultural efforts: Ilisimatusarfik University, whose counterparts are the Inuit Cultural Institute at Eskimo Point in the Northwest Territories and the now defunct Inupiat University of the North at Barrow, Alaska. The Institute of Eskimology at the University of Copenhagen is also an important contributor, as well as the Eben Hobsen Chair of Arctic Policy at McGill University in Montreal, established by the North Slope Borough of Alaska through a $500,000 endowment. In honor of an Inuk man who was prominent on Alaska's political scene, notably in the struggle that resulted in the Alaska Native Claims Settlement Act, and the founder of the Inuit Circumpolar Conference, the Eben Hobsen Chair "will focus on Arctic policy concerns as defined by the Inuit Circumpolar Conference and the North Slope Borough." The purpose of these Inuit-oriented institutions is to promote research on Inuit terms, as to direction, subject, dissemination of knowledge and use—not in the relatively disassociated manner in which outside research is usually done. So here one finds the kind of Native academic effort the Yupik educator and politician Tony Vaska was referring to in 1978 at the Northern Libraries Colloquy (now the Polar Libraries Colloquy) in Paris. (See footnote 5 for Chapter 7.)

The work of the Ilisimatusarfik in Nuuk includes research into the Greenlandic language and culture, combining knowledge about hunting and settlement life with archeological knowledge and language research, the study of present-day political relationships, and an exhaustive Greenlandic dictionary project inherited from the Institute of Eskimology in Copenhagen. (In 1995 we learn that this last project was never finished, and work on it has ceased.) The academic level is to be at the highest Danish university level, with small classes and a favorable faculty-student ratio. At first, Danish university methods of pedagogy will be followed, with a faculty half-Greenlandic, half-Danish. The living society will be both the source of projects and problems to address, and the recipient of its produced work. It is planned to exchange students and faculty with other such Inuit institutes.

When Home Rule started in 1980, the 17 *kommune* or county libraries became independent systems with their own headquarters and branch libraries. The Central Library performs some centralized functions, namely through consultancy and technical assistance. It also coordinates acquisitions and bindery functions. As mentioned above, notices of new Danish titles are sent out, and Greenlandic titles are distributed free of charge. The Central Library also organizes periodic training courses, which are held not only in Nuuk but in rural centers too. The nature of the training becomes more technical and advanced as one goes up in the library systems. Central county libraries often have part-time librarians. Due to the very young Greenland population, half of which is under 25, and the constant change it is experiencing, the demand for decentralized educational offerings is increasing. And the demand for library services is equally strong. Vocational training for some community librarians has been initiated since 1987.

In mid-1988 we received an update on the library situation in Greenland by way of replies to a number of questions that were submitted. Henriette

Aabo Hansen, then of the Nunatta Atuagaateqarfia (Greenland Central Library), provided the following information:

The annual publication rate in Greenland, as listed in the latest Greenlandic Book List, now totals about 85 titles. I believe this is a list of books that are by Greenlanders or about Greenland, that are published in Greenland or Denmark. Fifty of these were non-fiction, and thirty-five were in language and literature. Of the latter, six were about the Greenlandic language, and seventeen were "Greenlandic literature." it is not known whether authors were Danish or Greenlander, but almost all the titles appeared to be in Greenlandic. Two were translations of Danish works and one was a title in English, apparently copyrighted 1929, entitled *Skinboats of Greenland,* part of a series entitled "Ships and Boats of the North." The series is produced by the National Museums of Greenland and Denmark, in cooperation with The Viking Ship Museum of Roskilde.

Professional librarians in Greenland must complete a two-year period of study at the Ilisimatusarfik University, two years of courses at the Danish Library School in Copenhagen, and internships at various libraries in Denmark and at the Nunatta Atuagaateqarfia. At this time (1995) the Head and Vice-Head librarians of Greenland, as well as the librarian of the Groenlandica Collection, are Greenlander women professionals. More Greenlanders are studying at home to be librarians.

The Central Library's budget was reduced by four per cent since 1987. The block grants, which are distributed to both regional libraries and settlement libraries, vary in amount from kommune to kommune. Some microfilming is underway of Greenland literary and archival treasures in Denmark. Greenland now has its own National Archives, "Nunatta Allagaateqarfia." It is in the Central Library. The National Museum of Greenland, the Nunatta Katersugaasivia, also holds pictures and paintings.

Most settlement libraries are located in the local school and are closed during school holidays. Most of them have card catalogs. Some maintain a shelflist, or in any case the regional library does. New books are delivered shelfready from the "Copenhagen-situated filial of the Nunatta Atuagaateqarfia." Volunteers are not used in libraries, or rarely.

The Groenlandica Collections of the N.A. issued a computerized bookcatalog at the end of 1987. Plans were to update it late in 1988, when new computer hardware was to be installed. The Groenlandica Collection Database was expected to be accessible via Internet sometime in 1996. The classification system used is an "expanded version of the Danish DDC." The expansion is in classes "regarding Greenlandic issues," and there are no special subject headings for Greenland, except of course that the Greenlandic language is used alongside Danish. There are no plans for a special classification system for Greenland libraries. "Films and videos are collected by the Groenlandica Collection, but [are] not for lending. Later on the public library section might go into lending out videotapes."

Notes

1. Raycroft, Lois. "The Yukon Indian Resource Center," *Proceedings,* 8th Northern Libraries Colloquy, Edmonton and Whitehorse, June 1–6, 1980, p. 190.
2. Population figures in this section are taken from "9, Resources for Native Peoples Studies," by Nora T. Corley, *Research Collections in Canadian Libraries.* (In Bibliography and Reference List see under: Canada. National Library. Resources Survey Division. Collection Development Branch.)
3. Yukon Education. Libraries and Archives Board. *Annual Report 1985/86,* p. 2
4. Personal communication, Yukon Libraries and Services Branch. February 3, 1987.
5. From job description of Native Programs Coordinator.
6. "Agreement reached in Yukon Territory Indian land claims," *Tundra Drums* (Bethel, AK), 11-17-88, p. 26. "It involves more than $215 million in federal compensation plus 16,600 square miles of land, less than 10% of the territory. The Yukon's 6500 Natives comprise a quarter of the territory's population." Formal approval by both levels of government and the 13 Yukon Indian bands was still required. (On oversight of ongoing land claims negotiations, the Yukon Native Language Center, and the Aboriginal Language Service of the Yukon Government, see, for example, Hope in Bibliography/Reference List II.)
7. Information in the following paragraphs is drawn from pp. 669–671 of *Arctic,* Vol. 5 of the *Handbook of North American Indians.* Smithsonian Institution, 1984.
8. The standoff or siege atmosphere is everywhere prevalent: ". . . the current conflict mirrors decades-old differences concerning the north. The Indian seeks to regain the cultural benefits of a harvesting lifestyle, while the Euro-Canadians . . . , a group dominated by an extractive, development mentality that deems the land a commodity, not a way of life . . . , continue to search for means of developing the mineral potential of the northern lands. Though recent indications suggest a settlement of the land claims dispute at hand, the history of the Yukon suggests that Native-White relations in the territory will not be easily altered through signatures on a government sponsored document." *Best Left as Indians,* by K. S. Coates, pp. 333–334.
9. Reported in *Snowshoe,* the Newsletter of the NWT Library Association, Vol. 3, Nos. 1–2, p. 6.
10. For a discussion of the benefits of regionalization, see "Territorial Bureaucracy: Trends in Public Administration in the NWT," *Canadian Public Administration/Administration publique du Canada,* Vol. 27, No. 2 (Summer/été, 1984), pp. 242–252.

11. In 1988, on the occasion of the 20th anniversary of NWT public library services, an automated library catalog system was inaugurated. It also includes circulation and acquisitions modules, and combines a terminal plus compact disc memory that holds over five million titles. The system has multilingual capabilities and is expandable to include additional databases. Following that, a NWT government communication network will become accessible online by most NWTPLS regional libraries. The extraordinary advantages and power this gives territorial libraries can only be compared to the arrival of satellite television in the north.

12. Adamson, Edith. "Public Library Services to the Indians of Canada," *Canadian Library Journal,* Vol. 26, No. 1 (January–February, 1969), p. 49.

13. *Ibid.,* p. 49.

14. *Ibid.,* p. 53.

15. "Indian Information Centre Proposal." Dr. Blue, Althouse College, University of Western Ontario, London.

16. Adamson, *op. cit.,* p. 53.

17. "Problems Affecting Band Library Development in Northern Ontario," A Brief to the Minister of Culture and Recreation, etc. Nov., 1977.

18. Carlson, Judith Ann. "Library Services for the Native Peoples of North America: An Examination of Existing Services in Ontario and Recommendations for their Improvement." Ryerson Polytechnical Institute, Toronto, March 27, 1980.

19. *Report* to the "Ontario Public Library Review on Native Library Services in Ontario," Prepared by the Obonsawin-Irwin Consulting, Inc. under the direction of the Task Group on Native Library Services. Convenor—Earl Commanda. November, 1981.

20. "Ontario Public Libraries: the Provincial Role in a Triad of Responsibilities," the Report of the Ontario Public Libraries Programme Review for the Ministry of Citizenship and Culture. August, 1982.

21. Ontario Ministry of Citizenship and Culture, News Release/Communique. February 10, 1984.

22. *Ibid.,* October 15, 1984.

23. Quebec. Secretarist des activités gouvernamentales en milieu amérindien et inuit (SAGMAI). *Native Peoples of Quebec,* 1984. 172pp

24. This quote and the following paragraphs on the historical and developmental background of Quebec are drawn from two articles by Bernard Saladin D'Anglure in *Arctic,* Vol. 5 of *Handbook of North American Indians:* "Inuit of Quebec" and "Contemporary Inuit of Quebec," translated by the General Editor of the Handbook series, William Sturtevant.

25. "Inuit of Quebec," p. 504.

26. Avataq Cultural Institute/Institut Culturel Avataq. *Annual Report/ Rapport annuel, 1985/86.*

27. Personal communication, Yves Bernier, Direction des Nouveau-Quebec et service aux autochtones, Ministère des Affaires culturelles, Gouvernement de Quebec. February 5, 1988.

28. Institut éducatif et culturel Attikamek-Montagnais, Village des Huron, Quebec. *Les bibliothèques publiques en milieu Attikamek-Montagnais: savoir reponde a un besoin manifeste. (Mémoire),* April 8, 1987.

29. Personal communication, Manitoba Public Library Services, February 16, 1987.

30. Personal communication, British Columbia Library Services Branch, January 15, 1987.

31. Murray, John. "Indian Band Libraries in North Central Saskatchewan," Saskatchewan Native Library Services *Newsletter,* Vol. 2 (4), December, 1982.

32. ————.Personal communication, January 18, 1995.

33. Personal communication, Alberta Library Services, April 9, 1987.

34. Personal communication, Dr. Anne Anderson Native Heritage and Cultural Centre, Edmonton. January 18, 1988.

35. No less a non-Native library authority than the U.S. Library of Congress (or rather one division chief, to be precise) supports the principle of "Native-generated classification schemes." ". . . whatever organization of materials works best for a particular group of readers should be used. . ." Personal communication, January 16, 1987.

36. Personal communication, A. Brian Deer, January 22, 1988.

37. The following discussion draws on materials received from the Ojibway-Cree Cultural Centre. A similar scheme is used by the Assembly of First Nations Library in Ontario, and word from Inuit Tapirisat of Canada late in 1988 indicated that they were reorganizing their library using a Native classification scheme.

38. Personal communication, Susan Taylor, Central Filing and Library, Native Council of Canada, February 2, 1987.

39. *Report* of the Task Force on Library Service to Native People, October, 1986, p. 4.

Source Notes on Greenland

The term "Inuit" has become accepted as referring to all polar peoples in the remarkably extensive yet closely related Eskimo-Aleut language family. "Eskimo" acquired the erroneous definition of "raw flesh eaters" and is going out of use, both by Inuit organizations and by governments. Each isolated group had its own name for itself, of course, and these persist in the literature, and are reflected in such terms as Inupiat (Inuit of Northern Alaska),

Yupik (Inuit of southwestern Alaska and the Bering Strait area), Kalaaleq (Inuit of Greenland), etc. (From the *Handbook of North American Indians,* Vol. 5, *Arctic,* the Introduction by David Damas.)

General background on Greenland draws mainly from the following articles in *Arctic,* Vol. 5, of the *Handbook of North American Indians.* Washington, D.C.: Smithsonian Institution, 1984. Other articles in the same volume cover the aboriginal period.

—Kleivan, Inge. "History of Norse Greenland," pp. 549–555.
—Gad, Finn. "History of Colonial Greenland," pp. 556–576.
—Petersen, Robert. "Greenlandic Written Literature," pp. 640–645.
—Kleivan, Helge. Contemporary Greenlanders," pp. 700–717.

Information on Greenland library development and related subjects, in English and Danish, was drawn from the following sources, which are cited fully in the Bibliography/Reference List I in the back of the book: Andersen (1980); Aubert (1973); Dam (1972); Grode i den gronlandske bog-produktion; Gronlands Hjemmestyre (1980); Gronland og Sydslesvig (1980–84); Iversen (1983); Jorgensen (1983)—three articles; Lanken (1986); Lund (1987); Namminersornerullutik oqartussat, etc. (1980); Reymann (1982); Westermann (1975), (1976)—two articles, (1978), (1981); Westermann and Hoyer (1978). The *Groenlandica* catalogue, cited in the Bibliography/Reference List II and edited by Hoyer (1986), would also be very useful, but I was unable to include it because I received it near the end of research and updating efforts.

An entire, expanded issue of *Arctic Anthropology* (Vol. 23, Nos. 1 and 2, 1986; 422 pages) is devoted to Greenland, with articles ranging from archeology to museum laws, development under Danish rule, and Greenlandic home rule. Of special interest are articles on the Greenland Tukaq Theatre, and "Greenlandic Literature: Its Traditions, Changes and Trends," by Christian Berthelsen.

Some incidental information was taken from materials received from the Tourist Association of Godthab, Greenland (Nuuk Turistforening Gronland), as "published by the Danish Tourist Board, in cooperation with the Greenland Home Rule Association, Tusarliivik (Information and Tourism)." Additional details about individual collections and recent policies were taken from handouts made available by the National Library of Greenland. Greatly appreciated was information about Greenland libraries sent by Henriette Aabo Hansen, who is no longer with the Nuuk Central Library. Finally, I am most grateful for the current information, comments, and even sample books published in Greenland sent to me by the research librarian for the Groenlandica collection, Klaus Georg Hansen, research librarian for the Groenlandica collection. I had contacted him by mail following a referral from an American colleague who attended the 1994 Polar Libraries Colloquy in Rovaniemi, Finland (where Hansen presented a paper) and who saw my appeal on the Polar Librarians Forum (POLLIB-L) in the spring of 1995. The wonders of (computer) networking will never cease!

6.

Imperial Russia, Revolutionary Russia, and "Russia Reborn": Will Libraries Benefit Northern Nationalities?

[Inside the helicopter flying over the tundra] the old methodologist of the regional cultural brigade held a well worn rucksack tightly in his arms. Inside was a traveling library—books, brochures, fresh newspapers, audiotapes, and letters from relatives, [things that would] help [the reindeer herders] work much better. —from "A Song Flies over the Tundra" in *Toilers of the North in Life and Literature*

. . . The Leninka [Lenin State Library of Moscow] is probably the only great library in the world with two entire sets of catalogues, each occupying huge rooms; one of them a limited censored catalogue open to general readers, and the other, the full catalogue of the library's holdings, including the secret stacks . . . [early 1980s]. —Hedrick Smith's *The Russians*

It was a daunting prospect, due to the initial difficulties of access to enough information, to try to survey library development in the other half of the circumpolar north, in what was still the Soviet Union in 1985. But because I have Russian language background and had recently found that my translations compared favorably with those of other writers, I decided to go ahead. As pertinent sources were found on library services to the northern peoples, thanks to Lenin State Library (now the Russian State Library) in Moscow, which sent me special bibliographies and photocopied articles over a two-year period, I began learning more about conditions of "life and work" for those indigenous northern populations under Soviet domination.

Historically, Russian expansion across Siberia was completed in the seventeenth century, instituting the control of a remote Czarist authority and its Christianizing partner, the Russian Orthodox Church, which established monasteries and its onion-domed wooden churches. Though Czarist policies were benevolent toward Siberian and Arctic peoples to keep the fur collection high, such policies and decrees from distant Moscow were often subverted or ignored in the hinterlands. Provincial governors and their military garrisons ruled with quasi-autonomous authority and purveyed a tribute-driven trading economy, often just as capricious and corrupt in their relations with the motley Russian immigrant and exile populations as with the indigenous peoples. Subjugated and exploited for their fur-tribute (*yasak*) and labor, the Native population across the vast tundra and taiga of Siberia and beyond struggled to adapt and survive under the despotism and anarchy of the Russian frontiersmen; some remained defiant until the Bolshevik Revolution and the Civil War that followed.

In Czarist Russia as a whole the masses of peasantry and other lower classes were illiterate. Education was entrusted to church mission schools and was supplemented by a very select "library" situation, accessible only to a small fraction of Russian society: clerics, the intellectual elite, educated higher officials, and the landed and titled nobility of European Russia. At various times beginning under Peter the Great these privileged classes indulged in German, French, and English culture, as these influences reached into Russia or were brought there. Russian nobility sojourned in the West for education, training, and travel, acquiring whichever languages, literatures, clothes, and customs were in favor, often in dilettante fashion. In the nineteenth century Russian interest in Siberia and the Far East increased as border disputes with China in the Amur Region were settled.

The earliest libraries across the north of Imperial Russia were established by the Russian Orthodox Church and its missionaries, but these were exclusively religious in nature and had very limited use by anyone else, let alone that mostly illiterate portion of the local population being prosyletized by the church. Literacy was almost nil among the old Russian population, and nonexistent among the mostly nomadic Native peoples. Some early efforts were made by the church to produce Native orthographies, but these were solely for the propagation of the faith. In the decades just before the Revolution the church finally began distributing materials of a more general nature. On the other hand, the modest libraries and acculturating work of Czarist exiles across Siberia, both individually and through underground networks, introduced not only linguistic and cultural literary to local intelligentia, but also the seeds of political and revolutionary consciousness. Such subversive activities helped pave the way for the October Revolution, as well as future library development under Soviet rule. Although many of the exiles' book and pamphlet collections were confiscated, some of them survived to become the nuclei of Soviet northern libraries.

Following the 1917 Revolution, beginning in the 1920s and continuing into the 1930s and after World War II, the Soviet government imposed a whole range of socialist public policies along with ideological indoctrination. But, for a decade after the revolution, there was a period of civil war, with reactionary forces trying to stop the Bolshevik takeover in various parts of the north and Siberia, especially in the Far Eastern regions and in the eastern Archangel region. Foreign troops were involved (French, British, American, and Japanese, primarily), and Native peoples found themselves caught up in these struggles, one side or the other coming in with intimidating forces, conscripting Native fighters, and increasingly destroying Native lifestyle and pursuits. James Forsyth describes the scene after the dust had settled:

> At the end of the 1920s the general form of the USSR had been established in terms of national territories with varying degrees of nominal autonomy under the control of the Russian Communist Party (as it was called until 1925) in Moscow. The Civil War with all its horrors was over, having swept away most of the old social and cultural norms of Russia, but the country's fate was left in the hands of a party dedicated to paper schemes for a totally new society which were based on a combination of humanism in words and ruthlessness in practice, of ostensible rationality and speculative theories, of revolutionary élan and ideological pedestrianism, of conspiratorial cunning and culpable naivete. There was already cause for forboding in the ruling party's reversion to the concept of total economic planning after the respite of the "New Economic Policy" [initially encouraging free enterprise-ghh], its preparation of enforced collectivization of the peasantry, and its organization of a brutal system of terror for the suppression of all opposition by depriving citizens of their freedom, herding them into prisons and concentration camps and breaking them in body and spirit. The Russians of Siberia, in particular the peasants, had experienced these methods of Communist Party rule for a decade, but their bearing upon the indigenous peoples of Siberia had not yet become clear, as it would in the 1930s. (p.282)

A few paragraphs about the geographical and political composition of the Soviet Union until 1991 are in order. The continent-sized Union of Soviet Socialist Republics had a complex and highly centralized administrative structure. Territorially, there were two main subdivisions. One was the Russian Soviet Federated Socialist Republic (RSFSR), now the Russian Federation, which includes the Great Russian homeland in the west plus all of Siberia and the Russian Far East (north of China, Korea, and Japan). It is the northern and easternmost regions of this largest of the former republics with which we are primarily concerned. The rest of the former USSR was comprised of the 14 other republics in the west and south.

The RSFSR comprises about three-quarters of the area of the old USSR and just over half its population. Just after the October Revolution the population across the Russian Arctic was about 700,000. With northern resource development this multiplied to 4 million by 1959, and 9 million by 1980. About 80 percent of the population is Great Russian, and the remaining 20 percent is all other nationalities. Indigenous peoples in all home areas are now a fraction of the total population, with higher percentages in remote districts. Within the RSFSR were 16 of what were then called Autonomous Republics, which are the homelands of populous minority nationalities; 8 Autonomous Oblasts, smaller administrative units, like provinces, centered around a major city, for less populous nationalities; and 10 Autonomous Okrugs, which can be organized around a nationality smaller yet (formerly called "national areas"), or a regional metropolitan or industrial center. With the exception of Yakutiya (now called the Sakha Republic), or the former Yakutsk ASSR, these are the homelands of the "numerically small peoples" of the north. Due to its size and large Yakut population, in many respects Sakha is treated as a special entity unto itself.

Demographically, then, it should be kept in mind that everywhere in the Russian Federation today one will find a pluralistic society. As a rule, in all the areas we will examine, Russians are in the majority and, even in the okrugs named after them, the indigenous peoples are a minority. Further, these Native minorities will usually be found in the "back country," in villages, field collectives, and remote field brigades, rather than in the larger, urbanized villages and towns, although they may keep an apartment there. Except in the heavily industrialized and developed Russian homeland in the west and in certain industrial or regional centers across southern Siberia (on or within reach of the Transiberian Railroad), the population of the Russian Federation is scattered along major rivers and the Arctic and North Pacific coasts. Before 1960, when labor controls were in force, there was a high influx of new workers into Siberian areas of "new construction" (resource and infrastructure development like mines, oil and gas, dams, pipelines, housing, railroads, and cultural institutions); but later the Soviet government found it very difficult to recruit and keep new populations there. Many inducements and special benefits had to be provided.

Some terms need more detailed definition. A *kolkhoz* was the collective agricultural operation we've all heard about, in which the land was owned by the state but was leased permanently to a workers' association. A minimum remuneration for everyone was guaranteed, and profitability varied with the industrial operation. Salaries had a wide range, depending on the responsibilities, qualifications, and Communist Party controls. Some production quotas were required by the state, but the rest could be used or sold locally. Each kolkhoz member could have some livestock and a plot of his or her own, and a kolkhoz could resemble a village with all its amenities, including a library. The enterprises found on a kolkhoz can be of a variety, from row crops or livestock to logging or fur farming, depending on local resources and conditions.

The *sovkhoz,* or state farm, was "established to pioneer new methods and break in new land, besides setting higher standards generally." Sovhoz workers were state employees and were paid more than those in a *kolkhoz*. Following former Soviet Premier Mikhail Gorbachev's democratization, privatization, and new market-oriented economic policies of the late 1980s, radical changes and growing uncertainty began to replace the stability and guaranteed, though low, expectations of Soviet workers.

The *oblast* and the *okrug* are the largest administrative subdivisions in rural and remote areas of indigenous northern peoples. These are subdivided into several *raions*, or small regions, each of which contains a number of districts. A district refers to a localized area that holds a few villages and their outlying settlements. A village, if the center for an agricultural enterprise or industrial operations, is described as a "settlement of the urban type."

If the foregoing seems confusing, Yuri Slezkine uses Russian analogies in explanation. The Soviet Union was like a communal apartment, with Russia as the main hallway and kitchen, the 14 other republics having their own bedrooms. Within each "bedroom" there were other entities, not only geographic, but political and cultural, in terms of the 100-odd "nationalities" ("national" being the adjective). This

> "national demarcation resulted in a puzzling and apparently limitless collection of ethnic nesting dolls. All non-Russians were "nationals" entitled to their own territorial units and all nationally defined groups living in "somebody else's" units were national minorities entitled to their own units. By 1928 various republics contained national okrugs, national raions (small regions), national soviets (councils), Native executive committees, Native soviets, Native village soviets, clan soviets, nomadic soviets and encampment committees."!
> (p.430 of the article in *Slavic Review*)

Finally, under the Soviet government there were various types of economic regions (not to be confused with the aforementioned small administrative region), which may or may not cross the boundaries of major political entities. The smallest of these was the *kray*, the next largest was the Industrial Management Region, and the largest was the Major Economic Region. These became important when library systems within these regions, under the directives of higher library-type institutions (scientific-technical libraries, methodological institutes, etc.) attempted to organize interlibrary cooperation and networks in order to better serve specialists in a variety of settings, some remote, some urban. While this was going on, the economic regions themselves were oscillating between centralization and decentralization management policies.

Universal education for literacy included the creation of Native orthographies and the publication of materials in the Native languages of most of the 100-odd ethnic groups across the entire nation. The first Soviet census in 1926 identified 45 indigenous groups across the Russian north, but the 1929 Committee of the North reduced this to 26. In 1932 the First All-

Russian Conference on the Development of Languages and Writing Systems for Northern Peoples settled on 14 literary languages for which orthographies would be developed. Naturally this resulted in the loss of many dialectal subgroups, most of whom of necessity turned to Russian. But it took a generation for a significant portion of Native peoples to become literate, and then it was in Russian, rather than in Native orthographies, because from the 1950s to the 1970s "Sovietization" (i.e., Russification) was emphasized, Native languages were discouraged, and the population was concentrated in larger, permanent settlements. In rural areas, and especially among remote nomadic peoples, progress in "cultural enlightenment" and Russification was increasing relentlessly. (See Graburn and Iutzi-Mitchell, p.210–211) As elsewhere, due to the emancipating opportunities, these acculturating experiences opened up to both Russian and Native women, women's role in the community and society at large was steadily enhanced. To quote Forsyth: "As a result, by 1931 about one quarter of all deputies of soviets in the autonomous republics of Siberia were women." (p.286) The traditional life and its subsistence economies were collectivized, and Native lives ordered according to resolutions" from Party Congresses in Moscow and following directives from local Soviets with their Communist officialdom of *nomenklatura* (official designees of the Communist Party that occupied key posts at all levels of government).

Purges, ideological campaigns, and dislocations were to forcibly transform the indigenous life and culture. And, libraries and librarians were an integral part of the national system of indoctrination, the manipulation and denial of free information, and the intellectual isolation and stunting of the mind and will of the people, both individually and collectively.

The following series of condensed or paraphrased articles from 1957 through 1990 are a sampling of Soviet library literature concerned chiefly with library services to northern indigenous populations. A Commentary afterward will include other points of view, interpretations, and updating to late 1995.

1957, Likhovid—For a long time "library services" for subsistence peoples were meager and rudimentary. Rural areas were served by mobile "cultural enlightenment" detachments that carried a small quantity of books and other reading materials. In remote areas, transient parties of scientists and specialists might have time to expose inhabitants to literacy and reading through reading-aloud sessions. Later, between 25 and 30 cultural enlightenment centers or kultbazy were established in remote regions across the north. These were of a type never before seen. They combined a boarding school, social club, library, hospital, public baths, an agricultural experiment station, demonstration or model workshops, cooperatives, a radio station, and so on. So the "culture" they brought to the hinterland also included things like "soap and towels!"

To reach the most remote camps and nomadic peoples, "Red Detachments" or "Red Tents" of the most versatile mobility were utilized, employing dog teams in winter and a variety of boats in summer. These small outfits might carry a box or two of books.

Only with sedentarization (making homes in permanent settlements) by subsistence peoples could stationary libraries be considered.

Just before the "Great Patriotic War" (World War II), in which the Soviet people were invaded and lost tens of millions in dead, not to mention many times that in casualties, as well as appalling property losses, each national region had a central library. Development of city, children's and even village libraries were underway. Across the Far North, several hundred government people's libraries (not counting the Red Detachments) were started. Industrial operations that were part of the war effort brought tremendous changes, both material and cultural, to subsistence hunters and herders. After the war, library development gradually increased. Village libraries were established, along with school, departmental and trade union libraries.

One interesting statistic used is "number of readers," which would be roughly comparable to those holding library cards. It is cited along with circulation and size of collections, on an equal basis. In fact, numbers of volumes and numbers of readers are the most prominent statistics. Growth in these has multiplied dramatically, though on a more modest scale as one goes into the most rural areas.

Yet there are criticisms to be made, points out a sub-article entitled "Some Notes." Remote villages are very isolated, which really requires that each one have its own cultural-enlightenment services. These should be combined into one facility. Also, services overall should be more appropriate for the special environmental and economic conditions of the extreme north. And those who staff the club and library at the village level need special training for the same reasons.

Systematic support needs to originate closer to field operations, not from far-off regional or provincial (oblast) libraries. District libraries would be more appropriate. Materials should include information on northern economies, the benefits of Soviet policies, and on northern peoples of other countries. More well-illustrated and large-print books are needed, for those just learning to read. The volume of materials supplied to northern communities also needs to be greatly increased, and materials in Native languages should be sent directly to those areas where Native readers are concentrated. As it is, many publications in Native orthographies never reach Native readers.

1966, Slabin *et al.*—Among librarians, the development of natural resources in northern regions shares equal importance with the maintenance of suitable library services, to serve better not only the indigenous peoples, but the numbers of specialists and workers who take up residence there. Another aspect of this situation is that interest in the north is widespread, all over the nation, so librarians everywhere need to be better informed about developments in the north.

Conditions in northern Siberia are just as difficult as in comparable areas of North America. This impacts the work of a librarian, who must also be familiar with local history and daily life, and make regular reports on conditions to superiors.

A combined club/library can energize the library—and the librarian. Along with supplying outlying seasonal camps, providing children's services, and holding readings-aloud for the poorly literate, the active librarian in this more sociable context becomes an enthusiast and advocate, participating in club activities. On evenings of film showings he can present a talk or book reviews, for example. The librarian can organize thematic evenings where questions of the day can be clarified. On the other hand, practical demonstrations are also in order, such as the proper way to wash clothes or prepare fowl.

One disadvantage of such an arrangement is that individual reader's services tend to be neglected, as the stacks are open for random, casual browsing (self-service). Readers select their reading by chance, and are sometimes discouraged by what they end up with. [It would appear that unfocused serendipity was to be discouraged.]

A librarian needs to know his or her readers. Special groups should be identified and reading programs arranged for them. Women of ethnic minorities especially need help. Unfortunately, this hasn't been done very well. The library can instill good cultural habits in the family, to do with health, child-rearing and alcoholism. Though little literature is available specifically on these subjects, the librarian can take passages from general works and interpret this information.

Children's services have some serious deficiencies. These sections in libraries are often messy, and some materials end up in the adult section. And some librarians don't help teenagers at all. An ignorance of children's literature and lack of liaison with the school may be to blame. It is also unethical when a book clearly intended for older readers ends up in the hands of a youngster. For those who haven't finished their education, including older adults, libraries can help them do that. For example, some adults use children's encyclopedias or need well-illustrated or large-print books.

It isn't enough just to count the people using the library. One has to work with them regularly, to help them understand how to use reference books and cultivate the reading habit. Outside specialists who may be temporarily stationed in the area need to be made welcome.

Subsistence peoples aren't adequately served. Even the traveling Red Tents can't reach everyone. There aren't enough materials on subsistence economies, local history and ethnic heritage, or the peculiarities of local conditions in the north. And these materials are just as important and relevant for professionals working in the area.

Oblast technical service centers are responsible for any inappropriate or unneeded books sent to area libraries serving indigenous peoples. But these shortcomings are aggravated rather than helped when statistics in annual reports available to these centers aren't accurate, and don't say what is really needed. Technical Service Centers usually lack a northern specialist as well, and have no special plan to help remote libraries, nor any technical aids to make available.

The okrug library (serving a nationality) needs a professional materials corner, and a newsletter for giving advice. In the Nentsi (nationality) region this is done, and a couple of seminars a year are offered for librarians. In addition, village libraries keep records, have work plans and produce reports that show both failures and successes.

In one village there is a shelf of books about the local area. The librarian, who has found it more effective to work with small rather than large groups, also gives individual help. Bibliographical reviews are presented, and a display of photos of the best readers has been put up.

The club and the library can get together for some special programs. For example, just before the fishing season started, a program was held that included a colorful display about the local fish processing plant, its history and production goals. Local officials attended and there were games and other activities. The librarian's success in the village depends on knowing the community and getting a lot of volunteer help. The one in this village says he's also taken additional training and now works all year long.

1970, Langenbakh—Librarians have become involved in the phenomenal development that has taken place in the extreme north, as the influx of population, growth of cities and resource development have continued apace. Whole communities have been created which include new libraries. Such a renaissance has taken place among the Khanti and Mansi ethnic groups, for example, which are located in western Siberia along the middle Ob River basin, at the confluence of the Ob and Irtysh rivers.

A generation of local writers has come to the fore, and cultural activities overall have increased. Native librarians have achieved honors while matching the growth of schools, clubs, museums, Houses of People's Creativity and a proliferation of Red Tent units. Reader's advisory services are well established, for both groups and individuals. Supervisory librarians ran programs on themes such as "Every Book Has Its Home," or "Master Your Profession". Librarians naturally have close ties with the community and are very active, some even running for political office.

1971, Ledovskaya—In the Nentsi national area there are ninety libraries: 72 at the village level, seven children's libraries, three zone libraries, three district, four city and one provincial library. (The Nentsi homeland is the arctic coastal area east of the Kola Peninsula, directly opposite the arctic island Novaya Zemlya.) If libraries aren't filling the needs of an area, shifts and changes are made to serve a new population configuration, or a new community. Librarians are trained to be community-oriented and responsive. They organize veterans' evenings, mount displays, conduct informational meetings, and talk with reindeer herders to encourage reading. Here is a list of typical program titles: "Life Moves Along in Lenin's Orbit," "Today on the Tundra," "The Awakening Tundra," "Know and Love Your Land," "Oh North, Oh North—Our Rich Land," "North, North, My Love," "My Land, My Pride," "The Land—Where You Live," "Singers of Our Homeland," "Poetry of the North," "Lenin, The Book and Youth," "Why Do I Strive?" "From Conference to Conference," "The Prosperity of the Soviet People Grows," and so on. Some programs to promote reading amount to an "oral magazine." Recognition is given to those libraries which most actively promote government policies and objectives, or organize public information sessions on materials about party conferences.

In the extreme northern regions, just under half the population uses libraries (including Native peoples). Since most of them are located far from training centers and have few opportunities to take more training, steps are taken whenever possible to improve its availability. Demonstration projects are run, area cultural enlightenment centers are strengthened and regional libraries are used for additional and special training. Over half the library workers in these regions have received extra training.

Evaluations, reviews and advice come down through the library system. One question that arose was the mixing of training and bibliographic responsibilities. Experience has shown that these should be kept separate. In other words there are training cadre who do nothing else. And its not enough to have training originate only from distant, larger libraries. Training materials should be available at the local level as well.

1981, Shakhova *et al.*—In the Soviet Union, library development policies are directly derived from resolutions of the Communist Party Central Committee. For example, the 26th session directed, among other things, that agricultural production undergo continual improvement. The role for librarians was also indicated:

—to help in the fulfillment of plans for socioeconomic growth.
—to encourage socialist competition.
—to disseminate information on the achievements of science, technology and progressive methods.
—to effectively provide scientific-technical information to specialists.
—to render assistance to workers of all types, both in their daily work

and in raising industrial standards generally, allowing for differing educational levels and professional interests.

In the Magadan region, for example, the main agricultural economies are reindeer-herding, dairy husbandry and fur farming. In terms of library work and planning, agricultural collections building and information services to agricultural workers need to be closely monitored for relevance and currency. Reference collections could be more comprehensive, as well as better reflect local information needs. A local librarian should study the goal-oriented profile of the area's economy and culture, and the professional and educational needs of its residents. A card-index of subject requests should be maintained as an aid to collection development.

The typical system is one in which the central library and its branches form a single unified collection, making it possible for branches to request special subject sets, for example, and for village librarians to replenish their collections from a much larger collection base. Another benefit is that collection development takes into account all local needs, and a more efficient and systematic subject-acquisition plan is possible.

Gaps in a collection can be compensated for by using periodicals, which are the most digestible form of information. There is a selection of basic periodicals that the local librarian should have, which reflect the community profile, along with lists of other recommended periodicals. Collection unification also means that periodical subscriptions region-wide should be coordinated, to avoid duplication. To this end the Central Library and its branches should have exact information on who has what periodical and what the holdings are, and should put together a card-index (union list) that people can use. (The 'who' may well have included individuals like teachers and other specialists and their periodical holdings, though I'm not totally certain on this point.)

Various factors go to make up the correct distribution of periodicals among the branches: the number of branches, the profile of readers in the entire system as well as at each branch, and the needs of every group of readers. [So comprehensive is this system that] it takes into account private libraries and individual subscriptions, along with the sufficiency of and support given the agricultural section of a library's collection, and the quality of its newspaper, journal and book holdings overall. Evaluation of the periodical collection locally is used to determine which titles can be dropped, and which are needed. The "Summary Catalog of Periodicals received by Magadan Libraries" can be referred to, along with a retrospective catalog of the libraries' holdings from 1849 to 1972.

The Magadan oblast library sends an annual letter to all libraries in the region each year, giving subscription information and offering recommendations. Periodicals significantly impact library budgets. Recommendations from scientific and technical specialists are most needed, and help greatly. Various selection aids are available, including ones that take into account the size of a library's budget. But building a periodical collection and making it physically available is only half the job. Promoting and encouraging the use of periodicals is just as important. Specialists new to the region, for example, need to overcome a certain barrier as newcomers lacking local experience. Moreover, many other specialists simply aren't aware of all the special publications in their field, let alone how to use them.

The kinds of reader-groups in the oblast cover the following range: plant growers, machine operators, cattle and reindeer breeders, fur farmers, hunters, fisheries workers and poultrymen. Still others, in the specialist category, include agronomists, veterinarians, economists, livestock experts and certain other machine operators. Libraries can help all of these workers master their professions, raise their qualifications, and stimulate self-improvement.

Work with reindeer-breeders is a special case. Such traditional economies have undergone much reorganization and modernization, and library services have developed along with them. In the Magadan oblast in the 1970s, 45 special agitcultbrigades were active in the field. Though their work is very important for librarians, some difficulties have been experienced:

—insufficient coordination between the library and AKB (*agitatsionno-kultur'nyi brigad,* or *agitkultbrigade,* or cultural enlightenment brigade," which presented everything from literacy promotion, readings aloud, news intrepretations, musical and theatrical performances, and health and government services, as well as making library materials available to workers and specialists in rural and remote locations)

—no creative contact, and no mutual accountability to control quality

—operations managers don't understand the importance of library outreach

—librarians are not fully involved in the selection of literature for the AKBs. In terms of new titles and availability of other current literature, libraries don't (or can't) always qualitatively replenish mobile units

—studies weren't done to assess the reading needs of reindeer herders, hunters, fishermen, etc. And adequate information about the socio-demographics of the tundra is not available, so work tends to proceed without regard for the reader's actual situation

—there is no open and direct communication between libraries and the mobile units

—Finally, there is no reporting of the work of libraries in such outreach, and no evaluation of it.

The promotion of progressive work methods is an important task for librarians. This means publicizing, explaining and paying tribute to exemplary workers and the most productive methods. The library can plan evenings celebrating foremost production people, like anniversaries for record-breakers.

Displays can give not only results of production goals, but how productivity benefits everyone. Interviews can be obtained with foremost workers, and specialists can be consulted to learn more about the latest methods. In the library, a corner can be set up for this kind of promotion, utilizing posters, guides to literature, leaflets, book displays, photographs and explanations of party resolutions, etc. For cattle and reindeer breeders, places can be opened for collective reading, public readings by livestock experts can be encouraged, and meetings can be arranged promoting the latest methods, in which various specialists can participate.

Librarians should also participate in conferences of agricultural specialists. One innovative way for an exchange of views is the "conference by correspondence." This is carried out with the cooperation of the regional newspaper. First there is an appeal to area specialists regarding a particular subject, and contributions are solicited. Letters sent in are then published under the heading, "Readers' Correspondence Conference." Care must be taken not only to promote discussions of production aspects and so on, but to promote literature on the subjects being discussed, and how it may be obtained. A correspondence conference is usually summarized by the head specialist of the local party committee, but the entire conference is run by the regional library. The goal or desired result of such a program is that availability of up-to-date and progressive information leads to more effective work methods and therefore higher production and better quality products. However, this type of conference hasn't yet been tried in the Magadan oblast.

Another good format is the "radio-newspaper," in which news and propaganda (promotion, publicity, celebration, motivation) are read over the air, perhaps with excerpts from interviews. Or the "oral magazine" can be recorded on a series of audiotapes which can be duplicated, and copies widely distributed.

Regarding library services to individuals, there is a need to keep adequate and up-to-date records of their library use, including readers' evaluations of materials and even a record of when materials are refused. A special "feedback" coupon has been used in some systems to obtain information from library users on the effectiveness of library services. The telephone is also used for notification of new materials of interest, along with postcard mailings. The postcards can be accumulated by a reader as a file on recent literature available through the library.

Group library services need to utilize available current selection aids and promotional opportunities that reach groups of workers on a regular basis in convenient ways. For agricultural specialists it is vital that library propaganda address actual problems and issues of the day. A book exchange service can also be arranged. Books and magazines can be made available in a systematic way at both the workplace and the home. For transient agricultural workers, periodicals may be a more convenient way to obtain information. Literature surveys can also be exchanged with other library systems, for comparative evaluation. Special packets can be made up containing a selection of journal articles (in a variant of SDI, or Selective Dissemination of Information). A special type of display promotes a single journal, explaining in detail its features, usefulness and relevance for local readers. Such promotional efforts are often just as informative and stimulating for the librarian as for patrons. As mentioned earlier, specialists themselves, in their liaison with librarians, can be of great help in improving library services.

The bibliographical publication *Knizhnaya Letopis'* (Guide to Books) is an excellent source for comprehensive information about a wide variety of materials for agricultural specialists and the librarians serving them. Variety in the kinds of reader contacts stimulates more library use and, consequently, improved library services.

Typical advanced training sessions run by the Central Library for library workers last about two days. Trainers include managers of enterprises, and a wide variety of experiences is presented. For the first day, a school might be visited, area managers will give their perspective on information needs, the Central Library will explain the importance of planning and complete records, and a village library participant will be asked to give an analysis of how his library serves agricultural workers or selects materials for a mobile library unit.

For the second day a supervisory village librarian will explain information services to agricultural workers, then participants might attend a Day of Specialists or Day of Information for agricultural workers. (Keep in mind that the term "agriculture" here also includes the full range of what are called subsistence gathering activities: the conservation or husbandry and harvest of animal or plant produce, whether domesticated or in the wild.) A home assignment will be to plan and organize a literature survey display for agricultural specialists around a specific theme, or to carry out a Day of Specialists or Day of Information in one's own library. Afterward, a description of the program is sent to the Central Library. Another training session activity is Exchanging Experiences (or sharing experiences or ideas) on subjects like outreach services to agricultural workers, services to basic groups of workers in a village library, or special information services to specialists. Finally, the session ends with a talk by the head of training, going over successful results achieved through attendance at such training sessions.

In-service training is also available to library workers. Seminars are run, and include features like an analysis of past work with agricultural materials in area libraries, and a comparative discussion of basic indices or measures of such work. Both successful examples and failures are considered. Another feature could be an exchange or sharing of experience, covering individual reader's advisory services, library programs, promotion of progressive methods, how to attract readers, various promotional aids that are available, mobile library services, and joint work of librarians and specialists. Next, a survey of new bibliographical aids and how to use them might be on the agenda, followed by various take-home assignments, similar to those given during the two-day training sessions.

1983, Matlina—Helicopters are now commonly used by cultural teams, or agitkultbrigades (AKBs). [They are as common as small planes are in bush Alaska, but news from northern Chukotka is that the return of small planes and airstrips is anticipated, because they can take off and land in less favorable weather. Being limited to helicopters means that in winter weather some communities may be isolated for weeks on end.] In the Magadan oblast the AKBs work for both the library and local House of Culture, serving locations otherwise not readily accessible (without airstrips). These are places where subsistence gatherers are in seasonal camps (Chukchi, Eveni, Eskimos, and Yukagiri). Such brigades started in 1973 and there are now 56 of them in the oblast.

Even though nomadic peoples today have things like all-terrain vehicles, transistor radios and wireless radio sets, they still welcome visitors who bring the latest news. Library service points are also set up at each nomadic brigade, to keep in touch with stationary libraries.

AKBs work together with nearby village libraries, which are resupplied by central libraries. Though a librarian often goes with an instructor on AKB trips, brigade members have essential library knowledge, because AKB personnel and library staff usually attend each other's training sessions. A monthly regional newsletter now analyzes AKB/library operations.

A typical recent flight to Chukchi reindeer herders proceeded thus: Supplies are loaded: electrified speakers and amplifiers and packages of books, magazines and newspapers, among other things. The team today is comprised of the AKB instructor, area party representatives, and artistic groups from the local House of Culture. A variety of occupations is represented, as these sorties often carry a mix of artistic and occupational interests. As the loading continued and the helicopter warmed up, an accordion played for a little rehearsal.

Such trips usually have a thematic character, so the materials taken along and programs presented conform to the theme. On this trip, a village was visited on the way in order to pick up other personnel, and to drop off a special selection of materials for workers who had donated a day's earnings in a "peace watch." It was reindeer calving time, so some additional information on preventing calf losses and proper reindeer care at this time of year was also dropped off. All these preparations were done by the Central Library. Then the team stopped at a second village to pick up a doctor, along with some trading workers.

Finally they arrived at the remote camp, where five brigades were gathered for the occasion. There was a wooden building and a tent, and the agitkultbrigade was warmly welcomed. The sound system was set up, and other team members set up graphic aids and displays. It was disappointing to note that only about 20 books had been brought, which were mostly reprints of older authors. Nothing new. The Central Library certainly considers the individual and group requests of the reindeer herders, but unfortunately isn't able to fill all of them. About 60-70% of their non-fiction requests can be filled, and fiction only about 30-40%. One non-circulating copy of titles in high demand is always kept in the Central Library, by the way.

The barrier to sending most desired books out to the camps is that many are badly worn, or are lost or left behind as the brigades move from one seasonal location to another. The Central Library is unable to allow for such losses, so some titles are never sent. It's a vicious circle: the herders want books and the Central Library wants to send them—but it's impossible given past experience and economic realities.

Meanwhile, the building where we were setting up was filling with people, and a makeshift stage was contrived using reindeer hides. On a long bench the preschool age children were lined up expectantly. (Their school-age older brothers and sisters were away studying at the village boarding school.)

The program started with a report on the village workers who had made a "peace watch" gesture, giving up a day's pay. Then AKB members gave a briefing on international meetings that had been held, presented news of domestic affairs and talked about the selection of magazines that had been brought along. Then the entertainment started, which included various ethnic dances, such as Russian or Cuban ones. Requests were played. A nice festive atmosphere was created. Now an impromptu bazaar or trading market got underway, as homemade articles and garments made by the reindeer herders and fruits and other goods supplied by boat, plane and helicopter were laid out. There wasn't a single really good book to be seen, but the system prioritizes services to the tundra workers so that such offerings just aren't possible. However, selected passages from high demand books are recorded on audiotapes, which are circulated—a combination of book reviews, bibliographical information and factual talks. But this added service doesn't really fill the need for better books.

Central Library services are of high quality otherwise, but can field services be brought up to the same level? Villagers think so. But acquisitions need to be increased and the output from local publishing houses needs to be adjusted. Special "AKB sets" of books should be made up by the oblast collection-building department. These special sets could be the basic core book collection of AKBs, supplementing materials from the Central Library. In addition, special standards of preservation have to be implemented for tundra conditions, carried out on-site, and funded by the Central Library.

There is also much hidden talent out in the villages. It would be useful to be able to videotape some of these interesting and popular activities, but the video production equipment isn't yet available in the Extreme North, either at the local Houses of Culture or at central libraries.

Finally, books about the Chukchi national culture, along with works from the local School of Art, like students' drawings, could be utilized both in stationary libraries and out in the camps. Also, methods of propaganda among the Native subsistence workers could be made more meaningful, provocative and original.

1983, Gorbatykh et al.—A Northern Committee was established early on by the Soviet government to carry out Lenin's behests regarding development and "enlightenment" of the north. Staffed by "Communists and Young Communists," its goal was to be, for the "remaining nationalities, not teachers and nannies, but helpmates." Since 1954 the growth and expansion of library development among northern peoples, including the Magadan oblast, has continued as directed by resolutions of the Central Committee of the Communist Party of the Soviet Union.

These developments coincided with implementation of long-range plans for economic and social development. Naturally this implied a parallel long-term effort to further perfect the direction, goals and purposes of library provision.

Though there is a high percentage of Native as well as non-Native readers and a large collection of books to draw from, most of the books are in the Russian language. Books printed in the Native orthographies included the following (most to least): Chukchi—several thousand; Eskimo—just over 40; and Evenki—literally a handful. Distribution of books in the Chukchi and Eskimo languages came to over 2500 copies. Turnover (circulation) of these books was 58%. From 1976 to 1981 almost 4000 copies of books in the Chukchi and Eskimo languages were distributed, over half of these being social and political titles, the rest fiction and children's books.

Not all central regional libraries placed special emphasis on the acquisition of agricultural literature in the Native languages. These large, system-wide book collections weren't even evaluated with that in mind, let alone the demand by Chukchi and Eskimo readers for literature in their own languages. Such a collection was, in effect, insufficiently maintained, to put it mildly, which naturally had an impact on circulation and book returns.

Despite these impediments, library services reached an average of about 75% among Native peoples. Librarians have promoted surveys of new literature from local publishers on the radio, conducted individual advisories, sent out open invitations to register at the library, and organized house visits, and readings-aloud at production sites and on "Days of Culture."

Some Chukchi-speaking librarian/activists are especially prominent in this effort. One of them visited every family in his locality, studying their makeup, in the process learning about elderly people who spoke Russian poorly, and making friends with those having libraries at home. This permitted his library to significantly increase the scope of its services to the Native population.

Once it is learned what people want to read, both individually and in groups, a card-index of these titles and subjects can aid the librarian in book acquisitions. The oblast library issued bibliographical lists such as "What reindeer-herders are reading," "Chukchi Bone-carvers," etc.

Libraries promote literature in various ways, always addressing a multi-ethnic audience, as practice has shown that it is inadvisable to direct such promotion only to Native groups. Depending on the level of reader preparedness, a variety of forms and methods of library service is available. The composition of the nationality's audience must be considered too. Services to those Native elders who have a poor understanding of Russian are more successful if an interpreter is available, for example.

Work with Native readers in promoting literature, practically speaking, leads in all directions. Measures involving local lore or regional themes play an essential role in increasing the quality of ideological-educational work among Native peoples, as there is a great deal of interest and emotional involvement. Positive experience with these measures has been accumulated by oblast librarians through such programs as "lessons in courage," evening "portraits of foremost people," literacy hours, radio-newspapers and monthly or weekly propaganda about contemporary literature.

In the Anadyr region, village librarians have a variety of programs honoring workers, including some that focus specifically on Chukchi workers and families. Working in a small business economy (sewing and furrier shops, for example), librarians come up with service ideas that fit the situation. The same is true with fish processing and sea mammal hunting brigades. Over the years there has arisen a special form of propaganda called a survey-talk, for example. This combines elements of both a discussion or debate and a literature survey. In the future this should be developed and improved into a more formal and better organized program. Librarians also began to utilize audiovisual aids much more.

In one village there is a School for Culture and Life, with a variety of students using it, young and old. Instructional programs have to be suitable for all, including transient village visitors and women workers. The relaxed and comfortable atmosphere of tea-time, when everyone is more disposed to speak up and ask questions, makes for easy conversation. Discussions are held that respond to a wide range of listeners and their interests, with displays to match.

Almost 6,000 Native people in the Anadyr region of Chukotka lead the subsistence life; hence the importance of mobile library units. Seventy-one government libraries and 52 agitkultbrigades form a network that serves these users at the work site. The most widely distributed type of nonstationary library unit in the oblast, however, is the library service point or station, where a government employee of some kind represents the library. The other type is the mobile unit, utilized to a lesser degree because of the scarcity of means of transportation. Under the conditions one finds throughout the oblast, library service points are basic components in the provision of both individual and group propaganda regarding current political reading and production-oriented literature. There are 360 library service points serving 3600, mostly reindeer herders, throughout the oblast. Annual circulation reaches 40,000 (books and magazines), or an average of 12 items per reader. And often librarians themselves go into the field, to personally run popular programs.

A conference was held at the oblast level on library services to Native people, to clarify and strengthen policies. Forty-five attended, among them 18 from remote villages. Current issues of concern were discussed, such as a differentiated approach to services; ways to study and measure readers, their interests and circumstances; cooperation of libraries and AKBs in serving subsistence gatherers; ways village libraries can reach Native readers; and planning and directing a unified plan for library services to area populations. A survey by questionnaire was done of one area's libraries to obtain more information. Thus libraries, under the direction of the party organization, made a start toward improvement of library services to Native peoples of Siberia and the Far East.

Work should significantly improve in quality and effectiveness through thoughtful and tactful selection of those forms and methods that respond to local traditions, conditions and languages. Libraries will be under the guidance of the unified plan, which more precisely defines the zone of influence of every library. These improvements in Native library services will comprise a clear advance in the long-range growth of socialist competition [competition to serve the state, the people and the party's goals] between libraries of all systems and departments.

Village librarians need to pursue probationary work and practicums in the best libraries of the region. Advanced training schools need to concentrate more on services to Native readers. Agitcultbrigade book services always need review and improvement. The book requests of reindeer herders as a whole should be closely examined, and individual requests, especially from young people, need to be integrated into the acquisition process. The material-technical base of village libraries needs to be increased so libraries will be equipped with audiovisual media and other needed equipment, in order to raise the level of graphic propaganda. Accomplishing all these things will fulfill the directives of the 26th session of the Communist Party of the Soviet Union.

1985, Lesokhina—The state considers the library profession to be of profound importance in the achievement of national goals, and makes available

Siberian Yupik Eskimos launch a walrus skin boat for spring whaling, Gambell, St. Lawrence Island, in the Bering Strait. (Photo by Al Grillo, 1991)

Native women filleting red salmon for home use, hanging them on drying racks. Togiak, on Bristol Bay, southwest Alaska. (Photo by Doug Ogden, 1990)

Downtown Anchorage with the Chugach Mountains to the east, and Cook Inlet, an estuary of the sea, in the foreground. Of Anchorage's 250,000 population, over 20,000 are Native Alaskans. (Photo by Jeff Schultz, 1990)

A pow wow in Los Angeles' Indian community. The occasion? Halloween. Modern Natives have adopted holidays brought by non-Natives, and created many modern ones of their own. (Some are ignored or even protested, like Columbus Day.) Los Angeles has over 10,000 Native Americans in residence, representing over 120 different tribes nationwide. (Photo by Michael Burgess, 1988)

Small aircraft like this one on sea ice at Little Diomede in the Bering Strait provide transportation to isolated villages throughout Alaska and Canada, whereas helicopters are the work horses for remote locations across the Russian north. A snogo pulling a sled has come up alongside, and the pilot is probably the casual figure leaning against the tail. The dwellings on the hillside are modern, and the tanks hold winter fuel oil and gasoline, brought by huge ocean-going barges in summer. Big Diomede and Russia are a few miles to the west. (Photo by Jeff Schultz, 1985)

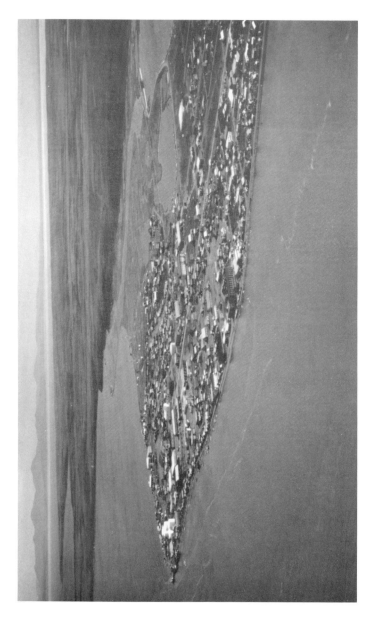

The modern regional center of Kotzebue at the top of the Baldwin Peninsula in Kotzebue Sound. The Baird Mountains are in the distance, and are the western end of the Brooks Range, which goes from the Bering Sea to the Mackenzie River in Canada, dividing the Arctic slope from the Yukon River basin, which parallels it to the south. (Photo by Jeff Schultz, 1990)

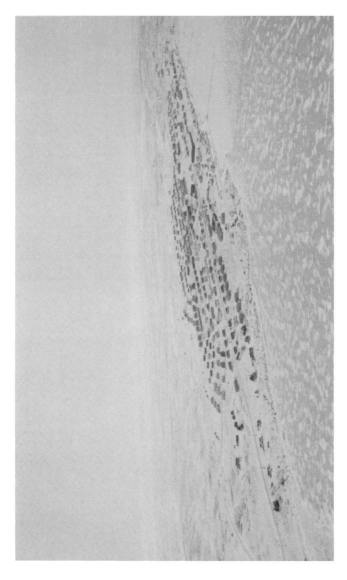

Baker Lake, Keewatin region, northwest of Hudson Bay in the Northwest Territories. Frozen Chesterfield Inlet in the foreground leads to Hudson Bay. There is nothing more desolate and forbidding than flying to such a remote arctic community in winter under marginal VFR conditions. Once on the ground, however, one is welcomed into an active, hospitable town life, with its own special atmosphere and environment. (Photo by Tessa Macintosh, 1986)

Entrance area of the Headquarters Library for N.W.T. Public Library Services in Hay River on Great Slave Lake in the southwest corner of N.W.T. N.W.T.P.L.S. is under the N.W.T. Culture/Communications department. (Photo by Tessa Macintosh, 1987)

School library on the Hay River Reserve. (Photo by Tessa Macintosh, 1987)

Inuvik, a regional center in the Mackenzie River delta at the extreme northwest corner of Canada and the N.W.T. This photo was probably taken at sunset——the bright reflections making it appear rather larger than it actually is. (Photo by George Herben, 1989)

Two youngsters reading. The table doesn't seem to mind a little soil from athletic footgear making itself at home. (Photo courtesy of Nunatta Atuagaateqarfia, 1990)

Sydproven commune library in 1987. Bound periodicals in the rear, children's picture books to the right, hospitality table at center. (Photo courtesy of Nunatta Atuagaateqarfia)

Library at Paamiut commune, 1987. Children's and youth collection. (Photo courtesy of Nunatta Atuagaateqarfia)

Uelen, on the Chukotka coast. This type of massive construction is found everywhere. In larger towns buildings can be as tall as three or four stories, with flat roofs and without elevators. Though individual homes are unheard of in the Soviet era, these buildings were well-designed for Arctic conditions. Heating, electricity, and plumbing are always operated from a central power plant. (Photo by Alim Kiryushin, Magadan)

A typical village library scene. They were used by Soviet authority for ideological control and indoctrination as well as literacy campaigns, which has compromised their public image in the post-Communist era. (Photo by Alim Kiryushin, Magadan)

"Elders willingly pass on their knowledge of the old arts to young people," notes the photographer of this picture. The mutual respect and affection of these teenage girls and their elder is radiant in its wholesomeness. The location is New Chaplino, Chukotka. (Photo by Alim Kiryushin, Magadan)

In New Chaplino, Eskimo language teacher Marina I. Sigunylik looks engagingly at the photographer during a break in activities at the water's edge. Though the stony beach, the treeless, snow-flecked hills and apparently empty sea present a bleak appearance, the warmth and vigor of northerners render such initial impressions of little relevance in human affairs. (Photo by Alim Kiryushin, Magadan)

A training workshop for village library aides held in 1982 in Aniak, Alaska. Left to right: Audrey Kolb of Alaska State Library; David Smart of Hooper Bay (deceased); Bill Schneider on oral history from the University of Alaska, Fairbanks; Marie Heckman of Pilot Station (deceased); Margaret Johnson of Mountain Village (replaced); and Tim Moffatt, who also assisted in training. Several other aides attended, but were not present for this photo. The high turnover of village library aides in the Yukon-Kuskokwin delta is attributable to many factors. (Photo by author)

Reindeer herder children from a Chukotka boarding school. Native peoples across the north are increasingly able to define their place in the modern world. Certainly these children will find their future more in their own hands than their parents did. (Photo by Alim Kiryushin, Magadan)

various levels of education and training. College training prepares "secondary qualification specialists," while higher qualification librarians, specializing in aspects of professional librarianship, acquire their training in institutes of culture and pedagogical institutes, as well as other universities. Each year a total of 20,000 librarians are graduated. Basically these are generalists who are able to adapt to dynamic social conditions, putting theory into practice and applying scientific methods.

In the college curriculum, a rational balance between general and special subjects is sought. Marxist-Leninist philosophy, political economy, history, scientific communism, as well as the humanities and pedagogy are studied—"the curricula for specialists with a high level of general culture and education, wide erudition, and a deep understanding of the social, moral and esthetic significance of their profession." Curricula are state-approved and the same across the entire nation. Textbooks are similarly provided. Changes are made after regular and systematic review.

Special attention is given to training librarians to serve in rural areas, because 70% of secondary librarians will work in rural areas and 40% of those with higher training will. All librarians return to work in their home area.

Librarians with specialist higher training also engage in research, in cooperation with secondary librarians, to bring the best scientifically trained specialists to work on improving library services across the nation. This approach also involves students, who participate in research at their institutions, and "take an active part in the work of scientific circles, students' scientific societies, and present their works at the All-Union and republic-level competitions."

The steadily increasing educational level of Soviet citizens has made the work and responsibilities of librarians more demanding. Continuing education is an integral part of the life of librarians, as well as other Soviet citizens. The forms and methods of such training will depend upon many variables. Evening and correspondance courses offer additional training for librarians. Advanced training is offered in a variety of ways, from longer institute and regional courses every several years to "seminars, applied science conferences and practical studies." "Active" forms of studying are the rule, which means study that is directly involved with the community or involves practical applications in the home area and their supervised evaluation.

All library education is paid for by the state, which also provides jobs for graduates, as well as a good living and working environment that fosters professional growth. The status of librarians is maintained at a high level, with state honors and medals are bestowed on special occasions.

However, there are deficiencies that need to be addressed. There are not enough highly trained librarians, and 40% of rural librarians don't have continuing education. There is also waste in having students with greatly differing educational credentials matriculate together. A system to accelerate training for better qualified students is needed. More emphasis should be placed on up-to-date training in computer applications and library automation. Some of the shortcomings along these lines arise from the situation in which higher education institutions are often subordinate not to one ministry, but to several.

1984, Zotova *et al.*—Since the 26th session of the Central Committee of the Communist Party, future goals for the USSR include the attainment of equal living conditions and cultural advancement for all peoples. In recent years the Party has devoted special attention to Siberia and the Far East, regarding joint problems in the development of natural resources and productivity, of which library development is considered an integral part.

The USSR Ministry of Culture has an interdepartmental commission for coordinating such plans in Siberia and the Far East, involving various local and professional organizations and cultural enlightenment institutions.

In the RSFSR, library provision has not kept up with rates of population growth, industrial production and scientific potential. Further improvement is called for. At the lowest level, special efforts will be needed to organize village library networks and to coordinate services to agricultural production areas.

The main problem in the organization of library networks appears to be the concept itself, where departments and branches feel isolated or disassociated from the idea, and are not used to interagency coordination, let alone seeing themselves as part of a needed network or unification. The absence of scientifically developed models for this kind of accommodation between libraries adds to the difficulty, and will prolong its implementation.

Zonal unifications (zone=economic region, which can be very large) created in Siberia and the Far East naturally focused the efforts of librarians on bibliographical work. However, the absence of enabling documentation concerning zone libraries impedes library cooperation within a zone. So real progress in this direction has to await action at the All-Union (USSR) level.

In recent years, significantly more attention has been devoted to acquisitions, and fulfilling more readers' requests. Central literature collections have been created for new Komsomol (Young Communist) projects, and various departments and organizations are releasing supplementary appropriations for books. Even so, there are deficiencies in such areas, due in large measure to the new demographics encountered—local situations that don't fit into the customary molds. For example, for a population that is younger and has a higher percentage of specialists, more reference and educational literature is needed, along with foreign scientific literature. More children's materials and art literature are also being asked for. The working collectives should have centralized library acquisition, including audiovisual materials and equipment; and some regulation of book acquisitions by residents and public organizations might be called for as well.

Another factor is the extreme remoteness of much of Siberia and the Far East from central and branch book warehouses. Interlibrary loan and cooperation take on much greater significance. In the case of foreign literature, for example, the main central collections are concentrated in European parts of the nation. A unified regional collection of foreign literature is called for, modeled after the Siberian Division of the National Academy of Sciences' Scientific-Technical Library.

A system of depository libraries should be established throughout the region, as organized by scientific training centers, which can determine the most appropriate profile of such collections, considering the special needs of areas they will serve. In the case of narrow subject and departmental literature, however, their respective branch depositories will continue to fill these requests most effectively.

Shared collection utilization and book exchange also means that combined or union catalogs are needed, and interlibrary loan procedures need further development. Here we encounter problems as well, because interlibrary loan has yet to be established between some libraries, and even information about the various collections involved is not freely shared.

Two other features of library services in new construction areas (with many young and specialist workers) are the great in-migration of workers, as well as a thinly deployed expeditionary work plan. Accordingly, all scientific training must be formulated paying special attention to work with the young, including the development of their political consciousness and cultural growth. The great number of enrollees in technical schools, schools of working youth and outside students, oblige libraries to uncover book needs that are linked with the educational training process.

Under conditions where libraries—especially small community libraries—are very remote from established cultural centers, more aggressive efforts will be needed in working with readers (through coordination with other cultural enlightenment institutions). This involves, for example, promoting art literature as well as art itself, in support of independent creativity. Analysis of contemporary cultural development in some areas of the region indicates the need for a systematic study of cultural progress among readers.

Regional specificity matches library services to the particular population and region served. Types of readers have to be identified, and this will determine the kind of book promotions used, as well as work with labor collectives.

Interlibrary cooperation will also be affected. This involves scientific-technical institutes serving specialists and professionals, along with specialized information services and services to important territorial industrial complexes in the area. Libraries should also interact with other cultural institutions and with periodicals, not only for ideological and aesthetic purposes, but to assist scientific training centers to fine-tune regional bibliographies and bibliographic indicators for use in planning, forecasts and regional management.

Twenty-two nationalities with a population of 158,000 live in Siberia and the Far East. Scientific-training centers now have policies that provide support for the optimization of library services to ethnic minorities of Extreme Siberia. The supporting resolution of the Central Committee of the Communist Party of the Soviet Union is entitled: "On the means of enabling long-range social and economic growth in residential areas of Northern peoples."

In many regions not only are the basic economies of the settled population improving (reindeer breeding, hunting, fishing and fur farming), but the rich natural resources are being developed, along with large-scale enterprises and energy and transportation units. All this obliges libraries to consider serious involvement in efforts supporting full employment of Native peoples in the national economy, as well as their professional training, while allowing for cultural traditions and subsistence needs.

Library services to Native populations of the Far East involve complex problems, and their solution is possible only through ensuring the strength of scientific collectives in the spheres of sociology, pedagogy and culture. The role of living and working conditions of ethnic minorities in the organization of library work, such as the acquisition and use of collections, helps to clarify sociological research, which includes studies of the need for literature in Native languages.

Long-range improvement of coordinated administrative policies at the central library level should take into account local conditions for the Native peoples, the enormous distances involved, and the available means of communication. The organization of customized forms of cultural services to local populations by agitcultbrigades and other means of cultural enlightenment delivery is also called for. Clarification of details in mobile club/library operations is needed, along with development of methodological and instructional materials for their improvement. Resolution of these problems is complicated by the fact that many librarians who come here don't know the Native language, or the peculiarities of local life. Accordingly, it's important to carefully select persons of local nationalities to administer special training programs in library education, and to provide special training for working librarians along these lines. Many problems of library services to Siberian peoples can be resolved through special policies and programs administered by the leadership of the RSFSR (Saltykova-Shchedrina) Republic Library, and with the participation of oblast and krai (territorial) libraries in the 12th five-year plan.

Training for library workers at the local level needs to be more readily available. Scientific training centers in Siberia and the Far East have been developing library training for cadre at the middle and higher ranks. Not infrequently, gifted young people pursue their studies at library educational institutions at the expense of their livelihood, so correspondence courses have been set up. However, the numbers of library cadre receiving such training remains low, and librarians in new project areas experience a severe shortage of adequately trained staff.

So raising of qualifications and improving expertise in libraries of the region awaits more systematic help from All-Union (USSR) and branch instructional centers. The goals of scientific-training of library cadre include the following:

—consider new training ideas
—provide a broad range of assistance that better prepares library education faculty in the region
—find the optimal system for the improvement of qualifications of library workers, one that takes into account regional factors and utilizes highly qualified specialists of All-Union (USSR) and republic libraries;
—prepare realistic learning aids and instructional recommendations that respond to the actual working responsibilities found in libraries.

Research for the next five-year plan will assist "librarians as a socio-professional group." This includes improving not only their working conditions, but their living conditions as well. Retraining and probation of instructors in special disciplines of library education faculties for Siberia and the Far East has already begun, as in the Moscow State Institute of Culture and Leningrad (Krupskaia Memorial) State Institute of Culture. In regional institutes of culture, lectures on real-life problems in library work are being offered by leading specialists.

A new plan has been created that will promote the coordination of training throughout this vast region, guaranteeing the capability of libraries and methodological centers to jointly resolve both theoretical and practical problems, thus fulfilling party programs and accelerating natural resource development.

1984, Gorbatykh—The few thousand copies of books available in the Chukchi and Eskimo languages are mostly socio-political titles, a third of them being fiction for both children and adults (mostly translations of short Russian and Soviet classics). It is obvious that literature in Native languages is insufficient for raising the general educational and cultural level. Not only does the quantity need to be increased, but the content needs to be diversified. No less important is the need to increase the output of small local presses.

Until now, there haven't been general materials reflecting contemporary readers' interests in the Far North, except in individual regions and villages. In the selection of materials and their distribution for any one population point the typically multinational character of the clientele needs to be considered ("not just the indigenous people"). Propaganda methods have to be appropriate in other respects as well, such as the kind of economy pursued. Small production units (sewing and furrier shops, etc.), and library service points of a seasonal character (fishing and sea-trapping brigades, or the courts) are some examples.

"Survey-talks" include elements of both thematic literature surveys and lively conversations. These are prepared using regional materials obtained from party and soviet institutions, and from other literary sources, including newspapers and magazines. Various themes are used, for example: "The Magadan Oblast from Party Conference to Party Conference"; "Northerners—Delegates to the Party Conference", "Geologists—Discoverers of Chukotka"; "Hero of the Five-year Plan." The Magadan oblast library renders differentiated instructional help to libraries in search of effective methods of book propaganda. Thus, collective reading points are organized in production units where mostly Native workers are found. Audiovisual materials are also becoming more useful in libraries which have special interest clubs.

Lately, classes have been successfully carried out in "Culture and Life" schools in areas of settled (Native) population. Library workers select literature for study, make up book displays, conduct discussions, participate in the work of soviet schools and, together with club workers and agitcultbrigade instructors, determine the best propaganda methods. For example, in the Ust'-Belaya village in the Anadyr region, the School of Culture and Life has been in operation for more than fifteen years. The academic program is differentiated according to age and education.

About one-third of the settled population in Magadan oblast follows the subsistence economies, so the system of remote library service takes on more importance. Library service points are the most widely distributed, 360 being found throughout the oblast. Mobile libraries are used to a lesser degree due to the lack of appropriate transportation.

With the goal of greater satisfaction of reindeer breeders' needs in mind, the oblast office of culture made the decision to increase library acquisition of literature for the reindeer breeders' brigades, and to organize these services through the agitkultbrigades (AKB). Materials are ordered centrally, and the chief collections librarian uses the thematic plans (as directed from above, and having little to do with actual public demand or need) of publishers in selecting acquisitions. The AKB itself performs as a mobile cultural complex, existing as an independent sub-unit for regional and village Houses of Enlightenment. The central library librarian or the cultural enlightenment instructor usually carries out book propaganda, for which the field services section entrusts book displays and recordings of reviews or discussions with readers working on the tundra. Library service points carry not only new offerings by the AKB, but also literature from the collections of regional and village libraries. Within the walls of the library, oral magazines, bibliographic surveys, readers' conferences and literary evenings are recorded on tape, then these recordings are played for the reindeer herders brigade or other field units. Regional libraries give a lot of attention to the creation of talking-books for reindeer breeders. Five brigades of one kolkhoz heard an evening program called "Literature of the Chukchi." Older students heard Chukchi poetry in the original language.

A joint task force needs to survey the status of northern library services. The expertise for such a survey already exists. The information thus generated could serve as the basis for a series of instructional aids, as well as bibliographic indicators that would help both scientific training centers and libraries carry on their work under the special conditions of northern areas.

The document "Special Purpose Joint Programs of Scientific-Training Aid to Libraries of Siberia and the Far East from 1983–1990" should help raise standards. We should consider creating a separate regional scientific-training center that would help guide the growth of library infrastructure in regions of resident northern nationalities. It could also work closely with scientific centers of the USSR Academy of Sciences located in Siberia, the Far East and the Extreme North, which are preoccupied with the regional problems encountered in opening up new territory. It is also necessary to improve relations with sociologists and teachers, in order to more effectively fulfill long-range library goals, as indicated in the policy entitled "On Measures for the Long-Range Social and Economic Development of Areas of Resident Nationalities."

1984, Isayeva—Representatives of regional instructional centers took part in work on courses raising qualifications for managers of service departments and field librarians of the Magadan oblast library. This involved a combined, many-faceted study of problems with readers, in particular a discussion of the various mobile forms of library service to Native populations.

The Magadan oblast (Pushkin Memorial) library is the initiator of special long-range joint programs, and the organizer of coordinated arrangements for the scientific-methodological maintenance of library-bibliographic services to readers. Librarians serving children and young adults also participate, along with representatives of scientific-training centers for cultural enlightenment, the House of Political Enlightenment, and the main library of the Oblsovprofa (Council of Professional Unions).

Joint special programs arranged by the Pushkin Library complement the work of other informational and cultural enlightenment institutions of the region. In other words, they are an integral part of comprehensive plans for oblast library services. As a local example, village branches promote books in close collaboration with Houses of Culture, music schools, art schools and even law enforcement organs, etc. Another good example, emphasizing the great possibilities of such joint arrangements, are the "Agitkultbrigade Weeks." These were highlighted at the 60th Jubilee of the USSR, which also included representational art, bibliographical book surveys, performances of local folklorists and amateur talent activities, all enabling a fuller and more graphic display of the original culture of our nation.

In implementing the decisions of the 26th session of the Communist Party, librarians noted the intensification of both traditional and new directions of food and agricultural production. Differentiated readers' services meant sub-dividing them into groups: reindeer breeders, hunters and fishermen, dairy and poultry specialists, gold-mining industry workers, and so on. Concrete proposals were addressed to each group during special "Information Days" that were organized for brigades and specialists of the region's model-production economy. Assisting were "foremost readers," who helped with preparations.

Including bibliographical and informational work with traditional library services is one of the features of work with readers in the oblast headquarters library. A bibliographer in service sections of central libraries is occupied with reference services for subscribing readers, making up displays and booths, and helping to organize popular programs. In such a headquarters library, and most importantly in rural branches using publications of organs of the Scientific-Technical Institute in work with readers, card indexes of recommended bibliographical aids and regional indexes are used to fill professional requests of workers' committees of kolkhozes, mining and other enterprises.

In library training courses of more than ten hours, the theme "Bibliographical and Informational Methods of Book Propaganda and Reading Guidance" is regularly featured. Practical methods of bibliographical searching are learned through real-life exercises, which add significantly to retention.

1985B, Yelepov *et al.*—The nature of library resource development in any specific region is largely dependent on historically determined socio-cultural conditions and the economic and scientific potential found therein. A survey was done of library resources in Siberia and the Far East. Present use was analyzed and compared with the rest of the RSFSR. Improved development of library resources is the result of increased development generally, including construction of the Baikal-Amur (BAM) railroad, the multiple increase in town size and the sharp population growth of recent past. [The population of the north tripled between 1926 and 1959—various sources.] However, cultural growth has lagged behind. The surge in growth brings with it a higher percentage of specialists, most of these being in the agricultural fields.

The level of education is also increasing. More students go on to middle and higher special training than elsewhere in the USSR. Increased information needs in the new construction areas are linked to this increase in training demand, as well as more highly qualified specialists and new specialities.

Given this situation, how are libraries able to meet these needs? First of all, the actual number of libraries has increased by over a third, most of these being government public libraries. However, this new library construction has not kept up with area growth. The problems include widely separated settlements, and an imbalance in the distribution of special libraries in relation to particular types of readers.

Although the combined collections of the region increased threefold in ten years (1971-81), the average collection is not impressive, due to the very large number of small libraries. Books per capita in Siberia are 12.8, and in the entire RSFSR, 17.3. Increased services are linked not only to new libraries, but to the increased load on existing libraries.

Staffing has improved, and absolute number of library workers have increased. But the quantity of better trained people hasn't risen enough, especially in the north, where one notes an "outflow" from libraries. It's hard to attract library specialists to new areas of settlement, especially young people.

Sixty-five per cent of the population of Siberia and the Far East are covered by library services. Of all readers, 80% go to government public libraries (any library with public access—may be various types), nine per cent to libraries of middle and higher educational institutions, six per cent utilize technical libraries, and five per cent use scientific libraries. Of the readers, 33.4% are specialists in local industry. Of the small percentage of near non-users, it was found that about eight per cent of agricultural specialists and from 3.2 to one per cent of specialists in public education, public welfare, science and culture used libraries one-third to one-quarter of the time that the vast majority of other specialists did.

When specialists aren't within reach of a special library, they turn to the nearest government public (-access) library. The best agricultural libraries are located in large towns, leaving about 11% of the agricultural specialists making do with local public libraries.

The flow of scientific information into a region goes through the All-Union centers as well as the institutions. It is all one integrated system, however, and the principle of resource-sharing—a contemporary trend—is applied. Internal as well as interregional sharing of information affects all areas of life and work. Increased liaison will create more unity in area networks, as well as strengthen their interaction.

The Siberian region is breaking up into smaller economic regions, such as Eastern Siberia, Western Siberia and so on. Under these constantly changing conditions, it's difficult to maintain a stable pool of workers. Then, with the further division of these new regional configurations into sub-regions of economic development, there is really a need for large library networks on the basis of interdepartmental unification. This also implies raised standards of service by both libraries and other cultural institutions.

Some factors indicating the degree of satisfaction of cultural and information needs include the number of libraries and library workers, and the volume of book expenditures per 1000 inhabitants. Once the actual norms of service are determined, it is essential to hold to the principle of aligning or equalizing library and information service in the various regions of the nation. The norms we are proposing are far from being set, and do not sufficiently allow for regional peculiarities.

A Coefficient of Services can also be applied (as well as various other quantitative coefficients), but this calculation is only useful for the construction of government public libraries. It takes into account the number of workers in all types of work (including libraries), how much territory is required before a library might be constructed, and what the size of a library collection should be. Simply expressed, the satisfaction of cultural needs is a function of economic development, and in this respect Siberia and the Far East are behind the rest of the nation. Rather than more libraries, it is better to strengthen those already in place through multifaceted interaction within existing networks. Sometimes special links are called for to guarantee this liaison, and these may include compulsory features.

In the future, there will be "library giants" created with exclusive or dedicated technological circuits within each region. The appearance of new information media and means of communication also makes possible independently operational library systems in larger political units, such as the krai, oblast, and autonomous republic. This assumes, of course, that all libraries and information services, to the lowest level, will be equipped with technological aids, from photocopiers and microform readers to telecommunications, making possible access to resources of other libraries and sci-tech organs at any level.

1986, Maksimova—This short yet concise article, written in an informal style, again cites the list of complaints we've heard before, regarding the inadequacies of library services to northern populations: too few copies of popular or indispensable titles; services to brigades in the field are inadequate; transportation is in short supply, and delivery and pick-up of books is by chance; service networks in remote areas are more difficult to maintain; improvements in management and planning at the level of central libraries are still needed—a long-standing complaint; the need for scientific methodology is brought up again and again, yet it takes so long to be applied in practice; planning and cost-analysis are essential, yet are little used; there are too few Native workers, and the level of qualifications is too low; there is insufficient orientation in the special conditions and needs of Native people; local libraries aren't getting needed support from libraries higher up (for example, a much vaunted series of special publications never materialized); and collection development staff aren't paying enough attention to actual area needs.

Despite this impressive, not to say overwhelming litany of complaints, there is good news from the same informant. Certainly work in the north is not as easy as people think. Conditions are very difficult, and there are many different clienteles. But special forms of service have been created, and manage to keep even the smallest place informed of broad issues facing the nation.

There are puppet shows for kids, for example, discussions are combined with bibliographical surveys to make for a more lively presentation, and clubs are very popular and have many variations.

The bottom line is this: readers in both towns and remote locations are still waiting for new books, really stimulating reviews and some genuinely innovative and popular measures.

1986, Landina—In the northernmost parts of the Taimir National Okrug (located on the north central arctic coast, the farthest north mainland of Russia), library services started with mobile Red Tents and Kultbases, directed to the Dolgani, Nentsi, Nganasani and Yentsi peoples. Now these areas receive stationary library services from the USSR Ministry of Culture libraries, with a wide network of library service points (245) located at reindeer and fish camps, and fur farms.

Every year, through the Taimir Department of Culture, the okrug executive committee under the direction of party organizations, together with libraries of all systems and departments, puts on a month-long campaign to do with socio-political literature. Others, lasting three months, have for themes "Reindeer-herding—the Leading Front," and "100 Days of Attack—the Search for Fish," and so on. Participating in these campaigns are the book trade organizations, the society of book lovers, and young communist periodicals.

As recommended by the Dudinski Central Library (Dudinka is a town about 450 k. south of the arctic coast on the Yenesei River), annual plans of okrug libraries included measures preparing for the 27th Conference of the Communist Party of the Soviet Union. Among libraries of all systems and departments there unfolded socialist competition, and several schools of progressive methods were created for the occasion, modeled after the libraries of the sovkhoz "Polar" and the "Potapov" settlement.

To prepare libraries for the conference, methodological and practical help was provided by the Dudinski library through on-site visits and shipments of advisory materials. Included were plans for an evening's program devoted to the 55th anniversary of the formation of the Taimir Okrug, entitled "I Sing of Thee, My Snowy Land"; readers' conferences on the theme "The Figure of the Communist in Creative Literature"; a cycle of talks around the subject of the "Politics of Peace and Progress"; an oral journal called "A Word about the Working Class," and displays on themes of the "Basic Directions of Economic and Social Growth of the Okrug" and "New Horizons of Communist Construction."

In the early fall of 1985, a month's campaign on socio-political literature opened with the theme "The Week of the Propagandist." Book displays were set up. Days of Information were arranged, and selections of literature just received by the library were heard on the radio and publicized in the okrug journal, *Soviet Taimir.*

The second week of the month had the motto: "The 27th Conference of the Communist Party of the Soviet Union—a Worthwhile Meeting!" All libraries of the okrug conducted talks in working collectives on the theme, "Work Totals of Production Staff of Our Sovkhoz for Nine Months of the Final Year of the 11th Five-Year-Plan," finishing the week with an oral journal devoted to a "Day of the Constitution of the USSR."

In the third week Days of Information are presented for parents on "Alcohol and Children"; reading conferences are held on the books, *The Gray Mouse* by Lipantov and *The Atonement* by V. Tendryakov, and on the subject, "The Whole Family Goes to the Library". Surveys of publications are presented, information bulletins like "The Commission on the Struggle against Drunkenness and Alcoholism Reports . . ." are distributed, and book displays are set up on anti-alcoholism themes.

For the final week of the campaign a book for youth was featured, along with lessons on Lenin in libraries, talks on the culture of behavior and social relationships, and a debate on the subject, "Active Rest—What Is It?"

During the 27th Conference of the C.P. of the USSR, libraries of the okrug took part in a readers' conference on the book by G. Markov entitled *The Coming Century*. In the town of Dudinka, Communists debated the question: What traits of the main character of the novel—Anton Vasilevich Sobolev—should be inherent in contemporary party leadership? Such conferences also took place in Dikson, Khatang, and other settlements.

In reindeer-herding brigades during the next monthly campaign readings-aloud were held, on "These Days in the Kremlin Conference Halls." Reindeer herders participated enthusiastically in discussions of the delegates' speeches, which could be heard on the radio from Moscow.

Methodological sections of the central library helped rural libraries visit almost every reindeer brigade. Talks among the brigades were linked with the conference's proceedings, its resolutions, and the speeches of delegates. Also, the oral journal, "Landmarks of Creation," was presented, as well as thematic evenings of a literary and musical nature entitled "Of the Party of Our Sons." Other oral journals had titles like "The Food Program—Our Initiative," and "Man, Collective, and Society." Lectures were read on "The Essence and Basic Principles of the Collective Contract," and "Setting Work Rates for Subdivisions of the Collectivist Contract."

In the fishing brigades, discussions took place on "Summaries of Work of the 27th Conference of the C. P. of the USSR, and the Tasks of Fishermen in the Implementation of Its Resolutions," and on "Prospects for Development of Fisheries in the Okrug." Ninety-four mobile library service points distributed books to the fishing brigades, and an oral journal was produced on the theme, "The Party's Plans are the People's Plans." The Dudinski Library System gives methodological aid to library workers concerning food production literature and ways to disseminate information on progressive methods to reindeer-herders.

Thus, analysis of the Potapov branch serving reindeer herders resulted in study plans like "You, the Reindeer-herder," "Techniques for Reindeer-herders," and "Diseases of Northern Reindeer." Packets of journal and newspaper clippings enjoy great popularity among them as well, including articles like "The Monthly Campaign Goes on: 'Reindeer-herding—the Leading Front'," and "The Northern Muse." The same analysis showed that 70% of the herders read books by northern writers like Lyubov Nenyang, Olga Aksenov, U. Rytkheu and V. Sangi. Fifty percent show a preference for books in their own profession. In 46 reindeer-herder brigades, mobile library service points were created for the distribution of literature. (Each brigade may have from one to a few thousand reindeer.)

The next monthly campaign, "Reindeer-herding—the Leading Front," saw the inauguration of special displays and "nooks" focusing on this theme in branches of the central library. Library work now engaged in explaining and clarifying materials just issued from the conference. At the end of the campaign, a traditional Day of Reindeer-herders took place.

In a period of monthly campaigns, special responsibility lies with the office of the Agricultural Directorate's Sci-Tech Institute. However, a great deal depends on the librarians, who supply the agricultural workers with the necessary publications, and organize avid readers around such themes. For example, the library branch in the village of Potapov, in the Dudinski Library System, organized a school of culture and life. In this school, the most active presenters, other than librarians, were agricultural and medical workers. A chief veterinary doctor led the section on economic knowledge among the reindeer herders. Such specialists traveling with them during the summer are the librarians' main helpers in carrying out cultural work. Before the agricultural campaigns the librarian of the Potapov branch library prepared talks, surveys and lectures, and distributed these among activists in the schools mentioned above.

Work like this among the reindeer herders is interesting in many ways. An evening celebration called "The Reindeer-herder Is the Son of a Reindeer-herder" has been long remembered. The Dudinski Central Library recommended that such celebrations be carried out in other libraries of the okrug. Every reindeer-herder brigade holds a debate on their Day of Specialists, called "Thrift Is a Communist Trait."

During the three-month campaign called "100 Outstanding Days in the Fishing Season," librarians, assisted in their work by all sorts of aids and techniques, helped in the fulfillment of fisheries' goals. A plan for measures to be taken is readied by the Methodological Section, along with a schedule of departures to the production brigades. That year they took place every ten days.

An article by S. Kustyrko, "Taimir Conversations—Two Letters about Fish and Fishermen," elicited great interest in all the libraries of the okrug. It appeared in a periodical popular with okrug readers, *Northern Spaces* (1985, #6). In the newspaper *Soviet Taimir,* a roster of okrug library workers will be published, along with a review of library activities during the fishing season. Finally, traditional send-offs were organized by libraries, called "Good Luck, Fishermen!"

No small difficulties have to be overcome in providing library services to this population. The situation is complicated because literature in the Native orthography has barely begun—the first Dolgani dictionary is just being readied for publication—so libraries at present work only with literature in the Russian language. The average service zone of one public library comprises a territory of 125,000 square kilometers, and the distance between population points is sometimes from 500 to 800 kilometers. Roads are lacking, as well as telephone communication. Areas with very few workers (from 2–10) lead a nomadic lifestyle. Under such unusual circumstances, the main factor preventing the long-term improvement of library services to workers is the absence of essential transportation. Above all, northern libraries need to be equipped with mobile housing (girdered-type) which can be moved along with the reindeer-herders, and in which the librarian can carry on cultural enlightenment work. Other needs include the creation of Sci-Tech Institute study rooms at strong okrug libraries and, of course, an increase in the material support of libraries. (Out of 34 public libraries in the okrug, not even one could be found in a building specifically designed to be a library.)

A main theme at library meetings was the raising of official qualifications for librarians. In March, regional seminars of okrug librarians were held, where improvement of library activities was examined in the light of the 27th Party Conference. Specifically, questions on counter-propaganda were considered, as part of the effort to aid food production in the Far North.

All library workers in the okrug must pass official certification once or twice a year, for which they prepare in weekly studies through regional seminars. Knowledge of library workers about party and government decisions to do with cultural enlightenment work is checked, as well as that involving library science theory and practice, fulfilling socialist obligations, and plans for personal initiatives.

The most telling aid by branch and rural libraries is rendered at the time of on-site visits. Due to the multi-faceted nature of the many literary propaganda themes that were carried out, it became clear that a guide should be developed which could be followed during such trips. In 1985, co-workers at the Dudinski Central Library helped 164 rural library workers during a day of methodological and practical classes.

The work of the Dudinski Central Library, serving as a methodological center, is constantly controlled by the okrug department of culture of the Taimir okrispolkom (okrug executive political committee). Colleagues at the culture department heard a report "On the Work of the Methodological-Bibliographical Division of the Dudinski Central Library System, for the Improvement of Methodological Leadership by Okrug Libraries." A program called "At the Round Table" was featured over the okrug radio, in which colleagues from the okrug department of culture, the Methodological-Bibliographical Division and the library services division of the Dudinski Central Library System discussed plans for methodological work during the upcoming five-year plan. The main thing is to help the people of the Far North to fulfill in every way the tasks set down by the 27th Conference of the Communist Party of the Soviet Union.

1985A, Yelepov et al.—The expanse of Siberia and the Far East occupies two-thirds of the entire area of the Russian Soviet Federated Socialist Republic (RSFSR). This is comprised of three autonomous republics, four territories (krai) and eleven provinces (oblasts). More than a million people work in agriculture in this region. Their professional information needs are satisfied to a certain extent through a system of agricultural libraries—branch libraries of the National Research Institute, and academic agricultural libraries in upper and middle educational institutions. However, a large role in information maintenance for the agricultural complexes belongs to government people's libraries, a network of which predominates in the villages. At the present time agricultural specialists of the region are served by more than 10,000 such libraries, and 180 agricultural libraries. The oblast library, coordinating its work with the territorial organs regarding scientific/technical information, serves as organizer of all information for the specialists. This was especially emphasized in the Yakutsk ASSR and Magadan oblast, in the extreme northeast.

The Soviet North is inhabited by 26 indigenous nationalities with a total population exceeding 150,000. Each one of these ethnic groups has its own history, combining aspects of husbandry, culture and lifestyle. Therefore, a well-thought out organization of library service for these Native nationalities takes on an especially important significance.

In rural areas, enormous changes have occurred in the social milieu. It is entirely natural that cultural and spiritual questions and needs of the population should increase greatly, and in essence not differ from a city-dweller's circle of concerns. It follows that party organizations consider it important to unite agricultural production with culture, and every day concern themselves with questions to do with the ideological growth of kolkhoz workers and specialists in the economy.

For example, agricultural production in the Yakutsk ASSR or Republic (or Sakha Republic, also called Yakutiya) and Magadan Oblast are served by branch libraries of the central libraries. The work is conducted along three lines. First of all, reader interest is stimulated by the study of socio-political literature and periodicals. Secondly, rural workers have become accustomed to multi-ethnic Soviet creative literature. And finally, there is professional reading.

A single system of library and information services to agricultural specialists was established in the Yakutsk ASSR, which has functioned since 1980. The experience of libraries in the Buryat ASSR was taken as the guiding example.

The activities of all the remaining participants—district, oblast, republic and regional libraries, along with many others—are focused on the village library. Serving primarily village residents, it first of all takes advantage of the entire complex of resources available within the oblast. Secondly, it accumulates information about the interests and information needs of readers; and thirdly, it directs these data up to the district, and then the oblast center, so as to provide "feedback." The headquarters library for the entire effort is, of course, the Yakutsk ASSR (Pushkin Memorial) Library, located in the capitol of Yakutsk.

Study rooms for scientific-technical information have been set up at district libraries throughout Yakutiya. Their goal is the skilled selection of needed materials and their quick delivery to rural specialists. Such study rooms are operating in southern districts of the ASSR. The Yakutsk Interbranch Center of the Scientific Technical Institute provides these study rooms with scientific-technical information arranged by subject, tied in with the implementation of the USSR Food Program. In addition, the Yakutsk Republic Library and Scientific-Technical Institute's Interbranch Library send out informational lists of literature not only to district libraries, but directly to agricultural institutions in the republic. By such means, one out of four specialists in agriculture utilizes stock of a special library, and the rest have recourse to people's libraries.

The agricultural library of the Yakutsk Sci-Tech Institute plans its work together with the Pushkin Memorial Library and the Yakutsk branch of the USSR Academy of Sciences. The Yakutsk Scientific Research Institute for agriculture has been directed to accelerate advances in science and agricultural production. In working for these goals, all information learned is transmitted to the central scientific-technical library, which provides it to the agricultural specialists. The Scientific-Technical Institute (STI) organization, which originated with a series of state farms, was called upon to inform specialists about recommendations worked out by the scientific institutions.

The experience of the Ordjon-Kidzev District Library is a good example of services to agricultural specialists. After studying the economic specializations of the area and their long-range development, the central library objectively identifies local information needs. With the help of a cultural/economic profile, and also more details about the kind of work each specialist performs, individual interests can be addressed. These specialized services are offered in S.T.I. study rooms in district libraries and by library stations that are located right on state farms. More than 50% of the agricultural collection of the Ordjon-Kidzev central library is at the disposal of these stations.

Services to agricultural workers naturally take into account the ethnic character of the district. The Native population of the Ordjon-Kidzev District comprises the majority of the population, and this produces a definite imprint on aspects of library work.

Experience gained in the Yakutsk ASSR and Magadan Oblast during implementation of the party's directive entitled "On the Measures for Long-Range Social and Economic Development of Regions of Resident Nationalities of the North" foresaw the creation of a network of mobile agitkultbrigades. This was set up within existing government library networks, and effectively met the information needs of Native subsistence workers, including those pursuing nomadic lifestyles.

Every year each library working with an agitcultbrigade receives a supplementary amount of 150–200 rubles for the library collection. The Magadan oblast library takes measures to increase acquisitions of book collections on a particular subject for the reindeer herders brigade. An interesting experiment was completed in the Bilibin District (in hilly country of west-central Chukotka) of the Magadan region, involving joint work of libraries and AKBs. Of the 35 mobile library units of all types, 27 were in villages. The AKBs operate in Anyuisk, Omolon and Ilirnya. The acquisitions of mobile library units are arrived at by considering reindeer herders' and fishermen's brigade readers' profiles from a card index. Supplementing this, library employees working with the AKBs obtain materials for debates and lectures that are produced by state farm specialists of the tundra. Other kinds of materials adapted for this use are recorded on tape, such as literary reviews, talking journals and presentations of kolkhoz specialists.

The AKBs of the Yakutsk ASSR make extensive use of talking books in the Eveni and Evenki languages (works of Native authors recorded on tape), prepared by the "Literature of Northern Nationalities" section in the department of Yakutsk regional literature of the Pushkin Memorial Library in Yakutsk, the capital. Over the years of this section's existence, 2,725 residents of Yakutsk ASSR and the Magadan and Kamchatka oblasts have heard the talking books. In 1980 the section was visited by residents of the most remote population points in the Crednekolymsk, Monsk and Tomponsk regions. With the help of talking books, the reader has an opportunity to get acquainted with works of ethnic writers, as well as the best Soviet and foreign literature, in his or her own Native language.

The transportation now used by AKBs is the helicopter, which can reach the most remote locations. Every year the government gives 700-800,000 rubles for the helicoptered delivery of services to agricultural specialists of the Yakutsk ASSR.

Services to agricultural workers—reindeer herders and fishermen—located for long periods on remote pastures and with fishing brigades, could be made more effective by adding representatives of district executive committees, local newspapers, libraries and local managers to the staff of coordinating councils. These councils (soviets) could perform such tasks as adjustments in work plans and control over their implementation, organization of acquisitions for the mobile library units, and timely, systematic delivery of literature to the brigades. Continued improvement of the qualifications of library workers requires courses, practicums, probationary work, district and town seminars, and a school for progressive methods.

Living and working conditions for young specialists need upgrading, notably regarding housing. The stability of cadre is 50-60%. Formerly, young specialists didn't last. It should be remembered that, in the districts noted, the level of qualifications for library cadre is among the highest. In libraries of a third of the Yakutsk ASSR, specialists have the highest education, and in the Magadan region these comprise about 50%, with the majority having achieved the most advanced library education.

Now, in all the principal regions of the RSFSR, including Eastern Siberia and the Far East, there are educational institutions that prepare the library's cadre, who speak their national languages and are familiar with the culture and traditions of their people. Their graduates manage people's and school libraries, government libraries (republic, oblast, etc.), as well as academic and higher educational institution libraries. And they also successfully manage library affairs on a regional scale.

But not all problems have been resolved. A number of librarians know only one language, and therefore experience difficulties in services to a multilingual client-group of readers. For example, in the Yakutsk ASSR, there are thousands of northern residents (Eveni, Evenki, Yukagiri and those from Chukotka). So it is expedient to send young people from the indigenous peoples to training schools of the northern region as grant-aided students, and to develop correspondence study in every way possible.

1988, Maksimova. (In the Russian Bibliography/Reference List, see under: RSFSR. Ministerstvo Kul'tury. Gosudarstvennaya ordena Trudovogo Krasnovo Znameni imeni M.E. Saltykova-Shchedrina. *Formy i Metody Bibliotechnoi Raboty s Narodnostyami Severa,* 1988 [Forms and Methods of Library Work with Peoples of the North].)

The northern Native peoples are engaged in traditional pursuits: reindeer herding, hunting, fishing, sea mammal harvesting, fur farming, and stock raising. Some occupy themselves with "non-productive" work, such as education, culture, health care, consumer services, trade, and so on. About 10 percent are craftspeople, like ivory carvers and furriers, or souvenir makers of a culturally traditional nature.

Here are the living conditions of the Native people (as well as the working situation of librarians serving them): a severe climate, huge distances between population points, difficult communication and transportation (often no roads), subsistence-based economic pursuits, small groups working seasonally or intermittently while based in rural and remote villages with only a few hundred residents.

Reindeer herders are on the move for 9 or 10 months of the year with a relatively unchanging lifestyle; reindeer herding is unappealling to the young and a challenge for librarians. Book collections at the district level need to be strong enough to supply both AKBs with adequate library materials and the traveling methodologist with instructional and informational aids. In the absence of AKB service, a book fancier in the brigade is put in charge of a "microlibrary" that is shared by all. For the few months spent in the home village, appropriate programs and services are planned by the local library. These are arranged around state holidays and celebrations of the herders' work, and at these times individual readers' services can be applied. Programs needn't be very long, perhaps 15–20 minutes, and can be on very diverse themes. Herders aren't the most natural readers, especially elders, but one may point out material being read by their children, friends, and relatives.

Fishermen are based in a home village, and fishing is done intermittently during times of fish runs. Librarians can reach them in the field during rest periods or lunch breaks or where they unload catches, when a short talk and encouragement in fishing can be offered. In the village, many more elaborate programs and services are followed, and discussions can be led by a fisherman-reader if not the librarian.

The hunters' working season is usually from October to May, and they go out on skis singly or in twos and threes, 30–50 kilometers from home. There are already little huts placed out there for their use, about 50–80 kilometers apart. Game hunted include blue and white foxes, squirrels and sables. In the field, services can only be provided by skis or helicopter, so these are very limited. The usual way is for one or two books to be taken when the hunter leaves on his long seasonal treks. Otherwise the best time to catch them is when they return home to rest and get paid. Again, a variety of programs and services are implemented, including individual help, which focuses on the life of the hunter, his accomplishments, and goals.

As for craftspeople, which include men and women at home, they will visit their local library and be presented with the usual variety of programs and services, wherever possible utilizing book lovers and preeminent craftspeople as discussion leaders and presenters.

Finally, library services for Native women, who mostly stay at home, deserve special attention. First of all, they usually aren't producers. Secondly, as their children grow up, they are either in child care centers or off at boarding schools. Because the men are away working, the women have a lot of free time and few responsibilities. The librarian makes the rounds of houses as well as arranging pleasant programs in the local library, offering tea and refreshments. Initial programs shouldn't be too "heavy," or some women might not return. But, over time, more purposeful conversations and discussion can be introduced. Maybe a club or interest group can be organized, and administration help, social organizations and women's councils taken advantage of. Activist women need to be identified; through their example a goal-oriented club can be organized, that involves everyone. The name of a club should be attractive and original, so a competition could be held to choose the best one. Such a club can address household problems such as budgets, cooking, and child development or special projects of local interest. One women's club decided to look for and memorialize the graves in their locality of victims of the Great Patriotic War. In other words, library work with Native women helps them become better homemakers and productive members of the community.

1989, In the No. 11 (November) issue of the national monthly library magazine, *Bibliotekar'* (Librarian), there appeared an insert entitled "Draft of a Concept for the Development of Library Affairs in the RSFSR to the Year 2005." It was produced by a large committee of library representatives and specialists. Its recommendations were as follows:

1. Decentralization of library authority nationwide, granting more autonomy and control to republics and oblasts, including planning and construction.
2. Financing of libraries, instead of being solely provided for by a distant and unresponsive central authority, will have the stimulating benefit of local funding options, such as selective additional services for a fee.
3. Local library management policies will be directed by a combination of community input, professional librarians' expertise and experience, and evaluation of actual services provided. For example, the array of periodicals received by a local library should be locally determined.
4. Networks and other interlibrary cooperation will be primarily based at the republic and oblast level. They must be flexible, meet real information needs, and be efficiently managed. Strengthening of languages and literatures of every nationality should be based at this level as well.
5. Technological advances must become a normal part of library operations, from one end of the RSFSR to the other, and should eventually reach modern standards (automation, information processing and searches, photoduplication, microforms, etc.). The role of the electronic media in information provision needs to be considered, as well as the growth of home libraries.
6. Where indicated, new types of libraries or forms of library services should be added that reflect all the dynamic sociocultural changes now going on in the Soviet Union. Mechanisms must be set up to enable library users and readers to be formal participants in the determination of library policies.
7. Training of library personnel must include new skills that reflect

changes in Soviet society and how libraries respond. Methodological work (inspection, regulation, etc.) will be reduced, giving line libraries leeway for independent analysis and selection. Special training is needed for certain library services, such as for the blind and handicapped. Continuing education for library workers should be more realistic, responding to the information demands of the community.

Information found since the Soviet Union began disintegrating politically in 1991 is incorporated in the following commentary. See Russian Source Notes and Reference List at the end of the chapter for all Russia-specific materials utilized.

Commentary

One should first be reminded of cross-cultural considerations specific to the Soviet Union, a vast, multicultural nation that in many ways resembles more a Third World empire than a monolithic world power. Throughout their history the Russian and then the Soviet people have experienced one invading migration or army after another, overwhelming and punishing its population and mostly rural landscape. This goes back to the Mongol hordes overrunning Kievan Russia beginning in the 13th century, and continued most recently with Napoleon in the early 19th and Adolf Hitler in the mid-20th century. There has always been a natural and understandable xenophobia, a suspicion and fear of foreigners and their influence. There is also a great sensitivity to the fact that Soviet technological applications have not supplied the Soviet consumer with the amenities of life equal to those in North America, western Europe, Japan, Australia, etc.

Rather than immediately adopting a monocultural and judgmental view of Soviet librarianship, however, from the point of view of competition and comparison in the international marketplace of ideas and the practicable application of standards that are "state-of-the-art," let us first try to accept and understand Soviet accomplishments on their own terms. In a cross-cultural relationship, we can learn a great deal more by observing and listening in order to understand, than by reacting and criticizing in order to claim superiority.

We may learn, for example, that Soviet libraries adopted some special and very appropriate (for their purposes, as well as to reach every reader) measures for providing library services, though highly ideological rather than state-of-the-art technology, or what their readers really wanted. And when it comes to other benefits for the Native peoples of the Soviet North, progress in specializations, literacy, improving the status of women, infrastructural development, and exploiting subsistence resources were at least the equal of that provided to northern peoples by other circumpolar nations. Yes, it was highly ideological and Russianizing, culturally destructive, and a brutally closed and totalitarian system, but then one could certainly describe the comparatively benign policies prevailing in Alaska and Canada as being, for many, many years, neglectful and biased and brutal in their own way—racist, paternalistic, and neocolonialist. And in North America, there has been *no* major, ongoing effort to educate and train Native professional, administrative, and technical specialists for service in their homelands, and the University of Alaska is still under fire in the mid-1990s by accreditation authorities for neglecting Native and rural education. The northern Native peoples of both spheres, the Russian and the North American, suffered the holocaustal consequences of contact and domination: the decimation of generations in the epidemics, the loss of lands and resource access and use, humiliation and deprivation as the result of juvenile potential "culture-carriers" being exiled and deculturated in distant boarding schools, coercive Christian proselitization by missionaries (who were usually handmaidens of the government), and the scourge of alcohol-plying, often unprincipled traders.

In 1970, Terence Armstrong of the University of Alaska, Fairbanks stated:

> Comparing the Soviet situation with the Alaskan, it is clear that the Soviet Union has gone considerably further than the United States in working out relations with the northern peoples. This is not surprising in view of the longer history of Russian contact with these peoples, of the greater Soviet interest in the north as a whole, of the much larger number of Natives involved (nearly 20 times as many), and of the wide range of accomplishment among them. It would seem that education has been the most important single factor in the successes that the Soviet Union has achieved. In providing this, the Soviet motivation has been that of missionary, and the missionary has had the full resources of the state behind him. (p.32 of Armstrong, cited herein on p.212. I would replace "missionary" with political zealot.)

Among severely disruptive policies of the new Soviet regime was the forced collectivization of the 1930s, which Armstrong claims was probably milder among the Native subsistence communities. Still, the Soviet's own figure of almost one-quarter of all reindeer being lost during that time is testament to just one small though key aspect of the havoc it caused. There is ample additional documentation of the heavy-handed and uncompromising implementation of Soviet socialist reforms among the small peoples of the north, and of their subjugation and subservience to these policies. Subsistence resources were taken over for collectivist management, and most traditional customs were purged and cast aside, along with those more well-off (and successful) Natives, who were either ostracized or liquidated. This was the negative side of the Sovietization of the small nationalities of the north, initially managed idealistically by the Committee of the North, which allowed for some tribal representation, flexibility and fairness.

Under Soviet power, state-imposed concepts and enterprise characterized all development in Siberia and the Far East (along with revolutionary fervor), and libraries were an integral part of it. We will use the Chukotka Autonomous Okrug (Chukchi National Area) as an example, which includes some Siberian Yupik coastal Eskimos (with Alaskan relatives across the Bering Strait). There were cultural bases (Kultbazy) in this easternmost part of the USSR before the future oblast capitol of Magadan was established in 1930 (Chukotka, the homeland of the Chukchi and some coastal Eskimos and the eastern half of the Magadan Oblast, asserted its greater autonomy in 1990. Ten years later there was a network of government peoples libraries in place, with its headquarters the Central Library of Anadyr, the capital. In 1944 a regional library was established in Lavrentiya on the coast of Chukotka. Starting after World War II, in 1949 a special group of more sophisticated "Red Tent" units was mobilized, to better serve reindeer-herding brigades. The Kultbaza concept was resurrected for the same reason, but in an abbreviated version. In these more streamlined stations the club, or house of culture, would be combined with the library, one staff member serving a dual role.

In 1954 the main Magadan library, with 88,000 volumes, was designated the oblast or provincial library. From that point forward, through various resolutions passed by central and oblast authorities, library development accelerated throughout the entire region. Material support greatly improved, along with the quality of library services, and collections grew in multiples. The concept of open access to book stacks was started around 1960, and by this time all village libraries had a library council. The goal during this period was to reach "every family" with library services. Library organization in Chukotka became progressively more complex and specialized, both as to type of library and interlibrary cooperation. Village libraries, for example, began separating from combined club/library operations. Centralization was implemented for certain types of libraries, such as trade union and government peoples libraries.

By 1970 in the Magadan Oblast altogether, there were 92 libraries of the RSFSR Ministry of Culture, which included the Pushkin (Oblast) Library in Magadan city and the Okrug Library in Anadyr (for Chukotka). Then there were four city libraries, including the central youth library. Also, eleven regional libraries (later reaching seventeen—one for each administrative region in the oblast), 62 village libraries, six children's libraries (in regional centers), and six libraries in clubs. In addition there were 134 professional (trade, specialist) union libraries, 123 general school and vo-tech school libraries, eight libraries of specialized educational institutions, 12 technical departmental libraries, and 16 Party Committee libraries. Naturally many of the remote or special libraries were quite small, and we leave out the mobile and rotating-type library services serving the urban workplace, as well as those in the field.

One is struck by a number of characteristic features of library development and services in the USSR, both generally and for the Northern ethnic minorities. There was the bureaucratic complexity of the centralized governmental structure that governed and supported libraries in the nation as a whole. Yet there was a fragmented character to it, with a stream of resolutions, directives, approvals (or denials) originating from distant and remote central planning ministries, filtered through republic-level councils, and diverse ministries competing with each other and other governmental organs, each one at every step of the way being accountable to the Communist Party. Still, despite these negative aspects, one has to be impressed by the variety of ingenious and creative methods librarians utilized, along with other agencies, in their "cultural enlightenment" campaigns and other library work.

There are other aspects worth noting. There is the evidence that library education, as in the West, seemed to have difficulty staying relatively modern and sophisticated on the leading edge of Soviet sociocultural efforts. There were difficulties in providing library services of equal quality to rural and urban areas, a situation shared by colleagues in Western countries. There seems to have been more libraries and library service units per capita and a nationwide commitment to try to reach entire populations no matter how variegated, specialized, or remote. Yet deficiencies and derogations were unceasing. Soviet libraries below the republic level in general appear to have lacked indispensable modern aids like photocopiers and microforms, and there was a scarcity of audiovisual equipment, except perhaps movie projectors. Buildings housing libraries were often inappropriate and poorly equipped. State-of-the-art technology, such as video playback and production equipment or computers and telecommunications, were unavailable certainly beyond Moscow for use in libraries, major scientific institutions, and the largest republic libraries. As late as 1989, for example, the Anadyr Regional Library had one television monitor for public viewing, which received two government channels, and orders for photocopying had to be sent hundreds of kilometers to the oblast capital, Magadan.

Many measures aimed at increasing library capability, efficiency and use in the broadest sense are discussed, and in the (theoretically) ideal mode library workers are seen as proactive, rather than just assertive and dutiful. Not that this has been the common experience in the Soviet Union; the articles are replete with complaints, criticisms, exhortations, recommendations and plans for reorganizations of agencies and their working relationships that reflect a seemingly chronic inadequacy of library services to perceived needs. Here and there exemplary progress is noted, by regions, individual libraries or library workers. Family or house-to-house surveys were done by volunteer "library activists," or specialists and professional workers who offered their time and energy as Party members. Later, follow-up and delivery could be performed by *Komsomol* youth (as old as in their mid-twenties). The goal striven for was to have the best possible (and ideologically correct) library services provided to every single Soviet citizen, no matter who or where, everyone on the same level in terms of library service quality. But the reality was otherwise. Interethnic inequities and class discrimination were maintained in the service structure, favoring the well-placed and Party-privileged, urban-centered and Russian-acculturated citizenry.

Libraries and the many variations in library service delivery were an integral part of the socio-cultural, political and economic life of the USSR, but the national library bureaucracy was overstaffed with heads and functionaries diffidently exercising limited powers, with apparently little linkage with their peers and colleagues in other library institutions. Liaison, cooperation, mutual accountability and good coordination, both vertically and horizontally, were evidently difficult to achieve, and the development of horizontal networking and cooperation, at all levels, although not a recent phenomenon, were never as productive or responsive as planned. Library services overall have been utilized significantly less in recent years, and some of the reasons for this include the increased availability of trade books and other reading materials to the general public, more private libraries and subscriptions, the proliferation of television, drastic funding losses since 1991, and possibly the identification of libraries with Soviet ideological indoctrination. Privately-owned books are now, nationally, several times the total of library holdings.

Library education is very European in that the same curricula are offered by state colleges everywhere, along with the same textbooks. However, as academic institutions as well as state publishing houses have more latitude in selecting teaching materials and textbooks are depoliticized, this may change dramatically. Under the Soviets, although the library profession was rewarded with medals and some librarians became politically prominent, at least in their service area, it is clear that library work was well coordinated with related "cultural enlightenment" and other quasi-political educational activities. Whether by choice or necessity, they were intellectually far more conservative and repressed than librarians in the West. In addition, the fact that the state provided all the education, professional training, and opportunities for research, as well as a job and a living situation, must have required undeviating loyalty from the recipient, including pressure to join the Communist Party. This would have had a stifling effect on initiative and creativity, unless one were ideologically correct in one's progressive ways. When acquisitions are constantly screened by military, literary, political, and security censors, there is no room for comfort! Add to that periodically changing tolerance for various authors, titles, and subject matter that resulted in secret stacks (even at the local level) and burning of books offensive to the current regime, as well as purges of librarians unable to shift accordingly or who inadvertently say or do something that is "incorrect", and the situation would be deadly indeed.

In the Soviet library world there was no equivalent word for "outreach," as far as I know, at least not as we use it in the United States. The extension of library and information services to every element and corner of Soviet society was, from the beginning, considered part of normal, mainstream policy. The only things special about it were the logistical and material problems in physically being able to reach the most remote camp and the most transient specialist or nomadic band with sufficiently appropriate support, or particular enclaves of Native speakers and newly settled populations in distant resource development projects. In the highly developmental situation that Soviet society was in, right through the "Great Patriotic War" and since 1945 (not to mention the herculean efforts and sacrifices needed for sheer survival and reconstruction after the war) the Communist-wrought social landscape was perforce the ideological workplace for Soviet librarians in this relatively new, modernizing nation. Keep in mind that the Russian Revolution, which took place only three generations ago, faced appalling universal problems in every area of social need. Yet during the first fifty years of the Soviet regime there was never any question about the essential role of library, information and allied cultural enlightenment services—promoting sanitary personal habits, personal as well as professional self-improvement, general and special education, political indoctrination and propaganda in Marxist-Leninist values, encouragement and support of maximum productivity for Soviet workers, and therefore the greater glory and advancement of Soviet society.

However, surely the fact that all credentialed library workers had to return to work in their home area (unless they were among the top students who were given more privileged options, or chose to go to areas of "new construction" in remote locations), would seem to have a deadening effect on at least some individual career aspirations, as well as encourage a parochial and reactionary view toward "life and work." On the other hand, employment was assured, as well as more or less tolerable living and working conditions, along with rewards for exemplary service and recognition of the industrious and those who developed "progressive methods." However, much of this kind of remuneration seems to have been more symbolic and laudatory than material in nature, though added privileges—if one had party approval—might bring some of that, too. Other articles cite cross-cultural difficulties with librarians who are strangers to Native areas, and, knowing as we do that Russification was the usual or default policy in any choice regarding cultural emphasis, whether for budgetary, political, or administrative reasons, one may conclude that there was probably a shortage of Native librarians in most communities—another problem held in common with Fourth World areas of Western countries, where, with the exception of Greenland, the ratio has been and continues to be much worse.

Statistical measures and indicators used in Soviet libraries include: the number of (registered) "readers," number of library visitors, number of books in a collection and its rate of growth, proportion of titles held in subject areas most appropriate for a given service area, number of various types of programs held and the attendance, number of agitkultbrigades (cultural teams), number of library units (stationary, mobile, service points, etc.), number of libraries of various types (government, public-access, people's, special, trade union, children's, school, sci-tech, academic, mobile units, industrial service points, etc.), numbers of library workers with continuing education or special training, numbers of books "returned" (circulation), numbers of books "read" (borrowed) per capita and per library "reader," percentage of books actually used out of a collection, percentage of readers' requests filled or not filled, and the number of graduates in library education (which is broken down by educational level and ethnic groups), percentage of librarians receiving advanced specialized training, and so on.

We have learned, however, that statistics submitted from all levels were routinely falsified, padded, omitted, or distorted, in order to tell higher authorities what they wanted (or needed!) to hear. This factor affected statistics of every kind, from the grossly national and macroeconomic to the most mundane daily figures from the local library. Statistics from the Soviet era simply cannot be trusted, without a great deal of investigation, qualification, and analysis.

Some special gauges used in library planning are worth noting. One is the Coefficient of Correspondence between book distribution and the scope of the collections involved, which determines the subject specialization needed in a given library. Another is the Coefficient of Proximity of Population Points, used as one indicator to determine where to site libraries in sparsely populated northern areas. Such indicators are a reflection of the "scientific" methodologies employed in Soviet library planning and development.

There are also various ways in which library services are qualitatively monitored. There are reviews and evaluations from above, articles in the general as well as the library press, various conferences for the exchange of views and promotion of new policies, analysis of the statistics cited above, studies of the changing socio-economic situation and the corresponding need for changes in library and information services to accommodate them, and the solicitation of readers' comments on services provided. House-to-house community surveys also bring a great deal of detailed information about individual readers to the attention of the local librarian.

Questions and criticisms concerning libraries in Native settings or for Native users in general are very similar to those being encountered in the west: not enough Native library workers; importance of library staff serving a multicultural population to have, as a unit, a multilingual capability; providing materials in Native orthographies; the uselessness of inappropriate, duplicative and outdated materials and the necessity to provide enough appropriate and up-to-date materials; difficulties of delivering services to remote settlements and nomadic camps; the importance of educating non-Natives outside Native areas or new to them about Native cultures; and the need to cultivate pride of nation and pride in individual Native cultural heritage.

However, library materials in Native orthographies were never commonly available, except for children. In the earliest years there was a sincere desire by those closest to the scene, especially idealistic Russian scholars and conscientious researchers of the northern peoples, to educate and publish in Native languages so as to preserve and sustain the Native cultures and their subsistence lifestyles, though in 'socialist forms.' But eventually the Russian language was always emphasized, if not overtly then inadvertently or by default, according to information found in various sources, for example at the end of chapters in the standard classic, *Narody Sibiri* (*Peoples of Siberia*), by M. G. Levin and A. P. Potapov (1956). The Russian language is everywhere the official and most commonly used language. A visit to the Anadyr, Chukotka area in 1989, including a Chukchi reindeer brigade in the field, found only Russian being spoken by all Natives encountered. Of course, most Native people are found in remote villages and work sites outside the larger cities and towns, working in collective field industries that derived from subsistence pursuits of old.

Other shortcomings in Soviet librarianship reflect many failures forthcoming titles announced yet never published, or issued in such small printings as to be nearly nonexistent; too few copies of popular, current or indispensable titles; services to field brigades were inadequate; delivery and pick-up of books was often determined by chance, rather then need; transportation was and still is in short supply; service networks in remote areas are more difficult to maintain; proposed improvements in management and planning never seemed to materialize; scientific methodologies are cited and invoked time and time again, yet implementation and practical application were too long delayed, if they ever happen at all; well-founded planning and cost-analysis are claimed to be indispensable, yet are little used; there is insufficient orientation to the special conditions and needs of Native people; local librarians aren't getting timely and appropriate help from higher up; collection development staff aren't paying enough attention to actual local needs; interlibrary cooperation and coordinated services too often seemed to be frustrated by slavish and hidebound bureaucracies; as in the one case, where a much vaunted series of special publications never appeared, and so on. And now, with substantial reductions of government subsidies, funding for libraries and librarians has become decentralized and very difficult. Many periodicals founded under Soviet rule have ceased, such as the two favorites *Severny Prostory* (Northern Spaces) and *Ruskii Yazyk za Rubezhom* (The Russian Language Abroad).

A few articles discuss ways of coordinating library planning, administration, training and local operations throughout the vast, continental expanse of Siberia and the Far East. Area library unifications at all levels are proposed, as well as centralized and/or specialized reference services, from the national level on down. These involved were to be restructuring for joint planning and demonstration projects, retraining, and new configurations for logistical and material support. Where needed, special library systems or networks were to be territorially organized to serve an economic region, metropolitan area, or major project site.

The professional goal was to ensure that progressive and modern methods of library and information science management were efficiently passed on and effectively implemented for all libraries and library field units. What made this admirable long-range and universal approach so complex and overwhelming was its being a systematic plan to create working networks and interlibrary cooperation, both vertically and horizontally, while simultaneously coordinating them with the larger national effort toward greater work productivity and improved economic performance in all sectors. There was no separating one from the other in the orthodox Soviet view. It was undoubtedly this integration in the pursuit of national goals, along with other constraining factors cited, that made local adaptation and individual initiative so difficult, unless it could be shown within the established system of working relationships to result in success in every sense of the word, an unlikely prospect under the severely restrictive and pervasively dogmatized conditions of "life and work" in the old Soviet state.

At the same time, the long-range view emphasized appropriate library services for every client group, including the northern ethnic minorities, which again involved complex interlibrary and interagency coordination schemes. And all this was to be directed, of course, by the far distant Lenin State Library, the headquarters or main library for the entire, vast, multiethnic society that was the USSR. Belatedly, the Soviet policies of perestroika (restructuring) and glasnost (openness), were intended to eventually bring less decentralized and more democratized, modern and appropriate library services to the local level. Instead, launched on the dual rails of an educated public finished with utopian dreams shattered and Communist Party domination, they helped bring about the fall of the C. P. from power, and the collapse of Soviet political structures. But libraries now suffered from their close seventy-year marriage with Soviet "cultural enlightenment," and it will require years of reasonably stable socioeconomic conditions for them to recover.

There are technical papers in some of the library source books examined that analyze in surprising detail various conventional policies and procedures in library services. For example, the concept of open access to book collections, which was introduced in Soviet libraries in the 1960s, receives close examination because of the loss of control in reader's guidance (along with loss of a librarian's status). Other articles are dutifully preoccupied with the diligent propaganda, political dicta and moral susasion we find throughout much of Soviet library literature. Few articles on aspects of technical processing were found in general library literature, except that acquisitions policies and the distribution of book supplies are under constant review. Recent periodicals have more articles on automation and computer applications, as well as realistic concerns of free librarianship, and totally lack propagandiziing.

Only certain Soviet periodicals could be subscribed to beyond national borders, and technical publications, collections, and monographs generally still have a very limited printing and are no longer available once out of print. The continuing rarity of photocopiers makes it difficult for users to obtain copies from local libraries. In 1990, payment by foreigners for photocopied material was still made through "exchange of materials," not cash. In 1995, this is no longer the case, at least from my own experience. In 1989, the Anadyr Central and Headquarters Library in Chukotka had to send materials for photocopying to Magadan, the provincial (oblast) capital 870 miles distant. The librarian claimed this was no inconvenience at all, and there was no great need for photocopying anyway. (I can recall hearing that kind of comment when photocopiers were first available in the United States!) Back files of Soviet serials are extremely difficult to find on the open market and are usually very expensive. Also, no mention was made anywhere of audiovisual materials being borrowed or used by patrons. Librarians used them internally and for library meetings or club programs. Undoubtedly they, along with microforms, had some specialized use in major research and special libraries, but economic constraints since 1991 have kept any plans for further modernization very limited.

As for ideological propaganda, one article describes monthly campaigns conducted by librarians, popularizing resolutions passed by periodic conferences of the Communist Party of the USSR, or exhorting field workers at pivotal times of the year to increased productivity of harvests. Another is devoted to descriptions of special training days and conferences for library workers serving agricultural specialists. One article discusses the need for more coordination between libraries serving a particular service area or community, and the need for regional networks of sci-tech libraries serving specialists. (In 1975, I unsuccessfully tried to do something similar in Tacoma, Washington State, by circulating a newsletter among its 26 postsecondary, public and special libraries. Now with computer listservs, it would be much easier.) A unified territorial reference collection is described, in existence since 1979 and involving 15 libraries. One paradox about Soviet libraries was their seemingly great variety—yet all under a complex central pyramid of government planning, funding, supply, administration, production quotas, and Communist Party oversight.

A striking feature of Soviet librarianship, then, was the high degree of bureaucratization and politicization in the planning, implementation, and maintenance of library services of all types and for all client groups. Library workers were seen as co-laborers and comrades with all other specialists, who often shared each other's training sessions, and sometimes worked as members of various joint teams serving a common purpose in some aspect of administration or public service. And the final accountability of a Soviet librarian's work was this: Has it increased the "cultural enlightenment" level of as many people as possible? Has it raised socialist political awareness and pride of heritage and nation, as well as the level of "socialist competition" (for the common good instead of individual gain)? And finally, has it increased both productivity and the quality of that produced, contributing toward the fulfillment of Soviet goals on both domestic and international levels? Our own reply must be two-sided: "Yes, it did support Soviet ideological goals in the past" and "No, productivity and quality of life, including the standard of living, did not improve, except of course for those with Communist Party affiliations and the nomenklatura elite."

In the highly structured work environment of the past, however, how could the individual library-worker feel comfortable about offering ideas for change to superiors? Yet there apparently were such opportunities, at conferences and training sessions, when an "exchange of experiences" often took place, as a regular feature of the formal agenda. Thus, some new ideas might be presented in a depersonalized way, based on experience rather than as personal views. But whether any concrete changes might come as a result was always, at least until now, an unknown.

In comparing these issues on a theoretical level with ones asked by western librarians of their own mission and work, there is little matching of them. Only on special, rare occasions do organized librarians in the U.S. and Canada, for example, declare such things as national goals to be operative, and these are not harnessed directly to economic goals for economic achievement, although other national cultural goals, desirable in principle, may be cited in passing. Not that there isn't obvious indirect linkage between, say, school libraries and better education, or special libraries and more profitable corporations, or law libraries and more effective courtrooms and attorneys. But the links beyond that, to national achievement and idealistic goals, are absent. The goals of organized non-Native librarians in the U.S. and Canada as the mostly print purveyors of knowledge for a populace cajoled and harassed by the electronic media, are almost always focused on their library work. On the other hand, library development in Greenland and Fourth World areas of North America is of necessity more nationally, tribally integrated, because modernization and economic development within the albeit weakening framework of the traditional culture is widely accepted and cultivated, and in fact describes national (or tribal) library development policy in every instance that I am aware of.

As a Soviet librarian of the past, one would seem to have the certain knowledge that one was a participant in the national effort to meet specific objectives improving the lot of everyone, and striving toward common goals, ones with an officially recognized and lauded national importance. On the other hand, there were insuperable bureaucratic barriers and impedimenta, ideological conformities to follow, some problems regarding a librarian's authority and discretionary latitude, especially at the lower levels, and a constant shortfall in the supplies of appropriate library materials and equipment. It was the picture of a profession under pressure to do a good, dutiful job "correctly", and whose services were an integral part of personal and public life in the USSR.

However, the importance and status of librarian's work has undergone a steady diminution in the past couple of decades. In all the documentaries done on various aspects of Soviet life for U.S. television over the past several years, I don't recall seeing anything about frequenting the library or receiving library service. From the literature one gains the impression of a strongly "community-oriented" profession, but with strong direction from above to implement broad policies decreed by national Communist Party conferences, utilizing officially approved "progressive methods" to carry out officially "recommended" measures. But along with this comes the close community orientation of training and work, at all times accountable to real-life situations—at least in so far as this complements governmental and party requirements.

A durable yet obsolete stereotype of the librarian in the West (still found in actuality in some rural areas) has been a worker who is kept busy with many manual or maintenance duties, someone who is inadequately trained, print-oriented, unassertive, yet jealously if not imperiously guarding the library's somewhat dated treasures. In the Soviet Union and much of today's Russia, where computers, automation, or even in-house photoduplication have not yet reached the everyday library world, it could be said that the average librarian, certainly in rural northern areas and the Native homelands, is still found in this mode, but without the closely coordinated integration of state-directed, ideologically "correct" goals dictated by distant library institutions and central ministries. Now, any such inspiration must arise from individual librarians and libraries, professional organizations, library networking and mutual consultation, and voluntarily from the community, when it can be elicited.

But we must qualify the "print-oriented" nature of the Soviet rural librarian stereotyped above. The Soviet government expediently recognized the oral tradition of the Native peoples, utilizing not only films and radio and television broadcasts in Native languages for purposes of social control and indoctrination, but also special audio recordings and graphics and dramatic visits by helicoptered cultural teams (including librarians and performers) to serve subsistence and nomadic camps in remote areas. This latter kind of "home/work-visitation" was also found in health care, where healthcare providers of various types even now can make house calls, a luxury American doctors dispensed with decades ago.

In the Soviet Union and today's Russia, members of the very smallest nationalities that have been assimilated into neighboring larger ones may speak three languages: their own, that of the host ethnic group, and Russian. Such gradual, or "natural," assimilation (as some sources describe it) means that Russification continues inexorably, although in the early decades of Communist rule most Native languages had their new orthography and seemingly every community and national region its newspapers and journals with articles in Russian and one or more area languages, no matter how small the readership.

In Siberia and the Far East, where economic, demographic and infrastructural growth has been intensifying since the 1950s, there still remains the remoteness, isolation and closeness to nature that engenders a more flexible and independent lifestyle, as in Alaska for example. One has to admire the persistence and creativity of library services provided to these modern Soviet pioneers. And although there apparently were surveys and statistics kept (of dubious validity), assessments and exhortations presented (if slanted and ideological), and methodologies honed to the tasks at hand (if disregarding the real needs and desires of Native northerners), the goal being to better serve what we in the United States call the "unreached majority" of the population.

Looking at the approximately 30-year span of the Soviet articles, it was striking to me how similar many of them were, as to message and even style. In a few cases it was like reading an article I'd already seen elsewhere, in another periodical or under another title, either by the same author or someone else! (In paraphrasing or condensing the articles for inclusion here, many repetitive and redundant portions were dropped.) It was only after 1991, when I began receiving articles and papers for the earlier period that I'd never seen or heard of, that I realized how much had been missed by appealing to Soviet librarians under the eye of the Communist regime.

By way of illustrating, in another field, the consequences for specialists of going against the grain in the old USSR, I remember a television program I viewed in 1990 (copyrighted 1987) of the NOVA series on educational television in the United States. It was entitled, "How Good Is Soviet Science?" The format involved an American scientist fluent in Russian who had visited the USSR every two years for the previous fifteen years. The purpose of the filmed trip was to gauge the progress of Soviet science. A riveting five-minute segment in this hour-long program dealt with access to scientific information in major Soviet libraries in Moscow. Using the example of *Science* magazine, issues from the U.S. were compared with the translated versions in Soviet libraries. The articles missing were those to do with political issues in science. Even one on officially sanctioned scientific exchange programs was excised. The American scientist learned that foreign scientific literature was censored, and scientific conferences outside the USSR were very difficult to attend. (One recalls the rare attendance of Soviet library representatives at Northern Libraries Colloquies—even though the Arctic is half Russian.) He met with the community of Soviet scientists who had been removed from their work and ostracized into a closet scientific group, meeting informally on their own. Individually, over the years, they had chosen to question official policy, procedures or priorities. Soviet science, we were told, was still entrenched in theoretical research, with technological applications widely neglected—let alone their implementation in industry and public services. Those who expressed dissatisfaction with current policies and procedures were moved out.

After the failed putsch of entrenched Communist elements and a few unenthusiastic army units in August 1991, the Russian social, political, cultural, and economic landscape has been rent and riven by a rising crescendo of drastic changes, upheavals that reflect all too realistically the title of a collection of essays on Mikhail Gorbachev's policies: *Revolutsiya*

Prodolzhaetsya (The Revolution Continues). The democratizing invitations of *glasnost* (openness) and *perestroika* (reconstruction) always assumed a continuing Communist Party leadership, but such tentative steps toward a more expressive society, freer economy, and responsive government are now only confusing echoes reverberating off the crumbling walls of the Soviet past.

With the disintegration of the union of 15 Soviet republics into a loosely linked and mutually suspicious Commonwealth of Independent States followed by the formation of a dominant Russian Federation (basically the former RSFSR) headed by President Boris Yeltsin, efforts have gone forward to establish a Russian-style democracy under a new constitution, with an elected though strong executive, representative legislative bodies, and a fairer judiciary. But the forces of reaction (Communists, Monarchists, Fascists, Anarchists, etc.) continue to struggle to undermine Russia-Reborn.

Since 1992 there has been a liberalization of fiscal and economic policies aimed at establishing lines of credit, stabilizing prices, and making the ruble directly convertible in the international marketplace. Severely reduced military spending and inflation due to overprinting of rubles in order to subsidize struggling industry and agriculture undergoing privatization have created an inconsistent and unstable economy, common criminality and corruption, and consequently widespread hardships for the diverse peoples of the former USSR, most of whom are very poor, though a few entrepreneurs are getting very rich. Some progress is being made, however, and analysts agree that the reforms must continue and the democratic movement needs the unstinting aid of judicious loans and grants as well as trade and investment from the United States and other First World nations.

Librarians began organizing their own professional associations during the Gorbachev era and lobbying for support from the community, as well as offering services and materials that their clients really needed and wanted. Libraries since 1990 are also being encouraged to try "self-financing" options, offering selected new services for a fee, and even bonuses to productive and proactive library workers. Letters to the editors of library periodicals indicate that such innovative steps are having invigorating results. The days of guaranteed budgets and salaries are gone and the very survival of many libraries and library jobs is at stake.

Library literature on the situation in the mid-90s across the Russian north among the Native homelands speak eloquently of the difficult conditions in every aspect of library work as the general media report on an array of appalling economic and political crises. Simultaneously, the media promotes (in the Native homelands), a return to subsistence economies, local government control, independent joint ventures with foreign investors, Native sovereignty, environmental protection, and preservation of Native cultural integrity, including the languages.

Epilogue

Throughout 1995 I continued in various ways to learn of current conditions for libraries and library workers across the Russian north, in particular in the Native homelands of the numerically small peoples. Though direct reports were not available or forthcoming from any sources regarding the current situation in local areas, enough "intelligence" could be obtained from a variety of indirect sources to assess conditions for library work. (There seemed to be no lack of information about major and scientific libraries, mainly through American sources emphasizing research and interlibrary cooperation at the highest levels.)

Statistics provided by Z.P. Sokolova, head of the Siberian Peoples Section of the Miklikho-Maklai Institute of Ethnology and Anthropology, describe the library scene across the Siberian and Far Eastern regions. From 1981 through 1993, the numbers of libraries in northern Native homelands remained fairly steady, though with significant increases in the Khanti-Mansi area of western Siberia and the Yamalo-Nenets region of the western Arctic. The numbers of residents and readers (card holders) per library varied slightly from region to region over time, with a few experiencing big decreases by the 1990s. The Sakha Republic (Yakutiya) seems to have had the most library development and the Chukotka and Kamchatka regions, the least.

Holdings of books in Native languages, emphasizing children's literature, were very high in the Sakha Republic and very low elsewhere, the lowest being in Kamchatka and the Archangel region of the far northwest Arctic, homeland of the Ugrians and Samoyeds.

Budgets are a constant struggle at the local level, with funding for any acquisitions and decent pay for workers a chronic problem. The automatic, top-down budgeting from remote and ideologically oppressive ministries no longer exists. Buildings need repair and renewal. Books and other media are in short supply, and old collections need replacement. Appropriate titles in subjects of interest and need for northern readers, Native or not, are hard to come by, especially in Native orthographies. The publishing industry is hard pressed to print small runs of such titles. More Native library workers are needed as is training for them. The "material-technical" base of district and regional libraries badly needs modernization, though major republic, regional, and scientific libraries are slowly acquiring the latest technology. Computers applications, including e-mail, for example, are beginning to come into use at this level.

For the Native peoples, there are Native sovereignty associations and cultural as well as subsistence advocacy movements. People aren't afraid to stand up and protest or to lobby their government representatives at all levels to respond to their needs. With the increasing democratization and slowly growing market economy since 1991 and before that under former Premier Mikhail Gorbachev, the socio-cultural environment of Russia, as well as the other republics is undergoing profound changes that will take decades to reach equilibrium. The most profoundly burdensome legacy to be overcome (if desired by the Russian people), is the cumulative mental ennervation, stultification and fear engendered by a thousand years of Czarist and Soviet central authority. Expectations and impatience are high, and individual and corporate initiatives are only beginning. Until sufficient stability and confidence characterize the general population, which is comprised nationwide of some 120 nationalities, the prospects for "rational" change will remain volatile. The "numerically small peoples" are like other Fourth World people around the circumpolar north, also finding their place in the national scheme of things, with more autonomy and control over their lands, waters, and resources.

On the positive side, probably most important and reassuring is that there is no longer the Moscow-based, Communist-led and fed command structure to oppress regional, ethnic, and local library hopes and expectations. Censorship, book-burning, secret stacks, banned titles and politically purged library advocates are not encountered any more. Controversial authors and publishers are no longer imprisoned, brainwashed, or "liquidated." And communication, exchange, and technical and consulting support is steadily increasing through foreign contracts even though foreign acquisitions are limited to only the largest and most central depository libraries. Russian libraries and librarians of every kind are joining the world community, and representatives of the Native peoples from all across the north, no longer confined and isolated to their homelands, are among them.

Russian Source Notes and Bibliography/ Reference List on Library and Related Development among the Numerically Small Northern Peoples and Yakutiya

1. Russian Source Notes

The Soviet material was difficult to get in hand at the beginning (late 1980s) and continued to come in after long searches and direct requests for help from colleagues at the Lenin State Library. This last appeal resulted in a large packet arriving after almost a year, in May, 1989, containing photocopies of every unfound article I had asked for, taken from three pages of citations the library had sent me two years earlier! (Using the "book exchange" method of payment then required, I supplied them with two titles, one on minor national political candidates in the United States, the other on something to do with Jews abroad.) They ranged from a number of individual articles in periodicals to excerpts from monographs and annuals.

Card catalog citations and a SPRILIB printout received from librarian Valerie Galpin of the Scott Polar Research Institute in 1986 revealed "nothing specifically indexed concerning libraries," but a fair amount of material on cross-cultural experiences. A fall 1994 search of Arctic databases (which include the SPRI holdings) brought up more Russian material, though again, nothing on library services among northern peoples.

In 1990, while in Seattle, I searched LISA, INSPEC, and Information Science Abstracts in DIALOG. In 1994 while in Anchorage, I searched POLARPAC (includes SPRI), COLD REGIONS (comprised of ASTIS and BOREAL), DISSERTATION ABSTRACTS ONDISC and ERIC at the University of Alaska, Anchorage. A search of LISA was made through the University of Washington Suzzallo Library. Only a few entries for the Russian north were found, and none were library-related.

The first quotation at the beginning of this chapter is from the vignette entitled "A Song flies over the tundra" on pages 75–76 of *Truzheniki Severa v Zhizn' i Literature (Toilers of the North in Life and Literature),* a Handbook for Teachers in the Magadan Oblast by E.D. Shevlyakova (Magadan Book Publishing, 1986). The second quotation is from Hedrick Smith's *The Russians,* on p.480 of the 1984 revised Ballantine Books edition.

In the 1990s, national and international "networking," or communication with one's colleagues through a variety of telecommunications applications, is increasing steadily. E-mail (electronic mail) and data retrieval or downloading from remote databases and information services from home or the workplace is readily available once one has the requisite equipment and application programs, or hardware and software, respectively. In the winter of 1994–95 I learned from the International Research and Exchange Board (IREX) of Washington, D.C. of library colleagues who were accessible in Russia and elsewhere in eastern Europe by e-mail (electronic correspondence by computer networks). (For more information on IREX, see under *News in Brief* in the following Reference List.) After six months of following these and many other referrals and sampling three or four international forums or newsgroups in an effort to learn about current library conditions across the Russian north, I finally achieved success. First I subscribed to slavlibs

(Slavic Librarians Forum), then relcom-sci-libraries (the Russian
Newsgroup), and finally pollib-1 (Polar Libraries Colloquy listserv). All
this networking finally resulted in my receiving, on one singular day,
substantive information and offers of help from three Russian library
colleagues. I have cited their generous help in the Acknowledgements,
and thanks to them the Reference List below has been nicely augmented
and updated.

For a terse and altogether critical summary of Soviet policy among the
Native peoples of the Russian North, see "Russian and Soviet Eskimo and
Indian Policies," by Richard A. Pierce. pp.119–127 of the *Handbook of
North American Indians,* vol. 14 *History of Indian-White Relations.*

2. Russian Bibliography/Reference List

*Aktual'nye Voprosy Bibliotechnoi Raboty, Teoriya i Praktika. (Current
Questions in Library Work, Theory and Practice).* Moscow. This is an
annual collection that is still being issued, though as of 1991 or so, under
another title *Massovye Biblioteki (Mass or General Public Libraries at the
Local Level).* I've been unable as yet to obtain copies of it since the title
changed. 75–100 pages.

Anthropology and Archeology of Eurasia, A Journal of Translations.
(formerly *Soviet Anthropology and Archeology).*
    This is a good source of articles and research on traditional cultures of
Siberia and the Russian Far East, including languages and how they are
changing.

Armstrong, Terence. *Soviet Library Development, with some Alaskan
Parallels and Contrasts.* Institute of Social, Economic and Government
Research. University of Alaska, Fairbanks. (ISEGR Occasional Papers,
No.2, October, 1970) 37pp.
    "Based in part on a series of lectures delivered at the University of
Alaska in March and April, 1970."

Artem'eva, E.B. *Bibliotechnye Obsluzhivaniya Narodnostei
Dal'nevostochnogo Severa. (Library services to nationalities of the fareastern
north)* Sov. *Bibliotekovedenie* 3:90 (1990), pp.64–71.
    Cites anew many longtime problems of library services to Native
peoples of Siberia and the Russian Far East that were never really addressed
during the Soviet period. Also, briefly covers difficulties of publishing for
the small peoples of the north in their own languages, now and in the past.
Concern expressed for survival of Native languages and cultures.

Artem'eva, E.B. "Osobennosti Raboty Bibliotek Dal'nevostochnogo

Severa i Formirovanie ikh Kadrovoi Bazy" (*Features of library work in far-eastern Siberia and formation of a skilled workforce*") from *Formirovanie i Razvitie Edinoi Informatsirovanno-Bibliotechnoi Sistemy Sibiri* From Formation and Development of a Single Library-Information System for Siberia. Collection of scientific papers, GPNTB SO RAN USSR (State Public Scientific-Technical Library, Siberian Section, Russian Academy of Sciences, USSR.), Novosibirsk, 1986, pp.93–118.

Artem'eva, E.B. "Spetsializatsiya Bibliotek i Model' Territorial'nogo Bibliotechnogo Obedineniya Yakutskoi ASSR" ("The specialization of libraries and a model for territorial library unification in the Yakut ASSR"), *Sov. Bibliotekovedenie* (*Soviet Librarianship*), No.3 (1986), pp.74–85.

Artem'eva, E.B. and A.N. Maslova "Bibliotechnye Resursy Sibiri i Dal'nego Vostoka v Nachale 90-kh gg." ("Library resources of Siberia and the Far East at the beginning of the '90s") from *Razvitie Knizhnogo Dela v Sibirii i na Dal'nem Vostoke (Sovetskii period)* (The development of book work in Siberia and the Far East; soviet period) (Collection of scientific papers, Sb. nauch. tr./GPNTB SO RAN, State Public Scientific-Technical Library, Siberian Section of the Russian Academy of Sciences, USSR), Novosibirsk, 1993, 179pp.

Austerlitz, Robert. "Folklore, Nationality and the Twentieth Century in Siberia and the Soviet Far East," *Journal of Folklore Institute* 12, no. 2/3 (1975): 203–210.
"Reasons for folklore dying out in view of industrialization and Soviet policy towards national minorities."

Avraeva, Y. "Patent na Tvorchestva" (A patent on creativity), *Bibliotekar' (The Librarian)* 7 (1986): 31–33.
"Results are discussed of a survey carried out in the library network of Far-eastern Siberia" (abstract).

Baeva, N.S. "Puti i Metody Tsentralizatsii Bibliotek na Krainem Severe, k itogem eksperimenta v Verkhoyanskom raione Yakutskoi ASSR." ("Ways and methods of the centralization of libraries in the extreme north, summary of an experiment in the Verkhoyansk Region of the Yakutsk ASSR") from *Problemy Tsentralizatsiya Bibliotechnoi seti. (Problems of the centralization of library networks).* Sb. statei (Collection of articles). Leningrad, 1978, pp.20–38.

Bibliotechno-Bibliograficheskie Resursi Sibiri: Sistema Informatsionno-Bibliograficheskogo Obsluzhivaniya. Sbornik Nauchnykh Trudov. GPNTB

SORAN USSR. Novosibirsk, 1984. 164 pp. (Bibliographical Information Resources of Siberia: A System of Bibliographical Information Services. Collection of scientific papers, State public scientific-technical library of the Siberian section of the Academy of sciences of the USSR)

Fifteen articles on various aspects of the subject, including SDI, ILL, etc. The use of abbreviations in Russian technical literature is common and, until one learns them, one needs a special dictionary of abbreviations (several hundred pages) to decipher many texts.

Bromley, Yu.V., and I.S. Gurvich, V.I. Boyko, Yu. P. Nikitin, A.I. Solomakha, eds. (1987) "Sovremennye Etnokul'turnye Protsessy u Narodnostei Krainego Severa" (Contemporary ethnocultural processes among the nationalities of the north) From: *Problemy Sovremmenogo Sotsial'nogo Razvitiya Narodnostei Severa* (Problems of contemporary social development of the peoples of the north). Novosibirsk: Nauka (Science). pp.159–168

Discusses the acculturation and assimilation of Native peoples with Russians as a natural development, denying any deliberate 'Russification' program. Russian is becoming the first language. Cites economic and social problems for traditional way of life.

Cherkasov, Arkadi. "The Native Population of the Soviet North: Language, Education and Employment," *Musk Ox,* Vol. 30 (1982), pp.65–72

Gives useful background information, notably through comparison of various major and minor Native ethnic groups and their contact and mixing with each other. The effects on strength of Russian and Native languages are of special interest. Russian is the lingua franca, and the smallest Native groups tend to be absorbed by the locally dominant Native ethnic group.

Chojnacki, Karen Michele. *The Association of Northern Native Peoples: A Case Study of a Soviet Interest Group.* Carleton Univ, MA Thesis, 1991

Analyzes the newly established Association of Northern Native Peoples in the Soviet Union, comparing it to the Inuit Tapirisat of Canada.

Dimitrieva, E.I. "Povyshenie Kvalifikatsii Bibliotechnykh Rabotnikov Respubliki Sakha (Yakutiya)" (Raising the qualifications of library workers in the Sakha Republic, or Yakutiya) (p.125–133 From: *Knizhnaya Kul'tura Respubliki Sakha (Yakutiya).* Sb. nauch. tr. GPNTB SO RAN (Book culture of the Sakha Republic, or Yakutiya. Collection of scientific papers/State public scientific-technical library, Siberian section, Russian Academy of Sciences), Novosibirsk, 1993. 158pp.

Dunn, Ethel. "Educating the Small Peoples of the Soviet North: the Limits of Cultural Change," *Arctic Anthropology,* Vol.5 (1968), No.1, p.1–31

"Argues that Soviet educational policy has damaged traditional native culture." (SPRILIB abstract) Gives relevant and detailed background on schooling, as well as progress in literacy in Russian and Native languages, setting the scene for library development.

Dunn, Ethel. "Education and the Native Intelligentsia in the Soviet North: Further thoughts on the Limits of Culture Change," *Arctic Anthropology,* Vol.6 (1970), No.2, p.112–122
"Assessment of Soviet education policy towards small native groups in the north." (SPRILIB abstract) Ponders the future of traditional Native economies in a setting of Soviet northern development, with accompanying educational, employment and modernizing influences.

Dunn, Stephen P. and Ethel Dunn. "The Transformation of Economy and Culture in the Soviet North," *Arctic Anthropology,* Vol.1, No. 2 (1963), p.1–28
A detailed look at the lives of the numerically small peoples as they have become acculturated and assimilated under difficult cultural as well as socio-economic conditions and changing policies of the Soviet regime.

Fedorov, A.I., and M.V. Epova, V.I. Boyko, Yu.P Nikitin, A.I. Solomakha, eds. "Zadachi Izucheniya Sotsial'nykh Problem Dvuyazichniya" (The tasks of studying the social problems of bilingualism) From: *Problemy Sovremennogo Sotsial'nogo Razvitiya Narodnostei Severa* (Problems of contemporary social development of nationalities of the north), Novosibirsk: Nauka (Science), 1987. p.203–209
Describes process and discusses problems of gradual changeover of Natives from Native languages to Russian. "Illuminates need for preserving Native languages as cultural media, and draws attention to role of various institutes in developing dictionaries and other aids to literacy . . . (also the) problem of different dialects of same language hindering formation of single written form, and language problem in schools." (SPRI abstract)

Forsyth, James. *A History of the Peoples of Siberia, Russia's North Asian Colony 1581-1990* 1992 New York:Cambridge Univ. Press (Paperback edition, 1994). 455pp
Presents the experience of the Siberian peoples over historical time, including that of the numerically small peoples of the north. Covers all aspects, and subheadings within chapters and a detailed index make this volume very useful as a general reference. Good companion volume to Yuri Slezkine's dissertation.

Gorbatykh et al. "Obzor Raboty Bibliotek Magadanskoi Oblasti s Korennym Naseleniem" (Survey of library work with the Native population in the Magadan Oblast), *Biblioteka i Chitatel'* (The library and the reader), Magadan, No.24 (1983), 9pp.

Gorbatykh, I.S. "Socio-Economical Transformation and Modern Ethnical Development of the Inhabitants of the Siberian Polar Zones of the North-Eastern Regions,": *Circumpolar Problems, Habitat, economy, and Social Relations in the Arctic.* A Symposium for Anthropoligical Research in the North, September, 1969. Edited by Gosta Berg. Oxford: Pergamon Press, (1973), p.53–60
   Comprehensive description in English of the relative status and cultural integrity of indigenous peoples of the Siberian northeast.

Gorbatykh, T.I. (1984) "Sovershenstvovanie bibliotechnogo obsluzhivaniya v raionakh prozhivaniya narodnostei severa (na premere magadanskoi oblasti" (Improvement of library services in areas of settled population of the North [with the example of the Magadan Oblast]) *Sovetskoe Bibliotekovedenie,* no.3, pp. 77–81.

Grant, Bruce M. *Memory and Forgetting among the Nivkhi of Sakhalin Island.* PhD. Dissertation, Rice University, Houston, Texas. 1993
   Though not included among the numerically small peoples of the arctic, the Nivkhi are a numerically small and isolated Native people very similar to them in general terms. I include this source because there is so little current documentation of this kind on the small peoples. It traces the historical experience of the Nivkhi in being oppressed and exploited by the Japanese, Chinese, Koreans, Russians (both Czarist and Soviet), and even Americans. The Soviet period is the most appalling, in terms of the destruction of Nivkhi society and culture, and the decimating, arbitrary purges of the 1930s. (I was reminded of Solzhenitsyn's *Gulag Archipelago,* whose massive documentation of Soviet oppression and purges I was simply unable to finish reading.) Some interesting features include a list of instructions for implementing a local purge, and a list of slogans used to hype production and ideological fervor. Mr. Grant was apparently fluent in Russian, and his personal visits to various locations on Sakhalin were, by turns, poignant, bizarre and haunting. I presume one could justifiably extrapolate the Nivkhi experience to that of at least some of the northern small peoples.

Gurvich, I.S. and Ch. M. Taksani. "Sotsial'nye Funktsii Yazykov Narodnostei Sever. i Dal/nego Vostoka SSSR v Sovetskii Period" (The social function of languages of the peoples of the north and far east during the Soviet period), *Sovetskaya Etnografiya* (Soviet ethnography), 1985, 2:54–63
   "Influence of changing social conditions, welfare and cultura development. Analysis of implementation of written languages, local language-Russian bilingualism, and teaching of national languages in schools." (abstract)

International Work Group for Indigenous Peoples. *Proceedings,* Association of the Small Peoples of the Soviet North, First Meeting, Moscow, March 30–31, 1990. Copenhagen: International Work Group for Indigenous Affairs (IWGIA). IWGIA Document No.67, 56pp, ill., table, maps

General introduction and report; opening speech by Chuner Taksami citing needs of northern peoples; ways of future development and legal measures proposed to RSFSR Supreme Soviet; Declaration of Congress, Statutes and Program of Association. The Association met in the following years (1990 and 1991) and expanded to include the Russian Far East.

Isayeva (1984). Bibliographical information on this citation was lost, and I was unable to provide it by publication deadline.

Karlinsky, Simon, ed. *The Nabakov-Wilson Letters, 1940–1971.* New York:Harper and Row, 1979.

In his introduction, Karlinsky disabuses us of the notion that Stalinism was a "betrayal of Lenin's policies." At age 21, Lenin tried to prevent food from reaching starving peasants during a famine (hoping thereby to create more revolutionaries). In the 1920s, he unleashed "a wave of indiscriminate terror unprecedented in modern times," "reinstated the censorship of books in a far more sweeping form than had ever existed under the Czars," "issued an index of prohibited books," "allowed his wife Krupskaya to ban from public libraries a long list of anti-artistic and counterrevolutionary literature," (which brought international as well as domestic protest and a subsequent reduction of the list), "staged a series of exemplary trials," "set up quotas of (subversives) to be convicted in advance," and "promised to expel from the Communist Party those judges and prosecutors who fail to fill their quotas." (p.13) Josef Stalin simply continued what Lenin had begun.

Kazarinova, L.F. *Knigoizdanie na Yazykakh Korennykh Narodov Sibirii i Dal'nego Vostoka.* (Publishing in the languages of the native peoples of Siberia and the Far East) Novosibirsk: GPNTB SO AN SSSR (State Scientific-Technical Library of the Siberian Section, USSR Academy of Sciences), 28pp, 1990.

"Examines problems of publishing small numbers of publications under new system of self-finance and self-support. Suggests ways of optimizing output of material in Native languages." (SPRI abstract) I later received a copy of this article, and it is discussed at length in Chapter 3.

Kazarinova, L.F. *Chitatel'skie Potrebnosti i Perspektivy Knigoizdaniya na Yazykakh Malochislennykh Narodov Sibiri i Dal'nego Vostoka v Sovremennykh Usloviakh* (Readers' needs and long range prospects for book publishing in languages of the numerically small peoples of Siberia and the Far East under contemporary conditions), Preprint 91–5,

GPNTB SO RAN USSR (State scientific-technical library, Siberian section, Academy of sciences, USSR), 1992, 23pp
Detailed historical and analytical discussion of the subject, which is summarized in Chapter 3.

Kenez, Peter. *The Birth of the Propaganda State, Soviet Methods of Mass Mobilization,* 1917–29. Cambridge U.P., 1985
Discusses the press, books, publishing, films and the cinema, posters, 'cultural enlightenment' efforts, and literacy campaigns.

Khudaverdyan', V. Ts and Kh.D.Khamrakulova "Est' li Budushchee u Natsionhal'nogo Knigoizdaniya?" (Does nationality publishing have a future?) *Knizhnoe Delo* (Book work) 1994, No.5(11), p.16–19
The article claims that it has if thorough market knowledge is obtained, desireable and pragmatic materials are produced in attractive formats, and outside subsidies are available at least until the economy improves at all levels.

Kimmage, Dennis, ed. *Russian Libraries in Transition,* An Anthology of Glasnost Literature. Jefferson, North Carolina and London: McFarland, 1992
This collection of "26 articles that appeared in Soviet journals and newspapers between 1988–1991" is a compendious look at the abuses in Soviet librarianship of the past, what democratic changes have occurred since Krushchev, the difficulties still to be overcome, and goals for the future. Pages 92–148 are especially enlightening of the inhibiting role that censorship, control of publishing, destruction of materials deemed ideologically at variance with 'state security,' and "Special Stacks" of restricted materials in libraries have had on learning, education, science, and intellectual life generally, not only in the pre-glasnost USSR, but in the post-Gorbachev nation, as it struggled to democratize and modernize library and related services. Libraries were part of enforcement of ideological conformity during the Soviet period, and this is a major cause of the poor image and low priority libraries and librarians are trying to improve.

Kondakov, I.P. "Library Services for a nation covering a large geographical area: the Soviet Union" A paper presented at the 33rd Session of the IFLA General Council, Toronto, Canada, August, 1967), *Libri,* 1967, No.3, p.202–209

"Kontseptsiya Razvitiya Bibliotechnogo Dela v RSFSR do 2005 Goda (Proekt)" (Concepts of Library Work Development in the RSFSR to the Year 2005 {Draft}). Found as an insert in the November, 1989, No.11, issue of *Bibliotekar'* (The librarian).

"Kraevedcheskaya Rabota Biblioteki. Metod. i Bibliogr. Materialy. Iz

Opyta Raboty Bibliotek obl." (Regional folklore work of a library. Methodological and bibliographical materials. Drawn from the experience of Oblast libraries), *Biblioteka i Chitatel'* (The library and the reader), Magadan 1978, No.18, 71pp.

Kuzmin, Evgenii. "At a Crossroads, Russian Libraries Face the Future." *Wilson Library Bulletin,* January, 1993. p.52–58, 118
    A candid and realistic description of libraries under Soviet Communism, and the problems and prospects for future democratization and solvency of Russian libraries.

Kyzlasov, L.R. "Mladopis'mennye Literatury Narodov sibiri i Istoricheskie Osnovy ikh Formirovaniya" (The newly recorded literatures of the peoples of Siberia and the historical bases of their formation), *Akademiya Nauk SSSR, Sibirskoe Otdelenie.* (USSR Academy of Sciences. Siberian Section.) *Izvestiya* (News), 1982, No.6, Seriya Obshchestvennikh Nauk. Vyp. 2 (Social Sciences Series. Publication 2), p.124–128
    "Ancient influences on literature and its development." (abstract)

Landina, N.T. "Organizatsiya Bibliotechnogo Obsluzhivaniya na Taimire: (The organization of library services in Taimir), *Sov. Bibliotekovedenie* (Soviet librarianship), 1986, No.6, p.84–88

Langenbakh, N. "Bol'shoi Put' Malykh Narodov" (The big path of the small peoples", *Bibliotekar'* (The librarian), 1970, No.4 p.39–41

Lebedeva, A.N. and A.N. Maslova. *Ratsional'noe Rasmeshchenie I Ispol'zovanie Bibliotechnykh Resursov v Strane* (Rational distribution and utilization of library resources in the nation) Collection of scientific papers. Magadan, 1984 p.123–130

Ledovskaya, A. "Za Polyarnym Krugom" (Beyond the polar circle), *Bibliotekar'* (The librarian), 1971, No.7, p.52–56

Lesokhina, Valentina S. "Problems of Training Library Personnel in the USSR", *Journal of Education for Library and Information Science,* Vol.25, No.3 (Winter, 1985), p.200–206

Lever'eva, G. F. "Mesto Natsional'noi Biblioteki v Sotsial'no-kulturnoi Zhinzi Yakutskoi-Sakha SSR" (The role of the Yakutsk National Library in the sociocultural life of the Yakutiya-Sakha ASSR) p.94–116, from *Razvitie Bibliotechnogo Dela v Sibiri, (Sovetskii period).* (Development of library work in Siberia [soviet period] Sb. Nauch. Trudov/GPNTB SO RAN (Collection of scientific papers/State public Scientific-technical Library, the Siberian Section of the Russian Academy of Sciences), Novosibirsk, 1992. 198pp

Levin, M.G. and A. P. Potapov, eds. *Narody Sibirii* (Series: *Narody Mira*, ed. S.P. Tolstov) (Peoples of Siberia, from the series, Peoples of the World). Moscow-Leningrad:USSR Academy of Sciences Pub. House, 1956. 1083 pp

Levin, M.G. and A.P. Potapov. *People of Siberia.* Translated by Scripta Technica, Inc. Translation editor, Stephen P. Dunn Chicago:Univ. of Chicago Press, 1964. 948 pp

Leybzan, L. "Prezidenta budet Tanya" (Tanya will be President), *Severnye Prostory* (Northern Spaces), No.1:7–8. 1990
    Same content as under Tuyen, T. herein.

Likhovid, F.A. "Bibliotechnoe Delo na Krainem Severe" (Library work in the extreme north), *Bibliotekar'* (The librarian), 1957, No.11, p.50–56

Likhovid, F.A. "Nekotorye Voprosy Bibliotechnogo Obsluzhivaniya Narodov Krainego Severa" (Some questions on library services to peoples of the extreme north), *Biblioteki SSSR, Opyt Raboty* (Libraries of the USSR, work experience), 1958, No.9, p.24–42.

Likhovid, F.A. "Razvitie Bibliotechnogo Obsluzhivaniya Malykh Narodov Krainego Severa" (Growth of library services among the small peoples of the far north), Transactions of the Lenin State Library, Vol.3, (n.d.), p.3–66

Lincoln, Tamara P.K. "Let Them Read!: The Socio-Political Education of the Indigenous, Native Siberian Child, A Didactic and Dogmatic Approach to Reading," *Proceedings,* 12th Northern Libraries Colloquy, Boulder, Colorado, USA, June 5–9, 1988, p.119–120

Lincoln, Tamara. "The Unexplored Siberians: A Literary Perspective of the Native Minority Writers and their Connection to the Regional Folklore Tradition," *Proceedings,* 11th Northern Libraries Colloquy, Lulcia, Sweden, June 9–12, 1986, 18pp.
    The acculturation of Native authors of school texts and children's books in Siberia's northeast corner, nearest Alaska, through their upbringing in Soviet education, creates a literature for youth that, with the passing years and progress in school, becomes more Soviet and less Native. Even the visual images become increasingly Sovietized, and the trappings of Native life and ways are seen less and less.

Luk'yanchenko, T. V. and N. N. Novikova. "O Rabote Uchreditel'nogo S ezda Narodnykh Deputatov ot Malochislennykh Narodov Severa, Sibiri i Dal'nego Vostoka" (On the work of the Conference of Peoples Deputies of the Numerically Small Peoples of Siberia and the Far East), *Sovetskaya Etnografiya* (Soviet Ethnography) No.6 (1991), p.134–138.

Observations on the second meeting of this new organization, which begins the movement toward self-determination and more sovereignty of the numerically small peoples of the north, not to dominated by outside authority as in the past.

Maksimova, G. "Na Krainem Severe" (In the far north), *Bibliotekar'* (The librarian), 1986, No.4, p.33–34

Maksimova, G.V. and E.V. Nevogatisova. "Mobile Library Services for the Nations of the USSR Extreme North" ?*Proceedings* of the 1991 IFLA Conference, Moscow? (official translation)

Maksimova, S.V. "Bibliotechnoe Delo v Yakutii (Sovetskii period)" (Library work in Yakutiya; soviet period), p.91–121, from *Razvitie knizhnogo dela v Sibirii i na Dal'nem Vostoke (Sovetskii period)* (Development of book work in Siberia and the Far East; soviet period) Sb. nauch. tru./GPNTB SO RAN (Collection of scientific papers/state public scientific-technical library, siberian section of the russian academy of sciences) Novosibirsk, 1993, 179pp

Maslova, A.N. and E.B. Artem'eva. "Regional'nye Problemy Bibliotechnogo Dela" (Regional problems of library work) Preprint 93–5, GPNTB SO RAN, or State Public Scientific-Technical Library of the Siberian Section of the Russian Academy of Sciences (formerly GPNTB SO SSSR), 1994, 66pp (including 40 pages of library statistics from 1976–91 for Siberia and the Russian Far East, by republics, oblasts, krays and okrugs.)

Under the current difficult economic conditions, the GPNTB SO RAN is playing a key role in consulting, and in the acquisition of many depository titles, especially foreign ones, because regional and local libraries are unable to do so. Planning and coordinating of interlibrary cooperation and emphasis on regional and local initiatives will be emphasized. The languages and cultures of numerically small peoples will be strengthened. Options for publishing small runs of titles in Native languages are cited.

Matlina, S.G. "Vertolet nad tundroi" (Helicopter over the tundra), *Bibliotekar'* (The librarian), 1983, No.9, pp.23–24

Matlina, S.G. "Kursy povysheniya kvalifikatsii i.t.d." (Courses for raising qualifications, etc.), *Sovremennoe Bibliotekovedenie* (Contemporary librarianship), 1984, No.1, pp.120–122

"Metodiko-Bibliograficheskie Materiali v Pomoshch' Propagande Literatury o Krae" (Materials on bibliographical methods for the promotion of regional literature), Magadan, *Biblioteka I chitatel'* (The library and the reader), 1984, No.12, 58pp.

Mitchell, Alison. (*Newsday*) "Heroes from Western World Invade Siberia via VCR," *Seattle Times/Post-Intelligencer,* Sunday, September 17, 1989, p.A6
   Reports on the proliferation of pirated and imported videotapes and mini-video theatres in the Siberian city of Novosibirsk.

News in Brief, Newsletter of the International Research and Exchanges Board, 1616 H Street, NW, Washington, D.C. 20006.
   "The principal purpose of IREX is to serve the interests of the American scholarly community engaged in individual and colaborative research and intellectual exchanges in the successor states to Eastern Europe and the Soviet Union." I was sent special lists of librarian contacts in Russian and eastern Europe, Russian and eastern European librarians visiting the U.S., and American librarians visiting Russia and eastern Europe.

Nielsen, Poul Thoe. "An Appraisal of the importance of the national languages among the north Siberian peoples," *Folk,* Vol.14–15 (1972–73), p.205–253, illus.
   "Lists 28 languages and traces development of written form. Attitude of central government, particularly as regards school policies. Based on study in Moscow and Leningrad." (abstract)

"Les peuples du Kamchatka et de la Tchoukotka," edited by Boris Chichlo. *Siberie III,* Questions siberiennes. (From the series: Cultures & societes de l'Est, 5 [1993], p.23–33, English version.
   Reports on findings of the "first international expedition" of 'World Scientists Contribution to the Siberian Far North, organized by the Leningrad Association of Polar Scientists and the Siberian Research Center in Paris,' conducted in the winter and summer of 1991. Pollution, closing of some local shipping lanes (such as in the Anadyr area); deteriorated housing and adverse health conditions were found everywhere, and though the Native languages were not being spoken, signs of their revival were reported. Lack of qualified teachers. Precarious subsistence economy of 'national' villages was found, along with waste in management and processing of harvests. Hygiene in rural areas "absolutely deplorable." The many years of collectivization have lowered expectations of the subsistence way of life, though increased autonomy of Native communities and the formation of organizations of indigenous peoples are prompting a revival of interest in Native crafts and culture generally. Kamchatka is worse off than Chukotka.

"O Putyakh Sovershenstvovaniya Obsluzhivaniya Chitatelei" (1987) Sb. st. (On ways of improving readers' services). From: Collection of Articles, Yakutsk, p.76

"Organizatsiya Raboty v Bibliotekakh s Mestnym Naseleniem" (1970).

(Organization of work in libraries serving a local population). Magadan, *Biblioteka I Chitatel'* (The library and the reader), No.12, 58pp.

Petrushkin, Arkadii A. *Korennye Narody Taimyra i Osnovnye Pokazateli Razvitiya Traditsionnykh Otraslei Khozyaistva (Kratkaya Spravka).* (Native peoples of Taimyr and the main indicators of the development of traditional livelihoods {A short guide}) No publisher. (1991) 41pp, tables, maps. Unpublished thesis.
    "Reviews history, changes in population sizes and traditional economic activities of Dolgani, Nentsi, Ngansi, Evenki and Entsi, and discusses briefly their social and economic problems. Presents extensive statistics on population size, social and economic activities, including reindeer herding, fishing, compiled from field work." (SPRI abstract)

Poppe, N.N. "Puti Povysheniya Rechevoy Kul'tury Zapaadnykh buryat" (Ways of improving the culture of western Burats) *Zapiski Instituta Vostokovedeniya Akademii Nauk SSSR,* Tom 2, Vypusk 3 (Memoirs of the Institute of Eastern Studies, Academy of Science of the USSR, Vol.2, Publication 3), p.107–128
    "Nationality, cultural and language problems." (abstract)

Present-day Ethnic Processes in the USSR. Moscow: Progress Publishers, 1982, 277pp
    "Ethnic and ethno-linguistic processes, including changes in settlement, culture and social structure, and interaction of languages; administrative system in relation to national peoples." (abstract)

Problemy Razvitiya Bibliotek Sibiri i Dal'nego Vostoka v Odinatsatoi Pyatiletke (1982). (Problems of library development in Siberia and the Far East during the 11th Five-Year plan). Sb. Tr. GB, NTB AN SSSR. (Collection of scientific papers. Lenin State Library, scientific-technical library of the USSR academy of sciences, Magadan, 151pp.

Rossiiskaya Federatsiya. Ministerstvo Kul'tury. *Orientiry Kul'turnoi Politiki.* Informatsionnyi vypusk No.6 (Russian Federation. Ministry of Culture. Guidelines on cultural policy, information circular no.6) Moscow, 1994. p.3–21
    After citing the difficult conditions endured by the numerically small peoples of the north during Soviet rule, problem areas are listed and needed help and reforms are discussed. Libraries, club operations and museums have declined in many areas, especially those serving Native populations. Historic preservation of sites culturally significant for Natives is needed. Finally, as part of the UN International Decade on Native Peoples of the Earth, decisions of the Interregional conference (in

Tomsk, 14–16 December, 1994) on problems of development of the numerically small peoples are listed.

RSFSR. Ministerstvo Kul'tury. Gosudarstvennaya Ordena Trudogo Krasnovo Znameni Publichnaya Biblioteka imemi M.E. Saltykova-Shchedrina. *Bibliotechnoe Obsluzhivanie Malykh Narodnostei Severa, Metodicheskie Rekomendatsii* (RSFSR ministry of culture. The Saltykov-Shchedrina memorial state public library, of the order of the toiling red banner. Library service of the small peoples of the north. Recommendations on methods.) Leningrad, 1983. 56pp
————. *Formy i Metody Bibliotechnoi Raboty s Narodnostyami Severa, Metodicheskie Rekomendatsii* (Forms and methods of library work with peoples of the north, Recommendations on methods), Leningrad, 1988. 32pp
————. *Tsentralizatsiya Bibliotek v Raionakh Krainego Severa i Priravnennykh k nim Mestnostyakh.* (Centralization of libraries in small regions of the extreme north and localities comparable to them), Leningrad, 1980. 26pp

Rusakova, S.F. "Organizatsiya i Razvitie Bibliotechnogo Obsluzhivaniya v Magadanskoi Oblasti" (Organization and development of library services in the Magadan Oblast), *Nauchnye biblioteki Sibirii i Dal'nego Vostoka* (Scientific libraries of Siberia and the Far East) 1973, No.17, p.149–157

Rytkheu, Yuriy. "Dva Berega, Dve Sud'by" (Two shores, two fates), From: Chekhoyeva, S.A. and G.A. Baryshev, comps. *Prosveshchenie na Krainem Severe.* Sbornik 19. (Enlightenment in the far north. Annual 19). Leningrad: "Prosveshchenie," 1981, p.101–106
    "Links between Chukotka and Alaska in relation to education, and development of written form of Eskimo language." (abstract) Rytkheu is an internationally known Chukchi author.

Safronov, F.G., ed. *Formirovanie Sotsialisticheskoy Kul'tury Narodov Yakutsii, 1918–1937.* (Formation of the socialist culture of the peoples of Yakutiya, 1918–1937. Yakutsk: Yakutskoe Knizhnoye Izdatel'stvo (Yakut Book Publishing), 1982. 132pp.
    "Development of school education and literacy, orthography, literature, national theatre, musical and fine arts, printing and publishing, in the context of socialist culture." (abstract)

Sentsova, G.V. "Formirovanie i Perspektivy Razvitiya Fondov Natsional'noi biblioteki Respubliki Sakha (Yakutiya)" (Formation of and future prospects for the collections of the National Library of the Sakha Republic, or Yakutiya), p.110–124. From: *Khizhnaya Kul'tura Respubliki Sakha (Yakutiya).* Sb. nauch. tr./GPNTB SO RAN (Book culture of the Republic of Sakha, or Yakutiya. Collection of scientific papers/State public scientific-technical library, Siberian Section of the Russian Academy of Sciences), Novosibirsk, 1993. 158pp

Samsonova, V.A. "O Roli Bibliotek v Natsional'nom Vozrozhdeniem Narodov Respubliki Sakha, or Yakutiya" (On the role of libraries in the nationality renaissance of peoples of the Sakha Republic, or Yakutiya), p.6–21. From: *Knizhnaya Kul'tura Respubliki Sakha (Yakutiya).* Sb. nauch. tr./GPNTB SO RAN (Book culture of the Republic of Sakha, or Yakutiya. Collection of scientific Papers/State public scientific-technical library, Siberian section of the Russian Academy of Sciences), Novosibirsk, 1993. 158pp

Savoskul, S.S. "Social and Cultural Dynamics of the Peoples of the Far North, *Polar Record,* Vol.19, No.119, May, 1978, p.129–152

Savvin, E.M. "Nekotorye Voprosy Bibliotechno-Informatsionnogo Obsluzhivaniya Narodnostei Severa," V kn.: *Kraevedcheskaya Deyatel'nost' Bibliotek v Pomoshch' Kommunisticheskomu Vospitaniyu Trudyashchisya* (Some questions about library information services to northern nationalities. From the book: Regional folklore activities of libraries supporting Communist education of working people). Collection of scientific papers. Lenin State Library, 1981, p.80–85

Serov, V.V. "Puti Ulushcheniya bibliotechno-Bibliograficheskogo Obsluzhivaniya Detei i Podrostkov" (Approaches to the improvement of library bibliographic work with children and teens) *Sov. Bibliotekovedenie* (Soviet librarianship), 6 (1983), p.17–29

Shakhova et al. "Biblioteki v pomoshch' Sel'skokhozyaistvennomu Proizvodstvu (Libraries to the aid of agricultural production), *Biblioteka i Chitatel'* (The library and the reader), Magadan, 1981, No.21, 22pp.

Shlapentokh, Vladimir. *Public and Private Life of the Soviet People,* Changing Values in Post-Stalin Russia. New York: Oxford Univ. Press, 1989
    An engrossing, many-faceted survey, in which the following reference to libraries is found (on p.183, quoted from the periodical *Nedelya* (The week), No.33 {1987}, p.3): "The 300,000 libraries in the Soviet Union have lost the importance which they once had in the lives of the people. Now they contain eight times fewer books than the citizens themselves, 5 billion against 40 billion." Shlapentokh is a former Soviet sociologist and pollster, and came to the U.S. to teach. Most of his data is taken from numerous polls, many of which he helped to design and conduct. He also comments that museum and theatre attendance was down, due in part to the spread of television, which now includes videotapes and VCRs.

Slabin et al. (This source is actually comprised of four short articles published together, on adjoining pages.) Slabin, S. "Krai Bol'shikh Bogatstv" (Land of great riches); Trutneva, N. "V Osobykh usloviyakh" (In special circumstances); Khatanzeiskaya, T. "Nasha Pomoshch' " (Our help); Zolotukhina, T. "Nafstrechu Chitatel' " (Meeting the reader). *Bibliotekar'* (The librarian), 1966, No.2, p.28–33

Slezkine, Yuri. *Arctic Mirrors, Russia and the Small Peoples of the North.* Ithaca, NY:Cornell University Press 1994. 456pp.
   This is, according to the author, a greatly expanded edition of his dissertation (see below), and brings his account of the experience of the small peoples up to the early 1990s. Of special interest are two sections analyzing the Native experience through fiction that Native authors produced during the Soviet period (323–335, 352–371), which I found quite illuminating. Lengthy bibliography.

Slezkine, Yuri. *Russia's Small Peoples: The Policies and Attitudes towards the Native Northerners, Seventeenth century-1938.* PhD. Dissertation, University of Texas at Austin, 1989. UMI, 614 pp.
   This is an excellent source for tracing the historical experience of the small peoples of the Russian North. The role of libraries is not addressed, but most every other cultural and social aspect is. Lengthy bibliography. The author's engaging, sometimes amusing approach makes it a 'good read', a rarity among dissertations.

Slezkine, Yuri. "The USSR as a Communal Apartment, or How a Socialist State promoted Ethnic Particularism," *Slavic Review* 53:2 (Summer, 1994), p.414–452
   An excellent, thoroughly documented (from original Russian sources) and illuminating essay on the complexities of Soviet political, social, cultural and linguistic organization. Emphasizes that Lenin and then Stalin used ethnocultural strengths of nationalities as a vehicle toward socialization of the country as a whole, linguistic identities (and their preservation) being the main criterion. ('Ethnic form for socialist content.') Russian nationalism was neglected in the first decades, but later rose to dominance, along with Russification of smaller nationalities.

Smith, Hedrick. *The Russians.* (revised edition). New York: Ballantine Books, 1976.
   This interesting best-seller of its time looks at life in the USSR in the early 1970s. It has many illuminating pages on libraries, censorship, periodicals and the information media generally. Quite arresting is the revelation of restricted collections within libraries, and restricted distribution of materials deemed not supportive of the Soviet ideology. In 1989 librarians in Anadyr denied me, a Russian-speaking American librarian, access to their classification scheme, asserting pleasantly though firmly that it was for staff only.

Smith, Hedrick. *The New Russians* New York: Random House, 1990. 621 pp.

The sequel to *The Russians* is primarily a study of the momentous political and economic changes that were brought about in the Soviet Union under Mikhail Gorbachev from around 1985 to 1990, preceded by brief background on the Khrushchev effect and the Brezhnev era. Unlike Smith's previous book, above, social and cultural developments are not described in as relevant detail for librarians or about the northern nationalities, although improving conditions for publishing are noted. The drastically changing and tumultuous national climate is vividly described, which helps one better understand the profound difficulties Russia and the Commonwealth of Independent States will continue to endure for many years to come.

Sokolova, Z. P. "S"ezd Malochislennykh Narodov Severa (Vzglyad etnografa)" (Conference of the Numerically Small Peoples of the North {view of an ethnologist}), *Sovetskaya Etnografiya* (Soviet Ethnography), No.5 (1990), p.142–146

Reports on this first meeting of the organization, which asserted among other things the sovereignty and need for self-determination of the small peoples, and that Native languages should be taught in schools, Native television developed, cultural and historical centers and Native 'malokomplektnye' schools set up, and publishing of textbooks, manuals and literature (including magazines and newspapers) in Native languages be facilitated. The quality of education generally needs to be improved so that it incorporates traditional subsistence ways of life. A Native University of the North should be established, so that the numbers of Native specialists can be increased, and the problems of northern peoples addressed more effectively. Further, an independent Native land should be delineated across the North, with each northern people having its own region. A State Committee on Northern Affairs should be appointed.

Stepanov, P.D. "New Forms and Methods of Library Service to Ethnic Groups and Minorities in the Far North of the USSR," *Library Trends,* Fall, 1980, p.317–323

Sudakov, V. "A Written Alphabet for 800 People," *Soviet Union,* 1983, No.12, p.21–23, illus.

"Article on Yukagiri of Yakutiya, and description of school in village of Andryushkino." (Abstract)

Tokarev, T.S. "Razvitie Bibliotechnogo Dela v Yakutii za gody Sovetskoi Vlasti" (Development of library affairs in Yakutiya during the years of Soviet power), *Scientific Libraries of Siberia and the Far East,* (Novosibirsk?), 1972, No.9, p.280

Teplitskaya, Helen. "Librarianship in the USSR" From: *The Whole Library Handbook,* George M. Eberhart, Comp. Chicago: American Library Association, 1991. p.424–429

Trutneva, I.V. "Nekotorye Voprosy Bibliotechnogo Obsluzhivaniya Naseleniya Krainego Severa" (Some questions about library services to populations of the far north), *Biblioteki SSSR. Opyt raboty.* (Libraries of the USSR. Work Experience.), 1966, No.33, p.90

Tuyen, T. "Kul'turnaya i Etnograficheskaya Nepreryvnost' u Korennykh Narodov Severa: Nekotorye Antropologicheskie Podkhody" (Cultural and ethnic continuity of the indigenous peoples of the north: some anthropological viewpoints). *Sovetskaya Etnografiya* (Soviet Ethnography), No.5:56–64, 1990
    "Report of First Conference of Peoples of the North in Khanty-Mansysk, subsequently named Conference of Native Peoples of Khanty-Mansysk, whose main aim is preservation of Finno-Ugrian culture and peoples. Describes some problems of region and peoples with particular reference to pollution and health. Gives account of interview with manager of factory on future of traditional cultures." (SPRI abstract)

Volkov, G.N. "Problemy Sovershenstvovaniya Gospital'noi Raboty" (Problems in the improvement of hospital work), From: Chekhoyeva, S.A. and G.A. Baryshev, comps. *Prosveshchenie na Krainem Severe.* Sbornik 19. (Enlightenment in the extreme north. Annual 19)

Ylepov, B.S., A.N. Lebedeva and A.N. Maslova. (1985B). "Razvitie Bibliotechnykh Resursov Sibirskogo Regiona" (The growth of library resources in the Siberian region), *Sov. Bibliotekovedenie,* (Soviet librarianship) 1985, No.6, p.21–29

Ylepov, et al. (1985A). "Spetsialistam Sela" (For Village Specialists), *Bibliotekar'* (The librarian) 1985, No.4, p.5–6

Zharaeva, T.A. "Bibliotechno-Bibliograficheskoe Obsluzhivaniie Truzhenikov Krainego Severa Yakutskoi ASSR. V Kn.: *Problemy Razvitiya Bibliotek Severa I Dal'nego Vostoka v Odinatsatoi Pyatiletke.* (Library-bibliographical services to workers in the far north of the Yakutsk ASSR. From the book: Problems of library development in the north and far east during the 11th Five-Year plan). Collection of scientific papers. Lenin State Library/Scientific-Technical Library of the USSR Academy of Sciences, Magadan, 1982, p. 117–121

Zotova et al. "Metodicheskiye Tsentry Bibliotekam Sibiri i Dal'nego Vostoka" (Methodological Centers supporting libraries of Siberia and the Far East), *Sov. Bibliotekovedenie* (Soviet librarianship), No.2, p.15–27

7.

A Potpourri: Culture Shock, the Author's Background, and Multicultural Librarianship

It is somewhat difficult for us to recognize that the value which we attribute to our civilization is due to the fact that we participate in this civilization, and that it has been controlling all our actions since the time of our birth; but it is certainly conceivable that there may be other civilizations, based perhaps on different traditions and on a different equilibrium of emotion and reason, which are of no less value than ours, although it may be impossible for us to appreciate their values without having grown up under their influence. The general theory of valuation of human activities, as developed [through] anthropological research, teaches us a higher tolerance than the one which we now profess.[1]

To an Outsider an ethnic group appears homogenous. The reality . . . is much more complicated.[2]

The reasons for being "culture-bound," of being incapable of understanding or accepting the ways of another culture, are almost by definition characteristic of much monocultural conditioning itself, which acts both as a reinforcer and defense against unwanted change. Looking at the encounter between Native North Americans and those recent invaders of European ancestry, Andy Tamas of St. Paul, Alberta echoes Boas:

Most of us are largely unaware of our own culture. We have habits and thought patterns that are distinctive products of our own upbringing, and we deal with the world in the manner to which we have become accustomed over the years. . . . We seem to live by a complex set of largely invisible 'rules' which we acquire as we mature. We become aware of these rules most frequently when they are 'broken,' i.e. when things don't fit our accepted or accustomed patterns of behavior. . . . The education of Native people has (sometimes by design, but, I suspect, sometimes by default) subjected Indian students to an educational system rooted in the Western European, Judeo-Christian tradition. The implicit goals of this system have been and continue to be to indoctrinate students into an industrialized middle-class lifestyle, including wage employment in the market economy. . . . Native values, which have been developed over centuries of a subsistence lifestyle with a rich spiritual and social tradition, are very different. . . . It has been shown that education or social change activities based on values and beliefs which are at variance with community norms are destructive to community well-being and will tend to make people want to leave their communities.[3]

One might observe here that in many cases they may not leave their communities, but they will leave the traditional cultural ways (which can amount to almost the same thing), drifting into the new cultural consciousness, to the consternation and despair of the older generations. Good cross-cultural intentions on the part of educational authorities, giving Native people some "input" into the decision-making process—like enabling them to run their own schools—aren't always the obvious answer, as Tamas indicates:

> Even those schools controlled by Native communities and employing Native teachers have to contend with the methods and values acquired by their staff during their training in the mainstream cultural milieu of urban university-based training programs. Regardless of statements to the contrary, the implicit goal of most universities' Native teacher training programs is to help Native students acquire those values and competencies considered the norm on campus. . . . The content of instruction, which is often confined strictly to a curriculum determined by state authority, rarely relates to helping students make the psychological adjustments faced in coping with the contradictory value systems they deal with in everyday life.[4]

The solution is to reinforce the validity of Native values and culture, which can be a very difficult, costly and complex task, because there are so many cultural systems in the Native world. Interpersonal communication skills have to be stressed, along with trust, honesty and acceptance of diversity, adds Tamas. Ideally, a bicultural learning environment is the best, and "success is possible with ethnocentric instruction if the context of education provides opportunities for students to clarify their personal structures of meaning and to work out their own cultural ambiguities in an atmosphere of trust, mutual support and cooperation."[5] It is just as important for the dominant society instructors to be aware of factors in the Natives' background that impinge so strongly on attitudes and expectations, for example the "colonized society" and "poverty-ridden environment" they've grown up in, along with the "atmosphere of chronic economic depression."

Lastly, Tamas points out that the ultimate solution lies with the Native communities having total control over their own educational process. And from what we have learned thus far, exactly the same is true of library services in Native communities.

According to George M. Foster,[6] the root cause of (professional) culture shock for the non-Native field worker is an array of unexpected limitations encountered in a strange place by the community developer, that are outside his or her ken. In the Third or Fourth World environment of Native communities, these include the limitations of a non-Euroamerican and somewhat colonial socioeconomic setting, the professional pride (sometimes arrogance) of the highly trained specialist in one particular aspect of community development ("professional compartmentalization"), significant if not severe communication problems (often including a foreign language), and an overwhelming feeling of isolation and inadequacy.

The signs of culture shock, Foster continues, are "precipitated by the anxiety that results from losing one's familiar cues." Some of the factors working to eclipse the usual constellation of cues are: a lack of local control over funding, no legal authority to take needed action, illiteracy of various kinds, the absence of Euroamerican leadership patterns and trained, experienced Native cadre, the absence of familiar models of cooperation and co-ordination, poor economic conditions, inadequate or inappropriate technical services in "health, agriculture, education and the like," a prevalent attitude of low self-discipline (in terms of the dominant society's ethic), and a pervasive feeling that nothing can (or should) change, that conditions will inevitably revert to how they were, or should be.

In the broader, more popular sense, any encounter with foreigners in a foreign place can have its own shocking, disturbing or puzzling revelations for the sensitive observer. (To some degree this used to be called—before the jet age made travel so easy and one's arrival so abrupt—the "travel experience.")

Any non-Native working on an Indian reservation or in Native areas is in for an initial shock, because these locations are characterized by features on the clichéd checklist we've heard so often, but which in fact reflect the real-life situation, at least from the point of view of the average, middle-class non-Native: poverty, unemployment, isolation (not to say ostracism) from the dominant society's socioeconomic life, low educational levels and high dropout rate, alcoholism, rising birth rate and, in certain areas, a very high rate of suicide and violent crimes. In the 1990s, there is little change. Almost all of the average 100 mostly young Yupik men incarcerated in Bethel's regional jail, with a handful of Whites, were there on "alcohol-related" crimes, and a new juvenile detention center next door was nearing capacity. These young Eskimos could be said to be in cross-cultural shock, unable to cope with the changes splitting their social and personal self-concepts, and with the consequent loss of roots and purpose in life.

Keep in mind that the non-Native professional's shock is usually based

on a relatively superficial knowledge of Native culture and community conditions, and represents a situation more to be understood, appreciated and
learned from, intrinsically, than something to be deprecated out of hand.
But the author's own first look at Native culture was very different, and
somewhat theatrical, perhaps in the 19th century tradition of the Victorian
chronicler and photographer of the Native American, Robert Sherif Curtis.

In the summer of 1962, I had a full experience with Native American
culture re-enacted from the past, though ironically it was a fellow Caucasian
who made it possible. From time to time I've met Natives who have also
learned something significant about their culture from non-Natives, the
oral tradition through elders having long ago been eclipsed by the culturally homogenizing public school system and culturally destructive actions
of the dominant society in the late 19th and early 20th centuries. Thus a
renaissance of Native culture has on occasion been aided through the usually scientific, sometimes charitable or legal efforts of Caucasians, some of
whom even prefer to live among the Native people.

After being in Europe for a few years on the GI Bill following the army
and marrying a Seattlite who was also a student there, we returned to the
States, ending up in Seattle. I spent the summer working at the former Hen-
derson Camps at the southern end of Lopez Island in the San Juan group
that occupies the border waters between Washington State and British Columbia's Vancouver Island. This was a summer camp for boys and girls, and
had a Native American character to its operation. Everyone lived in tipis,
arranged in clusters through light woods on a small peninsula at the island's
southeast corner. Though plains-type tipis are certainly not traditional
Northwest Native coastal dwellings, this oblique detail was more than compensated for by a Northwest coastal Indian cultural program run by the
summer resident counselor, Bill Holm, who has since become a published
author of several books on Northwest coastal Indian crafts and culture, as
well as serving for many years as the Curator of Native American collections
at the University of Washington's Burke Museum.

He had built an authentic longhouse on the shore fronting the camp,
near the small bouldered point that is its main feature on a protected cove.
There was a great deal of carving inside and a totem pole outside, plus a real
Chinook canoe, everything carved and built by Bill himself from cedar and
other woods. At first I paid little attention to the longhouse's details, inside
and out, as I had other things on my mind at the time, in addition to my
work. But this was to change during the last week of August, when Bill and
the campers he'd trained put on a salmon bake and potlatch.

When it became dusk, and everyone had had his fill of delicious baked
salmon, our attention was directed out to the darkening water, behind the
small point. Everyone fell silent, and suddenly around the point ghosted the
Chinook canoe, the paddlers quietly bringing the craft shoreward, with a
man standing on the prow, singing a song with a hand drum. He was

dressed in Kwakiutl regalia and a cedar fiber cape, with a strange carved mask covering his head. In the gathering darkness, this apparition truly seemed to be arriving from another world. When they came ashore, the costumed man spoke only Kwakiutl, we were told, and let us know we were to meet with them in the longhouse. Once inside, with night closing in behind us, we found a crackling fire in the center, and took seats on benches that ringed three sides of the interior. The fragrance of wood and perhaps sweet grass filled the nostrils. One narrow end, opposite the entrance hole we had come in, was a sort of stage, flanked by carved posts with impressive beaked figures at their upper ends. The smoke from the noisy fire was going out a hole in the center of the planked roof.

After an opening welcome and introductions of some Kwakiutl Indian guests who had come south from Vancouver Island for this occasion, an announcement was made that the evening was dedicated to Chief Mungo Martin, who had passed away not long before. For the next few hours we were immersed in songs, rituals and dances of the Kwakiutl, with various startling sights and special effects that made one gape with wonder and surprise. All the time the fire in the center was being fed, and great shadows gyrated around the vertical plank walls, hinting at other spirits in attendance.

It was an unforgettable experience, and everyone was impressed. The curious fact is that save for the few Indian guests, none of the participants were Native people. Yet the culture seemed to be there, at least to one new to such experiences. I have since seen real Native cultural activities on many occasions in diverse settings, but this first exposure was exquisite and total, involving all the senses at once, as a childhood experience might be. I was hooked on the Native heritage, which I have subsequently shared with Native peoples elsewhere in North America. My career in libraries has been profoundly affected, and at times literally resurrected through contacts with the Native community. I have learned that the Native heritage of blood and place is everywhere, under our feet and in the air, conveyed in the waters, if we will only recognize and learn from it, and listen to the Native people.

Earlier still, it was around 1943–45, from age 12 to 14 that my awareness of racism and discrimination toward minorities first made itself felt. Even in those tender years I was at once struck by the cruel prejudice directing aversion and ridicule against seemingly anyone of the colored races or minority religions. I also immediately gauged the emotional intensity that underlay these beliefs, and equally so the inherent injustice. In later years I belonged to a college fraternity which, much to the frustration of the liberal clique to which I belonged, "blackballed" time after time any candidates for membership from the colored races, as well as Jewish students in the early 1950s at Cornell University; even Catholics had a tough time being accepted as brothers. To my knowledge there were no Black American men or women on campus, which also meant that our intercollegiate athletes were then made up exclusively of white students. I was also struck by the fact that the organized major Christian churches seemed to countenance this status quo, and I soon dropped tenuous liberal church affiliations I had intermittently tried to cultivate.

During the 1960s and early 1970s, I was what was then called a civil rights activist, participating in many actions supporting minority rights to employment, housing, access to higher education, and apprenticeship training in the trades. Later, while working as a Library Assistant at the University of Washington Libraries, I became involved in the anti-Vietnam War movement, and joined in advocacy of equal pay and promotion for women librarians, a profession I was soon to join.

The next issue to come along locally was treaty fishing rights for western Washington Indians. One year in the late 1960s there was a militant (armed) fish camp on the Puyallup River in the heart of Tacoma, on Puget Sound, and I accompanied a couple of friends who were hauling food and other needed supplies and equipment down from Seattle on weekends. The rather startling thing for me was to see armed Indians determined to assert their 100-year-old treaty subsistence fishing rights, or at least access to part of them, in the face of overwhelming odds. A few weeks later the camp was "busted" by a combination of local police, Federal Marshals and the FBI (some with automatic weapons), and the site bulldozed over. But the issues were not so easily buried, and later the famous Boldt Decision[7] came out of the Federal courts, giving Indian fishermen rights to half the harvestable salmon on many tidewater rivers in Washington State.

This situation unfortunately created much ill will against local Indians. While working in Tacoma at the public library from 1974 to 1976, I had a tipi pitched in my backyard. I had just returned from working as librarian at Montana State Prison, where I had befriended a number of Indian inmates and become interested in tipi culture. That Halloween I would greet children at the door, and invite them to sit around the fire in my tipi out back, glowing and flickering like a magic hat on that night of surprises, after which I would distribute treats to them all. I simply wanted them to have the experience of sitting in a real tipi, to see how nice it was, and I'd briefly add some background and lore about the tipi, as the nervous kids nudged each other around the blazing fire, their shadows dancing on the canvas walls. I had taken one group of children to the tipi, and was talking to them seated around the fire, when a parent suddenly stepped through the oval-shaped door. Without a word to me, the woman looked around, wrinkled her nose and said: "C'mon kids, if you stay here much longer you'll smell like an Indian!"

My career as a librarian has had its ups and downs. I guess I was too restless, eventually becoming dissatisfied with one job, moving on to another after two or three years. My résumé was a little disjointed from these nomadic moves. At one point, after leaving a job, I found it seemingly impossible to find my next librarian position. I think the very bureaucratic and subordinate nature of a librarian's work would periodically get me down. I concentrated my job-searching efforts in western Washington, which I loved, but which is also a highly competitive job market. The jobs were there, but so were many young, eager applicants, every bit as qualified as oneself, drawn to the attractions of the Pacific Northwest.

Perhaps libraries weren't for me after all. Then came a desolate period of almost four years when all I had was a series of temporary and seasonal non-library jobs while I wrote the first draft of an autobiographical novel, occasionally drawing unemployment and working as a library volunteer, hoping this last gesture might bring me a library job. Then a point was reached when I felt I had to get back into libraries or it was finished, because it seemed I really had nothing else to offer, occupationally speaking. Having had such a poor experience of job-searching in western Washington, I wanted to expand to the entire Northwest. But I also needed something new, an angle to exploit. I thought of a Crow elder I knew only distantly, but whose unsolicited spiritual mailings I received now and then and hadn't given much attention to. (He had been a computer specialist, by the way, before retiring.) He lived in Seattle, so I gave him a call. I just wanted to talk to someone sympathetic and knowledgeable, to get my confidence and bearings back. My current unemployment benefits were about to run out, and I was frankly pretty desperate.

I took the cross-town bus and arrived at his ground floor apartment door. He lived in low-income city housing, overlooking park-like lawns. He and his wife were home, but she withdrew to the kitchen. We talked for a while over coffee, then went for a stroll, to sit on a bench and talk some more.

He simply suggested that I contact the larger Indian tribes of the region, introducing myself and offering my services as a librarian/researcher. I sent out ten letters, and within two weeks received two offers of employment: one with a small coastal tribe, the other with a Montana tribe. I heard from the coastal tribe first, and immediately accepted their job offer. I learned about the other job after my mail was forwarded out to the coast—that's how quickly I moved!

Out at the Bay Indian reservation, on the Pacific ocean, it was a new world, within sight and sound of the ocean surf a mile away across salt marshes, yet I immediately felt accepted and at home. The environment was more natural and unspoiled, with plenty of space. The atmosphere in human terms was quiet and compatible, unhurried and casual. My work was interesting, and I had a lot of latitude in pursuing it. The weighty personal concerns of the recent past seemed to dissipate into the air, just as the coastal fog does as a summer morning comes on and the sun rises higher. It seemed to be the beginning of a new era. And there was so much to be learned, for it turned out that I knew next to nothing about the real Indian community. It took years of living among them, listening and asking, watching and sharing, to begin to see how life was with them, both now and in the past. I was vexed why I, as a native-born Euroamerican, knew so little about Native peoples. The impression I got was that they were either romanticized or ostracized so much by the dominant society that the true reality was well closeted within the Native community itself, beyond the reach of even intrusive federal and state agencies who attempted to regulate every aspect of their lives.

Now here I was, sharing their lives as a librarian/researcher, of all things. I remembered back in graduate library school, during a course of International Librarianship (which actually was a course in comparative librarianship), being threatened with a failing grade by the long-tenured professor, who shook his finger at me in front of the class, warning me that I should fail if I couldn't find enough information "on libraries" in several former French colonies of sub-saharan Africa. (I had learned French while in Europe during the Algerian revolution and was interested in learning more about the developmental problems of libraries and related institutions in Francophone Africa.) What the professor was ignorant of was the multifaceted, multidimensional nature of Third World development and its implications for "libraries." It involved problems of literacy, documentation, education, urbanization, modernization, centralization, standardization—not to mention the cross-cultural character of all these things. What would he say now, seeing me in this dilapidated trailer-office on a tiny but beautiful coastal reservation, helping to "salvage the heritage" of one of the nontreaty tribes, without a library to take care of? Yet to some extent—and in challenging ways—I *was* working as a librarian. . .

I lived in an all-weather tipi[8] year round, bought a canoe, and was even written up in the area newspaper's Sunday magazine as the "Tipi Man," a white man come to help the Indians find out about their heritage! But I wasn't a total fool. I was constantly aware of how little I knew about the Native people hereabouts and their heritage. The coming years would see me coming back again and again, to try to learn a little more. I sometimes wished devoutly to have some Indian blood in me somewhere, so I might be accepted more completely. I remain a "Poston," a "Kussaq," a "Kabloona," a white man—The Man, a charter member of the dominant society.

But probably the most profound experience, the most complete immersion was to come in western Alaska, when I jetted out to work in a library development project among the Yupik Eskimo villages and stayed three years. This experience has been discussed in detail on the library side in chapter 2, but there are some other considerations and lessons to share.

It was my first experience with Native people who are still actively pursuing the subsistence life-style, about 70% of their needs, on average, being derived from hunting, fishing, trapping and gathering. In the remote villages there were very few cash jobs, and the only reason modern community development had come to them was because oil revenues starting in the

1970s enabled the state of Alaska to be generous in its development assistance throughout the state, in the form of a continuous stream of appropriations and grants for capital projects and technical assistance. Housing projects replaced the old, half-subterranean houses in the late '40s and 1950s, modern medical care was brought close at hand, and K-12 schools were available in even the smallest village, at great financial cost. No longer would high schoolers have to travel the thousand or more miles to Mt. Edgecombe school to southeastern Alaska, or further yet to Chemawa School in Oregon.

In the space of a generation, the Yupik Eskimo villages had gone from post-aboriginal living conditions, very isolated, traditional, Yupik-speaking, dependent totally on subsistence economies, to relatively modern community convenience. But the problems that came with all these changes, which are covered elsewhere in this volume, especially chapter 4, were equally numerous and ineluctable. Yet, as one older Eskimo woman was quoted by a visitor to the north, if we can paraphrase her gentle chiding: "You white people shouldn't worry so much about us, you know. We've lived out here for a long time. We've seen a lot of changes. Sure there's lotsa problems, but we're enjoying life and we can take care of ourselves. You white people worry too much!"

On my first visits to remote villages, I was struck by the predominance of an insular subsistence life—all the signs of fishing, hunting, trapping, gathering, wood retrieval and cutting, home repair of snogos and boats, generators and water pumps, the primitive methods of sewage disposal and an airstrip being the "road out of town." Then the dressing out of game carcasses and all kinds of fish, preparation of foods for storage and skins for making winter clothes, weaving of decorative baskets and mats and making ivory jewelry for sale, mostly to whites. Some things took acculturating on my part, such as seeing many animals and fish and fowl as necessary food in quantity, and not as discrete "wild game" to be hunted for fun. Learning to run a dog team starting the first winter taught me the discipline, work, patience and hardship that this traditional activity required. And I also learned a lot from working and living with the dogs themselves, just as I'd learned from the tipi years before. I really wondered, at first, where the village library would fit into all this.

In cross-cultural community development work, one runs great risks in not taking the time and opportunity to learn about the cultural ways, the living conditions, the issues from the Native point of view, and something of the Native language. Trust and respect come only with time and acquaintance. To ask for trust "out front" is phony and cynical at best, deceitful and exploitative if calculating. Trust should not be granted without shared knowledge, genuine understanding and mutual respect, experiences which need to be weighed and depended upon, and tested repeatedly over time. Knowledge is traded, understanding is mutually acknowledged, and thereby trust is earned and justified. It has always been that the ascendant culture assumes its superiority and ethnocentricity. But this is a cultural delusion. Work in Native communities can be much enhanced and made more effective by taking time to know the people individually and to be known by them, by attending community functions and being helpful, by accepting hospitality and invitations without reservation, and by taking an interest in community conditions, events and the heritage. To a notable degree cross-cultural librarianship turns one into an amateur applied anthropologist and community development specialist, in addition to the quasi-social worker role that many public service librarians are accustomed to.[9]

Wearing more than one hat in cross-cultural or multicultural service is an advantage, but it goes against the prevailing emphasis on technical specialization. The advantage is that one hopefully responds to the entire community and its situation, its wants and needs as *it* conceives them. The disadvantage, or danger, in being a single-minded, myopic specialist, say, in "library development" per se, is that

> specialization . . . by its very narrowness and isolation . . . becomes less and less responsive to the living experience. . . . It often brings with it a self-importance tainted with arrogance. It is this intellectual arrogance that separates the applied scientist from the richness available within our own tradition of the humanities, the social sciences, and the arts.[10]

—not to mention the people themselves and the real, full lives they are living.

As a versatile and adaptable student of other communities and cultures and the people they have nurtured, one is constantly attached to reality—chameleon-like—and becomes a student of it. In the Yukon-Kuskokwim delta, where I was working on this book in the winter of 1989–90, living in a log house with twenty dogs and some newborn pups outside, there is a major concentration of Native population in Bethel and 50-odd remote villages. The climate, topography and lack of inter-village roads prolong a subsistence lifestyle. Dog teams are still scattered around the villages, though the majority are owned by whites in Bethel, who use them only for racing. However, along with the popularity of dog-team racing, the depressed Alaskan economy in the late 1980s making snogo purchase and maintenance more difficult, subsistence dog teams have come back in some villages. Many Native people don't trust the dependence on oil for heat and fuel. Elders still prefer dog travel. As one only half-jokingly expressed it, "With dogs, at least you know you'll get there!"[11] Even in the rare event one got lost, with dogs there is always food, and some warmth. With an inoperative snogo, there is nothing except a very long walk home, which has proven lethal for many a lone snogo driver. Another example of this pragmatic approach is in new housing. Throughout the delta this has included both wood and oil stoves in each dwelling, to allow for the inability of many villagers to purchase heating oil all the time, or simply to save money in burning the driftwood that is usually available down the rivers and sloughs and coast every spring with breakup.

Making an attempt to learn the Native language of the area one is working in is significant, regardless of what the non-Native authority says. In the delta, I got some special tutoring in Yup'ik from the Adult Basic Education Center, with the idea of making a phrase book I could use on my village visits. I had gotten tired of being embarrassed while visiting certain villages where few Native chose to speak what broken English they knew, and I sometimes had to rely on an interpreter. Sitting in a village office surrounded by Yup'ik speakers, conversing and looking me over, made me feel even more "remote" than the village itself ever was. In later years I took the Asher TPR course, "Yup'ik Made Simple" (see p.82).

One feature of cross-cultural work to be noted well is the portrayal of Natives as being somehow less intelligent, especially those Natives for whom English is definitely a second language. Time and again, while working in Native or Indian communities, I've had them described to me, both as a group and individually, as being a people less discerning and capable than my own kind (Caucasian), but later, through my own personal experience and working relationship, found them to be very astute, demanding (of higher standards) and conscientious promoters of the best and most appropriate library services for their village. Critics of the Native way almost never have any knowledge of, for example, the Native language, and therefore couldn't converse with them if their lives depended on it (In this case it's their credibility and job performance that do.) But knowledge of the local language isn't required in order to be tolerant, respectful and gracious, a student of the Native ways, and to be accepted.

I've lived in France and attended French universities as a French student, and also have had to speak Russian in an all-Russian setting. I know very well how inadequate one feels trying to express oneself fully in a second language. In western Alaska the tendency of many whites (mostly the transient ones) was to judge the intelligence of Eskimos by how well they spoke English, or their demeanor in personal encounters. The more closely their speech patterns, body language, and cultural literacy matched those of whites (who speak no Yup'ik at all, with a few rare exceptions), the more the Eskimos were accepted as being "sharp" and "together" individuals. An eskimo speaking English falteringly and with strong Yup'ik speech patterns was often considered "slow," and perhaps even "not quite all there."

Even scientific professionals can err on the side of ethnocentricity and unintentional racial bias, if they are too culture-bound. An article by Julia S. Kleinfeld points out the slanted character of much "scientific" testing for intelligence, testing which is

> . . . in large part responsible for the consistent findings of 'intellectual inferiority' among most culturally different groups. This result occurs because

general intelligence tests were developed historically not on the basis of any theory about the nature and structure of human abilities, but rather for a very specific practical purpose: to predict success. Success, that is, given the educational and occupational methods and selective traditions of western society. It should hardly come as a surprise, then, that members of the dominant society tend to be better adapted—perhaps through heredity, perhaps through socialization—to the particular demands of western culture than those who are members of other cultural groups. What other result could one reasonably expect?[12]

Then there is the matter of cultural literacy, and especially the particular bureaucratic literacy we Caucasians are used to. Some specialists and educators cultivate the most "trendy" jargon, to the point where staff members have to listen closely to "keep up." One wonders what the Native students and visitors from the villages think of this kind of white man's talk, when its disconcerting nuances might be another aspect of mismatch in cross-cultural communications, compromising the availability or continuation of a college program in the village, or a capital-project grant. In the Y-K delta in the early 1980s, non-Native educators in this de facto bicultural education environment spoke no Yupik whatsoever, but their "hip" managerial patois, sometimes garnished in private with epithets and prejudicial "war stories," seemed indispensable for macho bush work. This phenomenon can also be described as the closet paternalism characteristic of neo-colonialist policies, still found in the north, and to some degree seemingly inescapable under present Native-White relations.

In the Yukon-Kuskokwim delta, the folkloric view among an element of the white population conveyed the impression that Eskimos just weren't quite the equal of whites, and "had a long way to go" before matching the judgment, quickness (in speech, for example), sophistication, comprehension, vision and cultural advancement (especially in the professions) of their Kussaq neighbors and visitors. Yet to consider placing the white person in a totally Yupik setting is to see how ludicrous is the Eskimo stereotype of being slow, dumb, inarticulate and backward. Some Kussaqs, including many professionals, live among the Yupik people fully expecting them to adopt the whole cloth of Kussaq society and culture, with only token reciprocity toward the Yupik side—and no language facility. The author attended a meeting of a bilingual/bicultural committee of the local school district that was working on a curriculum that would teach the Yup'ik language both as a first and second language, according to the students' capabilities. The chair at one point startled some ears by stating: "Well, of course, we all know we're presiding over a dying language, but . . ." There were Yupik people present, and others who should have spoken up, but no one did.

When the state and federal authorities through benign neglect allow wholesale replacement of Yup'ik language and cultural ways to continue unabated, there will be only one possible outcome if this policy is allowed to run its course. The author shares the view of those who believe that the Yupik people in the Yukon-Kuskokwim delta need to be politically autonomous for these purposes, and revert to federal status.[13] Perhaps then Yup'ik could become the equal of English as an official language, Yup'ik teachers become the majority at a faster rate, instead of a lingering minority, and the college would require its faculty (all but two of whom in 1988 were non-Natives, along with a couple in the Yup'ik Language Center—by 1990 the situation had improved considerably) to learn to speak the language, or Yup'ik instructors would be found and hired. Trends as well as long-range plans of the University of Alaska suggest that this may happen, but progress year by year is agonizingly slow thus far. (In 1990 the local school board attempted to require non-Native teachers to take Yup'ik language courses, but key advocates were voted out.)

During my time in the delta I noticed the unstinting attention and prominence given to individual criminality and anti-social conduct by the regional newspaper, which was then owned and edited by non-Natives. Those booked by the police and not yet in court were all named. Over 90% of such actions are "alcohol-related" and involve Natives almost exclusively. The abundance of this kind of "spotlighting," personally embarrassing and publicly shaming to Natives, was matched, obversely, by the absence of column inches on the historical causes of this self-destructive behavior, and the role of obtrusive and rampant Euroamerican acculturation in its perpetuation. (The newspaper is now Native-owned, but the naming and trial-by-media continues, although there is more public recognition of the real and underlying causes. Cross-cultural issues and Native sovereignty issues are being more openly and candidly addressed by both the Native and White communities, in Bethel and throughout Alaska.)

At this point we should be reminded again that acculturation works both ways. The culture shock discussed earlier speaks to that. Since Europeans first thought of, first glimpsed, and first arrived on colonial shores, they have begun to alter and change, in every facet of their being. Long-time white residents of Bethel, many with Yupik spouses and close friends throughout the Yupik community, and pursuing subsistence ways side by side, have been "Americanized" in that way. The Native world has taken them in.

While a staff member of Kuskokwim Community College in the early 1980s, I participated in the college "self-study" that was part of the accreditation process for the Northwest Association of Schools and Colleges. I was also on the committee that drafted the mission statement, and in some respects the discussion was most interesting. For example, how should we describe the community served by the college? At first, to my disbelief, the college president put forth a community description that lacked any reference to the fact that it was overwhelmingly Yupik, and profoundly bilingual and bicultural. (Over 90% of the students are Yupik Eskimos from all over the region.) When some of us insisted on this being included in the mission statement, the president at first balked, then acquiesced to this bicultural identity of our service area.

Curiously, a Native member of the committee agreed with the president, commenting simply, shaking his head, "We're all the same . . ." It would be a hasty misinterpretation to believe that this person was a "white Eskimo," or was an administration pawn. The more likely explanation for his view is that many Yupik people still share the custom of accepting modern visitors no matter what their racial or ethnic background, although there were instances during the series of European-induced epidemics around the turn of the century when hostility ran high against whites in some areas. And even today, there are villages that would rather not have non-Natives present. In one village a couple of years ago a white woman teacher was ordered to leave. Many villages have opted to ban the possession of alcohol, and one village in the winter of 1987–88 achieved some notoriety because the elders decided that everyone arriving in the village should be carefully searched, to see if any alcohol was being brought in. Some non-Native specialists refused to travel to it, asserting that their personal rights were more important than alcohol availability, so devastating in these remote villages. Similar incidents continue to occur from time to time.

Racism was apparently the domain of only a few transient non-Natives and was certainly not in evidence, at least not overtly. There is, of course, a variety of unobtrusive pressures on those Natives who have regular contact with whites to lead, at least to some degree, "white Eskimo" lives, especially ones who are leaders in the Yupik community. The strain of this kind of balancing act has produced some individual tragedies. Until now, the vital subsistence resources have not been seriously impacted by a steadily growing Native population, more hunters and fishers and more effective hunting and fishing techniques, and a stronger urban-dwelling, non-Native sport hunting and fishing lobby statewide (most of the Alaskan population lives in Anchorage, Fairbanks and Juneau). But with oil and gas exploration continuing in the Bering Sea, and pressures on subsistence resources increasing, one wonders if the Yupik people's traditional tolerance will last forever. As mentioned earlier, by 1995 several villages on the Lower Kuskokwim had largely withdrawn from control by Alaska state authority and reverted to Federal tribal status, which brings more independence. Still others are watching this trend closely while others are split, which puts a strain on deltawide, intervillage relations when conferences are held. In October, 1994, when Alaska State Troopers flew into a village to arrest alleged criminal suspects, a group of villagers obstructed, protesting state interference in village affairs. Others supported the state's authority. Some arrests were made of protesters, but the controversy then moved to peaceful negotiations. In another, assertive actions by the high school principal, a white woman, in matters of alleged child abuse, badly divided the villagers—

some saying the policy was justified, others, that it was too intrusive into family and village life. In the 1980s, the state Judicial Commission observed that whites, especially the well educated, were being removed by peremptory challenge from jury pools in the Bethel court. The attorneys (all white), whether for the defense or the State, could then have cross-cultural leverage over mostly Native and less enculturated juries. This skew has apparently been corrected.

While in Bethel, I told stories over the delta radio station, KYUK-AM, for a short time. Some of them were what I called "cultural stories," as told from the point of view of a Yupik Elder watching the ways of a white man coming into his village. After one program, I was told that a Native woman at the radio station was critical of one story on certain points. I arranged to meet with her, and together we listened to my story again. Two of her objections were these: the Yupik people welcome visitors, no matter what their race and background. One isn't suspicious of them or their motives. The other observation was that a grandfather wouldn't keep secrets from his grandchildren, in asking one of them not to tell his parents something, even in humor. In cross-cultural gestures, one must always be on guard, lest one's cultural biases and assumptions interfere with and distort perceptions of the Native world view and values.

I recall a white principal-teacher in one of the remote villages stating emphatically that his primary responsibility was to give the students a good basic education, so that they might be good managers of the tribal resources and corporations under the terms of ANCSA, and be properly equipped and disciplined to succeed in college. He would accept the courses in the Yupik heritage desired by village elders, but he knew his main job. Regarding the importance and relevance of the Eskimo culture in the late 20th century, his attitude was condescending and cynical, as he didn't believe that traditional subsistence ways were long for this world. The subsistence economy would pass away, bringing on jobs in a cash economy, sustained by the gradual development of both renewable and non-renewable resources on tribal lands and waters. Four years later this conservative teacher became a high school principal in rural Alaska.

If one can stand back and objectively consider such a stance, it is fascinating how a professional of the ascendant culture can dismiss the long reliable and resourceful indigenous culture and relegate it to obsolescence and extinction, as if somehow during this lifetime the millenium has been reached, and this best of all worlds will continue indefinitely into the far future. But then, perhaps he is right, as every indicator points to a closer community of variegated human cultures on "spaceship earth," despite all its local warring, famines, overpopulation, hazardous waste and signs of a deteriorating world climatic shield.

But consider as well the Native viewpoint: From the beginning of time our people have survived and prevailed using the proven old ways, at least until the coming of the Europeans, who have been profligate and reckless, and take from the earth without giving in return. Why should we discard everything we have learned and embrace his ways, alien to both our flesh and spirit, as well as disrespectful of what we hold sacred.

KTOO-TV (Juneau) has produced an excellent four-part video series entitled *Communicating across Cultures,* hosted by the Russian Orthodox priest, the Reverend Doctor Michael J. Oleksa, speaking informally before a live audience. This aired on public television in Alaska during fall, 1994. Other KTOO projects are being worked on through the Alaska Staff Development Network, the Alaska Humanities Forum, and the University of Alaska, Southeast. They address Native empowerment and Native education respectively: *Our Gathering Place* and *Alaska Onward to Excellence.* This last one was done with the cooperation of the Yupiit Nation and other southwest Alaska school districts.

In Plains Indian country, when I'd go shopping off the reservation, if I mentioned where I worked I often encountered racist attitudes on the part of whites, even in the market towns bordering the reservation, which flourish because of their Indian trade. On the Washington State coast, there was much resentment against the Bay Indians due to a land claim dispute (land illegally taken from the reservation in the 19th century), and litigation being considered to reclaim access to some of the fisheries on the bay, long since taken away from the Indians and, in the case of some species, totally depleted, necessitating restocking with non-Native or otherwise imported species.

One of the hazards of being a white person working under these conditions is to always be courting the resentment and anger of some fellow whites. Either that, or they assume one is "on their side," and privately share their opinionated virus. All one can do is to keep one's own counsel, and do whatever one can to bring knowledge and better understanding to Native/white relations.

Native library development, or improvement up to the qualitative standards of libraries in the dominant society, is an integral part of the larger movement toward increased multicultural librarianship responsibility, throughout not only North America, but the world.

> The history of library services to ethnic and linguistic minorities is almost a century old but interest in the field started to grow only after the Second World War and became, in the 1970s, one of the most prominent and debated issues in librarianship.[14]

This was the case in some countries, and especially in the developing world, which was being aided with technical assistance through the United

Nations and Unesco, for example, but the author attended graduate library school on the west coast in the early 1970s, and it certainly wasn't prominent or debated then. It might have been an issue among our faculty, but as students we only heard it referred to, if at all, in general terms. There were no courses, workshops or guest faculty to help us focus on multicultural, minority or ethnic librarianship. We did have one conservative Black faculty member, but his presence had no apparent impact on the curriculum in terms of minority/women status and treatment in librarianship or library materials, nor on the approach that other faculty members took in their courses.

An arresting question is why it might be an issue at all, on this highly multicultural North American continent. Of course, until recently (the 1960s) libraries and librarians in the U.S. have lived and worked in a segregated society. Only since the midpoint of the 20th century has agitation and promotion of universal library services to all minorities been institutionalized in official library organizations, library education and among working professionals. The periodical literature and bibliographies from that time are well seeded with many articles, reports, studies and surveys, documenting the information needs of minorities and advocating more action by legislatures, library agencies and libraries, especially those working at the "public interface."

Yet the library profession has been slow to follow up on all the valid findings and pointed advice. Then, in 1979, the U.S. National Commission on Libraries and Information Science held the first White House Conference on Library and Information Services, which included a Pre-conference on Library Services to Indians on or near Reservations. Out of the White House Conference also came a new entity, the Task Force on Library and Information Services to Cultural Minorities, which was to explore the current status of library and information services for this major multicultural element. Why was this new study called for? Because the concept needed deeper institutionalization into the library-supportive bureaucracy nationwide, as this would provide official findings on which legislation for funding more minority library development could be based. The Task Force held hearings and issued a report, not all of whose recommendations were accepted by the National Commission, however, which generated some controversy. The Task Force was then disbanded. (For some provocative critiques of NCLIS and its performance, see articles by Josey and Moon.)

For Native peoples of the U.S., the 1979 Pre-conference was probably the most important single milestone. There were many meetings, it produced many papers, but most useful was probably the reinforcement among participants, which has continued afterward through networking. With the noteworthy exception of the Pre-conference, however, NCLIS has not been either a pacesetter or a good paradigm in multicultural librarianship. Looking over its annual reports for the 1980s, including its publications and fifteen-year review of accomplishments in the 1985–86 annual report, the near-absence of minority library matters is glaring. Until 1993 there was, on average, only one commissioner out of 15 that was of minority extraction. As of that year, the number grew to three. Looking over the photos of commission members of recent years shows only one minority member, an Asian. Because there can be as many as 17 or 18 members, it's embarrassing that almost no minorities are represented, though under Democratic President Bill Clinton this may well change. Of course, appearances are a poor indicator of intellectual, social, and political representation, and beginning in 1989 NCLIS began an extensive effort to learn about library services or the lack of them in Native American communities. Its massive, 610-page report (*Pathways to Excellence*) was issued in 1993, and because of the variety of source materials and information it contains, it is a useful and exhaustive sourcebook on Native American library service needs.

However, on looking it over, one finds little on the need to adapt *urban* library services more appropriately and effectively to the approximately one half of Native Americans who live in cities. Most conventional urban libraries are culturally alien for Native persons, and so the local Native American population, usually an invisible fraction anyway, no matter how numerous and tribally diverse it may be, is ignored in cross-cultural terms. As was pointed out in the 1979 White House Conference, NCLIS can help by proactively identifying such problematical areas that are not being addressed, and encouraging urban library systems to recognize the need to make adaptive adjustments in their service environments, promotional efforts, and liaison with existing Native American organizations. And the term "city" here is relative, because in western Alaska, for example, the regional centers for Bethel (pop. 4,500) and Nome (pop. 3,500) are metropolitan centers for scores of remote villages in their respective regions. Los Angeles now has nearly 100,000 Natives and Indians (1 percent of the total population), and Anchorage is Alaska's "largest Native village," with an estimated 14,000 Native American residents out of a total of 250,000 or so for the entire municipality.

In Canada, the Library and Information Needs of Native People Interest Group, founded in the mid-1970s and attached to the Canadian Library Association, seems to have been the coordinating entity around which much else to do with Native library services has gained support. The minutes of the group's mid-1985 meeting provide some criticism such as we hear in the U.S., Greenland and elsewhere—mostly directed toward library bureaucracies.

After emphasizing the need for reinstatement of the non-discretionary or per capita funding scheme at the federal level, asking for more support from CLA, as well as direct liaison between CLA and Native organizations, and suggesting the need for some kind of umbrella group for the many regional groups across Canada that are working for the improvement of Native library services, some negative aspects of the national scene in this regard are pointed out.

There was an absence of initiative from the CLA leadership, and awareness of the Native library situation within library systems nationwide was low. The CLA supported the interest group but didn't incorporate its policies into divisional programs. The hierarchy of CLA and other mainline library organizations tended to react, rather than initiate. And CLA should have had a centralized information source on Native library services and collections, etc.

In 1988, one was referred to many individuals across the country, and to various groups and organizations outside the mainstream library bureaucracies. In varying degrees the exceptions are provinces like Ontario, Alberta and Saskatchewan, along with the Yukon and Northwest Territories, which have offices specifically responsible for Native library services, and to some degree the federal department of Indian and Northern Affairs, which is the main national agency administering local discretionary funds, a portion of which go to Native libraries.

Inquiries to the National Library of Canada or the CLA refers one to the variety of above-mentioned unofficial, ad hoc and quasi-official entities. We should note that the original and continuing range of initiatives has come, not from levels of government or official librarydom, nor from library education—though individual faculty and students, along with a very few schools, have made significant gestures. It has come equally from Native bands and organizations themselves, individual librarians working in public and academic libraries, and ad hoc interest groups.

This again underlines the conservatism and benignity that librarians must work and survive within, let alone attempt to advance the "library and information science" profession. The situation has become all the more frustrating, not to say desperate, as the rate of technological, demographic and sociocultural changes have accelerated, and become more complex and universal. The information field has become integrated into everyone's life, making for unprecedented sophistication and intense competition for information control and delivery. Suddenly we librarians, birthing out of the age of print, find that in many rural locations we are still staffing an old-fashioned library with little more technology than a telephone and perhaps some microfiches. Yet, within the conventional mode, this suits the early developmental situation of most Native library uses quite well—but only initially. The necessity of up-to-date, complete, and appropriate information services requires the latest library technology, innovative documentation of Native life, archival and artifact preservation and display, and multicultural adaptability.

Internationally, in 1980 the first open meeting of the Working Group on Library Service to Ethnic and Linguistic Minorities of the International Federation of Library Associations (IFLA) was held. In 1986 this became the official IFLA Section of Library Services to Multicultural Populations, which published the *Journal of Multicultural Librarianship* (now merged with *Multicentural Review*). The Section and the periodical serve as a stimulant and reinforcement for networking, to further the cause of multicultural librarianship and to provide information on activities around the world to anyone interested. Their meetings at IFLA conferences, though only for the well-funded few to attend, nevertheless serve to keep multicultural librarianship an integral part of IFLA, the primary international library organization.

Beginning at about the same time, Australia and New Zealand, among the nations of the Second World, well-developed industrially, have been very active in the pursuit of multicultural librarianship in recent years. A National Conference on Multiculturalism and Libraries was held in 1981. Developments since then in Australia and New Zealand reflect a much heightened resolve and effort to generate appropriate library services for all aboriginal communities, as well as to provide for other minority ethnic groups.

How do these relatively remote developments affect library development in North American and circumpolar Native communities? They help create an international climate for public recognition and public action that supports hard funding and an official infrastructure that can help implement improved and appropriate Native library services. It is indispensable for working public service and academic librarians in the field to have some way of touching this network. Certainly library schools, most of all, need to have multicultural librarianship well-represented in their faculty meeting rooms and classrooms.

In professional library organizations, the compartmentalizing effect of having "roundtables," special committees, "interest groups" or sections on multicultural and Native/Indian library services is unfortunate, because this tends to relegate such progressive, client group-oriented and socially responsible aspects of the profession to "fringe" or even, in the early going, "cult" status. It is symptomatic of the professional status difficulties of the library and information science field, although the information scientists are, by definition and association, in a stronger position. Problematical as this situation is, it derives from the nature of library education and in part from the lack of realistic relations with Native communities, and includes its cohorts in archival and museum management, although there, accelerating progress is being made.

Library education, which we shall look at in the next chapter, emphasizes the core or required courses which are print-oriented (computer applications also being mostly print-oriented, as well as library-centered). Everything else, except children's services (a traditional specialty, probably inherited from the historical situation out of which former women teachers often became librarians), including such vital modern areas as public "outreach" or extension services, library budget management, grantsmanship and community relations, tend to be considered special subjects, even electives. This would be understandable for specialty subjects like cartographic, archival, institutional or corporate librarianship, but there is pure dereliction, to be blunt, in treating multicultural librarianship (which includes services for the Native peoples) as anything other than a required subject in the core curriculum of library education.

Notes

1. Boas, Franz. *The Mind of Primitive Man*. New York: Macmillan, 1922, pp. 208–209. Quoted in: Harrison, Barbara Gill. *Informal Learning among Yup'ik Eskimos:* etc., 1981, p. 3.
2. Simsova, Sylva. "Central and East Europeans in Britain," *Journal of Multicultural Librarianship,* Vol. 1, No. 3 (July, 1987), p.121
   A fascinating article reflecting the multifaceted and subtle work of the multicultural librarian. In some quarters Native librarianship is considered rather separate from multicultural librarianship.
3. Tamas, Andy. "Psychology of Culture Change and Education for Economic Development," in *Cross-Cultural Issues in Alaskan Education,* Vol. II. Edited by Ray Barnhardt. p. 47
4. *Ibid.,* p. 50.
5. *Ibid.,* p. 53.
   For an excellent sourcebook on just such a bicultural environment, see Julia S. Kleinfeld's *Eskimo School on the Andreavksy,* 1979.
   In the deliberations of the 7th Northern Libraries Colloquy in Paris, 1978, the Yupik graduate student Tony Vaska put forth the notion of "Native academics . . . giving the Native perspective":

> The development of Native academics has to take time. Going through the western traditional system, form the time you are six, even through graduate school, may not give you a Native perspective; it must be got from one's own life experiences, living at home. . . . The kind of work I am doing falls under something . . . classified as Native academic research. And it was difficult to get into, it was difficult to convince my academic committee that this . . . work . . . was needed right now. . . . Give us time, we will develop an academic perspective [that] will seek understanding and cooperation.

Vaska later became active in Yukon-Kuskokwim delta pulbic affairs, a state legislator, and remains a prominent figure in the Yupik area, if not the state.

Academic research by Native scholars on the history of Native acculturation to Euroamerican ways can take a view not only very much at odds with Europeanized accounts, but with anger and bitterness at the effects on Native culture and social experience barely contained. See, for example, *The Educational Experiences of the Residents of Bethel,*

Alaska: An Historical Case Study, by Elizabeth Anne Parent. Doctoral dissertation, Stanford Univ., June, 1984.

The indispensability of cross-cultural or bicultural scientific and technical efforts in the north is increasingly evident. Archeologists and anthropologists making surveys now routinely utilize local Elders in Native areas. The paper by E. Bielawski, cited under "Education, Research, Information Systems and the North" in the bibliography, describes the rationale and work of the Northern Heritage Society in the Northwest Territories, in integrating cultural views in northern research. "In so doing, we can facilitate both science and education by meeting needs for academic and vocational study, employment, and role models." [p. 61.]

In his book *The Siberians,* written in the late 1960s and based on prolonged visits to northeast Siberia, the internationally known Canadian author Farley Mowat describes many situations where Native professionals, specialists and technicians are staffing research and development institutions and projects in their homelands, and not as "minority" workers. In some areas they predominate, and Native administrators and managers are just as common. In this aspect of northern development (training Native specialists), the North American countries appear to be at least a generation behind.

6. Foster, George M. *Traditional Societies and Technological Change* (1973). Quotations and points cited in this discussion of Foster are drawn mainly from Chapter 7, "Psychological Barriers to Change," and Chapter 9, "Bureaucracies and Technicians."

7. "Boldt Decision" refers to U.S. v.Washington (1974). This landmark case and the litigation and appeals it 'spawned,' affirmed that "treaty tribes (in western Washington State) . . . were entitled to an opportunity to catch 50% of the harvestable fish that were destined to pass through their usual and accustomed fishing grounds and stations." It caused an "uproar" when issued by Seattle Federal District Court Judge George H. Boldt. (quotes are from Cohen, Fay, cited herein, who traces the struggle of many decades over treaty fishing rights in the region.)

8. There was no housing available for me, and I still had my tipi from Montana. In later years I rented a trailer vacated when an Elder passed away.

9. On returning from particularly demanding village visits in the Yukon-Kuskokwim delta, the author felt frustrated by, among other things, the difficulty of explaining and justifying his cross-cultural concerns.

10. Gamble, Donald J. "Crushing of Cultures: Western Applied Science in Northern Societies," *Arctic,* Vol. 39, No. 1 (March, 1986), p. 23.

11. From the videotape "The Way We Live," available from KYUK-AM-TV, Bethel, Alaska. This tape has several smaller tapes re-recorded on it, produced originally by the Lower Kuskokwim School District in a

bilingual instructional television project. The quote paraphrases remarks in the one entitled "Quimugciryaraq: Yuungnaqutek'-Laraat" (They use dog mushing as a way of life). (1981).

12. Kleinfeld, J. S. "Intellectual Strengths in Culturally Different Groups: An Eskimo Illustration," *Review of Educational Research,* Vol. 43, No. 3, pp. 341–359

13. In the Yukon-Kuskokwim delta of Alaska, where over 20,000 Yupik Eskimos live in a geographical enclave of their own, there are increasing moves being taken toward Native self-government. The Yupiit Nation united three villages on the Lower Kuskokwim in a move toward regional tribal government in the early 1980s. By 1990 a net number of 13 had expressed definite interest in this concept, and a planning grant was received from the Federal government. Included in planning is a circuit court system. Under Federal status, traditional councils govern individual villages, not the state-incorporated municipal councils, One of the first acts of the Yupiit Nation villages was to set up their own school district and to have primarily combined school-public library facilities.

14. Zielinska, Marie. "Report of the First Open Meeting of the Working Group on Library Service to Ethnic and Linguistic Minorities," *IFLA Journal* 8 (1982):1, p. 68.

8.

Jobs and Library Education vs. Native Communities

... concerns for ethnic minorities should be an integral part of all courses in library schools and they should be evaluated by the students from this point of view ... [1]

The very survival of libraries in the west as presently constituted remains most doubtful.[2]

As a group, viewed historically, the graduate library schools of North America have been laggard and passive when it comes to cross-cultural or multicultural librarianship, whether one considers the makeup of the administration, the faculty, the student body or the curriculum. In the early 1980s I contacted one school and suggested a workshop, institute or course on this subject, but was told that there were no plans to do so, the basic and essential offerings in the curriculum being all they could handle; it was suggested that this was simply a pet interest of mine. The reality of library work said otherwise, however; for decades previously one could have hardly found a single public service or academic librarian who wasn't serving a variety of minority or immigrant patrons, certainly in urban areas. Multicultural librarianship has long been a *normal* feature of actual library work. Yet, until recently, library education has spent almost no time, attention or resources establishing good liaison with Native communities or training its own students to effectively serve the ethnically diverse American public.

Related to this is the situation in library schools where faculty become tenured and teach for many years without ever returning to the field in a working capacity. It should be required that every library school faculty member spend one year out of five in a field position in an area of change. Otherwise the tendency is to become unresponsive or indifferent to the changing demands being made on the working professional. In addition, to cite another factor detracting from the graduate experience, there is often a predilection on the part of long-tenured and field-ignorant faculty not to accept MLS candidates as colleagues and equals. I recall, as a 40-year-old student in library school, often being treated as an uninitiated undergraduate in many situations, as if my life experience, library-related work background and other education didn't count for anything. Those who inhabit the cloistered halls and faculty offices of the graduate library schools must know the library work-place periodically, in order to gauge effectively the real dimensions of modern "librarianship"—if it is to survive as a professional field with its own graduate schools.[3]

Perhaps there are other, intrinsic barriers to open learning to be found in the university experience we remember so well. As one critic analyzes this bastion of concentrated European culture:

> . . . much of what university people do stems from a bourgeois appetite for success in the eyes of peers. . . . It is a 'rule-and-conquer' syndrome which affirms that: 'You meet academic standards, as we define them. You meet these standards via the strategies which we also define. That is the road to success.' Notwithstanding the inherent need for evaluative criteria, the prevailing ethos is essentially colonizing, subjugating, controlling. . . .
>
> The academic mind sincerely and arduously labors for years to acquire and develop its conceptual prisms, but also at the same time develops an infrequently unyielding compulsion to determine for everyone else what reality is, and to label or name that reality. As far as Indians are concerned, this strong tendency is all too often arrogant, patronizing, insensitive, over-systematized, ignorant of and impervious to other ways of knowing.[4]

But of course, there are gifted, perceptive faculty as well, offering strong liaison to the real Native world of today. But for those other academicized specialists, educators and consultants, who keep their own company, a healthy apprenticeship to the real community is needed, to keep mind and spirit whole, to press the moccasins into the real earth, to use the cliché. Perhaps even consultation with Elders might be appropriate. I say this because I've encountered highly rated consultants who were strong in a western rational objectivity when looking at Native community "problem-solving," but who reflected a weak or uncomprehending regard for the cross-cultural situation confronting them. All too apparent was their sensitivity to the fact that their employer was almost always an established non-Native institution. One has to look beyond the rules and regs, the policies and procedures, the agency's self-defined mission, and even the quantifiable. . . .

When I was a young student in a two-year, vo-tech institute after high school, we respected the faculty not only because they were enthusiastic and seemed to know their subjects, but because they had close and regular ties with the working world we would soon be entering, and spent summers with counterparts in their respective fields, sometimes as volunteers. They were shirt-sleeved faculty, and were self-effacing and modest when they compared their position with those earning their living out in the community.

In order that relevant courses be carried in the curriculum, especially the core curriculum, it is indispensable that a professional advisory group be active in the library school. Usually the alumni are recruited for this purpose, with various committees being set up, including one on library education. Not that such committees are truly representative of the community at large, or that they are really functioning. Sometimes their existence is not much more evident than on paper, or they have little or no real impact on school operations anyway. After all, the status and budgets of many library schools in the university community are under close scrutiny, and retrenchment seems always to be in the air. An advisory committee from outside is always at a disadvantage when survival of the library school for another biennium is the bottom line. Any significant shifts can also be read as a sign of lack of purpose and confidence. So an inherent dilemma to be faced is that, though the library schools must modernize comprehensively (not just focusing on certain areas in a trendy way), this can only be accomplished through confident and articulate leadership—whose academic integrity will be under constant review and evaluation by the university administration.

Among the many library schools across the North American continent, why there have been so few courses or even one-time institutes or workshops in minority or cross-cultural librarianship? (Later in this chapter we will discuss the findings of my 1987 survey of 85 schools, including all those accredited by the American Library Association.) Is it because of the demographics of the library work force, where so few minority librarians are to be found? Is it because of the underlying conservatism characterizing the field as a whole? Is it because such courses would be "outreach" into new and somewhat alien areas for most librarians, and we are not comfortable with this prospect? Or is it rather that there are simply so few community-oriented or activist minority library school faculty who might "raise consciousness" sufficiently? Is there an ignorance of Native culture and community conditions, despite all the literature available, all the studies, reports, papers and conferences? Is it because the bureaucratic character of the field makes everyone chary of making too many or too big waves? Or has it been because the so-called profession of librarianship (or library and information science) as we've learned and practiced it until now is outmoded and inherently incapable of across-the-board modernization?

On various occasions I've asked managers in Native communities if they thought that their library, whether serving a community or a college, shouldn't be run by a Native librarian, preferably from the home town. It would be nice if that were possible, but everyone recognizes that Native MLS librarians simply aren't to be found. In fact, one is usually lucky to find a Native with a bachelor's degree who's also interested in helping out with the library. In some cases one must use work-study students or whoever happens to be available on short notice. Because almost all the expertise—the academically accredited professionalism—is in the hands of non-Natives.

So if you want a librarian in a rural Native community, this may well mean a "virgin" non-Native librarian (who has never worked in a Native community before), or a Native with some college training who may have a modicum of library training. Such is the range of prospective candidates for the library job—that is, those who are interested in and prepared to perform such work. Further pursuit of this question turns up other possible reasons why representatives of the dominant society are so overwhelmingly in charge, and why so few Native degree-holders try for an advanced degree in library and information science—and why fewer actually get it.

Conventionally speaking, libraries are for literate, modernized communities, ones already functioning socioculturally and economically in the mainstream of society, or at least for those having sufficient revenue and taxable income to support such relatively low priority public services as libraries. Given the economically deprived character of most Indian and Native communities and their need for services providing survival, subsistence, basic welfare and essential public services, libraries and their ilk would seem indeed to be way down the list of priorities. But we really aren't discussing conventional library situations, and in our context, many Natives don't believe library and information services, and archives and museums in Native communities are low priority. Quite the contrary. But the problems are endemic and manifold, and we've tried to address some of them in this volume.[5]

The overwhelming majority of Native communities are starkly isolated and underdeveloped, not only in the literal sense, but even more so in contrast to the surrounding, dominant culture and its acquisitive economies. Higher learning and literate modern ways are usually held by individual Natives who have been able to leave the reservation long enough to acquire a higher degree, or advanced technical training and dominant society experience. It is ironic that such local Native resource people, who are able to make a real contribution toward progressive community development at home, are sometimes looked upon with suspicion by some traditional and conservative Native leaders. There may even be a period when the returned college-educated Native son or daughter will be, to some degree, somewhat ostracized and under scrutiny, to see what new or foreign (untraditional) ways of thinking and acting they have acquired, and how they have come through their acculturating experience in higher academe.

Yet the young Native professionals with western know-how, including ones with higher degrees and library education, must return home and become leaders in community development, if the economic life of their society is to improve. Perhaps, after all, there is more at stake in their returning home than just to bring professional expertise to bear on local problems. Robert Austlitz describes, in another part of the Native world, the "brain drain" that can also become a critical cultural depletion if it gains momentum:

It seems to me that the gradual westernization of the great Native preserve that is Siberia has implications for the gene pool of the area. If the capable members of an ethnic group (where capable means ability to integrate, survive successfully, and reproduce in the westernized surroundings) are siphoned off into the mainstream of Soviet industrial society, the less capable ones, one may assume, remain behind. This would imply a strong mainstream but a gradually weakening gene pool in the population. To put it bluntly, the talented segment would be siphoned off and eventually disappear through absorption, leaving the less talented at home, propagating itself, with the imaginable implications for the Native culture.[6]

The absence or rarity of commonly held high-salaried positions in libraries is a distinctly unattractive feature of the field. But this "comes with the package," to do with its weak definition as a profession—or to be more accurate, the difficulty of defining the profession with vigor and conciseness, a weakness in this day of confident and well-credentialed specialists. Devious pay practices detract from what jobs are available to Natives. Sometimes Natives are hired as clerical help, perhaps as an "affirmative action" gesture, but then are not given library training opportunities or pay raises in good time, as other staff would expect. This is more likely to happen in small libraries. Staff development funds should also be used to credentialize otherwise untrained Native staff in any way possible. It is easy to overlook the fact, for example, that newly acquired Native staff in a library serving a Native community or a multicultural community with a Native population bring the invaluable gifts of cultural affinity and perhaps a Native language fluency, something worth a great deal to the library's service capability. This should be factored in when determining the contribution of Native staff to the library's human resources, and should be reflected accordingly in salary schedules.[7]

In most library systems, Native patrons figure as a minuscule and invisible minority, mostly because they are found among the "unreached" majority of the population who don't regularly use libraries. Similarly, in the case of the missing Native MLS librarian, potential candidates are to be found among that tiny percentage who have acquired a bachelor's degree, but who for many reasons don't go on to take a master's or doctoral degree.

And here one should take a look at how Native adults, on or coming off the reservation, acquire the expertise and credentials to gain good-paying, highly responsible jobs. Often a start is made in one's own tribal community where, through good connections and some training, usually at a local community college or through a year or two at a four-year college, they become desirable candidates for the more responsible tribal management or Bureau of Indian Affairs administration jobs, assuming they have been politic in their relations with local leaders, elders, and families in power. The role of kinship and interfamily relations within a tribe, band or home village is very close and well-known to all, and one must work within this complex local network positively and shrewdly in order to make progress, both individually and collectively.

Then there is the question: Why be a librarian at all when it is a job that, at least in the conventional image, is really dealing exclusively with the Europeans' heritage, history and sociocultural development? Hence the need to transform, to modernize the library image, the librarian's image, into a multicultural one.[8]

Perhaps there is an obvious caveat to the Native person contemplating such a career, or simply a disinclination to immerse oneself so totally in the acculturating crucible of the white man's "higher education," culminating with receipt of "his" graduate degree. The strongest interest and encouragement is to stay at home, to do well under the albeit usually very limited career conditions of the reservation or home village. I suspect that, unless economic conditions improve markedly in the respective Native communities, a high percentage of Native librarians will be those who no longer have very close ties with home, who live in the cities or only visit home infrequently, and who feel comfortable moving around and working in new settings. In some very traditional and conservative tribes, a full-blood may be under strong pressure to stay home, or to come home and take a traditional leadership position. When away from home, the tendency is often to apply for those jobs within federal or state government, or the many non-profit corporations and foundations, that deal with Native services and resources.

Let us consider what the Native graduate student encounters in the "ivory tower" U.S. graduate school environment, deep within the Euro-american higher education system, far from the tribal band or home village support system. Although he or she has already completed a four-year program culminating in a bachelor's degree, graduate school is more intensified, more lonely. Probably the Native or Indian graduate student is the only one in the school. The concepts and subjects addressed become more esoteric, doctrinaire and specialized, and Native studies become a minor if not a peripheral part of even minority librarianship, if there are any such courses at all. As the only Native graduate student in the school, one becomes an instant authority, a living bench mark which faculty and fellow students may use to gauge their understanding of the library and information needs and world view of Native peoples without venturing therein themselves. It would be an exceedingly rare instance for there to be a Native faculty member, or any Native representation on any advisory board or among alumni of the school. Thus the student becomes, on a daily basis, his or her own role model, although there are Native MLS librarians scattered up and down the continent, literally less than a handful per state or province at this time.

I conducted a survey in 1990 that showed that there were several Native or Indian faculty members who were throughout graduate library education, at least in the United States. (Canadian schools do not supply information on the ethnic background of students and faculty, I was told.) But before discussing those results let's look at some sources of statistics for library education and the library profession generally, and what they say about the status of Natives and Indians in this field. The first is a periodical report from the American Library Association.

This is *Academic and Public Librarians: Data by Race, Ethnicity and Sex,* issued by the office for Library Personnel Resources of the American Library Association.[10] At the 1986 Midwinter ALA meeting, OLPR held hearings on minority recruitment, which identified "three major issues":

1. Minority enrollment in graduate library schools and the numbers and percentages of minority graduates have been declining,
2. Lack of scholarship money is sometimes a factor in the inability of the profession to recruit minorities, and
3. the status and image problems of librarians and the low salaries contribute to recruitment difficulties.

This report's random survey of academic and public librarians in the U.S. produced data on almost 19,000 librarians. Of this number, 42 (forty-two), or slightly over two-thousandths of one per cent, were "American Indian or Alaska Native." Because "the definition of librarian [was] left to each library . . . the statistics may include persons other than those with a Master's in Library Science degree." I know from my own experience that this is definitely the case, so actually less than the above percentage are Native MLS librarians. The 1991 edition of this same compilation indicates more than double the number of American Indian/Alaska Native librarians in academic and public libraries, from 42 to 91. Although these numbers are still tiny, the "trend" is gratifying. One would hope and expect that the 1995 figures may double again, if not more so, because many more library operations have opened in at least rural Native American community settings. But for a long time there will remain an enormous shortage of Native American as well as other minority librarians and library educators. Various strategies were suggested at these 1986 hearings, but the key one asserted that "the best method of recruitment appears to be one-on-one personal contacts between a librarian and potential recruits, with follow-up after initial contact." This has also been verified in comments received from library school heads during research on this book. The effectiveness of a mentor/role model librarian (whether Native or non-Native, but especially the former) still holds true, and this is cited throughout library literature and materials from the ALA.

During the first half of 1987 I conducted a survey of 85 U.S. and Canadian graduate library schools. The 1986 *American Library Directory* was used for address information. The object was to discover the status of cross-cultural, minority or multicultural librarianship, especially as it relates to Native people. Three mailings were involved, with a few schools being contacted further, as a result of our determination to obtain replies. The first mailing to all 85 schools was of the longer questionnaire, a sample of which is in Appendix B. The other two mailings were to those who had not responded the first time, and for these an abbreviated version of the questionnaire was used, also found in Appendix B. Each reply was acknowledged by me, often with a request for clarification, additional details, the school catalog, or other information. All ALA-accredited schools were contacted. These were 60 in number, or 71% of all those contacted.

Due to a tight budget, the accompanying letter, explanations and the questions themselves had to be combined on a single sheet of paper, an economy whose product elicited at least one complaint—along with the requested information.

In the end, 67 schools responded, or 79% of those surveyed. One of the schools (ALA-accredited) had closed, leaving 66 replies out of a base of 84 to consider. Of the 18 not responding at all, 12 (two-thirds) were ALA-accredited schools. A few of the more prestigious schools were among these, and most missed was information from a couple of southwestern universities, home of the Navajo and other important tribes. On the other hand, from the same region excellent responses were received that more than made up for any gaps. Non-response was so low and could be attributed to so many factors, and the overall response was so strong, that we can still learn a great deal about "the status of cross-cultural or multicultural librarianship in advanced library education, especially as it relates to the Native peoples" by examining the information received.

Of the 66 schools, 16 replied "no" or "none" to all questions. (Please refer to the questionnaires in Appendix B.) That leaves 50 who replied with more information. In a few cases office staff dealt with the questionnaire, though the head of the school was addressed. In all other cases either the head or a faculty member supplied answers, sometimes at some length, including enclosures to share. The schools more active in this area were more interested in giving details and sharing information and experience.

The next category numbered 18 and included those schools which, although not replying positively to the other questions, said that the subject of multicultural or cross-cultural librarianship as it relates to Native people was either not covered in a specific course, or was covered where appropriate throughout the curriculum, with no other details or clarification being given. These schools were given the benefit of the doubt, so if the reply was "no specific course," for example, it was assumed that the subject is touched upon at appropriate points in the curriculum. This category of minimal involvement also includes those that said they believed one Native student might have/did attend the school in the past five years. The fact that this awareness or degree of attention to the Native factor was in evidence was considered worthy of note.

The remaining group of schools to be considered offer more than minimal involvement. The impression received, as one looks over these 32 replies, is that here is evidence of some movement, a beginning response to the multicultural needs in U.S. and Canadian library provision. However, we should not forget that the other responding schools we left behind showed mostly no or very little interest or activity in this area, either within the school, or in liaison or outreach with the community—local, regional or beyond. But 32 out of 66 responding is certainly significant, and one must admit that this was something of a surprise. Admittedly, a sizable portion of these 32 were only modestly or tentatively involved, but a beginning or recognition—the trend—was there, and we can only applaud and encourage these progressive library educators.

Specific courses in cross-cultural, multicultural or minority librarianship are offered, and these schools have more than one Native graduate or currently enrolled Native students, some with fellowships, and are taking initiatives to effect a liaison with or assist the Native communities within their reach—though in one case even a far distant one was reached by jet travel. By the way, the reason given by a Canadian school for not replying—that because it serves only French-speaking students it couldn't serve English-speaking Inuit—isn't relevant. The large city in which it is located has a sizable Native population, some of those being Native people from northeastern Canada who speak French—or Native languages.

Types of general courses taught in these schools range from those on multicultural or minority librarianship generally, to others covering overall library services for Native groups of a particular area. The most common mode is to have such courses intermittently, or to have special institutes, seminars or workshops, sometimes out in the Native community. The University of Hawaii has "courses for Native Hawaiian and Pacific groups." One would expect also to find such courses in the southwest, where there are large tribal concentrations, but unfortunately information is lacking from two state universities for Arizona and New Mexico (though they were repeatedly contacted by mail), and a third responded negatively. Approximately twenty of these graduate library schools have regularly scheduled courses in multicultural or minority librarianship. And almost all of these respondents indicated that library provision for Native people was included in these courses.

Those schools with Native graduates or students during the approximate five-year period, 1981–1986, also numbered twenty, almost all of them coming from those schools with courses in multicultural/minority librarianship. The number of graduates was slightly less than the number who enrolled over roughly the same period. Two schools listed doctoral candidates or graduates, and two schools specifically mentioned students being on U.S. federal Title IIB fellowships (Higher Education Act of 1965).

Liaison, outreach and consultancies out in the Native community were the next area of activity most indicated by graduate library schools. Approximately twelve schools had a variety of such activities, ranging from having a Native alumnus who advised to running a series of training workshops with a local tribe, or in one case, sending faculty to distant, out-of-state locations to give workshops and in-service training in Native communities. The University of British Columbia School of Library, Archival and Information Studies contacted the Open Learning Institute in Richmond, B.C., which offers distance learning utilizing not only correspondence school methods but also modern distance learning technology, to explore the idea of offering a "training package for library workers living on reservations." The liaison person for that effort was an alumna of the UBC library school who worked for Aboriginal Management Consultants, Inc. of North Vancouver.

Finally, the least involvement for Native people in graduate library schools was as faculty. On this question, anticipating a very low number, we also included those non-Natives with significant experience in Native communities. There were approximately three Native faculty and four faculty with Native community experience.

The survey, then, shows definite movement in multicultural/minority librarianship, a development which, though only in a few cases concentrated on library services for Native peoples specifically, can only help toward the day when Native MLS librarians and well-oriented non-Native MLS librarians will serve the Native people adequately. We should never forget that there are two equally important sides to the coin, in terms of balanced multicultural librarianship: relevant library education for Native graduate students, and relevant library education in Native library services for non-Native graduate students. This requires good Native community liaison, adequate financial aid for Native students, an appropriate and supportive learning atmosphere, relevant curriculum fare, and preferably Native faculty represented in the school, or at least the occasional presence of Native community members as guests, whether as presenters, advisors or lecturers. For non-Native students, some personal experience with Native community conditions and a consequent beginning of understanding of the Native point of view are indispensable.

Early in 1988 the Library Education Task Force of the Ethnic Materials Information Exchange Round Table (EMIERT) of ALA issued a report entitled "Ethnic and Minority Concerns in Library Education." After reporting the preliminary results of a survey of accredited graduate library schools by Dr. Rene Tjoumas of Queens College, City University of New York (CUNY), Graduate School of Library and Information Studies at Flushing, New York, many recommendations were offered to improve the status of multicultural aspects of library education. The Summary/Recommendations were as follows:

1. Ethnic librarianship should be included as a component of the core curriculum of library schools.

2. Continued emphasis on the recruitment of ethnic and minority students and faculty should be undertaken by library schools.
3. Cross fertilization of library school curriculum with other ethnic and minority related departments should be encouraged, as well as tie-in with undergraduate level programs.
4. Summer work programs in libraries for ethnic and minority students should be developed and supported.
5. Scholarships sponsored by library organizations for those interested in minority and ethnic concerns should be provided.
6. Library school faculty and administration, as well as students, should be sensitized to ethnic and minority needs and concerns through practicum, colloquia, and other types of relevant continuing education activities.
7. Research grants should be provided for studies specifically in areas relating to ethnic librarianship, ethnic and minority library concerns.
8. Practicing librarians, especially those working with ethnic communities, should establish relations with library schools in their area.
9. Language skills should be encouraged in library and information science education.
10. Courses in interpretation and assessment of community information needs and interests should be developed and offered.
11. Use of internships involving work with ethnic and minority communities should be stressed.
12. Evaluation of faculty teaching should involve intercultural sensitivity and awareness, as well as inclusion of ethnic and minority concerns as part of its focus of interest.
13. The ALA Committee on Accreditation should include ethnic and minority concerns as part of its focus of interest.
14. Guidelines should be presented to library schools concerning specific ethnic and minority topics related to each area of the core curriculum; the elements of ethnic literacy.
15. A list of consultants and adjunct faculty willing and competent to teach specific courses in ethnic librarianship or to provide input or guidance in the integration of ethnic and minority concerns throughout the curriculum should be developed.

I would comment that there is reflected here an absence of: 1) ethnic or minority (including Native) community participation and advice in library school policy making; and 2) the ways and means suggested for graduate library education institutions to increase their multicultural scope, including the more field-oriented recommendations, nos. 2, 4, 8, 11 and 15, are still too oblique and indirect, insulated from actual contact and dialogue with people in these communities. In effect, we see here an idealized community of librarians responding to the needs of multicultural America. Where is the place of ethnic and minority communities in this equation—equally passive?

In item no. 8, *librarians* from the community are urged to keep in touch with library schools in their area. Nowhere do we read where these communities are being directly contacted and involved in the process of democratizing library education. Or if this is supposed to be implied, we must again depend on the individual administrator librarian, or faculty member to take some kind of initiative. Field experience by faculty is needed. The ALA Committee on Accreditation should include ethnic and minority *members,* in proportion to the demographics, not just "concerns as part of its focus and interest," although one must agree that being of minority blood is no guarantee or assurance of responsiveness to minority concerns. There is also the caveat that being a non-minority liberal or closely tuned and experienced civil rights advocate is no guarantee of sensitivity, actual knowledge or understanding regarding the reality of the minorities' lives.

Overall, then, one has the distinct impression that library academe in this report is being chided by the tentative admonitions of fellow library educators. We are left looking at the library school from outside, from the street, as it were, waiting for them to respond to one another. An institution training professionals to serve the community should ideally be a vigorous arm *of* that community, organically joined to it, not separate and theoretical, because there is always the danger of elitist, condescending, and "imposed" methodologies when this is the case (the Soviet Union being the prime example). Perhaps my impatience and distrust is prompted by the long record of unmet recommendations, countless "workshops" and "round tables," and sporadic "cries in the wilderness" that have littered the library literature terrain over the decades since World War II. One must support and encourage the work of such professional committees and groups, hoping all the while that they will be "working themselves out of a job," when Natives/Indians and other minorities are well represented in the library profession and well and appropriately served by it. And, of course, libraries and librarians are in some measure always beholden to majority public opinion and bias, so any radical changes are subject to criticism and curtailment by reactionary elements and authority. Many people would like libraries and librarians to never change, and remain just as they remember them in their youth, but the world around us and its youth are constantly changing, and if we want to be a viable part of that world, we must change too, becoming not only unified *with* them, but also *growing* with them.

The same school at Queens College offered a useful example of a program that helps those in the field to be better multicultural librarians, through a grant-funded institute[11] that has been offered twice. Aimed at working librarians in the greater New York City area, it had thirty three-hour sessions spread out over nearly a year. With excellent and well-planned field trips, and a variety of top-notch (even nationally known) speakers, it produced various video and audio training materials. It also had sessions on Native Americans. While very few libraries could expect or would need to mount such an ambitious multicultural library education project, there are many ideas herein for any smaller project.

Information on financial aid available to minority students in the U.S., at least for starting an MLS program, is collected in the American Library Association's publication, *Financial Assistance for Library Education.*[12] Looking at data for the 1988–89 academic year, we find about 29 sources, either library schools or library organizations, most of which amount to several thousand dollars, and many sources also include a tuition waiver. It isn't possible to determine how many of these went to Native North American students, but it's safe to say that it was a fraction. ALA's Office of Library Personnel Resources (OLPR) also issues an annual guide entitled *Financial Assistance for Library and Information Science Studies.*

The ALA's OLPR can help library administrators and supervisors do a better job in multicultural librarianship. Its staff makes available a variety of materials very pertinent to helping redress the balance in services, collections, Native and minority community liaison, hiring and training, and more realistically serve their diverse client groups. A noteworthy OLPR program is "Each One Reach One," the aim of which is to bring minority people into the library career field, and they have many successful case histories to share. (For examples, see *Bringing Us Together, Library Personnel News,* and Jones-Quartey et al. in Bibliography/Reference List II.)

Another useful guide was *Sources of Financial Aid Available to American Indian Students,*[13] compiled by Roxie June and Preston Thomas. Though centered on the southwest quarter of the U.S., it had information and advice useful for any Native American student.

The Library Programs/Library Development staff of the U.S. Department of Education states that from 1973 through 1985, 52 Native Americans received fellowships for graduate study in library science. That's an average of slightly more than four per year. In 1986, 38 schools had 68 Title IIB fellowships, but the number taken by Native Americans wasn't known at the time of our inquiry. These fellowships for "minorities, disadvantaged, handicapped and women" amount to $8,000 for a master's degree student and $12,000 for a doctoral candidate.

As for Federal aid to Native libraries, the U.S. Department of Education also administers Basic and Special Grants under the Library Services for Indian Tribes Program, Title IV of the Library Services and Constructed Act (LSCA), which provides funding for a wide variety of public library activities among the tribes. In 1986 there were 17 Special Grant projects among 16 tribes, the grants ranging from $745 to $213,445. The types of projects covered outreach, materials access and preservation, computerization, interlibrary networking, materials acquisition, training, library construction, vehicle purchase, building renovation and equipment purchase. In one case funds paid for a needs assessment, materials purchase, and partial salaries for participating staff. Basic Grants for 1986 totaled over $606,000 for 185 awards. A significant percentage of these funds went for "personnel." In 1985, there were 18 Special Projects Awards for 17 tribes, ranging from

$3,750 to $420,343. Basic Grants were applied for by 130 Indian tribes, in the amount of $3,498 each. An additional Basic Grant for 13 library projects for Hawaiian Natives totaled $590,000. As one example, the Plains Indian Community College (discussed in chapter 1) received one of the Basic Grants, which was used to purchase microfilmed backfiles of a number of periodicals and almost 50 reels of microfilmed government records from the National Anthropological Archives on the tribe.

By 1993 the Nisqually Tribe, which is within the Tacoma Public Library service area (discussed in chapter 1), received an LSCA Special Project grant to develop library and related services. And in 1994 the Bay Indian Tribe (also discussed in chapter 1) received a similar Special Project Grant to develop library services to that isolated coastal community. Since 1986 the total amount for both Basic and Special Project grants has remained around $2.4 million, with slight fluctuations up or down each year.

Earlier we mentioned the fact that library schools are declining in number (ten less than in 1978). A dissertation by Marion Paris,[14] completed in 1986, looked at four such closings, and perhaps the conclusions drawn can help shed some light on the present-day predicament of graduate library schools (those offering the 5th-year degree).

In the first place, there were too many schools, as the 1960s and '70s produced an excess. And being ALA-accredited was no guarantee of survival. The interdisciplinary nature of library and information science makes it a problematical and vulnerable field (in this era of extreme specialization emphasis in education), especially in times of declining enrollment, changing student populations, rising tuition and dwindling resources. This overall situation is described as retrenchment, and in times of retrenchment library schools are in a precarious state as a university redefines its mission.

Paris cites many negative aspects of advanced library education that are noted by university administrators and deans, and even by faculty from other departments. Traditional library education is largely obsolete, and though the former service emphasis has given way to a technological emphasis, by way of moving "library and information science" education toward the end of the 20th century, curricula are still often irrelevant, with indecision predominating in curriculum revisions. Others observe that there is a lack of minority recruitment, students and faculty are of lower caliber, the thesis programs are poor, and, above all, leadership is lacking. Some describe library school faculty, curriculum and networking as "out of touch with reality," isolated and insulated from the local academic community. One dean who served on university committees with library school faculty commented that, as scholars, they seemed "out of date." Library schools also rated low in grant-seeking and research, showing a lack of creative and imaginative grantsmanship.

But the weak leadership factor, and an accompanying lack of purposefulness on the part of these graduate library schools, were the underlying and very political reasons for their tenuous position in the academic community. "What exactly is information management, or studies? What is 'library and information science'?" Library school faculty themselves couldn't adequately define their instructional domain, among these four that went under.

Paris concludes that there is a need for imaginative and diplomatic leadership, and a strong mission, or sense of "self." Ancillary needs would appear to include improvement in all the areas cited above. Other ways to improve library education, in the author's view, and with Native library provision in mind, would include: much closer ties to and input from librarians in the field, including using them as guest instructors; spend money on better faculty, who must take a sabbatical every five years, to work or do research in a problematical field situation (not a cushy consultancy); go out in the service community at large—including the Native community—and establish regular liaison contacts and exchanges; and encourage publication and research by faculty, especially the future-oriented kind, making every effort to generate grants for their research. It is not difficult to link the findings of the Paris dissertation with the state of either multicultural or Native librarianship.

Norman C. Higgins[15] of Arizona State University made a list of final recommendations for "Improving Library Education for Selected Minorities" (Spanish-speaking and Native American). It covers not only the needs of Native students in library education, but by extrapolation can be applied to library education and to the university community generally, regarding Native students. The following is quoted almost verbatim:

1. Enlist persons living in minority communities to persuade qualified individuals to apply for admission to the program [personal contact and follow-up].
2. Maintain personal communication with individuals who apply for admission to the program. Personal interviews get much valuable information, enabling students to be better advised and helped.
3. Use established program admissions requirements when selecting students. But be more flexible, and more discriminating in using non-standard measures of student achievement.
4. Use successful work experience in a library or other service area as one criterion for selecting students.
5. Admit applicants who are not fully qualified on a provisional basis.
6. Teach students competencies that are appropriate for the positions and situations in which they are likely to be employed.
7. Teach minority students basic library competencies in regularly scheduled library courses. Be flexible; perhaps fewer courses during time of taking basic courses. Content should be multicultural in scope.

8. Teach specialized library competencies in courses that are well-developed additions to the regular program.
9. Distribute practical work experience throughout the educational program.
10. Include regularly scheduled semiformal meetings as a part of the education program. Discuss topics of mutual interest.
11. Select faculty who are prepared to teach students to perform the competencies expected of them. Use several faculty for special courses. Don't compromise quality of instruction.
12. Conduct field-based training to reduce geographic barriers and provide appropriate settings for developing special competencies.
13. Provide extra-curricular activities to develop students' social skills and professional commitment. Additional support should include financial, social, personal and academic services.
14. Provide direct financial aid for minority students.
15. Provide personal counseling/advising services to help individual students.
16. Provide tutoring for students having academic problems (using peers or faculty).
17. Work with library administrators and community leaders to develop library positions.
18. Arrange follow-up assistance for graduates after they are employed.

We have repeatedly cited the needs of Native libraries, librarians and students. It is a recurring set of themes, woven in and out of a discussion of library institutions, library education, Native communities and the conditions in Native society. At the same time there are countless reflections of these themes in the overpowering if indifferent mirror of non-Native library society. We are not referring here to those individual library institutions and organizations, in and out of government, or to those individual librarians, that have responded to the developmental needs of Native libraries. As we have seen, a great deal has happened despite a predominant atmosphere of inertia. If libraries have been struggling to achieve some fiscal status and priority in society at large, then Native library development—until very recently—has had the same status and priority in the library world. But the education of Native librarians on all fronts is scandalously short-changed, and the education of non-Natives in multicultural and Native librarianship has been, until very recently, identically treated. Here are two sides of the same well-worn coin. Progress is being made, but much too slowly—another symptom of the chronic retrenchment seemingly endemic to library institutions. And undoubtedly this work environment is a contributing factor in our inherent disinclination or difficulty in keeping up with a faster changing modern world.[16]

As a class, librarians do not yet have the same status as teachers and professors. And this is because, until recently, librarians have not had to be intellectually accountable to anyone. Now we are accountable to the institution of which we are a part, to our clients, to the community at large, and most disconcertingly of all—to ourselves. The library field has been an ancillary one, the housewife to education or industry or other professions. Now we are asked to stand alone, to justify ourselves, to demonstrate integrity and project leadership not only within our profession, but in a concentric series of larger contexts. And it has been too much, all at once. But just as the Native communities have shown us the way in taking initiatives and demonstrating that they know what libraries and related community services can do, so we can gain a new orientation, a new impetus, a new motivation—one that involves the whole community. To achieve equity of Native library and archival services with the rest of the world, for example, the rest of the world (which means the "First" and "Second" Worlds) must embrace the multicultural society of which it is increasingly comprised.

Like avid baseball devotees seemingly obsessed with the arcane details of their vocation, and to meet the requirements of granting and other funding sources for quantitative measurements, librarians have traditionally chosen to attest to the fruits of their mostly publicly funded services by showing statistics for such quantifiable denominators as circulation (books and other materials loaned to users), size of collection and its rate of growth per budgetary period, number of periodicals subscribed to, library open hours, number of reference inquiries by day and by category (phone or in person), number of walk-ins, interlibrary loans (incoming and outgoing), etc. More qualitative "output measures" and public (not just user) assessments of library services are the rare exception.

Graduate library schools have had a similar onus, as editions of the *Library and Information Science Education Report* of the Association for Library and Information Science Education (ALISE) amply demonstrate. A perusal of the 1986 and 1994 editions of these *Reports* can add to an understanding of the status of library education, as well as reveal its shortcomings.

The 1986 edition, 266 pages in length, shows tables for no less that 206 quantitative indices. An overview of the information in this report reveals some unsettling trends. Library schools were becoming fewer in number, the percentage of tenured professors and their age was increasing. "Schools in response to decreasing enrollments and changing economic conditions have shifted direction. They have become more general in their curricula in order to make (sic) to a broader audience. This shift has emphasized information management and the use of information technology." (p. 263) The number of new courses added was more than courses dropped, but there was a surprisingly long list of "experimental" courses, which means they are one-shot affairs, "testing the market." The editors "noted the astonishing scope and breadth of continuing education offerings," which was seemingly a response to the "decline in students over the past several years." Yet the actual number of continuing education activities has steadily declined. Further, "less than half the reporting schools offer continuing education units." Most schools had a curriculum committee, but only a small minority included alumni representatives on these committees. There was no information on liaison with or advice from the community at large. On the whole, it appeared that a retrenching trend was operative, although the ALISE report editors point out that many of their figures must be considered as tentative, due to "internal inconsistencies" in the reporting.

The 1994 edition grew by 52 pages to 318 with a net gain of two indices, to 211. The tables are bigger and much easier to read. In this edition, ALISE worked jointly with the American Library Association's Committee on Accreditation, which "refined" some of the figures. However, the Conclusion points out that "the statistics should be shaped to enable cohorts of like schools to more readily identify one another." Many should be "collapsed" into summary tables. Looking at the many indices in this physically impressive publication, all quantitative, and the small numbers involved, one has the impression of digits scattered over the academic landscape in discrete anonymity. What do they really mean, and what usefulness have they for "managing change" in library education?

Looking at some of the indices noted in 1986, the trends continue through 1993, with subtle shifts. There has been a slight increase in minority faculty overall. The numbers, total percentage and placement of minority students, are still but a tiny fraction, whether graduate or paraprofessional, although figures from 10 out of the 11 non-ALA accredited schools were lacking. There has been little change in several years, and the Summary and Comparative Analysis asserts that "there is not a whisper of reasons for growth, decline or change in enrollment patterns." This amounts to a "No comment" stance. Distance education declined overall, but I know that in some places it is significantly increasing through televised and correspondence courses and computer networks. Conferences and meetings have dramatically increased, probably through audio-conferencing, the Analysis suggests, yet this important development isn't mentioned. Contextual details just aren't there, and we are out in a statistical landscape somewhere, called "library education."

The Comparative Analysis has chosen to emphasize suggestions for improving the *Report*. More sophisticated analysis is needed, identifying and comparing like institutions and providing more context. Sharing of curriculum evaluations and reviews, especially by outside visitors, would be more helpful. Why not look at "indicators of success and outcome measures" rather than only these barren statistical tables filled with meager numbers? Although almost all the ALA-accredited schools have reported figures for every edition, one has to wonder if some are "quantified out," to use the vernacular, or oversurveyed. Closer to the mark, maybe they are well aware that the most important factors determining the success of library education and management of needed change are not really quantifiable, and they become impatient or bored with the constant requests for numbers of every imaginable kind of statistical measurement. Such a host of tables with bare figures can be juxtaposed and manipulated any way one wishes, to show growth or decline or stagnation, improvement, or the need for improvement, or the lack of it. It has seemed obvious for many years that the report should be drastically shortened, with all indices reviewed for management usefulness, then summarized and related to one another. A second analytical or "qualitative" section could then be added, filling in with real context, significant variables, important new developments, trend indications, and areas of poor performance as well as success.

In 1973, "A Joint Policy Statement of the National Indian Education Association and the American Library Association" was made, establishing the "Goals for Indian Library and Information Service."[17] In 1985, the doctoral dissertation of Albert Franklin Spencer attempted to measure the progress of these library services as perceived by school and college administrators and librarians serving Indian students. The results showed that there were very few differences in the perceptions of these various educators, at least none that are especially relevant for our purposes. He reviewed the literature from as far back as 1935, analyzing scores of articles, reports, studies and surveys, and his findings were that there had been moderate to little progress in the 1973 goals to date. This dissertation, however dated, is an excellent evaluation of progress in Native library services, even though it concentrates on educational institutions serving Indian students, primarily secondary schools and tribally controlled community colleges. As for library services to Native peoples, both in Native and non-Native communities, modest progress has also been achieved, in the United States, Canada and Greenland, as we have seen. Russia's society and culture are undergoing such enormous changes currently that it will be decades before we can see the resultant condition of Native populations and their libraries.

Looking ahead, however, we must ponder with some apprehension the progress to come, not only in Native Library services, but in public libraries generally. Academic and special libraries have their established roles to play, not much changed in the past generation, except for a certain amount of client-oriented reform and technological advances. Librarians and information specialists generally have their professional parameters ineptly drawn for them in the graduate library school experience, and the standards of both library education and professionalism as continued in the field must be raised markedly in the future. Griffiths and King project the image of a rather different stereotype "librarian" and the professional world he and she will inhabit:

> The informational professional of the future will be much more outgoing and proactive, as evidenced by the perceived increasing importance of having a broad view of the profession; in anticipating needs (of both user and one's own organization); in having knowledge of ongoing research in the field; in

the development of interaction skills; and in a knowledge of career opportunities. This is parallel to recent trends in the provision of library and information services based on an active identification of actual, projected and potential information needs of various user communities.

[However,] unless there is a coordinated effort on the part of the majority of participants in the information professional education community to enhance and project a positive, proactive image of the profession and its leading role in the Information Age, we cannot expect to see an appreciable improvement in the competence of information professionals.[18]

Information professionals will have to be more communicative in all respects, to use untapped potential through self-initiatives to keep current and to grow, not merely in "the profession" as we've known it, but, in the expanded, forward- and outward-oriented version, in knowledge of and communication with their client communities and the conditions they contend with, and in their own intellectual capabilities, especially in perceiving and scoping future worldwide human needs for information. And in this inclusive rather than exclusive definition of future librarians and information professionals, library services by and for Native communities, in the north and elsewhere, will be an integral part—as they are already starting to be.

Notes

1. Zielinska, Marie. Director, National Library of Canada Multilingual Biblioservice. Reporting on the American Library Association Conference, June 28–July 3, 1986. Comment refers to the program conducted by the Ethnic Materials Information Exchange (EMIE) Roundtable. *Journal of Multicultural Librarianship,* Vol. 1:2 (1986), p. 56.
2. From Adolphe O. Amadi's *African Libraries, Western Tradition and Colonial Brainwashing.* Metuchen, NJ:Scarecrow Press, 1981, p.193.
3. The same state of affairs has been documented in Great Britain. See "Working in a Multicultural Society: Education and Training for Librarians and Information Scientists," by Judith Bowen, Pat Hiley and Ed Walley, *IFLA Journal* 12 (1986) 3: pp. 192–202.
   In Canada, "it is regrettable that the multicultural education of professional staff remains a low priority in Library and Information Science Departments." See "Canadian Multicultural Library Services—A Selective Bibliography," by a Subgroup of the Metro Toronto Multicultural Services Committee. *J. of Multicultural Librarianship,* Vol. 4, No. 3 (July, 1990). Official Canadian librarianship apparently distinguishes between Native library services and multicultural (immigrant European, Asian and South American) services.

4. Couture, Joseph E. Department of Native Studies, Trent University, Peterborough, Ontario. "Next Time, Try an Elder!" in *Flower of Two Soils: American Indian Youth in Transition,* edited by M. Beiser. Seattle: University of Washington Press, 1979, p. 12.

5. I was brought up short by the indignant statement of one highly placed Canadian Native librarian, regarding any doubt of the relevance of libraries for Native peoples:

   "It appears that the stereotyping of libraries is coming into play here. It seems that libraries are always terribly misunderstood. Why should libraries be bad? How can people make judgments of this nature when the services provided by libraries/resource centres [are] to preserve documents of historical significance on a specific group of people. . . . I personally feel that anyone who [believes] that libraries are bad [does] not understand the functions of a library, nor realize the value of the services it provides." Personal communication, Stella Etherington, April 23, 1987.

6. Austlitz, Robert. "Folklore, Nationality and the 20th Century in Siberia and the Soviet Far East," *Journal of Folklore Research,* Vol.12, No.2/3 (1975), pp. 203–210.

7. The author learned of one case where a Native library worker who spoke the language remained at entry level in a library assistant position for five years before friends encouraged her to bring the subject up with her supervisor. When the library's budget was faced with possible reductions, both Native workers (later there were two) were advised that the hours of one might be cut, and the newer worker laid off.

8. For an excellent exposition of the minority recruitment dilemma in libraries, and refreshing ways to approach it, see for example: "The Recruitment of People from Minority Ethnic Groups into the Library Information Workforce," a report by Judith Elkin of a one-day seminar held at Birmingham Polytechnic Department of Librarianship and Information Studies on Monday, January 18, 1988, sponsored by the British Library: *Journal of Multicultural Librarianship,* Vol.2, No.2 (March, 1988), pp. 61–68. Although addressing the situation of "blacks and other ethnic minorities" in Britian, regarding library services, library employment and access to library education, the wide-ranging discussion provides many cues for realistically dealing with the situation of Native people and libraries.

9. *ALISE Library and Information Science Education Statistical Report 1986,* edited by Timothy W. Sineath. State College, PA: Association for Library and Information Science Education, 1986. 266p.

10. American Library Association, Office of Library Personnel Resources. *Academic and Public Librarians: Data by Race, Ethnicity and Sex.* Project Director: Jeniece Gay. Chicago, 1986. 34p.

11. Cohen, David. *Performance Report for Ethnicity and Librarianship Institute 2: Multiethnic Library Materials, Programs and Services in New*

York City and its Environs—Long Island, Westchester, Connecticut, New Jersey. Queens College, City University of New York, 1978. 155p.

12. American Library Association, Standing Committee on Library Education. *Financial Assistance for Library Education, Academic Year 1988–89.* Chicago, 1987.

A readable general guide to student funding sources and how to manage financing for the student is the U.S. Dept. of Education's *The Student Guide, Financial Aid from the U.S. Dept. of Education: Grants, Loans and Work-Study* (annual).

13. Indian Resource Development (IRD). *Sources of Financial Aid Available to American Indian Students.* Las Cruces, New Mexico, January, 1987.

14. Paris, Marion. *Library School Closings: Four Case Studies.* Indiana University, 1986. (For further analysis and other viewpoints, see also these entries in Bibliography/Reference List II: Boyce, Biggs and Biggs, "Dean's List:", and Josey. Also, Bennett and Josey in List I. All of Josey's articles apply.)

15. Higgins, Norman C. *Improving Library Education for Selected Minorities.* Arizona State University, 1979.

16. " . . . [B]ureaucrats are not anxious to believe that they can profitably be studied. Nor are they, in most instances, anxious to be observed and questioned as they go about their chores. Even when they are interviewed with great tact, and even when they have been well briefed as to why a study is being carried out, friction and hard feelings may develop. For some of them the mere fact that questions are being asked implies the suspicion of an unsatisfactory performance. . . . For most employees in a bureaucracy the line between performance evaluation and disinterested research seems rather fine." Foster (1973), pp. 198–9.

17. Spencer, Albert Franklin. *A Perception Study of the Accomplishment of the Goals for Indian Library and Information Service in Native American Educational Institutions.* Florida State University, 1985.

18. Griffiths, Jose-Marie and Donald W. King. *New Directions in Library and Information Science Education.* Published by Knowledge Industry Publications for the American Society of Information Science, 1986, pp.259, 262.

Source Notes I (Mostly to 1990)

A variety of agencies and organizations concern themselves with Native library services, either for them alone or along with library services to other ethnic and racial minorities. The following were found to be helpful during our research.

The American Library Association has at least four divisions, affiliates or round tables with which one should be familiar, in looking at Native/Indian library services. There is the American Indian Library Association, organized in 1979, which was an outgrowth of the White House Pre-conference on Indian Library and Information Services On or Near Reservations. The ALA Office for Library Outreach Services (OLOS) publishes the quarterly *American Indian Libraries Newsletter,* which should be received by every American library serving Native patrons.

The Ethnic Materials Information Exchange Roundtable of ALA circulates the *EMIE Bulletin,* published quarterly in cooperation with Queens College Graduate School of Library and Information Studies, City University of New York. As well as coordinating the exchange of information about library materials for ethnic and racial groups, it recognizes the concept of multicultural librarianship and encourages its development.

The Office for Library Personnel Resources of ALA provides the most up-to-date, useful statistics and other information about library workers in the United States. Publications of this office include several "kits" on aspects of personnel for libraries. The OLPR also has many materials available that can help library systems add Native and other minority employees, recruit and support them to go through library education, improve services and collections for Native and minority communities, as well as initiate or improve liaison with them.

Conferences of ALA also result in a variety of information and publications relevant to Native/Indian library services and related subjects. The Publications Office of ALA should be addressed.

The National Indian Education Association makes available various publications, notable for libraries being the series of 12 booklets produced by Project ILSTAC, listed in the bibliography.

The most productive subject heading in Library and Information Science Abstracts (LISA) was RACIAL/ETHNIC GROUPS. Others used were CANADA, GREENLAND, CONFERENCES and RURAL LIBRARIES.

As will be seen in the bibliography, a very wide spectrum of periodicals was utilized, on libraries, the north, community development, anthropology, linguistics, education, cross-cultural studies, literary issues and the social sciences generally. We have not exhausted the available periodical or government literature, but drew on what we could find within range and as time permitted.

Comprehensive Dissertation Index, international in scope, provided citations in the Social Sciences and Humanities volumes, Part I, under Library and Information Science. More useful was *Dissertation Abstracts International,* the volumes under: The Humanities and Social Sciences. Looking under Communication and the Arts, we checked the Library Science subheading. All entries are abstracted. Both these sources are produced by University Microfilms International.

The Native American Research Information Service (NARIS) is a specialized off-line computer database service that contains Native-related citations from many sources. It is operated by the American Indian Institute at the University of Oklahoma. Searches are run at no charge for libraries serving Native people (especially Native libraries themselves).

The Polar Libraries Colloquy (formerly the Northern Libraries Colloquy) is a loose-knit association of those concerned with Northern library activities everywhere in the circumpolar north, though to date there has been little participation by Soviet librarians. The Alaska State Library has edited and published the *Polar Libraries Bulletin* (formerly the *Northern Libraries Bulletin*) about twice a year. It concerns itself with "furnishing information on northern libraries activities, development and cooperation, serving as an informal link for a northern libraries network." Since the Colloquy's beginnings in the early 1970s, Phyllis DeMuth and the Alaska State Library edited and issued the *Bulletin.* In 1987 the editorship was passed on to Nancy Lesh of the University of Alaska Library at Anchorage. The *Bulletin* also gives news about the colloquies, annual from 1971 through 1976, biennial since 1978, which are held in a different location each time. The proceedings from each colloquy are published by the host institution. Thus far there have been 16 colloquies (through 1996), with proceedings available for most of them. For information about availability and where to write for copies, see p.453 of the 10th Northern Libraries Colloquy *Proceedings,* or issues of the *Polar Libraries Bulletin.* (For updating particulars, see Source Notes II.)

The Archives and Documentation Services of the Unesco Library in Paris also operates a database service, which will run searches. Up through 1987 there was no charge for this service. Its worldwide scope produces some interesting citations, especially for Third World countries.

The International Federation of Library Associations and Institutions (IFLA), based in The Hague, Netherlands, now has the Section of Library Services to Multicultural Populations, which was formed in 1986. Concerned with library services to *all* minority populations around the world, the original *Journal of Multicultural Librarianship* carried stimulating articles about library services to indigenous populations. In 1991 the new quarterly periodical *Multicultural Review* assumed the role of the Section's periodical, and the *Journal* ceased publication. By 1994 some old *Journal* fans might miss its more informal, personalized character, as the *Review*'s American address is reflected somewhat in its contents and glossy personality, though the *Journal*'s diversity and directness are still there, with many more useful features. Occasionally the IFLA Section will issue special publications, such as *Multicultural Communities: Guidelines for Library Service.*

The Scott Polar Research Institute in Cambridge, England had a library and database search service (SPRILIB) which produced citations from all the circumpolar nations for a fee. In 1994 this database, now called SPRI, was in the new, combined POLARPAC database, available in some academic libraries on CD-ROM. The Institute charges for this service. The Institute Library uses its own Universal Decimal Classification for Polar Libraries.

The Boreal Institute for Northern Studies Library at the University of Alberta in Edmonton was relocated and its name changed in 1991. It is now the Canadian Circumpolar Library, and it is housed in the main Cameron Library of the university. Although SPRI UDC was used for Polar Libraries by the old Boreal, it, as well as subject headings and other index tools, are under review. The collection should continue to grow and, hopefully, to provide excellent service. I was fortunate in 1989 to be sent actual copies of many books and other materials in large packets from the Boreal Library, which I expeditiously went through and returned by air from my remote location in western Alaska. Though undoubtedly such personal service is invaluable, it has the risk of loss. I equate my experience with the oldtime home-visits of doctors! Of course, now there are a variety of electronic ways to send many texts, whether in print form or from one computer memory to another, and the communication is much more expeditious, often mere hours or even minutes.

In the 1980s, QL Systems of Calgary provided online access to a few northern databases. Now the Arctic and Antarctic Regions interdisciplinary database (Cold Regions) incorporates these and others from the United States, Canada, and Great Britain: Arctic Institute of North America (U. of Calgary), Cold Regions Bibliography (U.S. Library of Congress), C-core (cold oceans, U. of Newfoundland), Citation (glaciology, Colorado U. at Boulder), SPRI (Cambridge, G.B.), USGS (Antarctic place names), Boreal (Canadian Circumpolar Library C.C.L., U. of Alberta), and Boreal Northern Titles (also C.C.L.) Another major northern database is POLARPAC, begun in 1993, a database of international polar library materials, containing in 1994 over 165,000 full bibliographic records. In making the acquaintance of these and other computer databases, I've utilized the resources and help of the staff at the University of Alaska, Anchorage, Consortium Library, and in particular a useful guide to them by staff librarian Clara L. Sitter, entitled *Plugging into the Electronic Library,* which made the burgeoning database landscape much more negotiable.

In the opening pages of chapter 3, on the oral and written traditions, my approach was strongly influenced by the theories of Claude Levi-Bruhl and other writers of similar views who have studied the evolution of human consciousness from aboriginal to modern times, as demonstrated in the arts, literature, psychology, sociology and other disciplines. All sources have been cited in Bibliography/Reference Lists I and II.

Bibliography/Reference List I (to 1990)
Selectively Annotated

Adamson, Edith. "Public Library Services to the Indians of Canada." *Canadian Library Journal,* 26:1 (Jan–Feb, 1969), pp.48–53.

Ahenakew, Chief David. Federation of Saskatchewan Indians. "Indian Control of Indian Information." An Address to the Canadian Library Association Conference, June 19, 1978. 6pp.

Aikio, Marjut. "The Position and Use of the Same Language: Historical, Contemporary and Future Perspectives." *Journal of Multilingual and Multicultural Development,* Vol.5, nos.3–4 (1984), pp.277–292.

Alberta Education. Native Education Project. *Native Library Resources for Elementary, Junior and Senior High Schools.* March, 1987. 61pp.

Alberta Municipal Affairs. Native Services Unit. *A Guide to Native Organizations in Alberta.* Sept, 1986. 35pp.

Aleybeleye, B. "Oral Archives in Africa: Their Nature, Value and Accessibility." *Int. Lib. Rev.* 17, pp.419–424.

Amadi, Adolphe O. *African Libraries, Western Tradition and Colonial Brainwashing.* Metuchen, NJ: Scarecrow Press, 1981.
An eye-opening look at the role libraries play in Native communities, and why they must integrate the oral tradition.

American Indian Reader - Education. San Francisco, CA: The Indian Historian Press Inc. American Indian Educational Publishers, (1972). Organizing and Maintaining a Native American Reference Library, "Prepared at the request of Indian students, by the American Indian Historical Society," pp.275–291.

American Library Association. *American Indian Libraries Newsletter.* 1977 to date.
A valuable source of current news and views on U.S. Native library affairs, including funding, urban library services, archives, and developments with individual tribes, etc.

——— Office of Library Personnel Resources. *Academic and Public*

Librarians: Data by Race, Ethnicity and Sex. Project Director: Jeniece Guy. 1986. 34pp.

———— *Report of the Racism and Sexism in Subject Analysis Subcommittee to the RTSD/CCS Subject Analysis Committee.* Midwinter 1980. 3rd revision, June, 1980.
Appendix 2, as well as some comments in the text of the report, address questions to do with Native peoples.

———— Standing Committee on Library Education. *Financial Assistance for Library Education, Academic Year 1988–89.* Chicago, 1987. 52pp.

———— *Traditional and Non-traditional Delivery Systems for Remote Areas.* Proceedings of the Public Library Association, Small and Medium-sized Libraries Section, Rural Library Services Committee. American Library Association Annual Conference, Los Angeles, 1983. 41pp.

Andersen, Marianne Krogh. "Gronlands biblioteksvaesen overtoget of hjemmestyret" (Greenland's Library System taken over by home rule), *Bogens Verden* 7/80, p. 342- (3 pages).

Andrewartha, Graham P. Northwest Territories. Department of Social Development. "Training of Indigenous Non-professionals: An Analysis of Eskimo Welfare Workers' Perception of their Role." *The Social Worker-Le Travailleur Social* 1 (1976), pp.2–6.

Angaiak, John. "I'm Lost in the City." (phonodisc) 33rpm. Eskimo Language Workshop, Dept. of Linguistics and Foreign Languages, University of Alaska, Fairbanks.

Armstrong, Terence and George Rogers, Graham Rowley. *The Circumpolar North, A Political and Economic Geography of the Arctic and Subarctic.* London: Methuen and Co., Ltd., (1978). 303pp.
A useful handbook on all aspects of circumpolar regions.

Association for Library and Information Science Education. *Library and Information Science Education Statistical Report 1986,* edited by Timothy W. Sineath. State College, PA: Association for Library and Information Science Education, 1986. 266pp.

Aubert, Vilhelm. University of Oslo. "Greenlanders and Lapps: Some Comparisons of their Relationship to the Inclusive Society," in: *Circumpolar Problems, Habitat, Economy, and Social Relations in the Arctic.* A Symposium for Anthropological Research in the North, September, 1969. Edited by Gosta Berg. Oxford: Pergamon Press, (1973). Wenner-Gren Center International Symposium Series. pp.1–8.

Auerbach, Eric. *Mimesis, The Representation of Reality in Western Literature.* Translated by Willard R. Trask. Princeton, NJ: Princeton University Press, 1953. 563pp.
An engrossing introduction to western literature as it reflects the world view and self-consciousness of a writer in his/her particular sociocultural and historical milieu.

Austlitz, Robert. "Folklore, Nationality and the 20th Century in Siberia and the Soviet Far East." *Journal of Folklore Research,* Vol.12, nos.2/3 (1975), pp.203–210.

Avataq Cultural Institute/Institut culturel Avataq. *Annual Report/Rapport annuel 1985/86.*

Axtell, James. *The European and the Indian, Essays in the Ethno-history of Colonial North America.* New York: Oxford Univ. Press, 1981.
The concluding chapter trenchantly summarizes both the effects of European culture on Native Americans and how Native American culture altered the beginning Euroamerican culture.

BBC-TV Productions. "A Matter of Fact." 60 min. television program. Narrated by James Burke. 1988. (Series: The Day the Universe Changed.)
Describes and discusses the merging of the oral tradition into the print mode in Europe and Great Britain. Writing itself was a mystical act, and for the scribes toiling in monasteries, copying documents by hand, even the tools and materials at their disposal—the nib, pen, knife and parchment—had religious significance. Formerly ". . . the young looked up to the old, who were living records. . . ." In fact, their memories served as legally binding verification in court proceedings. Early printing shops brought together those of all class backgrounds, from royal patrons to writers, local clerics and officials, teachers and tradesmen (and undoubtedly an occasional librarian). Burke comments that "electronics sent us back to the village," an intensively interactive community, and for librarians and information specialists, cross-indexing, for example, came at "the speed of light." He adds that the ascendance of the print tradition was perhaps the time when our modern emphasis on youth began—with print establishing records of the past and universal education spreading literacy and knowledge to more and more people, the young "no longer needed to go to elders. . . ."

Barnhardt, Ray and the X-CED Staff, Cross-Cultural Education Development Program, eds. *Cross-Cultural Issues in Alaskan Education.* Center for Education Research, University of Alaska, Fairbanks. July, 1977. 165pp.
The word education is applied in its broadest sense. Useful bibliography at the end of each chapter. (X-CED stands for Cross-Cultural Education Development, a program originally intended to train rural Native elementary school teachers, primarily to obtain a bachelor's degree in Education. It has been expanded to include a non-teaching degree in rural human resource development, for those interested in state-wide Native affairs, and a Masters program. Information from Darnell and Hoem, cited herein.)

Barnhardt, Ray, ed. *Cross-Cultural Issues in Alaskan Education, Vol.II.* Center for Cross-Cultural Studies, University of Alaska, Fairbanks. September, 1982. 206pp.

Battiste, Marie Ann. *An Historical Investigation of the Social and Cultural Consequences of Micmac Literacy.* Ph.D. Thesis, Stanford University, 1984. 212pp.
"Results of a study of the transformation from an aboriginal ideographic literacy system to a western literacy system. . . ." Literacy in Native or-

thographies, unless incorporated into Native sociocultural forms, has various negative consequences, especially if confined to classes in the schools.

Bell, Daniel. *The Coming of Post-Industrial Society, A Venture in Social Forecasting.* New York: Basic Books (Harper Torchbook), 1973, 1976. 507pp.

Benge, Ronald Charles. *Cultural Crisis in Libraries in the 3rd World.* London: Clive Bingley; Hamden, CT: Linnet Books, 1979.

Bennett, George E. *Librarians in Search of Science and Identity: The Elusive Profession.* Metuchen, NJ: Scarecrow Press, 1988.
A well-documented study tracing the origins of the present ambiguity in the status of librarians.

Berger, Peter, Brigitte Berger and Hansfried Kellner. *The Homeless Mind, Modernization and Consciousness.* New York: Vintage Books, Random House, 1974 (1973).
Stimulating and arresting analysis of humanity's social and psychological adjustments in the face of relentless urbanizing and modernizing trends, comparing the industrialized nations and the Third World.

Berry, Franklin, ed. *The Collected Papers of the Northern Cross-Cultural Education Symposium,* University of Alaska, Fairbanks, November 7,8,9, 1973. UAF, Fairbanks, Center for Northern Educational Research. May, 1974. 285pp.
A few papers are of interest in this collection: "Special Problems of Reading Comprehension in the Education of Eskimos and Indian Pupils," by Arnold A. Griese; "British Columbia Indian Language Project," by Randy Bouchard; "Local Input and Local Control," by Elaine Ramas; and "The Way—and Why," by Raymond Obomsawin, from which we quote:

. . . the vested interest of the great army of Indian-Eskimo specialists, professional scholars, overstaffed bureaucratic Indian Departments, along with all other Native do-gooders, must recognize as their goal the very self-destruction of their involvement, to be replaced by Native independence and self-sufficiency. (p.2.)

Blue, Dr. Althouse College, University of Western Ontario, London. "Indian Information Centre Proposal." (no date). 5pp.

Boas, Franz. *The Mind of Primitive Man.* New York: Macmillan, 1922.

Bowen, Judith, Pat Hiley and Ed Walley. "Working in a Multi-cultural Society: Education and Training for Librarians and Information Scientists." *IFLA Journal* 12 (1986), pp.192–202.

Brox, Ottar. Department of Social Anthropology, University of Bergen. "'Conservation' and 'Destruction' of Traditional Culture," in: *Circumpolar Problems, Habitat, Economy, and Social Relations in the North,* September, 1969. Edited by Gosta Berg. Oxford: Pergamon Press, (1973), pp.39–44.
Cites the paradoxical character of social changes that appear to support either traditional or modern economies among Native populations.

Emphasizes the key roles played by Native adaptability and community control.

Buffalomeat, Nellie, Maxine Edmo, Lotsee Smith and Minerva White. Profiles of Four Indian Library/Information Programs. "Papers prepared for the White House Pre-Conference on Indian Library and Information Services On or Near Reservations." Denver, CO, October 19–22, 1978.

Burnaby, Barbara. *Promoting Native Writing Systems in Canada.* Toronto: Ontario Institute for Studies in Education. (Occ. Paper 24.) 1985. 222pp.

Canada. National Library. Resources Survey Division. Collection Development Branch. *Research Collections in Canadian Libraries* (9, Resources for Native Peoples Studies, by Nora T. Corley.)
Statistics are cited from "a memorandum, Data on Native Peoples, by Pierre J. Hubert, Census Provincial Liaison Office, Statistics Canada. January 28, 1983."

Carlson, Judith Ann. *Library Services for the Native Peoples of North America: An Examination of Existing Services in Ontario and Recommendations for Improvement.* "Prepared for Mr. M. E. Morgan, Instructor, Dept. of Library Arts, and Mr. R. Wall, Instructor, Dept. of Business and Technical Communications. Ryerson Polytechnical Institute, 50 Gould Street, Toronto. March 27, 1980." 89pp.

Carter, Jane Robbins. "Multi-cultural Graduate Library Education," *Journal of Education for Librarianship,* Vol.18, No.4 (1978), pp.295–313.
The state of this aspect of library education in the late 1970s in the U.S.

Chang, Henry C., Principal Investigator. Bonnie Isman and Adele Zenchoff, Project Staff. *Virgin Islands Demonstration Library Network Study: Exploring Library Networking in Remote, Disadvantaged Areas.* Bureau of Libraries, Museums and Archeological Services, POB 390, St. Thomas, US Virgin Islands, 00801. Jan. 31, 1978. 39pp.plus 29 unnumbered pages.

Chaytor, H.J. "Reading and Writing," *Explorations,* 3 (1954), pp.6–17.

Clow, D.V. "Consultancy Roles in Library Development," *Int. Lib. Rev.* (1984) 16, pp.5–20.

Coates, Kenneth Stephen. *Best Left as Indians: Native-White Relations in the Yukon Territory, 1840–1950.* PhD. Thesis, Univ. of British Columbia, March, 1984.

Cohen, David. Dept. of Library Science, Queens College, City College of New York. *Performance Report for Ethnicity and Librarianship Institute 2: Multiethnic Library Materials, Programs and Services in NYC and Its Environs—Long Island, Westchester, Connecticut, New Jersey.* 1978. 155pp.ED 188 636.

Cohen, Felix. "Americanizing the White Man," *American Scholar,* Vol.21, no.2 (Spring, 1952), pp.177–191.
The author was a famous attorney for Indian rights and wrote classic works on Indian law.

Coldevin, Gary O. "Some Effects of Frontier Television in a Canadian

Eskimo Community," *Journalism Quarterly,* Vol.53, No.1 (Spring, 1976), pp.34–39.

Cole, Douglas. *Captured Heritage, the Scramble for Northwest Coast Artifacts.* Seattle: Univ. of Washington Press, 1985 (1995 ed. now available).

Coles, Robert M.D. *Eskimos, Chicanos, Indians.* Vol.IV of *Children of Crisis.* Boston:Little Brown and Co., 1977, 587pp.

Couture, Joseph E. Dept. of Native Studies, Trent Univ., Peterborough, Ontario. "Native Training and Political Change—Future Directions." in: *Popular Analysis, Popular Action: Canadian Readings in Adult Learning for Political Change,* by T. Jackson and B. Hall, eds. Toronto: International Council for Adult Education, 1979. 28pp.

Couture, Joseph E. "Next Time Try an Elder," in: *Flower of Two Soils: American Indian Youth in Transition,* edited by M. Beiser. Seattle: Univ. of Washington Press, 1979. 18pp.

Crampton, C. B. "Native and Academic Natural Science," *Arcana Poli,* Vol.1, No.1 (July, 1988), pp.10–13.

"If Native experts can forgive past affronts and respond to new attempts to understand their traditional knowledge, if academic and commercial scientists will consider the social as well as the economic implications of their own work, and if both sets of experts can rise above the short-term considerations that self-serving bureaucracies, Native and White, impose upon their employees and associates, we may look forward to innovative solutions to old problems that are reflected in the ever-changing northern landscape." p. 12.

Creed, John. "The Electronic Chalkboard, 'Telelearning' System Brings Concepts Home to Far-flung Students," *Anchorage Daily News,* November 5, 1987, pp.E–1, E–2.

Cruikshank, Julia M. *Legend and Landscape: Convergence of Oral and Scientific Traditions with Special Reference to the Yukon Territory, Canada.* A thesis submitted in partial fulfillment of the requirements for the Diploma in Polar Studies. Cambridge, England: Scott Polar Research Institute, 1980. 91pp.

The Native oral and Western written, scientific traditions merge in the Yukon, and the lessons to be learned. Lengthy, stimulating bibliography. This work was the catalyst that impelled the author to look further into the oral and written traditions.

Cruikshank, Julie. "Getting the Words Right: Perspectives on Naming and Places in Athapascan Oral History," *Arctic Anthropology,* Vol.27, No.1, 1990, pp.52–65.

This intriguing article takes one along while visiting with Indians in the border area between the Yukon Territory and British Columbia. After summarizing the debate around the value of oral history and recent research, "it shows the variety of ways in which six individuals use named locations in space to discuss events in time."

Cserepy, Frank A.E. Chief, Language Bureau, Dept. of Information, Northwest Territories. Native Languages in the NWT. "Notes for a Round-table Discussion on "Native Languages—A Precarious Heritage," at the National Symposium on Linguistic Services, Ottawa, Ontario, Oct. 9–12, 1984. 10pp.

Dam, Ole. "Education in Greenland," *North* (periodical). Canada Department of Northern Affairs and National Resources. Northern Administration and Lands Branch. Ottawa. Vol.19 No.1, (1972), pp.39–42.

Darrell, Frank and Anton Hoem. *Taken to Extremes*, Education in the Far North. Boston:Scandinavian Press, 1996
Examines the consequences of schooling on northern Native populations. Geographical scope is circumpolar, not including Russia.

Deloria, F. Sam. *Strategies for Funding of Library, Media and Information Services on Indian Reservations.* A paper prepared for the White House Pre-Conference on Indian Library and Information Service On or Near Reservations, Denver, CO, October 19–22, 1978.

Deloria, Vine, Jr. *The Right to Know.* A paper presented for the White House Pre-Conference on Indian Library and Information Services On or Near Reservations, Denver, CO, October 19–22, 1978.

Denmark. Prime Minister's Office. Greenland Department.
Greenland in Figures. 1987. 44pp. Small, pocket-size booklet. Demographic and economic information of interest, but no library-specific information.

Dicks, D.J. *Impact of Communications Services in the Eastern Arctic.* Final Report: 15 May 1975. Dept. of Electrical Engineering, Queens University, Kingston, Ontario. 142pp.

Distance Education in the Canadian North: An Annotated Bibliography. (Occasional Paper No.12) Ottawa: Association of Canadian-Universities for Northern Studies, September, 1984. 28pp.

Distance Education Library Courses. (calendar) Library and Information Technology, Rural Library Training Project, Southern Alberta Institute of Technology. Calgary, Alberta, (1987). 35pp.

Dorson, Richard M. "Oral Traditions and Written History: the Case for the United States," *Journal of the Folklore Institute,* Vol.1 (1964), pp.220–234.

Du Mont, Rosemary Ruhig. "The Future of Public Library Service: A Behavioral View," in: *Communications and the Future,* edited by Howard F. Didsbury, Jr. Bethesda, MD: World Future Society, 1982, pp.190–197.

Du Mont, Rosemary Ruhig. "Race in American Librarianship: Attitudes of the Library Profession," *Journal of Library History, Philosophy and Comparative Librarianship,* Vol.21 (3) Summer, 1986, pp.488–509.

Dunn, Ethel. "Education and the Native Intelligentsia in the Soviet Union: Further Thoughts on the Limits of Culture Change," *Arctic Anthropology,* VI-2 (1970), pp.112–122.

Education, Research, Information Systems and the North. "Developed from Proceedings of the ACUNS meetings in Yellowknife, 17–19 April 1986." Editor: W. Peter Adams. Association of Canadian Universities for Northern Studies and Trent University. 362pp.

This excellent resource volume has many articles helpful for students of cross-cultural issues in the North. Among these are: Michael Shouldice of the ICI on a "museum based cultural teaching centre"; E. Bielawaski's paper on "the role of the scientist in human development in the Northwest Territories," which shows how the Northern Heritage Society in the NWT fostered culturally integrated studies in northern Canada: "In so doing, we can facilitate both science and education by meeting needs for academic and vocational study" (p. 61); Alice Abel's paper, "Pot of Written Gold, The Dene Nation Library/Archives, Yellowknife, NWT," which links with "Further Observations on the Dene Nation Library/Archives" by Leith Peterson.

Egan, Kieran. "Literacy and the Oral Foundations of Education," *Harvard Educational Review,* Vol.57, No.4 (November, 1987), pp.445–472.

Includes a comprehensive bibliography.

Elliott, Pirkko. "The Relationship Between Public Libraries, Other Relevant Agencies and Self-Help Ethnic Minority Organizations," *Journal of Librarianship* 18 (4) October, 1986, pp.223–241.

Makes key suggestions for library cooperation with ethnic minority organizations.

Etudes/Inuit/Studies. "Journal published twice yearly by the Inuksiutiit Katimajiit Association, Inc., with encouragement of Department of Anthropology (Laval University), and financial assistance of Ministère des Affaires culturelles du Quebec and Social Sciences and Humanities Research Council of Canada."

Vol.6 (1982), No. 1 features "Communications," with articles in English and French on new communications technology in the north, effects of television, use of interactive satellites, and Inuit-controlled production and broadcasting. Kalaaliit-Nunaata Radioa—To Be Master of One's Own Media Is to Be Master of One's Own Fate," by M. Stenbaek-Lafon, is an excellent article on the long-time role of Radio Greenland in the preservation of Greenlandic ways.

Ficek, Richard. *Community Services Practicum: Information Needs of Native Peoples in the City of Toronto.* Faculty of Library Science, Univ. of Toronto, May, 1974, 60pp.

Fienup-Riordan, Ann. *Navarin Basin Sociocultural Systems Baseline Analysis.* Prepared for Bureau of Land Management, Outer Continental Shelf Office. (Alaska OCS Socioeconomic Studies Program, Final Technical Report No.70.) January, 1982. 576pp.

The obfuscating title the bureaucracies have given this document successfully hides the fact that it contains the most comprehensive single description of contemporary Yupik communities on the Lower Kuskokwim and adjacent Bering Sea coast and their subsistence economies. The author is a well-known anthropologist and the author of several books, most of which are about the Central Yupik area. Copies may be obtained either through the National Technical Information Service (NTIS), or the Program Coordinator (COAR), Socio-economic Studies Program, Alaska OCS Office, PO Box 1159, Anchorage, AK 99510.

Fisher, Edith Maureen. "Minority Librarianship Research: A State-of-the-art Review," *Library Research* 5 (1983), pp.5–65.
Portions on the American Indian are very helpful.

Fleckner, John A. *Native American Archives: An Introduction.* 1984. Society of American Archivists, 600 South Federal, Suite 504, Chicago, IL 60605.
Concise, compendious introduction for anyone interested in the subject. Many tribes now have formal archival programs, and the S.A.A. has a list of them.

Forbes, Norma. *Television's Effects on Rural Alaska.* Summary of Final Report (of Social and Cognitive Effects of the Introduction of Television on Rural Alaskan Native Children, by Norma Forbes, Clark Ashworth, Walter Lonner and Danuta Kasprzyk. Alaska Council of Science and Technology, Center for Cross-Cultural Studies, Univ. of Alaska, Fairbanks. March, 1984). 11pp.

Foster, George M. Univ. of California, Berkeley. *Traditional Societies and Technological Change.* 2nd edition. New York: Harper and Row, (1973).

Frosio, Eugene T. "Comments on the Thomas Yen-Ran Yeh Proposals," *Library Resources and Technical Services,* Vol.15, No.2 (Spring, 1971), pp.128–131.
See also: Yeh, Thomas Yen-Ran

Gamble, Donald J. "Crushing of Cultures: Western Applied Science in Northern Societies," *Arctic,* Vol.39, No.1 (March, 1986), pp.20–23.

Giffen, Naomi Musmaker. *The Roles of Men and Women in Eskimo Culture.* Chicago, IL: Univ. of Chicago Press, 1930. (reprint.)
Although descriptive of traditional roles, there are clear and useful indicators for the altering roles of Native men and women in the modern world, and those who live and work with them under these highly acculturative and trying conditions.

Gove, Chris Moyers Leddy. *The Conflict Between Persistence and Acculturation as It Affects Individual Behavior of Northwestern Alaskan Eskimos.* A Dissertation Presented to the Graduate Faculty of the School of Human Behavior, United States International University. In partial fulfillment of the requirements for the Degree of Doctor of Philosophy in Sociology-Anthropology. San Diego, 1982.
"Twenty-six Eskimos were interviewed . . . : . . . Verbal descriptions by the subjects of their own behavior closely conformed to the nomemes of the dominant culture, while their observable behavior more closely resembled traditional nomemes. . . . This dichotomy was identified in the areas of child rearing, sexual relationships, family relationships, family structure, and female role behavior. . . . a greater degree of acculturation has occurred in the area of material culture, religion, and language." (from the abstract.)

Graburn, Nelson H. H. and Stephen Strong. "The Samek (Lapps)," in:

Circumpolar Peoples: An Anthropological Perspective. Pacific Palisades, CA: Goodyear Publishing Co., 1973, pp.11–32.

Greenfield, Louise, Susan Johnston and Karen Williams. "Educating the World: Training Library Staff to Communicate with International Students," *Journal of Academic Librarianship* 12:4 (September, 1986), pp.227–231.

Griffiths, Jose-Marie and Donald W. King. *New Directions in Library and Information Science Education.* White Plains, NY: Published by Knowledge Industry Publications for the American Society of Information Science, 1986.

"Grode i den gronlandske bog-produktion" (Growth in Greenlandic Book Production).

"Gronlands hjemmestyre": Cirkulaere nr.11/80: Cirkulaere om folkebiblioteckerne i Gronland. (Greenland's Home Rule: Cultural and Educational Board Circular No.11/80: Circular on Public Libraries of Greenland).

Gronland og Sydslesvig. 1980, 1981, 1982, 1983, 1984. (Yearly reports for Greenland libraries.)

Gurstein, Michael. *Urbanization and Indian People, An Analytical Literature Review.* December, 1977. 44pp. Bibliography, 7 leaves. Ottawa: Indian and Northern Affairs Canada, 1983.
A useful review because it goes over all the routes Native people take in becoming urbanized, whether visiting, passing through or settling in larger towns and cities, and what this means in terms of personal and social problems, and their remedies. Options of all parties affected are cited.

Gynther, Bent. *The Use of Greenlandic and Danish in Greenland Schools, 1950–1978.* Occasional Publication No.5 of the Association of Canadian Universities for Northern Studies. 1980. 59pp.

Handbook of North American Indians. Vol.4, *Arctic.* David Dumas, volume editor. Washington, DC: Smithsonian Inst., 1984. 829pp.
An excellent background sourcebook on Native peoples and development of the circumpolar north. Some articles refer indirectly to factors affecting library development, though the index has no reference to libraries. Lengthy bibliography. One article of special interest is Robert Petersen's "Greenlandic Written Literature."

Handbook of North American Indians. Vol.5, *History of Indian-White Relations.* Wilcomb E. Washburn, volume editor. Washington, DC: Smithsonian Inst., 1988. 838pp.
A comprehensive survey of the subject, both geographically and by its variety of aspects. Emphasizes historical background, which inevitably casts deep shadows over all subsequent development in Native communities. Religious, literary and film treatment of Natives are also covered.

Hanks, Christopher C. "Perception and Utilization of Television: A Comparison between a Saulteaux Reserve and a Rural White Community," *The Musk Ox,* No. 28 (1981), pp.20–25.

Hanks, Christopher C. *et al.* "Social Change and the Mass Media: the Oxford House Cree, 1909–1983," *Polar Record,* Vol.1, No.134 (1983), pp.458–465.

Harris, Jessica L. and Doris H. Clack. "Treatment of People and Peoples in Subject Analysis," *Library Resources and Technical Services,* Vol.23, No.4 (Fall, 1979), pp.374–390.

Harrison, Barbara Gill. *Informal Learning among Yup'ik Eskimos: An Ethnographic Study of on Alaskan Village.* Ph.D. dissertation, University of Oregon, 1981. 253pp.

Havelock, Eric. *Preface to Plato.* Cambridge, MA: Belknap Press of Harvard University Press, 1963. 328pp.

Hennepin County Library. Minnetonka, Minnesota. *Cataloging Bulletin.* Sanford Berman, ed. and Chief Cataloger.
A source for alternative subject headings, and the dialogue that goes with more appropriate treatment of Native peoples in matters of library organization schemes.

Higgins, Norman C. *Improving Library Education for Selected Minorities.* Tempe, AZ: Arizona State University Dept. of Educational Technology and Library Science, 1979. 55pp.ED 781 911.

Hills, Alex and M. Granger Morgan. "Telecommunications in Alaskan Villages," *Science,* Vol.211, January 16, 1981, pp.241–248.
A discussion of the State of Alaska Satellite Project, with "social impact and local control" being touched on. Useful bibliography on both technical aspects and significance for Native communities.

Hippler, Arthur E. "The Demographic 'Youth Bulge': One Reason for Acculturative Difficulties among Alaska Natives," *Polar Record,* Vol.18, No.114 (Sept, 1976), pp.304–306.

Hippler, Arthur E. *Eskimo Acculturation, A Selected Annotated Bibliography of Alaskan and Other Eskimo Acculturation Studies.* Institute of Social, Economic and Government Research, University of Alaska, College, Alaska. ISEGR No.28. August, 1970. 209pp.
A very useful document, giving a survey look at the subject in literature dating from the early 19th century to about 1967. The annotations include some value judgments, and comparisons with similar works. One lesson one comes away with is that the nature and issues of acculturation were perceived very early, and little new has been added since.

Hippler, Arthur E. *Final Report to the Commissioner of Public Safety on the Village Public Safety Officers Program.* Institute of Social and Economic Research, Univ. of Alaska, Fairbanks. October, 1982.

Hirsch, E.D. Jr. "Cultural Literacy," *Innovation Abstracts,* Vol.VIII, No.10. Regarding the "background information that a [citizen] should know . . . We all know that our continuing failure to achieve a high level of national literacy insures a continuing lack of subtlety in the communications that we can transmit. . . . Plain literacy skills are not enough, and substantive knowledge of history, culture and contemporary issues is indispensable to effective citizenship." There are now a number of articles and books available on this subject. Though not cross-culturally sensitive on the face of it, this concept can also be applied to kinds of literacy in Native communities.

Hobfall, Stevan E., Robert Morgan and Raymond Lehrman. "The Development of a Training Centre in an Eskimo Village," *Community Development Journal* 15:2 (1980), pp.146–148.

Hofbauer, Jenna. *Information Access through Library Services: A Handbook for Native Groups.* Canadian Association in Support of the Native Peoples, 1978. 18pp.

Holden, Madronna. "Making All the Crooked Ways Straight, The Satirical Portrait of Whites in Coast Salish Folklore." *Journal of American Folklore,* vol. 89 (1976), p. 272–293 Relates how some informants, for amusement, sometimes altered or falsified stories they told to anthropologists.

Hughes, Charles Campbell. "Under Four Flags: Recent Culture Change among the Eskimos," *Current Anthropology,* Vol.4, No.1 (February, 1965), pp.3–69.
Seminal article on cross-cultural development among all Eskimo peoples.

Indian Resource Development (IRD). *Sources of Financial Aid Available to American Indian Students.* Compiled by Roxie June and Preston Thomas. Editors Marjorie Burr, Lance Lujan and Kathryn Tijerina. Indian Resource Development, Box 3 IRD, Las Cruces, New Mexico 88003. Funding for this book is from the State of New Mexico. January, 1988. 45pp.

Institut educatif et culturel Attikamek-Montagnais, Village des Huron, Quebec. *Les bibliothèques publiques en milieu Attikamek-Montagnais: savoir répondre à un besoin manifeste.* (Mémoire.) April 8, 1987.

International Federation of Library Associations and Institutions (IFLA). Section on Library Services to Multicultural Populations. *Multicultural Communities: Guidelines for Library Services.* 1987. 14pp.

Inuit Broadcasting Corporation. *Position Paper on Northern Broadcasting,* Revised, October, 1985.

Iversen, Mogens. "Gensym med Gronland efter 23 ar," *Bibliotek* Vol.70 (1983), No. 21, pp.583,585.

Jackson, Miles M. "Distance Learning and Libraries in the Pacific Islands," *Int. Lib. Rev.* (1983) 15, pp.177–184.

Jaynes, Julian. *The Origin of Consciousness in the Breakdown of the Bicameral Mind.* Boston, MA: Houghton-Mifflin Co., 1976. 467pp.
A plausible theory of how the self-conscious, subjective mind of modern individual humans evolved from the collective and integrated social consciousness of prehistory.

John, Magnus. "The Language of Formal Education and the Role of Libraries in Oral-Traditional Societies," *Int. Lib. Rev.* 16 (1984), pp.393–406.

John, Magnus. "Libraries in Oral-Traditional Societies," *Int. Lib. Rev.* 11 (1979), pp.321–339.

Joint Commission on Indian Education and Training. Kwiya. *Final Report* (sponsored by the Yukon Minister of Education and the Vice Chair for Social Programs of the Council for Yukon Indians). August 28, 1987. 41pp.

Jorgensen, Torben. "Boger og bygder" (Books and Settlements), *Bibliotek,* Vol.70 (1983), No. 1, pp.16–18.

——— "Boger pa gronlandsk er fortsat en mangelvare" (Books in Greenlandic are continually in short supply), *Bibliotek,* Vol.70 (1983), No. 2, pp.44–46.

——— "De vil skrive gronlaendernes egen historie" (They want to write the Greenlanders' own History), *Bibliotek,* Vol.70 (1983), No. 13, pp.318–319.

Josey, E.J. "Library and Information Services for Cultural Minorities: A Commentary and Analysis of a Report to the National Commission on Libraries and Information Science," *Libri* 35:4 (December, 1985), pp.320–332.

Josey, E.J. and Marva L. DeLoach, eds. *Ethnic Collections in Libraries.* Neal-Schuman, 1983. 361pp.

Eighteen essays, nine of which describe major Black, Hispanic, Asian and Native American (including Caribbean and Pacific Island peoples) collections, with the remaining essays on "archives, programming, Federal policy and linkages," and "forging a partnership with professional ethnic associations."

Jousse, Marcel. *The Oral Style.* Translated from the French by Edgard Sienaert and Richard Whitaker. (The Albert Bates Lord Studies in Oral Tradition, Vol.6.) (Garland Reference Library of the Humanities, Vol.1352.) Translation of *Le style oral rythmique et mnémotechnique chez les verbomoteurs.* New York: Garland Pub., 1990 (1981).

Stimulating study of the physical and gesticular origins of the oral tradition, and how the entire body is conditioned to be expressive and responsive in communication, something largely repressed and lost among moderns, who have become "disassociated" from the stimuli of natural surroundings. Disassociation occurred when consciousness was born, and ideas were verbalized. The bulk of this intriguing book is comprised almost entirely of quotations from other authors.

KYUK-AM-TV(POB 468, Bethel, Alaska 99559). KYUK Catalog Video Productions. KYUK is a non-commercial, non-profit regional radio/television station with special status, in that it carries all commercial network programming plus Public Broadcasting Corporation as well as local Yupik programming.

Kaufert, Joseph M. and William W. Koolage. "Role Conflict among 'Culture Brokers': The Experience of Native Canadian Medical Interpreters" (Research Note), *Social Science Medicine,* Vol.18 (1984), No. 3, pp.283–286.

Kim, Choong H. "The Mini-Library Movement in Rural Korea: A

Successful Experiment with a Rural Public Library Alternative," *Int. Lib. Rev.* 11 (1979), pp.421–440.

Kleinfeld, Judith. *Effective Teachers of Indian and Eskimo High School Students.* Institute of Social and Economic Research, Center for Northern Educational Research, Univ. of Alaska, Fairbanks, 1972, p.74.

Kleinfeld, Judith Smilg. *Eskimo School on the Andreavsky, A Study of Effective Bicultural Education,* (Praeger Studies in Ethnographic Perspectives on American Education.) New York: Praeger, 1979. 185pp.
This concerns a Catholic boarding school at St. Mary's on the Lower Yukon. Its approach was the fusion of bicultural values in a highly supportive sociocultural setting, with a high teacher/student ratio. In the years following provision of K-12 schools in all Alaskan rural communities, enrollment steadily declined and the St. Mary's School closed in 1987.

Kleinfeld, J.S. "Intellectual Strengths in Culturally Different Groups: An Eskimo Illustration," *Review of Educational Research,* Vol.43, No. 3, pp.341–359.

Korhonen, Salme. Librarian, Lapland Department, Rovaniemi, Finland. *Literature Concerning Instruction in the Lappish Language in the School Systems of Finland, Norway and Sweden.* Ottawa: Association of Canadian Universities for Northern Studies, 1980. 5pp.
A bibliography on the subject. Most of the entries are in Scandinavian languages.

Kotei, S.I.A. "Some Variables of Comparison between Developed and Developing Library Systems," *Int. Lib. Rev.* 9 (1977), pp.249–267.

Krauss, Michael E. *Alaska Native Languages: Past, Present, and Future.* (Alaska Native Language Center Research Papers No. 4.) 1980. 110pp.

Kularatne, E.D.T. "Library Education and Training for Subprofessionals in Developing Countries," *Education for Information* Vol.3, No. 4 (December, 1985), pp.283–290.

Lanken, Dane. "Inuit Cousins, but Oh How Different!, Life in Frobisher Bay, NWT and Nuuk, Greenland," *Canadian Geographic,* Vol.106, No. 2 (April–May, 1986).

Lentz, Tony M. "The Medium Is the Madness: Television and the Pseudo-Oral Tradition in America's Future," in: *Communications and the Future,* edited by Howard F. Didsbury, Jr. Bethesda, MD: World Future Society. pp.322–336.

Library Trends (quarterly periodical). University of Illinois Graduate School of Library Science, Urbana, IL. Fall, 1980. "Library Services to Ethnocultural Minorities." Issue Editor, Leonard Wertheimer.
Most of the articles deal with aspects of the subject as found in countries other than the U.S. Of special interest are: David Cohen's article, "Ethnicity in Librarianship" (U.S.); "Library Training for Services to Minority Ethnic Groups" (Great Britain) by Sylva Simsova; "Public Library

Services to Ethnocultural Minorities in Australia" (in which aborigines are briefly treated); P.D. Stepanov's article on "New Forms and Methods of Library Service to Ethnic Groups and Minorities in the Far North of the USSR"; and "Public Library Service to Native Americans in Canada and the Continental US" by Richard G. Heyser and Lotsee Smith.

Linkola, Martti. University of Jyvaskyla, Finland. "The Snowmobile in Lapland—Its Economic and Social Effects," in: *Circumpolar Problems, Habitat, Economy, and Social Relations in the Arctic.* A Symposium for Anthropological Research in the North, September, 1969. Edited by Gosta Berg. Oxford: Pergamon Press, (1973).

Lorentowicz, Genia. "Planning a Workshop on Multicultural Service," *Canadian Library Journal* 41(3) June, 1984, pp.125–126.

Lotz, Jim. "Northern Alternatives," *Arctic* Vol.28, No. 1 (March, 1975), pp.3–8.

Lund, Keld. "Det Grondlandske Landsbiblioteks for Bibliotekarer ansat i kommunerne," *Nunatta Atuagaateqarfia.* July 16, 1987.

Marshall, John. Professor, Faculty of Library Science, University of Toronto. *Library Service for Native People, A Brief to the Ontario Task Force of the Education of Native Peoples.* Nov. 20, 1975. 14pp.

Mathews, Virginia H. *Opportunities and Needs: The Current State of Funding for American Indian Library and Information Services On or Near Reservations.* A Paper prepared for the White House Pre-Conference on Indian Library and Information Services On or Near Reservations, Denver, CO, October 19–22, 1978.

McIsaac, Marina Stock, with Radford Quamahongnewa and Ruth Finneman. "Native American School Library Professionals: An Unmet Need," *School Library Journal,* Jan, 1984, pp.38–41.

McPhail, Thomas L. Associate Professor, School of Journalism, Carleton University, Ottawa, Ontario. *The Impact of Broadcasting Technologies on Northern Native Communities in Canada.* A Paper prepared for the International Communication Association Annual Conference, Chicago, Illinois, April 24–28, 1975. 20pp.
A brief, early overview on the effects of radio and television, including satellite and interactive forms of TV. Useful bibliography.

Metoyer, Cheryl. *Community Information Needs and Library Potentials.* A paper prepared for the White House Pre-Conference on Indian Library and Information Services On or Near Reservations, Denver, CO, October 19–22, 1978.

Miyaoka, Osahito. Otaru University of Commerce. "Alaska Native Languages in Transition," *Senri Ethnological Studies,* 4, 1980, pp.169–203. ("Papers presented at the Second International Symposium, National Museum of Ethnology, Osaka. August, 1978.")
Until recently, assimilationist policy governed schooling in Alaska for

Native language speakers. "Apparently there was no recognition whatsoever that the best medium for teaching a child is his mother tongue, and that assimilation may mean dispossession . . . to switch to English and to abandon one's mother tongue would not lead directly to his acceptance in a non-Native or white group. It would be quite possible that by so doing he would end up being a marginal man who is ostracized by both groups." Bilingual/bicultural programs emphasizing language maintenance are now mandated for schools serving Native populations, but there are so many cross-cultural factors involved that the outcome in terms of the survival of Native language in either oral or written form is uncertain. This paper looks in particular at the situation in the Central Yupik area of southwestern Alaska.

Moon, Eric. "Our Commission, Our Omissions, An Assessment of the National Commission on Library and Information Science (NCLIS)," *Library Journal,* July, 1984, pp.1283–1287.

Morton, W.L. "A Centennial of Northern Development," *The Polar Record,* Vol.15, No. 95 (1970), pp.145–150.

Mowat, Farley. *The Siberians.* Baltimore: Penguin Books, 1970. 360pp.
An intriguing tour of a number of towns and settlements in NE Siberia in 1966 and 1969, giving a Canadian's view of the Siberian environment, lifestyle and challenge.

Muller-Wille, L., P.J. Pelto, Li. Muller-Wille and R. Darnell, Editors. *Consequences of Economic Change in Circumpolar Regions.* Papers of the Symposium on Unexpected Consequences of Economic Change in Circumpolar Regions at the 34th Annual Meeting of the Society for Applied Anthropology in Amsterdam, March 21 to 22, 1975. (Published by the) Boreal Institute for Northern Studies, The University of Alberta, Edmonton.
This collection of papers is typical of such literature. The apparently scientific and objective title disguises the fact, however, that every one of the 24 papers is about the effects of western cultural contact, intrusion and dominance on circumpolar peoples. Areas of concern covered are: Northern Environments and peoples: some definitions; Changes in Native economy, equipment and resources; Implications of disturbance of northern ecology: the hydroelectric experiment; Emerging new settlement patterns and their consequences; and Socio-cultural and political implications of North-South contact. Canada and northern Scandinavia are the geographical emphasis, with one article each on the USSR and Greenland.

Murin, Deborah Lee, Editor. *Northern Native Broadcast Directory.* Runge Press Limited, 1988. 95pp.

Muensterberger, Warner and S. Axelrad, eds. *Psychoanalytic Study of Society.* New York: International Universities Press, 1960.
Some articles are interesting and relevant to an understanding of the Na-

tive cross-cultural experience: "'Culture Shock' and the Inability to Mourn," by Howard F. Stein, Vol.11, pp.157–172; "Eskimo Social Control as a Function of Personality: A Study of Change and Persistence," by Arthur E. Hippler, Vol.10, pp.53–89; "The Subarctic Athabascans of Alaska: The Ecological Grounding of Certain Cultural Personality Characteristics," by Hippler, Boyer and Boyer, Vol.7, pp.293–329; "The Mackenzie Delta Eskimos: Problems of Adaptation to Changing Social and Economic Conditions," by Joseph M. Lubart, Vol.7, pp.331–357.

Myers, Beatrice. "Literature for Preliterate Linguistic Minorities," *Phaedrus* ("an international journal of children's literature research"), VII, No. 1 (Spring/Summer, 1980), pp.43–46.

Namminersornerullutik oqartussat/Gronlands hjemmestyre (Greenland's Home Rule). Kulturimik atuartitsinermillu aqutsisut/ Kultur- og undervisningsdirektionen (Cultural and Educational Board). Cirkulaere nr:11/80 (Circular No. 11/80) Cirkulaere om Folkebibliotekerne i Gronland (Circular on the Public Libraries in Greenland). March, 1980. 9pp.

This is the original Home Rule statute that governs public library services in Greenland.

National Commission on Library and Information Science. Task Force on Library and Information Services to Cultural Minorities. *Hearings.* San Francisco, CA, 1981.

National Commission on Library and Information Science. Task Force on Library and Information Science to Cultural Minorities. *Report.* 1983.

National Indian Education Association. Project ILSTAC. *Adult Education and Indian Libraries,* by Virginia H. Mathews. (Guide No. 6). 15pp.

———— *Alternatives to Classification,* by Laura Wittstock and John Wolthausen. (Guide No. 4). 14pp.

————*Assessing Indian Needs,* by Elizabeth Whiteman Runs Him. (Guide No. 9). 17pp.

———— *Establishing Indian Library Service, Working with Indian Communities and Agencies to Establish Indian Library Services,* Part I, by Rosemary Christiansen. (Guide No. 1, Part I). 15pp.

———— *Establishing Indian Library Service, Working with Indian Communities and Agencies to Establish Indian Library Services,* Part II, by Hannis Smith. (Guide No. 1, Part II). 16pp.

———— *Generating Information in Indian Libraries,* by Charles T. Townley. (Guide No. 8). 10pp.

———— *In-service Training,* by Lotsee Smith. (Guide No. 11). 13pp.

———— *Materials Selection,* by Rosemary Christiansen. (Guide No. 10). 13pp.

————*Promoting Indian Library Use,* by Charles T. Townley. (Guide No. 7). 10pp.

————*Staffing for Indian Library Services,* by Margaret Wood. (Guide No. 3). 15pp.

———— *Urban Indian Library Services,* by Marie Jones and Edith Casaday. (Guide No. 5). 10pp.

Native Counselling Services of Alberta. *Creating a Monster—Issues in Community Program Control.*
What happens when a community-based program has its local control and direction gradually taken away by established institutions; in this case a program intended to keep minor offenders and fine-defaulters out of the court system, using other alternatives to imprisonment. The lesson learned is that local community control should be precisely that and not be replaced or bypassed.

Native Library Advocate (periodical). Library and Information Services, Assembly of First Nations, 47 Clarence Street, Ottawa, Ontario. K1N 9K1. Annual since 1985.

Nickels, James B., ed. *Studies of Expected and Effected Mobility in Selected Resource Frontier Communities.* Project Work Force, Center for Settlement Studies, The University of Manitoba, Winnipeg, Manitoba. 163pp.

Nilles, Mary E. and Dorothy B. Simon. "New Approaches to the Multilingual, Multi-cultural Students in Your Library," *Catholic Library World,* Vol.55, No. 10 (May/June, 1984), pp.435–440.
Impassioned plea for a cosmopolitan, cross-cultural approach to school librarianship in the US.

Northern Libraries Bulletin (now the *Polar Libraries Bulletin*). Northern Libraries Colloquy. Currently edited and issued by Nancy Lesh, Library, University of Alaska-Anchorage, 1828 Bootlegger's Cove Road, Anchorage, AK 99501. (*See* Source Notes preceding this bibliography.)

Northern Libraries Colloquy. *Proceedings.* Biennial, various locations. (*See* Source Notes preceding this bibliography.)

Northwest Territories. Legislative Assembly. Special Committee on Education. *Learning, Tradition and Change in the Northwest Territories.* 1982. 168pp.

———— Department of Information. *Analysis of the Dene Language Information Review.* Prepared by M. Devine December, 1983. 50pp.

———— Education. *Language and Society.* (1983).

———— *Response to the Recommendations of the Task Force on Aboriginal Languages.* October, 21, 1986. 13pp.

Nowak, Michael. "Subsistence Trends in a Modern Eskimo Community," *Arctic,* Vol.28, No. 1 (March, 1975), pp.21–34.

O'Connell, Sheldon. "Television's Impact on the Eskimo," *North,* Vol.22, No. 6 (November/December, 1975), pp.34–37.

O'Connell, Sheldon. "Television and the Eskimo People of Frobisher Bay," *Arctic,* Vol.28, No. 3 (Sept, 1975), pp.155–158.

Okko, Marjatta. Professor, University of Tampere, Department of Library and Information Science, Finland. "Public Library Services in Sparsely

Populated Regions: Report on a Nordic Seminar in 1986," *Scandinavian Public Library Quarterly,* Vol.20, No. 1 (1987), pp.4–9.
Although not directly discussing library services to Saami areas, the points made are relevant for such services.

O'Neil, John D. *Is It Cool to Be an Eskimo? A study of Stress, Identity, Coping and Health among Canadian Inuit Young Adult Men.* Doctoral thesis, University of California at San Francisco, 1984, 321pp.UMI 84-11072.

Ong, Walter J. *Orality and Literacy, the Technology of the Word.* London and New York: Methuen, 1982.

Ontario Public Libraries Program Review. Special Task Force #9. *Native Library Services in Ontario.* Prepared by Obonsawin-Irwin Consulting Inc. under the direction of the Task Group on Native Library Services, Task Group #9. Ontario Public Libraries Program Review, 1981. 75pp.

Ontario Public Libraries: the Provincial Role in a Triad of Responsibilities. The Report of the Ontario Public Libraries Programme Review for the Ministry of Citizenship and Culture. August, 1982.

Opening the Literate Mind. (Three audiocassettes.) "Five Powerful radio half hours . . ." Western Media Concepts, Inc. POB 100215, Anchorage, AK 99510. Annotated.
This is a stimulating and wide-ranging discussion of kinds of literacy, and the evolution and implications of each for moderns. A lengthy, annotated reading list is also available, as well as a discussion guide.

Ortiz, Professor Roxanne Dunbar, and Simon Ortiz. *Traditional and Hard to Find Information Required by Members of American Indian Communities: What to Collect; How to Collect It; and Appropriate Format and Use.* A paper prepared for the White House Pre-Conference on Indian Library and Information, Denver, CO, October 19–22, 1978.

Paine, Robert, ed. *Patrons and Brokers of the East Arctic.* (Newfoundland Social and Economic Papers No. 2.) Institute of Social and Economic Research, Memorial Univ. of Newfoundland. Univ. of Toronto Press, (1971). 111pp.
Illustrates and discusses many variations of bicultural/bilingual "agents" for change in Native communities.

————— *The White Arctic, Anthropological Essays on Tutelage and Ethnicity.* (Newfoundland Social and Economic Papers No. 7.) Institute of Social and Economic Research, Memorial University of Newfoundland. Univ. of Toronto Press, (1977). 419pp.
A quoted personal communication in the preface sums up the emphasis of this excellent book about Native/White relations in the Canadian Arctic: "Don't waste your time with the Eskimos, it's the whites you should really be studying!" For example, Anne Brantenberg's chapter, "The Marginal School and the Children of Nain," is informative on the social and psychological split experienced by the Native child, between traditional ways at home and the acculturating ways of the white-staffed

school, between the Native language and the majority language in Fourth World education.

Pape, Marion L. "NWT Public Library Services: The Giant Leap to Resource Sharing," in: *Glaciological Data,* Report GD-22, INSTAAR Special Publication, 12th Northern Libraries Colloquy, 5–9 June, 1988 (Boulder, Colorado, USA). Edited by Ann M. Brennan and Martha Andrews. World Data Center for Glaciology (Snow and Ice), University of Colorado, Boulder. August, 1988.
An illuminating review of the development of library services in the Northwest Territories, with a complete description of the new, fully-automated union catalog that will be available in 23 communities in COM or CD-ROM form, and on-line in six regional centers, with a telecommunications network linking most if not all libraries in the NWT. Appendices provide technical details.

Parent, Elizabeth Anne. *The Educational Experiences of the Residents of Bethel, Alaska: An Historical Case Study.* Ph.D. dissertation, Stanford Univ., June, 1984.

Paris, Marion. *Library School Closings: Four Case Studies.* Metuchen, N.J.: Scarecrow Press, 1988. 168pp.

Pelto, Pertti J. *The Snowmobile Revolution and Social Change in the Arctic.* (The Kiste and Ogan Social Change Series in Anthropology, University of Minnesota.) Menlo Park, CA: Cummings Publishing Co., 1973.

Pelto, Pertti J. and Satu Mosnikoff. "Skolt Sami Ethnicity and Cultural Revival." *Ethnos,* 1978, pp.193–212.

Pelzman, Frankie. "Native American Libraries, Ten Years Later," *Wilson Library Bulletin,* April 1989, pp.58–61.
The U.S. National Commission on Libraries and Information Science (NCLIS) visits pueblo libraries in New Mexico.

Penna, Carlos Victor. "The Interaction between Education, Libraries and Mass Communication, as seen by a Librarian," *Unesco Bull. Libr.* XXVIII, No. 6 (Nov.-Dec., 1974), pp.311–314, 324.

Philie, Pierre. "Infirmières et Inuit: des valeurs différentes," (Nurses and Inuit: Some Differing Values) L'Infirmière canadienne, Vol.27, No. 5 (May, 1985), pp.29–32.

Phillips, Susan Urmston. Univ. of Arizona. *The Invisible Culture, Communication in Classroom and Community on the Warm Springs Indian Reservation.* (Research on Teaching Monograph Series.) New York: Longman, 1983. 147pp.

Price, Neville. "Recruiting Staff from Cultural Minority Groups," *Library Association Record,* Vol.85, No. 9 (Sept, 1983), pp.305–306.

Problems Affecting Band Library Development in Northern Ontario. A Brief to the Minister of Culture and Recreation for the Province of Ontario. Presented by the Joint Committee of Representatives of the Four Northern Regional Library Systems and Grand Council Treaty #9. Nov, 1977. 8pp.

Puiguitkaat, The 1978 Elders Conference. Transcription and Translation by Kisautaq-Leona Okakok. Edited and photographed by Gary Kean. North Slope Borough, Commission on History and Culture. (Barrow, Alaska, 1981). 653pp.

Putnam, John J. "Greenland Feels the Winds of Change." Photographs by George F. Mobley. *National Geographic,* Sept, 1975, pp.366–393.
Topical theme is uncertainty and despair over loss of traditional Greenlandic ways.

Québec. Secrétariat des activités gouvernementales en milieu amerindien et inuit (SAGMAI). *Native Peoples of Quebec.* 1984. 172pp.

Raycroft, Lois. "The Yukon Indian Resource Center." *Proceedings* of the 8th Northern Libraries Colloquy, Edmonton and Whitehorse, June 1–6, 1980. (Miscellaneous Publications, Boreal Institute for Northern Studies, Univ. of Alberta, Edmonton.)

Reid, Sean. "Alaska Calling, Telegraphs to Satellite Transponders . . . Technology Tackles Alaska's Age-old Problem of Long-distance Communication," *Alaska Magazine,* May, 1982.

Report of the Task Force on Library Service to Native People. (Canadian Library Association), October, 1986. 13pp.

Report of the Task Force on Aboriginal Languages. Government of the Northwest Territories. February 28, 1986. 54pp.
The Report is in English, with a reverse duplicate section in Inuit syllabics. Executive summaries in several other NWT aboriginal languages. (For the Government's Response, see herein under: Northwest Territories. Response of the Government, etc.)

Report to the "Ontario Public Library Review on Native Library Services in Ontario." Prepared by the Obonsawin-Irwin Consulting Inc. under the direction of the Task Group on Native Library Services. Convenor, Earl Commanda. Nov, 1981.

Reymann, Ase. The Royal Library, Copenhagen. "Arctic Library Resources in Denmark—on Library Research and on the 'Grondlandsk avis-og Tidsskriftindex'," *Proceedings,* 9th Northern Libraries Colloquy, Tromso, 1982. pp.150–167.

Richardson, J. "Libraries and the Neoliterate," *Int. Lib. Rev.* Vol.15 (1983), pp.9–13.

Riesman, David. "The Oral and Written Traditions," *Explorations* 6 (1956), No. 2, pp.22–28.

Rowley, Graham. "The Canadian Eskimo Today," *The Polar Record* Vol.16 (1972), No. 101, pp.201–205.

Ruth, Grace W. "Selecting Children's Books to meet Multicultural Needs," *Catholic Library World* Vol.55, No. 4 (Nov, 1983), pp.169–173.
Practical advice with specific organizations and sources cited.

Salabiye, Velma S. "Library and Information Services, pp.197–232, Chapter 8 in: *Community-based Research, A Handbook for Native Americans,* by Susan Guyette. University of California, Los Angeles: American Indian Studies Center, (1983).

Schaefer, Otto. "Eskimo Personality and Society—Yesterday and Today," *Arctic* Vol.28, No. 2 (June, 1975), pp.87–91.

Schuurman, Hubert J.C. *Canada's Eastern Neighbor, A View of Change in Greenland.* Indian and Northern Affairs, Canada. 1977. 103pp.

Scollon, Ron. "Communicative style and research style: a problem in discovery, application and reportage." A paper presented at the 40th Annual Meeting of the Society of Applied Anthropology, March 19–22, 1980, Denver.

————— "Gatekeeping: access or retention?" Working Papers in Sociolinguistics, No. 59. Austin: Southwest Educational Development Laboratory.

————— "Human knowledge and the institution's knowledge." Final Report to the National Institute of Education.

Scollon, Ron (with Suzanne B.K. Scollon). "Cooking it up and boiling it down: abstracts in Athabascan children's story retellings," in: *Coherence in Spoken and Written Discourse,* by Deborah Tannen, ed. Norwood, NJ: Ablex Publishing Corporation.

————— "Ethnic stereotyping: some problems in Athabascan-English interethnic communication," *Method: Alaska perspectives,* Vol.2, No. 2, pp.15–17.

————— "Face in interethnic communication," in: *Language and Communication,* by Jack Richards and Richard Schmidt, eds. London: Longman.

————— "Literacy as focused interaction," *Newsletter of the Laboratory of Comparative Human Cognition,* Vol.2, No. 2, pp.26–29.

————— *Narrative, Literacy and Face in Interethnic Communication.* ABLEX, 1981. 209pp.(Vol.VII in the Series: Advances in Discourse Processes. Roy O. Freedle, ed.)

————— "The Problem of Language Problems in Alaska." (Alaska Native Language Center, Univ. of Alaska, Fairbanks). April, 1982.

————— "The Role of Audience in the Structure of Athabascan Oral Performance." (Alaska Native Language Center, Univ. of Alaska, Fairbanks.) Paper presented at the XLIII International Congress of Americanists, Vancouver, Aug 15, 1979.

Scott-Stevens, Susan R. *Foreign Consultants and Counterparts: Cross-Cultural Problems in the Transfer of Technical Knowledge.* Ph.D. Dissertation, Univ. of Colorado at Boulder. 1986. Ann Arbor, MI: University Microfilms International.
Study of the actual personal relations between consultants and their indigenous colleagues in 3rd World projects. Useful bibliography.

Scribner, Sylvia, and Michael Cole. "Unpackaging Literacy," *Social Science Information,* Vol.17, No. 1, pp.19–40.

Senungetuk, Joseph E. *Give or Take a Century, An Eskimo Chronicle.* San Francisco, CA: The Indian Historian Press, 1971. 198pp.

Shah, Aruna. "The Positive and the Negative of Multiethnic Provision," *Library Association Record,* Vol.86, No. 5 (May, 1984, pp.215 and 217.

Sharr, F.A. State Librarian for Western Australia. "Functions and Organization of a Rural Library System," *Unesco Bulletin for Libraries,* Vol.26, No. 1 (Jan–Feb, 1972), pp.2–7.

Simonson, Rick and Scott Walker. *The Graywolf Annual Five: Multicultural Literacy, Opening the American Mind.* St. Paul: Graywolf Press, 1988. This is a useful collection of articles by American writers of various nationalities (including Native American and Hispanic), trying to describe their respective ethnic outlook toward writing, learning and the dominant Caucasian, northern European society of North America.

Singer, Charles, E.J. Holmyard and A.R. Hall. *A History of Technology.* London: Oxford Univ. Press, 1954, Vol.I, pp.102–106.

Smith, Derek G. *Natives and Outsiders: Pluralism in the Mackenzie River Delta, NWT.* Ministry of Indian and Northern Affairs, Information Canada, Ottawa, 1975. 173pp.

Smith, Lorne. "The Mechanical Dog Team: A Study of the Ski-Doo in the Canadian Arctic," *Arctic Anthropology,* IX-1 (1972), pp.1–9.

Smith, Lotsee. "Affirmative Action for Native American Librarians and Library Workers," in: *Affirmative Action Handbook,* edited by John F. Harvey and Elizabeth M. Dickinson. Metuchen, NJ and London: The Scarecrow Press, Inc. 1983, pp.200–205.

Spencer, Albert Franklin. *A Perception Study of the Accomplishment of the Goals for Indian Library and Information Service in American Educational Institutions.* Ph.D. dissertation, Florida State Univ., 1985. 197pp.

Steinbring, Jack, Gary Granzberg, Cecil Pereira and Christopher Hanks. *The Impact and Meaning of Television among Native Communities in Northern Manitoba.* Univ. of Winnipeg, 1979. 253pp.

Tennant, Edward, and Audrey Kolb, consultants. *The Yukon-Kuskokwim Village Library Project, An Evaluative Study.* "Prepared for Kuskokwim Community College and the Alaska State Library." January 8, 1984. 93pp.

Thiel, Mark. *Native American Archives.* (Published in mid-1980s, and updated periodically.) Available from: Educational Services Institute, 5201 Leesburg Pike, Suite 600, Falls Church, VA 22041. Mr. Thiel has experience in developing archives for tribes and conducts periodic workshops for ESI around the US. On museums, he provided the author with a "Directory of North American Indian Museums and Cultural Centers," issued by the North American Indian Museums Association.

Tlen, Daniel L. *Speaking Out: Consultations and Survey of Yukon Native Languages Planning, Visibility and Growth.* "Prepared for the Government of Yukon and the Council for Yukon Indians. Whitehorse, Yukon. August, 1986." 76pp.

Totten, Herman L. "A Survey and Evaluation of Minority Programs in Selected Graduate Library Schools," *Journal of Education for Librarianship,* Vol.18 (1977), No. 1, pp.18–34.

TRAILS. *Final Report.* Training and Assistance for Indian Library Services (TRAILS). School of Library and Information Studies, the Univ. of Oklahoma, Norman, OK. Lotsee Paterson, Program Director. Sept. 10, 1985–Jan. 10, 1987. Produced as part of contract no. 300–85–0162, USDE. Office of Educational Research and Improvement, Library Programs.

———— *Tribal Library Administration Procedures Manual.* An excellent guide and reference for Native library management. Available from: Library Programs, OERI, U.S. Dept. of Eduation, 555 New Jersey Ave., NW, Washington, D.C. 20208.

Tundra Drums (newspaper). Weekly. POB 868, Bethel, AK 99559. Award-winning newspaper serving the residents of 50-odd Yupik Eskimo villages of the Yukon-Kuskokwim delta in western Alaska.

"TV—Better than Shaking Tents and Dreams," *Psychology Today,* March 1978, p. 109.

TV ONTARIO. *North of 60: Destiny Uncertain.* (television series in 13 parts). Ontario Educational Communications Authority. 1983.
A comprehensive survey of northern development in Canada, and the problems and issues it is producing. TV ONTARIO has also produced a number of other video programs and films on northern development and the Native Peoples.

US Bureau of Indian Affairs. *BIA Plan for the Improvement of Library/Media/Information Programs.* "Working Draft for initial action and discussion through the White House Pre-Conference on Indian Library and Information Services On or Near Reservations," Denver, CO, October 19–22, 1978.

US Center for Information and Library Services, US Dept. of the Interior. *Self-Determination Requires Information Power.* "The Report of Record on the White House Pre-Conference on Indian Library and Information Services On or Near Reservations," Denver, CO, October 19–22, 1978.

US Peace Corps. Office of Programming and Training Coordination. *Cross-Cultural Training for Peace Corps Volunteers, Core Curriculum Resource Materials.* December, 1981; April, 1982.

Vanderburgh, Rosamond M. "When Legends Fall Silent Our Ways Are Lost: Some Dimensions of the Study of Aging among Native Canadians," *Culture* (II) 1, 1982, p.21–28.
Citing the heterogeneity of broad Native groupings, the variety of aging situations, and increased urbanization, the author describes ways Ojibwa elders have been integrated back into traditional roles and status through programs of the Ojibwa Cultural Center on Lake Huron.

Vaudrin, Bill. "Native/Non-Native Communication: Creating a Two-Way Flow," in: *Cultural Influences in Alaskan Native Education,* edited by James Orvik and Ray Barnhardt. Center for Northern Educational Research, Univ. of Alaska, Fairbanks, 1974, pp.71–84.

Video in Libraries—an International Perspective, edited by Paul McNally,

IFLA Round Table on Audiovisual Media. (AV in action—5.) The Hague: Nederlands Bibliotheek en Lektuur Centrum, 1985. 121pp.
Although no articles deal specifically with TV in Native communities, there is much of interest in this interesting issue which includes a lengthy article on the comprehensive and Canadian audiovisual database, FORMAT, accessible through the database service, UTLAS (University of Toronto Library Automated Systems). Coordinated by the Canadian National Film Board and with many contributing members, it is described in a videocassette offered by the NFB.

Waddell, Eric. "The Hazards of Scientism: A Review Article" (review of the book, *Natural Hazards: Local, National, Global,* by Gilbert F. White), *Human Ecology,* Vol.5 (1977), No. 1, pp.69–76.
The book reviewed discusses "natural hazards" from the western scientific approach of "conquering nature," or at least controlling if not besting it, whereas the reviewer points out that, for traditional peoples who endured and thrived for millenia within the given environmental conditions of their ancestral domain, so-called "natural hazards" were in fact normal, and described a mostly dependable and supportive habitat and homeland . . .

. . . the basic assumptions and method [used by the author] are appropriate to the type of society for which they were originally conceived—a Western, urban-industrial, capitalist state characterized by a resolutely anti-environmentalist ideology, a population that both is massively mobile and has lost most of its sensitivity to the natural world, and a central government whose responsibility for managing environmental problems is ill-defined. The approach suits literate people, who are accustomed to thinking abstractly with respect to preferences and choices and whose reality is in flux. . . . [It] loses all credibility when it is applied to rural communities in other cultures, that is, unless one's view of the Third World is an ethnocentrically developmental one whereby traditional societies are regarded as incapable of coping with natural hazards and therefore as dependent on modernization and the transfer of know-how and technology for their future.

Wasserman, Paul. "Professional Adaptation: Library Education Mandate," *Library Journal,* April 1, 1970, pp.1281–1288.
Written during the anti-war and minority rights ferment of the 1960s in the U.S., this long essay, originally a speech to students, should be required reading for everyone wondering why change is needed in the library field. Its impassioned yet measured plea is, unfortunately, still timely and still a "voice in the wilderness."

Westermann, Hans. "Det Grondlandsk Biblioteksvaesen—et Historisk rids og lidt om Biblioteksvaesenets situation idog og imorgen." (place, date unknown, 1978?)
———Central Librarian, Greenland. "Greenland's Library Service through 150 Years," *Scandinavian Public Library Quarterly,* Vol.14 (1981), No. 1, pp.16–19.

The earliest historical details of Greenland library service are found in the *Scandinavian Public Library Quarterly,* Vol.2 (1969), nos.2 and 3.

———— Head of Godthab Public Library, Greenland. "Greenland's New National Library," *Scandinavian Public Library Quarterly,* Vol.9 (1976), nos.3–4, pp.98–101.

———— "Gronlands nye landsbibliotek" (Greenland's New National Library), *Bogens Verden,* 9/76.

———— "Libraries in Greenland," *Proceedings,* 5th Northern Libraries Colloquy, Rovaniemi, 1975, pp.149–153.

Westermann, Hans and Benny Hoyer, Librarians, Greenland National Library. "Changes in the National Library of Greenland," *Proceedings,* "Arctica," 7th Northern Libraries Colloquy, Paris, 1978, pp.273–277.

Whittington, M.S. "Territorial Bureaucracy: Trends in Public Administration in the NWT," *Canadian Public Administration,* Vol.27, No. 2 (Summer, 1984), pp.242–252.

Wilson, Thomas Clark. *The Role of Television in the Eastern Arctic: An Educational Perspective.* Master of Arts Thesis in Educational Technology, Concordia University, Montreal, Quebec. May, 1981. 151pp.

Yeh, Thomas Yen-Ran. "The Treatment of the American Indian in the Library of Congress E-F Schedule," *Library Resources and Technical Services,* Vol.15, No. 2 (Spring, 1971), pp.122–128.

Yukon Department of Education. Libraries and Archives Board. *Annual Report 1985/86.*

Zee, Nicholas and Marianne Winglee. *Who Reads Literature? The Future of the U.S. as a Nation of Readers.* Santa Ana, Calif.:Seven Locks, 1990.

Source Notes II
Supplemented and Updated
through late 1995

In late 1994 and early 1995 I began updating the original manuscript, though I had been collecting citations of new materials since 1990. At the University of Alaska, Anchorage, I searched the following computer databases: POLARPAC, COLD REGIONS, DISSERTATION ABSTRACTS ONDISC, and ERIC. POLAR PAC and COLD REGIONS are comprised of a number of northern databases, and one has to keep up with their growth and scope.

Then LISA was searched at cost with the help of the Suzzallo Library at the University of Washington, using terms reflecting this book's subtitle. This produced some 50-odd pages of annotated citations. The results were mixed though stimulating, and provided several new citations for the Source List below. Multicultural diversification and racism awareness in library education and the library profession were prominent, both in essays and conferences. LISA draws on some 450 journals. The search terms used are crucial, and any but the most concrete can misfire. Take the word "indigenous." Here are some uses of that word in abstracts that make life difficult for a computer search person: "... The U.S. needs to develop an indigenous strategy for . . ."; " . . . indigenous to (computer) program techniques . . . " ; ". . . a U.S. indigenous (church) denomination. . . ." But the worst example was the following: "A key to this search is the construction of a paradigm which engulfs a set of objects that is genuinely indigenous to MIS (Management Information Systems)."

I didn't go to more general social sciences databases or search terms because, although southern Canada and the U.S. "Lower 48" are selectively examined, either geographically or topically, this would have produced an unwieldy quantity of citations, and my approach is already quite interdisciplinary. Primary emphasis is on the north, and the scope is circumpolar. Of course, if by chance or through serendipity I noted something stimulating and relevant, I included it. I'm only human, and the elusive nature of the subject, like the intriguing effects of eating the cake had for Alice, suiting her for entry into Lewis Carroll's Wonderland, made me "curiouser and curiouser." For example, I discovered that the Directory of Awards, Fiscal Year 1994, of the (U.S.) National Science Foundation, entitled *Arctic Science, Engineering, and Education,* describes several current projects on cross-cultural issues around the circumpolar north.

The fall 1993 issue of *American Indian Libraries Newsletter* features "Native Networks." *Igloo Station,* Montreal, focuses on North American Indians but includes other indigenous peoples and has a message conference. *Dakota BBS* Rapid City, South Dakota, "promotes the self-sufficiency of American Indians and rural people." "NATIVEPROFS is a listerv for and about the American Indian and Alaska Native Professoriate." Those using it should be members of this organization. Arizona State University at Tempe is the sponsor. ENAN stands for Educational Native American Network and is sponsored by the U.S. Bureau of Indian Affairs; it is based at the University of New Mexico's Center for Technology and Education. It has e-mail, on-line conferences, access to ENAN libraries for downloading data, and interactive activities. *TRAILS* is a listerv at the University of Oklahoma's School of Library and Information Studies. The moderator is Dr. Lotsee Patterson, and prospective subscribers should contact her. More details are found in the *AILA* newsletter cited. *Ethnic newswatch* is a CD-ROM full text database for all minorities and includes periodicals. One should always assume the possibility of new computer databases and networks and never cease being on the lookout for them. Finally, I learned of the listserv *Native-L,* which is a "discussion list on issues pertaining to aboriginal people's," according to the *EMIE Bulletin* of ALA's Ethnic Materials and Information Exchange Round Table Spring 1994 issue. Finally, the March, 1995 issue of *Multicultural Review* has an article entitled "Multicultural Resources on the Internet," by Trudi E. Jacobson, and on p.47 of the article more forums, lists, and gopher sites for Native American studies are listed.

Bibliography/Reference List II Supplement and Updated through late 1995

Active, John. "Concept of Individuality devastates Native Tradition". *Anchorage Daily News,* p.B8, under Letters/Forum feature. September 16, 1992
   Native traditions of cooperation, communal sharing, respect for elders and learning by observation have been eroded, challenged and even punished in the non-Native educational system, which emphasizes competition between individuals toward a hierarchy of power and control. (The Yupik 'code' entails personal modesty, mutual respect, and an unwillingness to interfere--GHH) John Active is a Yupik news reporter for KYUK (Bethel, Alaska) radio and television, a storyteller, and cultural interpreter. His narrations have also been aired on National Public Radio.

Agranat, G.A. "Korennoe Naselenie Alyaski i Kanadskogo Severa: Sovremennye Sotsial'no-Ekonomicheskie i Politicheskie Problemy" (The native population of Alaska and the Canadian north: present-day socioeconomic and political problems). *Sovetskaya Etnografiya* (Soviet Ethnography), No.6, 1982, p.66–80

Alaska Native Tourism Council. *Alaska Native Journey,* A Special Guide on where and how to meet Alaska's friendly and fascinating native people. (periodical) Several pages. Alaska Native Tourism Council, 1577 C Street, Suite 304, Anchorage, AK 99501.
   This attractive, large format publication exemplifies efforts of Native communities and organizations throughout Alaska to garner jobs, income and goodwill from tourism in Native areas, which is bound to expand. A wide variety of tours and events are described, including transportation and accomodations. Illustrated.

Alaska Natives Guide to Anchorage. Municipality of Anchorage. SAFE City Program and the Anchorage Native Concerns Committee. (1994) 36pp.

A typical guide to services available for urban Natives or any other minority. The variety of basic as well as special services reflects the difficulties of city life. Includes "safety tips" and one library entry under "Points of Interest," with a phone number.

Alaska (State). Department of Education, Division of State Libraries, Archives and Museums. *Statistics of Alaska Public Libraries, FY 1992 and FY 1993 with FY 1988-FY 1993 Comparisons.* Compiled by Mary Jennings. 1995. 79pp

American Library Association. *Handbook of Organization, 1988–89.* Minority Concerns Policy. "Six Goals for Indian Library and Information Services."

American Library Association. Office for Library Personnel Resources. *Library Personnel News.* Bimonthly. Chicago, IL.
Don't be discouraged by the dry title of this newsletter. For any library system concerned to improve their personnel profile and capabilities, in all respects, this is an indispensable resource. The OPLR advises and makes available a variety of materials.

Beck, David. *The Chicago American Indian Community, 1893–1988,* Annotated bibliography and Guide to Sources in Chicago. Chicago: NAES College Press, 1988.
Illustrative of the extent and variety of Native community life in a large city, and where the documentation of it can be found.

Belay, G. "Conceptual Strategies for Operationalizing Multicultural Curricula," *Journal of Education for Library and Information Science* 33:4 (Fall, 1992) p.295–306
Attempts to define multiculturalism, as it relates to libraries, and as opposed to the "epistemological universality" that has reigned heretofore, encompassing "ethnocentrism" and "cultural monolothicism." I have some difficulty with jargon like "operationalization", but then it's sometimes hard for me to keep up with these newly coined words.

Bigelow, Jane M. H. "Library and Information Services for Native Americans," *Multicultural Review* 3:4 (Dec. '94) p.20–24
This is a brief, excellent review of the literature, citing many of the problem areas associated with library services to Natives and Indians, and that persist to this day. In fact, it is only now that most of them are being effectively addressed.

Biggs, Mary and Victor Biggs. "Library and Information Science Faculty: their Lives as Scholars," *Library Quarterly,* 63:3 (1993) p.282–317.

The authors found that "In job satisfaction, research collegiability, publishing volume, professional activity, respect for their own literature, and sophistication of library use, they are similar or superior." (to faculty from the humanities and social sciences). The data are "self-reported", but even so "it would seem that the criticism directed at library schools and their faculties is either naive or prejudiced, insofar as it assumes higher faculty standards and stronger faculty performance in the more traditional 'soft' disciplines." The authors have replicated a similar 1985 survey by the American Council of Learned Societies "survey of scholars." In both of these, one has the impression of an inside evaluation of one's colleagues that begs objectivity and output measures.

Blair, Maude. "Native Professionals face Icy Reception upon returning Home to work," *Anchorage Daily News,* October 30, 1994 (Lifestyles section feature, entitled "Reconciling Two Worlds"), p. M1, M2
     Conflicting emotions confront the Native specialist returning to the home village: distrust, jealousy, resentment, accusations of having 'become White', of placing individual status above the community, youth above elders, etc. The benefits include being a resident role model for the young, serving as a resource person and cross-cultural interpreter, potential leadership, being completely at home in the Native language (if still spoken) and community pride in a son or daughter, raised in the village and known to all, come home to live and work.

Boulanger, Andre. "Le centre de documentation du Grand Conseil des Cris du Quebec" (The Documentation Centre of the Quebec Grand Council of Crees), *Documentation et Bibliotheques* October–December 1987 (33:4) p.127–129.
     "The Council was set up in 1974 to assist and defend the political interests of the Cree Indians. The Documentation Centre dates from 1981: material is divided into three sections—a library, a map library, and archives." The Centre has developed its own cataloging and classification systems. (abstract) The article is in French.

Boyce, Bert R. "The Death of Library education," *American Libraries* March, 1994 p.257–259
     Advocates tougher and consistent accreditation standards for all graduate library schools, to improve their overall performance as educators of professionals.

Bringing us Together: A Selected Resource Guide to Cultural Diversity Activities in the Library Community. 1992: American Library Association, President's Committee on Cultural Diversity, Chicago, IL.
     This booklet includes the 1992 ALA Summer Conference program

schedule on "Cultural Diversity," activities in a variety of libraries, library schools and other organizations in cultural sensitivity and recruitment of minorities, and a list of consultants specializing in cultural diversity assistance.

Brody, Hugh. *The People's Land,* Eskimos and Whites in the Eastern Arctic. Harmondsworth, Middlesex, England: Penguin Books, 1975.
Useful and stimulating look at living conditions and White-Native relations before the current period of self-determination and land claims settlement began.

Brown, Lorene B. "Students Admission and Multicultural Recruitment," *Journal of Library Administration* 16: 1/2 (1992), p.109–122
"Explores the utilization of demographic patterns of minority students as a tool for the management of student admission and multicultural recruitment." (abstract)

Burgess, Roxanne, Coordinator. *American Indian Community Survey,* Summary. Presbyterian Church (USA), 1988.
Over 800 respondents provided detailed information on the Los Angeles area Indian community. The purpose was to learn interest in Presbyterian or ecumenical worship, but information of interest to other service organizations was obtained. Two thirds were women, unemployment was about 50%, 70% were high school graduates, almost all wanted to have an Indian community center and two-thirds wanted "to be more aware of issues affecting Indian people." Over *120* tribes from all over the USA were represented. The total Indian population of Los Angeles County was variously estimated at around 100,000, or about 1%, with Indians/Natives comprising a disproportionate 5% of those on "Skid Row", according to Tom Lippert of the American Indian Resource Center in Huntington Park.

California Powwow (periodical) Karen Wright, Publisher-Editor, POB 359, Brisbane, CA 94005-0359. Issued every six months or so, continuously updated.
Exhaustive guide to Native American events and resources in California. In June, 1992, for example, 51 events were scheduled. Lists books, bookstores, cultural and social services, museums, library and information centers specializing in Native Americana, radio and television shows, films and videos, magazines and newspapers, stores and vendors of Native American fare, etc. This is a model guide for any state, province, national area, or metropolitan region.

Chadley, Otis A. "Addressing Cultural Diversity in Academic and Research Libraries," *College and Research Libraries,* 53:3 (May, 1992), p.206–213

Discusses the current state of affairs and reports on a survey conducted of academic libraries by the author in 1991. Recruitment of librarians, services to students and collection development are reviewed, and suggestions offered. The situation has improved, but much remains to be done. "A culturally diverse library environment is its own best marketing tool to attract diverse groups to the library and to librarianship." (concluding sentence)

Chavers, Dean. "The Native Media are Growing," *Glacier Reporter* "Official Publication of Browning and the Blackfeet Reservation" (Browning, MT) October 27, 1994 p.15 (under the feature "Around the Campfire.")
Reviews the history of Indian journalism in the US. Also looks at Indian/Native radio and television, journalism education and the Native American Journalism Association. Indian computer networks, new, few in number and struggling, are briefly mentioned. The most viable and active ones seem to be regional in scope.

Chen, C. "Computer Technology to Preserve and Access endangered Oral History Recordings in Alaska," *Microcomputers for Information Management* 1992 (9:3), p.191–195.
"Describes Project Jukebox, a multimedia computer system providing access to the oral history collection of (6000 individual audio and video) recordings of Alaska's history through the University of Alaska, native historical recordings, pioneer accounts, interviews with political figures and recollections of important events." (abstract) See also Chugach Conference herein.

Cherkasov, Arkady Ivanovitch. "Environmental Problems and Native Self-Government: Northern Peoples in the Russian Federation and Canada," *Musk-Ox* No.40 (1994; Final issue of *Musk-Ox.*) p. 54–58
After citing the major environmental responsibility Russia and Canada have in possessing about one fifth of the earth's land surface and forty percent of the entire Arctic, the author emphasizes the need for northern Native populations to be in charge of the fragile lands and waters they occupy, especially because they have a tradition of 'sustainable' development of natural resources. Hence the need for new educational institutions, to train Natives in essential administrative and technological skills. A major feature of the article is a two-page chart showing "aboriginal" peoples of the circumpolar north, and separately of Russia, giving location, population, (and additionally for the latter) language, number speaking Russian or their Native tongue, name of autonomous homeland, percentage who live in their homeland, and percentage of Natives to the total population of their home area.

Cherkasov, A.I. "Nunavut: The Canadian Experiment in Territorial Determination," *Polar Geography and Geology,* Vol.17 (1993), No.1 p.64–71
  Description of Nunavut negotiations and future administration and development of this new territorial government. Suggests that Russian entities should consider entering into joint ventures directly with Nunavut, rather than going through NWT or Canadian government. See also: "Formal Signing . . . " , and Dickerson, listed herein.

Christenson, John. "Native American Radio Stations," *American Indian Libraries Newsletter* (17:4) Summer, 1995 p.1–2
  Brief article that discusses the American Public Broadcasting Consortium's "new national, two-hour daily call-in talk show, news and cultural events radio program on Native American concerns." Listed are twenty-seven Native American community radio stations with addresses and frequencies that air the show, which is called *American Indian Radio on Satellite* (AIROS).

(The) Chugach Conference: Finding our Way in the Communication Age (3rd). 1991. Produced by the University of Alaska, Anchorage Department of Journalism and Public Communication.
  "The Chugach Conferences on the future of communication in Alaska are working conferences in which participants play as important a role as the speakers." Three have taken place thus far: 1989, 1990 and 1991. None have been planned through 1995, but one may be considered in the future, dependent on funding. For our purposes, the following presentations are of special interest.
  1990: Communication and Alaska Natives; The Issue is Control, Northern Communications in Canada; The Yugtarvik Museum Project (Using Hypercard and bilingual audio to produce a multimedia computer program for public education in the Central Yupik region, and elsewhere. The same approach is being used to produce Yup'ik language learning programs at the Kuskokwim Campus, UAF, Bethel, under the direction of Prof. Barry Sponder); Yupik Science.
  1991: Project Jukebox: 'We are digitizing our oral history . . . ' Broadcasting as a tool for Social Change.

Collis, Dirmid R.F. *Arctic Languages,* An Awakening. Unesco. 1990: Paris. 458 pp. Figures, maps and tables.
  Compendious guide to the subject, with historical sketches, numbers of speakers and location of homelands, status of oral and written language, use in the media, schools, etc. Latest citations are 1986–87, and Russian Arctic material is older than that on Alaska, Canada, Greenland and the Saami area by several years, reflecting theory and practice well before the Gorbachev era, easily spotted by utopian

assertions and the familiar Communist hyperbole about progress and happiness in a socialist state.

Condon, Richard G. *Inuit Youth: Growth and Change in the Canadian Arctic.* (Volume I, Adolescents in a Changing World Series) New Brunswick, NJ: Rutgers University Press, 1987.
    A cross-cultural study of teenagers in Holman, an Inuit community on Victoria Island in the west central Canadian high arctic. Useful for understanding changes and stresses that acculturating Eskimo adolescents are experiencing, and the implications for library and related services, although these are not mentioned directly. 'Adolescence' as a period of life and adolescents as a social class probably didn't exist in aboriginal or early post-contact communities, when subsistence, Native language use and the elders' value system and leadership were dominant. Physical maturation was much more closely matched with social acceptance and initiation into adulthood. Today, schooling, technological 'toys' (including TV programming), and the greater security of larger towns and modernization help to prolong childhood and create 'adolescence' sociologically. Greater anonymity, decreasing social cohesion, boredom and unemployment bring a sharp rise in anti-social and self-destructive behavior, primarily among young males.

Connerton, Paul. *How Societies Remember.* (Series: Themes in the Social Sciences) Cambridge UP, 1989.
    Cognitive and habitual social memory, through recurring ritual and concretely entrenching habits of dress and movement have conveyed ethnic identity from the past to the present (cult-enacted; 'collective autobiography' as an image of the past). But modernity in capitalism obliterates linkages with the past, and a disconnectedness comes to characterize newly formulated ritual. The implications for indigenous societies entering modern, westernizing society are chaotic and devastating. Of particular interest is the chapter entitled "Bodily Practices", which discusses both 'inscribing' and 'incorporating' bodily processes or experiences that condition the human body per se to new cultural capabilities and expectations. Looking at rituals, ceremony, habitual cultural actions and oral traditions of aboriginal communities, it is to be expected that the European written and scientific tradition will overlook the aboriginal record, and relegate its heritage to oblivion, or, at best, distort and selectively focus on fragmented and residual aspects.

Craige, Betty Jean. *Reconnection, Dualism to Holism in Literary Study.* Athens: Univ. of Georgia Press, 1988.
    Stimulating for anyone concerned with the status of library education, although she looks at academe as a whole, and her specialty is literary studies. She argues that the time of encapsulated and isolated academic

disciplines is declining, and the need for an interdisciplinary, generalist approach is at hand, a trend that began in the 1960s. Her discussions of the influence of the printing press and television on learning and our world-view are also illuminating for a librarian. "Literature has been merged into television, where the line between fiction and reality is 'only a frame away', when we are told the name of the program." A homogeneity is produced by the unchanging television viewing setting, and the fact that ads introduce and close each TV 'show'.

Cruikshank, Julia, "in collaboration with Angela Sydney, Kitty Smith, and Annie Ned." *Life Lived like a Story,* Life Stories of Three Yukon Native Elders. Lincoln:University of Nebraska Press, 1990.
    Good acculturating material for non-Natives who want to understand Native behaviors, thoughts and feelings, and the importance of life-storytelling. Many other such accounts by Native/Indian women are being published, and are noted and reviewed by such periodicals as *Multicultural Review.*

Cunningham, Keith. *American Indians' Kitchen-Table Stories,* Contemporary conversations with Cherokee, Sioux, Hopi, Osage, Navajo, Zuni, and members of other nations. (Series: American Folklore Series. W.K. McNeil, Gen Ed.) Little Rock, Arkansas: August House Publishers, 1992
    If you don't have Indian friends, and haven't lived on a reservation, this book is useful for getting acquainted with Indian thinking, manners and values. Illuminating for urban non-Indian librarians working with Indians/Natives. Topics covered include stories, medicine, legends, humor, cross-cultural considerations, and the "untranslatable."

Curtis, Jean-M. et al. "Symposium on the Summary Report of the White House Conference on Library and Information Services: Library and Information Services for the 21st Century," *Government Information Quarterly,* Vol.9 (1992), No.3, p. 323–363
    "Eight articles discuss the ramifications of the summary report of the 1991" conference. All perspectives are covered, including those of Native American library services. "47 references."

"Dean's List; 10 School Heads debate the Future of Library Education," Editors, *LJ. Library Journal* 119:6 (1994) p.60–64
    The field is in "tumult and transition," reducing its ties both to librarianship and to libraries per se, and the MLS degree is "exploding" into a growing array of specializations. But all the school heads were confident about the future of "information education."

Deaton, Deborah. "Schools try 'Yup'ik (sic) Way of Teaching', Bethel-area kids to get more traditional culture," *Anchorage Daily News,* July, 17, 1995. p.B1, B2.

With the help of Native leaders and Elders, the Lower Kuskokwim School District is completely overhauling the Yupik curriculum in its schools. Subjects taught in the Yup'ik language will be integrated, so that math, language, science and social studies will all be applied to studies of the Yupik way of life. A high percentage of students are Yup'ik-speaking, and a Yup'ik orthography has been taught for several years. The new method is similiar to one used in Canada. Dialectal differences and new science and math terminology in Yup'ik are being resolved.

Deer, A Brian. *Final Report of the Organization of the Files of the Kahnwake Combined School Committee.* August 31, 1990.

On procedures and method used in organizing the records of the school, which is located in the Mohawk community of Kanehsatake.

Dickerson, Mark O. "Commentary: A Blueprint for Change in the NWT?" *Arctic,* 45:3 (Sept, '92) p.iii–iv

The Beatty Report commissioned by the Northwest Territories government points out the 'overgoverned' status of the NWT (pop.56,000), with a budget of $1.1. billion and 6,000 employees. The need for decentralization and regionalization is underlined, and the creation of Nunavut may be the trend of the future. The government in Yellowknife needs to consolidate departments and perhaps the NWT needs to divide further.

Duran, Cheryl. "The Role of Libraries in American Indian Tribal College Development," *College and Research Libraries* September, 1991 (52:5) p.395–406.

"Presents a mode for assessing the role libraries play in meeting the institutional goals and objectives . . . " (abstract)

"Empowering People through Libraries." Library Services for Saskatchewan, Aboriginal Peoples Conference. Conference *Proceedings.* Coordinator, Lynne Hunks. 41 pp

"Copies of this publication available from: Saskatchewan Indian Cultural Centre, Library and Information Services, 401 Packham Place, Saskatoon, Saskatchewan S7N 2T7."

Evans-Pritchard, E.E. *Theories of Primitive Religion.* Oxford: Clarendon Press, 1965.

Of interest is the chapter entitled "Levi-Bruhl", p.78–99, which, as well as summarizing his theory on the nature of the aboriginal mind, comments on criticisms of Levi-Bruhl's position, and how it changed over time.

Fienup-Riordan, Ann. *Eskimo Essays: Yupik Lives and How We See Them.* Brunswick, NJ: Rutgers Univ. Press, 1990.
A very readable collection of writings by the well-known and well-published anthropologist of the Central Yupik Eskimo area. By looking at the subject from a variety of popular aspects, from media reinterpretation (movies and plays about "Eskimos", etc.) to the Yupiit Nation sovereignty movement, she connects aboriginal and post-contact traditions with modern Yupik lives trying to survive within a dominant outside society's persistently invasive culture.

Fitzhugh, William W. editor. *Cultures in Contact,* The European Impact on Native Cultural Institutions in Eastern North America, A.D. 1000–1800. 1985:Smithsonian Institution Press. 326 pp

Foderingham-Brown, M. "Education for Multicultural Librarianship: the State of the Art and Recommendations for the Future," *Acquisitions Librarian* 9\10 (1993) p.131–148
One article in an issue devoted to multicultural acquisitions. (abstract) Discussion of the implications for other aspects of librianship.

Fogel-Chance, Nancy. "Living in Both Worlds: 'Modernity' and 'Tradition' among North Slope Inupiaq Women in Anchorage," *Arctic Anthropology* 30:1 (1993), p.94–108.
This article reports on a mid-1980s study of how Native women adapt in bicultural ways to life in Alaska's largest city. (Similar studies are needed for Native men, who fare much less satisfactorily, in my view.)

"Formal Signing by Tungavik Federation of Nunavut Final Agreement," *Musk-Ox* No.40 (1994), p.85–91 (Selections feature), abridged from an article in Communique, Ottawa, Indian and Northern Affairs, Canada 1-9324.
This gives full details of the May 25, 1993 agreement establishing the Native land of Nunavut in the eastern Arctic, two million square kilometers in area, with summaries of the forty-two articles, and references for more detailed information. Implementation is planned for completion in 1999. (*Musk-Ox* ceased publication with this issue.)

Foster, Michael. "Library and Information Work in a Diverse Society: The Work of IFLA's Section on Library Services to Multicultural Populations." *Ethnic Forum,* 10, Nos.1–2 (1990), p.13–33.
The author was one of the founding members of the Section, and the editor of the Section's *Journal of Multicultural Librarianship,* now merged with *Multicultural Review,* which is published in the U.S.

Foster, Stephen P. "Victimization in Library School Closing Rhetoric: A Response to a *LQ* Symposium," *Library Quarterly* 63:2 (1993) p.199–205
A thoughtful analysis of three articles, including the one by Marion Paris (cited and discussed herein), to do with the closing of over a dozen graduate library schools from 1978 to date. The author's concluding comments add that library schools need not feel victimized in and of themselves. "The failure of a program to survive may simply be the result of a concentration of forces brought together by complex changes in society." This may be partly true, but some accountability surely belongs to those in library education. See also "Dean List; 10 School Heads debate . . . " listed herein.

Freiband, S.J. "Multicultural Issues and Concerns in Library Education," *Journal of Education for Library and Information Science* 33:4 (Fall, 1992) p.287–294
Focuses on the curriculum of graduate library schools.

Gagne, Marie-Anik. *A Nation within a Nation,* Dependency and the Cree. 1995: Black Rose Books, Montreal. 160p
Strongly argues against further assimilation. Her "four-step proposal involves political institutions accountable to the aboriginal electorate; territorial bases for aboriginal groups; self-government; and on-going fiscal support for increased social programs and economic development." (from the publisher's catalog)

Gallagher, T.J. "Language, Native People, and Land Management in Alaska," *Arctic,* Vol.45, No.2 (June, 1992) p.145–149, map
Natives in Alaska are obtaining increasing control over land in Alaska, but the main decision-makers are elders, who are less likely to be fluent in English. Translation and interpreting services are needed for the 20 Native languages in Alaska. Arguments are made why, and solutions offered.

Gaughan, Tom. "The Pulse of Library Education," *American Libraries,* Part I (Dec., '91), pp. 1020–1021, 1072; Part II (Jan., '92), p. 24–25, 120.
Optimistic though wary assessment of U.S. graduate library schools.

Getty, Ian A.L. and Antoine S. Lussier, editors. *As Long as the Sun Shines and Water Flows,* A reader in Canadian Native Studies. Univ. of British Columbia Press, 1983.
See the chapter "The Politics of Indian Affairs," p.164–187, which is abridged and updated from Chap. 17 of *A Survey of Contemporary Indians of Canada,* Part I, edited by H. B. Hawthorn. Ottawa, 1966. Somewhat dated, yet excellent background for understanding the changes in political conditions in Canada that resulted in steady improvement of Native library services since the late 1950s and 1960s.

Godwin, M.J. "ALISE meets in San Antonio," *Wilson Library Bulletin* 66:8 (April, 1992) p.40–41
Reports on the 1992 conference of the Association for Library and Information Science Education. Theme was 'The Ecology of Organizational Survival.' Compares changes in zoos' practices and library education, role of innovation, school designs, the experience of San Antonio and accreditation issues.

Goody, Jack. *The Domestication of the Savage Mind.* New York:Cambridge Univ. Press, 1977.

——.*The Interface between the Written and the Oral.* (Series: Studies in Literacy, Family, Culture and the State) Cambridge U.P., 1987

Hamilton, Lawrence C. and Carole L. Seyfrit. "Coming out of the Country: Community Size and Gender Balance among Alaskan Natives," *Arctic Anthropology* Vol.31, (1994) No.1, p.16–25
Through a study that examined outmigration of young Native women from fifteen rural communities to the city, it was learned that more women go to the city and do better, and more young men remain in the village and do worse. As a result there is a gender imbalance that impacts individual and cultural survival in many villages as well as the city. Youths raised in larger towns and cities acculturate more to the dominant White urban life and have more confidence in their future. Youth in villages are more split in their expectations, and young men especially are more likely to act-out their despair and frustrations. Village schools, through helping youth at home, increase graduation rates and serve as the main acculturating agents, but they may also leave students stranded in a socio-cultural limbo, ill-prepared for both village subsistence life and the intense pressures and stresses of city life, or college.

Hampton, Eber Lafayette Jr. *Toward a Redefinition of American Indian/Alaska Native Education.* Harvard University, EDD dissertation, 1988.
"Drawing on interviews with Indian participants in the American Indian Program at the Harvard Graduate School of Education and his own experience, the author suggests twelve standards that should be addressed by an Indian theory of education." (abstract) These are spirituality, service, diversity, culture, tradition, respect, relentlessness, vitality, conflict, place and transformation. I found his rationale and holistic theoretical basis illuminating. As seems inevitable in dissertations by Native Americans, as well as other American minorities, an intellectual indignation and anger clothes the final pages. A puzzling note arose when a copy was not found in either ALN or WLN databases, and it was not available from University Microfilm (late 1994).

Hanson, W.F. (Bill) "Indigenous Peoples' World of Two Realities: Implications for Future Development Initiatives," *Musk-OX* No.40 (1994) p.47–53
Maintains that future development schemes involving Natives should recognize the "dual realities" of Native life today: the pressures of acculturation and assimilation, and the psychic and spiritual heritage of traditional culture. By utilizing the strengths and benefits of *both* (rather than one or the other), Natives can better achieve a balanced life in the modern world.

Henry, Jessica. "Racism awareness . . . Training for Change," *Public Library Journal* 2:1 (1987), p.9–15
Points out the marginalization of minority library services, sometimes separated in their objectives, staffing and funding. Racism awareness training can help bring a more universal approach to serving the library's clientele. (paraphrased from the abstract)

Henze, Rosemary C. and Lauren Vanett. "To Walk in Two Worlds—Or More? Challenging a Common Metaphor of Native Education," *Anthropology and Education Quarterly* 24:2 (1993), p.116–134
Analyzes five misleading if not false assumptions of this metaphor, which ignores the complexity and variety of both the Yupik and Western cultures today, and the changes both are experiencing. Further, "the two worlds metaphor does not do justice to the complexity of choices facing native Alaskan and Indian students," and its reductionist approach, lacking realism and full of conflict, may be harmful. Study and appreciation of the real Yupik community today is needed, which has an "emerging unacknowledged identity."

Hess, Franke Snyder. *Explaining International Movements: A Study of Global Activism among the World's Indigenous Peoples.* University of Maryland, College Park, 1990. PhD Dissertation.
Analyzes nature of dominance of Native peoples by colonial and exploitative forces. Emphasizes the moral questions involved for the dominant groups, and ways to legally protect the Native moral and psychic community. Role of international conferences and organizations among the Native peoples is discussed, as well as the global implications of these changed relationships.

Hills, Gordon H. "Library and Related Services to Native American Inmates in Two Alaskan Correctional Institutions," *Proceedings,* 14th Polar Libraries Colloquy, Byrd Polar Research Center, The Ohio State Univ., Columbus, Ohio, May 3–7, 1992, p.336–344
The library, information and educational needs of Alaska Native prison

inmates in the Yukon-Kuskokwim (Bethel) and Hiland Mountain (Eagle River, outside Anchorage) correctional centers are assessed. Approximately 95% of those at the Bethel facility are Yupik Eskimo men, and about 20–25% at Hiland Mountain, a treatment facility, are Alaska Natives. The author's background is briefly referenced, along with some of the sources of psychological stress that Alaska Native men have been experiencing.

Hollaran, Susan. "Rural Public Library Service to Native Americans," *Rural Libraries* 1990 (10:1) p.31–48.
Relates Native American library needs and interests to "socio-economic and cultural position in the USA." (abstract)

Hope, Andy. "Canadian, Alaska Tlingits Explore Common Ties." *Juneau Empire,* July 29, 1992 (page?)
"The Council of Yukon Indians is a federation of First Nation tribes in the Yukon that provides oversight for the Yukon Native Language Center, the Aboriginal Language Service of the Yukon Government, and the on-going Land Claims negotiations with the Canadian Federal government."

Hoyer, Benny, Editor. *Groenlandica,* Catalogue of the Groenlandica-collection in the National library of Greenland. 1986: Nuuk. Nunatta Atuagaateqarfia (Greenland National Library). 585pp
This is an indispensable resource volume for anyone doing research on Greenland. There is an alphabetical listing of books in Greenlandic, a separate listing of "Books on Greenland and the Arctic" in other languages (mostly Danish and English), an alphabetical listing by author and title, and finally a classified listing using the Danish Universal Decimal Classification System. A sizable portion of the Groenlandica collection remains to be catalogued, and it is planned to have periodic supplements compiled in the future. It was not seen until just before I completed work on this book.

International Work Group for Indigenous Affairs (IWGIA). *Indigenous Peoples in the Soviet North* (Document 67) Copenhagen, 1990. 56pp
"In the last few days of March, 1990 indigenous peoples of the Russian Federated Soviet Republic met in the Kremlin to establish their first country-wide association. This document is from, and about, this meeting, which resulted in the establishment of the "Association of the Small Indigenous Peoples of the Soviet North." (book jacket note)

"Inuits offer Help," *Anchorage Daily News,* July 30, 1995. p.A1, B3
At the Inuit Circumpolar Conference in Nome, Russian Native northerners said that scarce commodities and gear for hunting and fishing,

high unemployment and rampant alcoholism make life very difficult. There are instances of food thievery, fining of desperate subsistence hunters and extremely high tariffs on equipment and supplies donated from abroad, which has had to be returned. The ICC pledged its help, and will ask the US State Department to intercede so humanitarian aid is not tariffed.

Jacobs, Andrei. "Mastering Today's Society Key to Yupik Survival", *Anchorage Daily News,* August 2, 1993, p.B-3
    In this short essay by a high school graduate in Bethel, AK, teenagers tell how they try to balance their lives between traditional ways and capitalism.

Jennings, K.A. "Recruiting New Populations to the Library Profession," *Journal of Library Administration* 19:3/4 (1993), p.175–191
    One article in an issue devoted to the theme: Libraries as User-Centered Organizations. Discusses ways in which librarians and library educators can attract minority users and workers.

Joly, Elisabeth. *Concept d'identite et pratique de socialisation croisee chez les femmes Inuit.* Doctoral paper, Universite Laval, Quebec, 1988–89. *Musk Ox,* No.39 (1992)
    Reports on research to study conceptions of the social roles Inuit women are asked to play, who have been raised as boys. Sex roles and gender identity are examined.

Jones-Quartey, Theo S. and Kit S. Byunn. "Ethnic Minorities in Librarianship: A Selected Bibliography," (On the Scene feature) *Special Libraries* 84:2 (Spring, 1993), p.104–111.
    This seemingly short article turns out to be a bibliographical treasure trove of recent library literature on the subject, containing over 120 sources under References, Statistics and Data, Ethnic Minorities and Library Education, Recruiting Ethnic Minorities for Librarianship (most entries), Multi-ethnic Diversity in Libraries, and Librarians of Color. Many are about Native Americans. (Also avail. as a handout from ALA OPLR)

Josey, E.J. "Education for Library Services to Cultural Minorities in North America." *Journal of Multicultural Librarianship* 5:3 (July, '91) p.104–111
    The author, of the Graduate School of Library and Information Science of the Univ. of Pittsburgh, completed a survey of multicultural library training in the U.S., and the results are discussed.

————."The Challenges of Cultural Diversity in the Recruitment of Faculty and students from Diverse Backgrounds," *Journal of Education for Library and Information Science* Fall, 1993 (34:4) p.302–311

"Observes that annual statistics of ALISE show that the percentages of (minorities) among U.S. library school students have not increased since the passage of the Civil Rights Act of 1964." (abstract) Urges that this situation must be reversed, as the minority U.S. population is steadily growing.

Keating, Elisabeth. *A Plea for Understanding:* The use of Native Elders and Spirituality in Cross-Cultural Counseling. MA Thesis, 1989. Univ. of Alaska, Fairbanks.
Emphasizes the trauma of epidemics three generations ago, during which *most* children died, and other losses, of land, language, spiritual relationships and rituals, and consequent self-respect and community integrity, and likens the legacy for Native peoples to a holocaust. Natives gather today for spiritual healing, and to communally share the grief and hurt caused by these felt losses, focusing on the devastation of alcohol abuse and sobriety. She uses her own close relationships with family elders— especially a grandfather medicine man, to underline the crucial role of landed roots and family ties in achieving a balanced life.

Knowles, Em Claire and Linda Jolivet. "Recruiting the Underrepresented: Collaborative Efforts Between Library Educators and Library Practitioners," *Library Administration and Management,* 5:4 (Fall, 1991), p.189–193
Much more cooperation is needed, and a proactive approach to the community at large and minority communities in particular, in order to attract candidates of color to the library and information science profession. Extra effort is called for, in other words, not merely a reliance on conventional ways of recruiting minorities to the field and the minorities to libraries, which have failed or had minimal effect. There is already an historical array of recommendations to consider, but little continues to actually be done. An exemplary Minority Internship/scholarship in Library and Information Science is cited, as well as a program at the UCLA library school, in which a Latino student is matched with a Latino librarian mentor, the object being to encourage the student to consider a graduate library degree.

Kolb, Audrey. *A Manual for Small Libraries in Alaska.* "For the Alaska State Library" 1987. Loose-leaf binder.

Kurbis, Susan M. *The Nentzy and the Inuit:* A Comparative Study. Bachelor's Thesis, Univ. of Waterloo, Ontario. 1990. Abstracted in *Musk Ox,* No.39 (1992)
Compares acculturation experience of these Russian and Canadian Native peoples, both before and after significant contact with western culture.

Langley, Elizabeth G. *The Development of a Literacy Program among the Navaho Indians. The Influence of Culture in beginning to set up a Literacy Program. A Proposal for Developing an English Literacy Program among the*

Navaho Indians, with Reference to present Motivations for Learning to Read. New York Univ., EDD degree, 1956. 235pp
Over half of this dissertation is devoted to a description of the traditional Navajo culture, emphasizing the pre-contact period. Then the author relates life needs of humans generally to the Navajo way, and how literacy can help fulfill these needs. Most interesting is the last portion, which illustrates how literacy can be dovetailed into traditional Navajo attitudes and desires for a full modern life. By her own work she emphasizes the need to know and understand the culture of any people thoroughly before embarking on any community development program. A corollary to this is certainly that a Navajo is best equipped to plan and implement such a program.

Language and Educational Policy in the North. Proceedings. Conference hosted by the Canadian Studies Program and the Department of Anthropology, University of California, Berkeley, March 13–15, 1992, UC Berkeley. (Working Papers of the Canadian Studies Program) Edited by Nelson H. H. Graburn of UC Berkeley and Roy Iutizi-Mitchell of Kuskokwim Campus, College of Rural Alaska, Bethel, who also organized the conference. 219pp
Historical and current assessments of Native language survival in the circumpolar nations, including "international perspectives" and citing effects of schooling policies. Native orthographies and publishing are also discussed.

Lenox, M.F. "Developing and Enhancing Multiethnic Understanding," *Journal of Library and Information Science* 34:3 (Summer, 1993) p.246–250
"Reviews recent initiatives at Missouri University at Columbia School of Library and Information Science, taken to strengthen understanding relative to racial and cultural diversity and their effects on libraries . . ." through various means.

Leonard, G.D. "Multiculturalism and Library Services," *Acquisitions Librarian* 9/10 (1993), p.3–19
One article in an issue devoted to multicultural acquisitions. Brief review of the historical relationship between libraries and minorities. Identifies issues, and underlines obligations and limits of libraries in serving minority communities.

LePan, Don. *The Birth of Expectation.* (Vol.I of *The Cognitive Revolution in Western Culture*) Houndsmills, Basingstroke, Hampshire, UK:Macmillan, 1989
Of most interest to me is his discussion of various theories about the

evolution of human consciousness and world-view, and his criticism of Levi-Bruhl's position, that aboriginals had an awareness and mindset that was distinctly *un*self-conscious for the individual, compared to moderns.

Lerner, Daniel. *The Passing of Traditional Society:* Modernizing the Middle East. Glencoe, IL: Free Press, 1963
One of the early studies that emphasized the role of the mass media in modernization of people of traditional cultures. (Not examined. Annotation paraphrased from *Becoming Modern,* Individual Change in Six Developing Countries, by Alex Inkeles and David H. Smith {Harvard U.P., 1974}, who point out that, "Just as wearing a watch is often the first dramatic sign of a man's committment to the modern world, so acquiring a radio may be the thing that really incorporates him into that world." p.29)

Levi-Bruhl, Lucien. *How Natives Think* (Les fonctions mentales dans les societes inferieures) Authorized translation by Lilian A. Clare. New York: Alfred Knopf, nd. Reprint by University Microfilms.
His theory on the nature of the aboriginal mind says that it is of a fundamentally different makeup from that of modern humans, being a collectivized consciousness that is integrated into the 'physical' world of the 'senses' (as science would say), whereas the modern mind has gradually become dissociated and objectified through intensifying socialization, to the degree that modern civilization is now defined and judged by the quality of the individual life, and how well he or she manages this awesome burden.

Lewis, Claudia. *Indian Families of the Northwest Coast,* The Impact of Change. Univ. of Chicago Press, 1970.
A study of reserve life on southern Vancouver Island and how it reflects personality formation and growth. Effects of Shaker faith, kinship parenting, merging of traditional and acculturating values, alcohol drinking, etc.

Lim, Coralie-Ann. *The Impossible Dream: The Library Media Technology Program at Northland Pioneer College.* Northland Pioneer College, Holbrook, Arizona. 1990. 10pp
"For additional reports on this program, see ED 305 080 and ED 305 931." (ERIC) Describes a flexible program in library education for isolated Indian library workers that combines classes in a central field center with remote audio and video support. Students are able to take two or more courses simultaneously, or have an Independent Learning Contract. A Certificate or an Associate of Applied Science Degree in Library Media Technology can be earned. Local community colleges are being approached

to host courses, and a Weekend Credential Program by videotape is also being considered.

Lincoln, Tamara. "Ethnolinguistic Misrepresentations of the Alaskan Native Languages as mirrored in the Library of Congress System of Cataloguing and Classification," *Cataloguing and Classification Quarterly* Spring 1987 (7:3) p.69–90.
    Critical of LC Classification's treatment of northern languages, offering an LC-compatible alternative developed at the Rasmuson Library at the University of Alaska, Fairbanks.

Long Range Program for Library Development in Alaska, 1995–1999. "Prepared by Alaska State Library, Governor's Council on Libraries in Consultation with U.S. Department of Education." 42pp
    Details of the goals of grant funding in Alaska made available under the Federal Library Services and Construction Act Titles I, II, III IV, V and VI.

Maybury-Lewis, David. "Tribal Wisdom, Is it too late for us to reclaim the benefits of tribal living?" *Utne Reader,* p.68–95 (From the book by the author, *Millenium:* Tribal Wisdom and the Modern World, New York: Viking-Penguin, USA, 1992)
    This alternative press article urges the importance of learning about and accepting one's ethnic roots, and of toleration of and respect for others' heritage. Emphasizes multicultural diversity and cooperation.

McCauley, Elfrieda. "Native American School Libraries: A Survey" *School Library Journal,* 4:91, p.34–38
    Makes strong appeal for Native American library professionals, building an accessible career ladder in library work, and attracting Native Americans to become librarians.

McDaniel, Sandi. "Village Support Networks aim to fuse Culture with Curriculum for Better Education," *Anchorage Daily News,* October 30, 1994 (Lifestyles section feature, entitled "Reconciling Two Worlds"), p.M1,2
    Advanced education may compromise and isolate Native teachers when they return to the home village to teach, and out of this has come the Alaska Native Teachers Association for mutual support, not only for newly returned teachers, but to make village education more appropriate and effective, and to help young adults live in both the Native and non-Native culture. See also Blair, Maude, herein.

McNabb, Steven. "Elders, Inupiat Iditqusiat, and Culture Goals in Northwest Alaska" *Arctic Anthropology,* 28:2 (1991) p.63–76

The role of organized elders in a 'mystical revitalization' of Eskimo community life in the Northwest Alaska Native Association region (NANA) is discussed. Testimony of elders on issues like alcohol, subsistence, welfare of children, cultural programs in schools, Native foods and the attitudes of parents and teenagers is quoted at length. See also Duran, Cheryl (1991).

Metoyer-Duran, Cheryl. "Native American Library and Information Services," *Government Information Quarterly* 1992 (9:3) p.359–362
   As part of a Symposium on the Summary Report of the 1992 White House Conference on Library and Information Services, discusses how this may impact Native Americans.

Metoyer-Duran, Cheryl. "Tribal Community College Libraries: Perceptions of the College Presidents," *Journal of Academic Librarianship* January, 1992 (17:6) p.364–369.

Minority Rights Group, ed. *Polar Peoples, Self-Determination and Development.* London: Minority Rights Publications, 1994 270pp
   Comprehensive assessment of northern peoples' current status and prospects, while continuing under intense and unrelenting pressures of acculturation. Geographical scope includes Greenland, the Russian North, Alaska, the Canadian Inuit, and the Saami of Northern Scandinavia.

Molloy, W. Thomas. "The Historic Foundation of Aboriginal Rights in Canada and the Basis of Current Discontent," *Musk-Ox* No.40 (1994) p.59–63
   A useful sketch of the historical policies of English, French and other European powers in dealing with land claims and sovereignty of Native peoples in Canada. Many land claims remain unresolved today, as well as subsistence issues, and even more problematic is the issue of sovereignty. The need for a "Native core of local decision-makers, professionals, and admisistrators" is underscored.

Monroe, Judith. "Public Library Service for Native Alaskans," *American Indian Libraries Newsletter,* (17:4) Summer 1995. p.1–3
   Compendious summary of the state of library services to Native communities in Alaska, mainly remote villages, and the many problems they face.

Morin-Labatut, Gisele. "Is there a User in the House? Connecting with the User Information Services," *Information Development,* 61 (January, 1990), p.43–48
   One article in an issue devoted to activities of the Information Sciences

Division of the International Development Research Centre. "Argues in favour of developing indigenous capabilities for collecting, and disseminating both locally- and externally-generated information and stresses the importance of socio-cultural factors in the communication of information, especially in societies with an oral tradition . . ." (abstract)

Morrow, Phyllis and Chase Hensel. "Hidden Dissension: Minority-Majority Relationships and the Use of Contested Terminology" *Arctic Anthropology* 29:1 (1992), p.38–53
Illustrates the misunderstandings and cross-purposes that occur when non-Native government representatives negotiate with Yupik fishermen on matters vital to their subsistence lifestyle, when the dominant "Euroamerican construction of reality is presented as a culture-free paradigm", and Natives are "pressured to defend their practices in a manner consonant with approved patterns of Western discourse and logic." ". . . (T)he negotiating parties often assume that contested terms represent congruent realities, and . . . this assumption may mask deeper cultural disagreements." (abstract)

Mueller-Alexander, J. M. "Researching Native Americans: Tips on Vocabulary, Search Strategies and Internet Resources," *Database,* April, 1994 p.45–46, 48–54, 56.

Napoleon, Harold. "Yuuyaraq, The Way of the Human Being," *Northern Notes,* No.111 (May, 1992), p.1–35
The author, a Central Yupik Eskimo ("I was born into a world that no longer exists."), explains how the devastation of early epidemics and later alcoholism reflect the profound shock experienced by surviving Natives in all the post-contact years. These holocaustal stresses were compounded by the *de*culturating impact of missionary and government schooling and authoritarianism, which eradicted traditional displays of spiritual and other cultural ways, as well as the language in many places. To rebuild the Native community psychologically, self-government and kinds of 'collective therapy' are needed.

"Native College leader chosen, Backers hope to establish school in Alaska by fall," by David Hulen. *Anchorage Daily News,* January 12, '94, p.D1, 3
Citing high Alaska Native college dropout rates and losses due to elimination of community college system and with approval for the second year by the Alaska Federation of Natives, a group of Native and non-Native backers of education have hired educators from a California system of mostly reservation-based educational programs to establish the college, possibly offering courses in 1994 or 1995, once a location, faculty and other resources are acquired. The curriculum will offer vocational training and college preparatory courses, and be "geared more toward Native

students." It will be available to urban and rural Natives, the latter by electronic means. It is presently called "Alaska Tribal College."

"Native Librarians form Group," *Windspeaker* (formerly AMMSA, Aboriginal Multi-Media Society of Alberta). May 1, 1987. p.2

Nick, Rose M. and Carol P. Okitkun of St Mary's. "Earn Your Respect" *Tundra Drums* (Bethel, AK), Mail Call feature, 5-27-93, p.A32
   This letter from two younger Yupik women of Pitka's Point, a small village on the Lower Yukon, urges elders to be good role models and they will be given respect. Asserts that young people are doing the best they can to balance Yupik ways with the Western cultural ways that Whites bring, and shouldn't be criticized so much for making that difficult effort. Compared to certain elders, who only complain or drink, not talking to the young much, some young adults are becoming better role models for children.

Northwest Territories. Culture and Communication. Public Library Services. *Activity Reports of the Public Libraries of the NWT, 1989.*
   Community by community report, with statistics. Some unusual program ideas include: dinner theatre, adults-only night, board games night, author visits, promotion of Inuktitut books, exchange book racks (for donated books), summer reading with merchants' prizes, visits by young offenders outside public hours, photograph exhibits, a volunteer day, flea market (bazaar), and a library program on the Inuit Broadcasting Corporation.Noteworthy items of administration include: high staff turnover, meetings conducted in Native language, hunters and trappers make local maps for youth, elders' involvement, videos popular with children.

————*1992.*
   Same types of information. Use of libraries is slowly rising (along with the population), and the holdings of the Public Library Services collection are now on CD-ROM and each library in the territory has electronic access to the headquarters library in Yellowknife. This service resource is very popular in some places. Rotating collections are sent out to remote communities periodically. High staff turnover continues. New program ideas include: prisoner services after hours, junior craft days, slide shows, visits by school classes, children's film festivals, donated book sales, setting up displays at community picnics, open houses, entering library floats in parades, story hours for various foreign ethnic groups in the community (French, etc.), and visits by children as part of summer camp. Library workers of individual regions got together to visit, compare notes and receive training, and some went to library conferences outside the NWT.

Oral Tradition. 1986 to date. Columbus, Ohio: Slavica Publishers. Biannual.

Pater, Joseph V. *The Acquisition of English Speech Acts by Native Speakers of Inuktitut.* Master's Thesis, Concordia Univ., Montreal, (1990?) Abstracted in *Musk Ox,* No.39 (1992)
   ". . .(P)resents an investigation of the relationship between socio-linguistic background and the use of a second language . . . (O)f special interest to . . . those concerned with the dynamics of cross-cultural interaction in the North, especially educators using English as the medium of instruction." (abstract)

Phillips, Natalie. "Natives get help claiming lost artifacts, Law forces museums, agencies to turn over items, information," *Anchorage Daily News,* October 19, 1995. p.B-1,3
   Reports how Alaska Native corporations are finding and filing claims for human remains, and artifacts of various types, with additional help from computer applications.

Puller, Gordon L. "Ethnic Identity, Cultural Pride, and Generations of Baggage: A Personal Experience," *Arctic Anthropology* 29:2 (1992) p.182–191
   Drawing on his own background and that of Alutiq people of the Kodiak Area Native Association (KANA), the author movingly discusses several major deculturating and destructive factors in Alaska Native and American culture: epidemics, separation of children from family through placement in institutions, an education system that portrayed Native cultures as inferior, the introduction of alcohol, and natural as well as human-caused disasters.

Rajan-Eastcott, Doris. *The Evolution of a Racism: First Peoples and the European Invasion of Canada.* Carleton Univ., Masters Degree, 1990.
   Exploitative policies of Europeans and their alleged superiority and actual dominance of Natives are discussed. "Aboriginal policy which served to provide ideological credence to the functioning of racism, expressed the objectives of control, appeasement and assimilation. Racism against the First Nations is still a very salient feature today as evident in their poor health and economic conditions, inadequate social and education services, and the state's refusal to entrench self-government in the Canadian Construction." (abstract)

Report on Violence against Alaska Native Women in Anchorage. Municipality of Anchorage. Municipal Department of Health and Human Services. Social Services Division. SAFE City Program, et al. "In collaboration with the Alaska Native Concerns Committee." October, 1994, 28pp.
   Though describing conditions of life for Native women in Alaska's largest city, with recommendations and proposals to improve the situation, it references life for men and children as well. Any social service worker in Anchorage, including librarians, should learn from its findings how better to serve this user/non-user group.

Rockefeller-Macarthur, Elizabeth Ellen. *American Indian Library Services in Perspective: From Petroglyphs to Hypercard.* San Jose State Univ., MLS degree, 1993.
Survey of Indian-White relations, "American Indian ways of knowledge," the role of museums, existing Library services and their funding sources, and future developments, including Hypercard.

"Saving Native American languages is conference goal," *Glacier Reporter* "Official publication of Browning and the Blackfeet Reservation" (Browning, MT) October 20, 1994, p.14
Discusses Native American Language Issues Conference, November 9–12, 1994, near Santa Fe, New Mexico

Schafer, Steven Allen. *An Investigation of Student Use of the Supplementary Materials List at Athabaska University (Alberta).* Univ. of Alberta, MLS degree, 1993.
"Athabaska University is an open university, with 18,000 students, that offers instruction at a distance. Currently 200 courses are offered through three faculties, leading to five undergraduate degrees and six university certificate programs." A mail survey showed that 87% of students knew that the university provided library services, but only 21% used them. Of these, 65% indicated that their course had a supplementary materials list. 64% of all students said they have access to a computer, and would search the library catalog if they had remote access.

Schoenhoff, D.M. *The Barefoot Expert: The Interface of Computerized Knowledge Systems and Indigenous Knowledge Systems.* (Contributions to the Study of Computer Science, no.3) Westport, Connecticut: Greenwood Press, 1993
Not examined, but sent to me was an excellent review, itself worthy of mention, by Patrick Wilson, in *Journal of the American Society of Information Science,* April, 1994. (Here follow my notes from the review-GHH.) Cross-Cultural transfer of technical expertise, scientific knowledge and foreign wisdom (from the First and Second Worlds to the Third and Fourth Worlds) is addressed, along with the many questions it raises. Local indigenous resource people and leaders need to create their own "expert systems," that benefit first and foremost the home country. The author prefaces her discussion with reviews of the literature on the "limits of science", background on Third World conditions, and a discussion of development theories. Indigenous knowledge systems and their modern potential are not sufficently discussed by the author, Wilson says.

Shearwood, Perry. *The Sociolinguistics of Literacy in an Eastern Arctic Community.* Doctoral paper, Ontario Institute for Studies in education. Toronto, 1991. Reported in *Musk Ox,* No.39 (1992)
Study of changing literacy patterns in a region where both Inuktitut syllabics and the English alphabet are used.

Shweder, Richard A. *Thinking Through Cultures, Expeditions in Cultural Psychology.* Cambridge: Harvard University Press, 1991. 404pp
  Stimulating series of essays, some done with another researcher, on how the human mind within one culture looks at life and people, and toward those of differing cultures and backgrounds. This is as much a 'self-study' of those within the western cultural milieu as it is a comparative psychological examination of others (with emphasis on the Third World) on the planet. On this point, see the example p.150–155.

Smithsonian Runner, A Newsletter for Native Americans from the Smithsonian Institution, Washington, D.C.
  News of the Smithsonian, and art, culture and publications of Native Americana.

Stairs, A. "The viability of Native Languages and the Role of Writing, the Experience of Inuktitut in N. Quebec" (in French), *Recherches Amerindiennes au Quebec.* Bulletin d'Information, Vol.15, No.3, p.93

Swann, Brian, editor. *On the Translation of Native American Literatures.* 1992: Smithsonian Institution Press. 242pp
  Twenty three essays by scholars in English, folklore, and linguistics.

Taylor, Rhonda H. "American Indian Library Association," *Ethnic Forum* 6: nos.1–2, p.128–132
  History of the AILA.

Torgovnick, Marianna. *Gone Primitive,* Savage Intellects Modern Lives. Univ. of Chicago, 1990.
  A fascinating study of how westerners have viewed Native populations over time, and how Native culture and art have influenced western thinking since antiquity.

Toronto Public Library. Board. *Library Service to Native Canadians, A Report.* "Prepared by Paula de Ronde, Community Outreach Coordinator." March, 1990. 16pp, 5 lvs.

Townley, Charles. "Encouraging Literacy, Democracy and Productivity: The Current Status of American Indian Libraries", *Journal of Multicultural Librarianship* 5:1 (Nov '90) p.26–32

Toynbee, Arnold. *A Study of History,* Vol.1, p.152–153. London:Oxford Univ. Press, 1939.
  Discussion of appellation "Natives" as used throughout history.

————. Vol.3, p.4–22. London:Oxford Univ. Press, 1939.

Discussion of Eskimos and Nomads as "arrested civilizations", due to the exigencies of "Mother Nature", and the encroachments of "sedentary civilizations" worldwide.

"Two Languages Better Than One, To preserve cultures, children should speak native tongues as well as English," by David Hulen. *Anchorage Daily News,* February 12, 1994. p.A1 and back page.
   Administrators of proposed Alaska Tribal College and others in Alaska assert that bilingualism and biculturalism are not only valid and healthy for young Natives, but result in better students of English and other subjects. (See also "Native College Leader Chosen)"

Travis, Robert. "Homelessness, Alcoholism, and Ethnic Discrimination among Alaska Natives," *Arctic,* Vol.44, No.3 (Sept, '91) p.247–253
   Focuses on Natives in Anchorage, who appear to be increasing in dislocation and social disruption, partly due to the boarding school experience, alcoholism and discrimination against them. "Feeling discriminated against seems to foster anger, frustration and self-blame among homeless Alaska Natives, who often come to see themselves as outcasts within the urban centers far from their homeland." (abstract) One can observe the same conditions in other large cities.

Troy, Timothy. "American Indian Materials in Microform: An Overview," *Microform Review* Spring, 1987 (16:2) p.112–117.
   Describes kinds of materials available in microform. This kind of archival material is especially useful for tribal libraries in support of tribal heritage programs.

"U.S. confers tribal status on Natives, Exactly what ruling means is unclear" by David Hulen. *Anchorage Daily News* 10-16-93, p.1, 12
   Ada Deer (Menominee), Assistant U.S. Interior Secretary for Indian Affairs under President Clinton, speaking before the annual convention of the Alaska Federation of Natives, "officially recognized more than 220 Native groups here and said they have many of the same legal powers as tribes Outside." Although many legal questions remain to be resolved, this policy makes it easier to claim in Federal courts that Native governments have certain special, federally protected rights, and adds strength to self-determination and sovereignty initiatives, weakening the position of Alaska State government regarding their affairs.

U.S. Education Department. Office of Educational Research and Improvement. *Library Services for Indian Tribes and Hawaiian Natives Program:* Review of Program Activities, 1990. Title IV, Library Services and Construction Act. Compiled by Beth Fine and Viola Woolen. Washington, D.C.
   Beth Fine has been the LSCA Title IV Program Officer of the

Discretionary Library Programs Division of Library Programs/OERI, U.S. Dept. of Education, for many years, which awards Basic and Special Grants directly to Native/Indian communities, that "encourage the development and improvement of public library services" to these populations. It has been a major stimulus and contributor to not only library services per se, but indirectly to archival, museum, documentation and educational efforts as well.

U.S. National Commission on Libraries and Information Science. *Pathways to Excellence: A report on Improving Library and Information Services for Native American Peoples.* Washington, D.C. December, 1992 610pp (numbered within sections)
   Contents include Summary Reports and Conclusions, Strategic Plan for the Development of Library and Information Services to Native Americans, Site Visit Reports, Hearing Transcripts, Commissioned Papers, Petitions and Resolutions, and photo portraits of Commission members. Comprehensive documentation of library and information needs of Native Americans is presented. "Ten major challenges" are put forward: improve funding, training, collections, access, interlibrary cooperation and partnership, museums and archival services, literacy programs and level of technology, "establish general Federal policy and responsibilities," and identify model programs. This is also a useful reference on the background and current conditions of library and related services in Native American communities. Hearing testimony gives detailed reports on most regions of the U.S.

Usabel, Francis de and Jane A. Roeber. *American Indian Resource Manual for Public Libraries.* Bulletin No.92429, Wisconsin State Department of Public Instruction. Division of Library Services. Madison, 1992. 160pp.
   Addressed to Wisconsin public librarians who want to expand their services to Native Americans. Covers materials and their selection and evaluation, Indian community contacts, resource collections and expertise available, programing, promotional ideas, demonstration collections, bibliographies, publishers, etc.

West, Sharon M. "Information Delivery Strategies and the Rural Student" *College and Research Libraries* Vol.53 (1992), No.6 p.551–561
   How the Univ. of Alaska brings information and library services to distance learning students through "information brokering and document delivery via the university's computer network, voice mail, and telefacsimile." (abstract) "26 references."

White House Conference on Libraries, Native American and Alaska Native Pre-Conference. February and March, 1991. *Resolutions.*
   Printed in the Summer, 1991 issue of *American Indian Libraries Newsletter.*

Whiteside, Don (sin a paw). "A Case for the Collection of Fugitive Material about and by Indians," p.71–75, 3rd Colloquium, The Bibliographical Society of Canada, National Library of Canada, Ottawa, October 19–21, 1978

Over a ten year period this Indian researcher collected a bibliography of over 7,300 items about Native Canadians, including some related Native American items. He argues that librarians have habitually collected primarily books through mainstream publishers in a small number of Native categories: general, specific histories, demography, values and crafts, and religion. Almost all of these are produced by non-Natives. The missed 'fugitive material' covers treaty rights, Indian law and administration, discrimination, politics and resistance, community and economic development, urbanization, education, health, housing, welfare, criminal justice, biographies, and foreign material. This timely and modern information is more likely to be produced by Indians and Natives, and is found in these formats: articles in Indian magazines and newspapers and regular newspapers, and mimeographed (now photocopied or videotaped) non-governmental speeches, reports, briefs, etc. It amounts to half the materials about Natives, who want information from the Native viewpoint and Native role models.

Wilson Library Bulletin. December, 1992

This special issue's featured section is entitled "Native American Library Services, Reclaiming the Past, Designing the Future." Most of it is devoted to articles, advertisements, resources and literature reviews to do with Native Americans. Government policies, legislation, conferences, typical Native American libraries, documentation projects and even tribal archives and museums are noted. (See also Metoyer-Duran)

————. December, 1993

This issue features a 23-page section entitled "New Zealand Libraries," including articles on library services to the indigenous Maori population and citing implications for library education, and other cross-cultural areas of concern.

Zakhar, Arlene Alice. *The Urban University and Native Americans in Higher Education.* Doctoral Dissertation, Univ. of Wisconsin, Milwaukee. 1987

Appendix A
Village Libraries, Native Style

By Gordon H. Hills

The flight was uneventful, except when we made our tightly banking turns to land. It wasn't like the jets! I walked the half-mile or so into the village, asked where the city office was, and for those people I had been told to contact. But right away, on that first trip, I had the growing sense of being out of place. What was I doing there, offering to help this village to set up a community library—even if they had requested it?

I saw signs everywhere of the subsistence life, the daily work to provide the necessities for survival: fishing, wood-cutting, moose-hunting, trapping, clothes-making, snogo and boat repair. I visited the school, and got a tour of the village by the major. Then we looked at community buildings where they thought to set up the library. None were suitable, really, so I made some suggestions. I would have to return later. My feeling was that it would be another year before this village had proper housing for a library. Yet I knew nothing about the economics of the village, their own needs for community services, what their budget was, and where their income and revenue came from.

For three years my job was to administer a library development project that eventually helped to establish small public libraries in 15 villages around the Yukon-Kuskokwim delta. My office and the base of operations as the village libraries coordinator was in the Kuskokwim Consortium Library out of the Kuskokwim Community College in Bethel. Actually, this library is a regional or "area center" library, coordinating library development and cooperation for the entire Y-K delta.

What we accomplished was due almost entirely to the villagers themselves. I had worked for Native people before, on the Washington coast, but nothing could have prepared me for my delta experience.

335

From the beginning I felt that a home-grown Native librarian should be doing my job. I had to start learning about village life and values from scratch. I was entering a new world, a different country, and one in which I didn't know a word of the local language.

I like the North, and was stimulated by the prospect of getting to know the Yupik people, the tundra environment—the vast marsh country with its endless maze of sloughs and lakes, and the climate. As far as my work was concerned, frankly I felt like a child, and looked to all these things as my special tutors. The simple fact that I would be doing a lot of small-plane flying to remote villages, for example, was totally new to me, an exciting prospect. And I would see the fabled Bering Sea! I also listened to my fellow Kuss'aqs (non-Natives) especially those at the college who had been working at the villages for years. What was it like working with the villagers?

There was no real briefing or orientation for college field workers, except the invitation to talk with this person or that who had years of village experience (all were non-Native). These conversations, though of general usefulness, did not address my specific need: what should one know and understand when going these Yupik Eskimo villages and working on a community development project? Was I going to have to learn by trial and error, chance advice and my own educational and intuitive efforts? Yes, and after three years, when I felt I was most effective, funding for the project ended! Experts on such development projects in the village assured me that this was not an uncommon experience—to have an innovative educational project cut off prematurely, often in rather arbitrary fashion, paying little heed to its effect on the people served, or the potential losses in funds invested.

What is a village library, Native style? I remember another village mayor taking me aside, as the wind swirled the snow around us. He looked concerned. "What is the library supposed to do? Can you make a list of the things that's supposed to be going on there? I have to pay the library aide and I need to know that." That brought me up short.

For the Kuss'aqs, a library is a storehouse of knowledge for wisdom. It is also a place of recreation—for the mind. The Kuss'aq is used to books, to reading alone—reading being a solitary activity. He is used to pursuing his or her own particular interests, whether it is to do with a job or a personal hobby. But for the library user in the Native subsistence village, this could be rather new, even a foreign experience. A library is one way the Kuss'aq keeps in touch with its own kind, his own heritage. The village library, therefore, has to be transformed into the same kind of place for the Native villager. It can be a place where he or she can learn practical things, information to do with corporate, resource and land management—even helpful information about subsistence. The printed page can speak to them, telling how to repair a snogo, write a report, learn first aid, make clothing from patterns, apply for a job and a variety of materials about the Yup'ik community and heritage—magazines and books, audiocassetes or video-tapes recording village activities, and films about Alaska and other Eskimos. A library is a place where a villager can vicariously or through make-believe learn life experience—though mostly life experience beyond the village. They can obtain movies from the village library. These are borrowed from another, bigger library, in Anchorage. The library, a collection of stored information, on a wide variety of subjects, can also help a student in the village. It can help that student learn more about the world outside the village, the world that is becoming smaller and smaller. Nowadays the speed of communication and travel worldwide is making the entire earth what some call a "global village." Many villagers are already having this experience on a daily basis, where they have access to programming from multi-channel cable TV systems.

Villagers like their own community library because it is a warm meeting place, conveniently located in the center of town, where there might be refreshments and company. Children have put pictures on the walls, and there is some music playing. There is an album of photos on the table, showing all the children of the village. A pile of contour maps of the area is also on the table. On the wall above, a carefully drawn map of the village is tacked, with all the houses and buildings labeled with people's names on them.

There can be career, vocational and educational guidance books, subscriptions to any kinds of magazines or newspapers, mail order catalogs, repair manuals and parts catalogs, telephone books, religious materials from the church, guides for community skills of all kinds, draft books and catalogs, pattern books, and materials about the village, the region, and Alaska.

Besides books, magazines and maps, there can be a television set in the library for those not able to have a TV at home. There could be a small computer, with educational and bookkeeping software and games for anyone to use. If there is also a VCR, movies could be rented from out of town for people to see. The library can maintain a collection of audiocassetes or phonograph records, available for borrowing by villagers. Children like the story-cassettes, and there are language and self-improvement tapes.

There will also be things the library aide could use, in helping villagers find books. The card catalog shows all the books the library has on its shelves. There will also be a set of Alaska Library Network microfiche and a microfiche reader. The ALN microfiche collection, which can be held in one hand, lists the several 100,000 books held by all major Alaskan libraries, and where they are located. Using this setup a villager can select and borrow any title they want through Interlibrary Loan. The library aide will send the request out by mail.

Then there are the programs the library can sponsor, and these will vary from village to village. Teachers can be invited to bring classes to visit the library. Storytelling sessions, held either at the library or someone's house, or a walk to historic locations around the village can be initiated at the library. There can be craft skill demonstrations and reading programs. In late winter, one of the men can show others how to overhaul and tune up an outboard motor or three-wheeler, in preparation for spring. The same for snogos in the fall. The library can sponsor audio or videotaping of community events and activities. These tapes should be carefully stored and made available for borrowing too. A variety of fund-raising programs can also be fun.

So what is a village library? It turns out to be a place of many purposes, but the main one is to provide community information services of any kind the village wants. The key phrase here is: WHAT THE VILLAGE WANTS.

The village library attempts to balance the Native heritage and its subsistence concerns with the western, written, scientific, and economically exploitative culture of Euroamericans, in providing the community with appropriate information resources and services. Both cultural traditions are essential, for the future good of the Native people and their children, yet by definition a library is non-Native, non-traditional. But the Yupik Eskimo villagers of the Y-K delta, for their part, have shown much innovative and imaginative skill in adapting the concept of a library to their own community needs.

In ways that will only be shown in the future, these village libraries will gradually take their place in the educational "delivery system" of the delta, a necessary cross-cultural and bilingual undertaking. The silent books on the shelves are learning to sing on winter nights.

Reprinted from *Alaska Native Magazine*, March–April 1986.

Appendix B
Three Questionnaires Used in Survey of 85 Graduate Library Schools

I

December 5, 1986
6515-15th Ave. NE
Seattle, WA 98115
U.S.A.

Greetings,

I'm working on a book about "Libraries and Native North American Communities, A Cross-Cultural Approach", which includes a chapter on advanced library education as it relates to Native North Americans. Specifically, I'm interested to know the following about your institution:

1. Since at least 1980 (optional to go back further), how many graduate students of Native North American stock have entered, and completed, your advanced library education program? (Please break out these two figures)

2. How many school faculty have been of Native North American stock in the same period, or have had significant experience with Native peoples, in the Americas or elsewhere? (temporary faculty like speakers and instructors at seminars, workshops, and institutes may be included). Please differentiate between the two kinds: Natives, and those with significant Native background, if it's possible to determine the latter.

3. During the same period, what courses in cross-cultural, minority or ethnic librarianship have been offered in the school, either as part of the regular curriculum or as part of special seminars, workshops, and institutes?

4. Does your graduate school of library education have any Native North Americans on the alumni, professional or community advisory committee or board, from your regional service area? (For example, a school in Idaho might have the Nez Perce Tribe represented. One in Quebec might have band members from the Cree nation advising.) If no such direct participation by local Native people in an advisory capacity is present, has the school established good, regular liaison with area Native communities or groups? Please briefly explain.

Canada and the United States are multi-cultural, democratic nations, and their public service and academic librarians have almost daily encounters with those of diverse racial and cultural backgrounds, including the variety of Native North Americans who are found in or near every community.

I look forward to hearing from you, so I can get a clearer picture of the status of cross-cultural librarianship in the graduate library schools, especially as it relates to the Native/Indian peoples.

Sincerely,

Gordon H. Hills

II

March 20, 1987
6515-15th Ave. NE
Seattle, WA 98115
USA

Greetings again,

This is an abbreviated version of a survey I sent to you three months ago, as part of research on a book entitled, "Libraries and Native North American Communities, a Cross-Cultural Approach." I'm sending it to those library schools that did not respond the first time around (half of 80 schools contacted). I hope you can take a few minutes to do me this favor, so I can have the highest possible response on which to base findings.

1. If your curriculum ever has any courses expressly devoted to multi-cultural or cross-cultural aspects of librarianship, especially as they relate to Native/Indian communities, could I please be sent a copy of their syllabi? (Otherwise, may I assume such considerations are routinely touched upon at appropriate points throughout the curriculum?)

2. If your school has any other significant multi-cultural or cross-cultural activities, regarding Native/Indian people, please briefly cite them.

(Examples might include: Native North American students, faculty, advisors or liaison people with area Native/Indian organizations; special workshops or institutes; consulting projects with area Native/Indian organizations, educational institutions, tribes, or bands; involvement in the provision of urban library services to Native/Indian people.)

Thanks,

Gordon H. Hills

III

June 4, 1987
6515-15th Ave. NE
Seattle, WA 98115
USA

Greetings,

This is my third attempt to contact your school with a survey I originally sent to you six months ago, as part of research on a book entitled, "Libraries and Native North American Communities, a Cross-Cultural Approach". I'm sending this abbreviated version to those library schools that did not respond the first and second time (34 out of 85 schools contacted in the USA and Canada). I hope you can take a few minutes to do me this favor, so I can have the highest possible response on which to base findings.

1. If your curriculum ever has any courses expressly devoted to multicultural or cross-cultural aspects of librarianship, especially as they relate to Native/Indian communities, could I please be sent a copy of their syllabi or brief descriptions? (Otherwise, may I assume such considerations are routinely touched upon at appropriate points throughout the curriculum?)

2. If your school has any other significant multi-cultural or cross-cultural activities, regarding Native/Indian people, please briefly cite them.

(Examples might include: Native North American students, faculty, advisors or liaison people with area Native/Indian organizations; special workshops or institutes; consulting projects with area Native/Indian organizations, educational institutions, tribes, or bands; involvement in the provision of urban library services to Native/Indian people.)

Many thanks for your time and attention in this matter,

Gordon H. Hills

Appendix C
Brief Notes on Native Library Provision in Northern Scandinavia

While pursuing research on the subject of this book, I ran across relevant material on the Saami (or Same or Samek) of northern Scandinavia (In some quarters Lapp is not considered the appropriate or accurate term, but it is still in use), though due to translation costs and the little material available in English, it has to be left a minor addition. This material was found in occasional articles and various abstracts and noted, but not pursued further in most respects. *LISA* abstracts in English on Scandinavian Native libraries were of articles published in Scandinavian language periodicals. The total population of the Saami peoples is something under 35,000.

The Saami have been in the unfortunate position of being pressed on all sides, even from the sea, for almost all historical time, by aggressive peoples and nations to the south and east. Differentiated as to cultural variation by habitat—the forest, the mountains and the lakes to the east in Finland—they have had to adapt and adapt again, taking good advantage of their intimate knowledge of local subsistence resources in order to survive.

Missionaries from the south brought the greatest changes to traditional society. As early as 1619 a prayer book was available in a Saami orthography. Throughout the 18th century, the governments of Norway, Sweden and Finland eventually established mission schools in Saami areas. The 19th and 20th centuries brought intensive colonization, various border disputes, warfare and occupation by invading armies. Today they are a minority in their own homelands, pursuing traditional economies "as inconspicuously as possible".

In 1995, late information on the Saami area was sent by Paivi Alanen of the Lapin Maakuntakirjasto (Lapland Regional Library) in Rovaniemi.

Several entries in *LISA* were noted:

From LISA 86/4985 and 86/4986 ("86" referring to the year 1986):

342

In Finnish Lapland, some villages no longer have Lappish speakers. A few are more traditional and Lappish is spoken. Lappish is taught in schools in Lapland. An added difficulty is that the Lapps speak three different dialects, with a separate alphabet for each. There is a publisher of Lappish books in Norway. Lapland covers parts of all northern Scandinavian countries. There is a shortage of qualified librarians, and many posts are unfilled.

From LISA 86/1749:
   The abstract of an article on outreach services in a Swedish journal points out that "much can be achieved with the help of Native-speaking colleagues, authors and other contact persons."

From LISA 85/115:
   An article points out the need for a Lapp National Library. Norwegian library budgets were too low and Lapp holdings suffered. Some libraries in Lapp areas have extremely few Lapp books.

From LISA 84/2114:
   An article mentions that literature about Lapps has increased, but books by Lapps and in Lapp are few.

From LISA 84/3392 to 3395:
   These cite articles from a special issue of *Bok og Bibliotek* (in Norwegian), which is devoted entirely to Lapp literature and library services.

   In 1990 and 1995, several entries in *LISA* were noted. (These are found under "The following items were found in English," below, provided by Paivi Alanen.)

Grosfjeld, Birgit. "Samisk bornelitteratur andet end Anders And" (Samek Children's Literature, Different than Donald Duck), *Bibliotek*, Vol. 70 (1988), No. 8, pp.331–332. This concisely written article indicates a trend in Saami literature that not only old legends and religious literature will be printed in the future, that young Saamis will be able henceforth to read titles about their daily lives and questions. In 1967 it became legal to teach in Saami; thus the boarding school experience in another culture and language is mollified. The Saami Publishing House in Norway is coming out with more offerings, geared more appropriately to the real lives Saami are leading. The Saami Cultural Council is playing an active role, and the Nordic Council is assuming obligations to the Saamic people. It is estimated that there are now from 600 to 900 titles available in Saamic. The cultural survival of the Saami is similar to that of other Fourth World peoples of the circumpolar north—how to grow and adapt to the ascendant cultures that bombard and press them from southern latitudes, yet retain that which is essential and valuable in the Saami culture. And building a modern tradition of documentation and expression in print and other media, in the Saami orthography, vision and voice, is indispensable to that continuity.

The following items were found in English:

For introductory information: Graburn, Nelson H. H. and B. Stephen Strong. "The Samek (Lapps)," pp. 11–32 in: *Circumpolar Peoples: An Anthropological Perspective,* (1973). Or "The North of the Old World: Lands of the Northeast Atlantic," pp. 210–231 and other material in: *The Circumpolar North, A Political and Economic Geography of the Arctic and Subarctic,* By Terence Armstrong, George Rogers and Graham Rowley (1978).

The 11th Northern Libraries Colloquy was held in 1986 in Lulea, Sweden. The *Proceedings* have the following papers of interest: "Ajtte—Saami Museum and Information Centre," by I.-B. Blindh; "Library Information Systems and Local History Literature in Northern Fenno-Scandinavia and the Kola Peninsula, Nordkalotten," by Tor Sveum; "Living within a Cold Region: The Kilpisjarvi Project," by Kyosti Urponen and Kerttu Vesterinen, Sveum's paper is especially illuminating, in terms of its closer look at the conditions for the refinement of library services in Nordkalotten (Fennoscandia and the Russian Kola Peninsula), given recent socio-cultural development, which include increased local opportunities in higher education and training, local history projects and museum associations. Computerization of Nordkalotten databases is finally bringing about effective bibliographic control of information and publications on the Saami area. By examining a particular village of a certain type, the paper entitled "Living within a Cold Region" describes in detail the quality of life in a Saami setting, in terms of both its natural and human environment.

The 12th NLC was held in Boulder, Colorado, USA, and the proceedings include the following paper: "Library Services in Lapland," by Erkki Pirjeta and Rainer Salosensaari of the Rovaniemi Public Library, Regional Library of Lapland, in Finland.

The 15th Polar Libraries Colloquy (formerly the Northern Libraries Colloquy) was held in Cambridge, England in 1994. The *Proceedings* contain the following paper of interest: "Arctic Know-how at the University of Lapland," by Liisa Kurppa and Lea Karhumaa.

Aikio, Marjut. "The Position and Use of the Same (or Sami) Language: Historical, Contemporary and Future Perspectives," *Journal of Multilingual and Multicultural Development,* Vol.5, Nos 3/4 (1984). And we quote:

. . . the opportunities for speaking Same are severely restricted and they are dwindling constantly—this is particularly the situation in Finland—in contrast to what the representatives of the majority and various decision-making bodies seem to be imagining in good faith. . . . In reindeer herding, the main element of traditional Same culture, it is increasingly difficult to use the Same language. In Sweden and Norway there is a possibility of using Same as an administrative reindeer herding language but not in Finland. . . . The effects of Finnish as the official administrative language in reindeer herding will in time prove disastrous for Same culture and, indirectly, for the use of the Same language.

Aikio, Samuli, *The Sami Culture in Finland*. Helsinki: Lapin Sivistysseura, 1994. 160p.
General information, including discussion of the status of the language and its use in the electronic and other media, p. 62–67.

Alanen, Paivi. "Public Libraries serving diverse populations in the North," *Antarctic Info* (1993?) p.2–4
Discusses revival of Saami language; improved status of publishing in the language; multi-national nature of Saami publishing; role of special Saami libraries in the various countries where Saami live, including joint efforts such as the Saami National Bibliography; increased use of tape-recorded Saami literature because many Saami can speak and understand the spoken language, but have little acquaintance with the written form; and "outreach" to remote villages and congregations of reindeer herders, etc.

Aubert, Vilhelm, University of Oslo. "Greenlanders and Lapps: Some Comparisons of their Relationship to the Inclusive Society," pp.1–8 in: *Circumpolar Problems, Habitat, Economy, and Social Problems in the Arctic.* A Symposium for Anthropological Research in the North, September, 1969. Edited by Gosta Berg. Oxford: Pergamon Press, (1973). (Series: Wenner-Gren Center, International Symposium Series, Vol. 21.) First of all, with respect to territory and language, the Saami are found in four countries and have some mutually unintelligible dialects, whereas the Greenlanders are on an island and have few dialectual impediments, though there are important variations to do with economies pursued in different regions. Few Greenlanders have been assimilated elsewhere, whereas the Saami have been under constant pressure in all spheres of life to change to the dominant society's ways. "Danish civil servants governed Greenland on the basis of an ideology purporting to protect the Greenlanders, while taking Danish superiority for granted." In other words it was a paternalistic relationship, but a "complementary one." On the whole, the Saamis have competed on equal terms with their outside and intruding neighbors. Greenland has had both the advantages and drawbacks of a very centralized administration, but the Saami have been dealt with in bits and pieces, depending on the area, the group, and the issue at hand. In terms of preserving a cultural integrity, the Saami have been able to accomplish more, yet have suffered more discrimination along with it. From the 1950s to 1979, Denmark's policy was strongly assimilationist, but since 1980 and Home Rule, Greenland has been more and more charting its own course.

Ayras, A. "Library Problems in Finland's Northern and Northeastern Developing Regions," *Scandinavian Public Library Quarterly*, Vol. 10, No.3 (1977), pp. 97–104. Written with an occasional humorous touch, this article addresses certain situations, such as the lifestyle in Lapland, problems in getting and keeping trained library staff in the remote areas, library administration considerations in northern regions of sparse (mostly Native) population, distribution of library funding, how remoteness must be overcome for access to library training, and why isolated librarians are always complaining about their miserable situation! One key subject not touched on at all is the availability of materials in Saami, or about the Saami. The vigorous approach of the author is stimulating, and some of the insights are refreshing.

Helander, Elina. "The Saami People; Demographics, Origin, Economy, Culture." p. 23–34 of *Majority-Minority Relations, the case of the Saami in Scandinavia*. p. 23–34 (1994). Available from the Nordic Saami Institute, P.B.220, N.9520 Kautokeino, Norway.

Paine, Robert. *Herds of the Tundra*, A Portrait of Saami Reindeer Pastoralism. Smithsonian Institution Press. 1994: Washington, D.C. This is a detailed study of the minority of Saami who are still reindeer herders. The area covered is primarily Norway, with incidental information on Sweden. Based on research the author did in 1960–61 while living with the herders; its latter chapters follow the impact of modernization and increased government controls through 1989, in which the Saami Parliament had little or no decision-making power. Reindeer herding is more problematical than ever, not only for the pastoral Saami, but because of the cultural significance of the reindeer for this northern people. Excellent reference on reindeer husbandry.

Pelto, Pertti J. and Satu Mosnikoff. "Skolt Sami Ethnicity and Cultural Revival," *Ethnos* 1978, pp.193–212. The Skolt Sami inhabit the extreme northeastern corner of Finland. After World War II, traditional territories of this group were ceded to the Soviet Union, thus drastically altering their subsistence patterns. Loss of the traditional domains, houses and buildings, reindeer herds, the winter village, and cultural exclusivity were compounded by the addition of snowmobiles and a highway into the region. Yet, these challenges to the old Skolt Sami heritage prompted a resurgence of traditional crafts (the catalyst being a growing tourist trade), a revival of traditional singing thanks to a well-known singer's efforts, and a return to use of the Skolt language.

Sammallahti, Pekka. "On the Roof of Europe," *Aktuumi* No.3 (1993) p.13.
Discusses the Saami studies program at the University of Oulu, Finland, which has existed since the early 1980s. This is an "English-language issue of the information magazine" of the university.

Seurujarvi-Kari, Irja. "The Status of Sami Culture and its Future," *Universitas Helsingiensis (UH)* 2/1991, p.5–7.
This is a multilingual quarterly of the University of Helsinki. The article discusses linguistic and cultural questions of the Saami.
The language has not returned to fluency, but to some integrity in a Finnish-dominant society. Old Skolt literature is being collected, young people aren't ashamed to speak Skolt any more, and a few Skolt periodicals and other publications, including dictionaries and grammars, are now available. Some news and commentary is now heard in Skolt on a regional radio station, and there is a clear prospect that Skolt may be taught regularly in the beginning grades in schools, as Native languages are treated in many other Fourth World areas of the circumpolar north.

The issue of Vol.14, No.1 (1981) of *Scandinavian Public Library Quarterly* is devoted entirely to library services to Saami peoples living north of the arctic circle.

The following citations of interest were found in the SPRLIB database in 1990:

Mead, W.R. *The Scandinavian Northlands.* Pamphet (Series: Problem Regions of Europe.) Oxford: Oxford University Press, 1974. 48pp.
Social, economic and political problems in northern part of Norway, Sweden and Finland.

Jones, Mervyn. *The Sami of Lapland.* Pamphlet (Report No.55.) London: Minority Rights Group, 1982. 15pp.
General account including present political and cultural problems.

Muller-Wille, Ludger. "The 'Lappish movement' and 'Lappish affairs' in Finland and Their Relations to Nordic and International Ethnic Politics," *Arctic and Alpine Research,* Vol.9 (1977), No.3, pp. 235–247.
Account of development of ethnic awareness and of native rights movement among Lapps in Finland, comparison with similar trends in Sweden and Norway.

Index

About the Author

Gordon Hills received a B.S. in agriculture from Cornell University and a M.A. in librarianship from the University of Washington. He has worked as a prison librarian, regional history librarian, research librarian for tribal heritage, community college librarian in an Indian community, and library development coordinator in Yupik Eskimo communities. He has also been a regional museum manager in a Native area, and a part-time Russian instructor. He "retired" in 1994, and now devotes all his time to writing projects and other pursuits, including playing the cello, oil painting, collecting books, canoe camping, bicycling, and occasional travel.